Understanding Art

A Sunday Afternoon on the Island of La Grande Jatte, 1884-85, by Georges Seurat was chosen for the cover design because of the luminous beauty of the work. Seurat began the work at the age of 25 and spent two years executing the final painting, which stands at six-and-a-half feet tall and ten feet long and includes 40 human figures. Before he finally completed the large canvas, he had done twenty drawings at the site or from models in his studio and thirty small paintings that were rapidly executed with broad brushstrokes.

An enterprise of this scope was unique among the painters dominated by the Impressionist vision. Most of them chose to work rapidly in order to capture fleeting effects in a short time. Apparently, under the dots, there is a layer of pigment that has been applied broadly, showing much the same technique as in his painting sketches. That is why white from the canvas does not show through.

The luminosity in Seurat's work comes about because of the technique he developed, which uses pointillist brushstrokes of pure pigment mixed in complementary and contrasting patterns to create optical color mixture in the eyes of the viewer.

Understanding Art

Gene Mittler, Ph.D.
Professor of Art
Texas Tech University

Rosalind Ragans, Ph.D.
Associate Professor Emerita
Georgia Southern University

GLENCOE

Macmillan/McGraw-Hill

Lake Forest, Illinois   Columbus, Ohio   Mission Hills, California   Peoria, Illinois

Send all inquiries to:
Glencoe Division, Macmillan/McGraw-Hill
15319 Chatsworth Street
P.O.Box 9609
Mission Hills, CA 91346-9609

ISBN 0-02-662286-6 (Student Text)
ISBN 0-02-662287-4 (Teacher's Wraparound Edition)

3   4   5   6   7   8   9   95   94   93   92

Editorial Consultants

Nancy C. Miller
Booker T. Washington High School
for the Performing and Visual Arts
Dallas, Texas

Jean Morman Unsworth
Art Consultant to Chicago
Archdiocese Schools
Chicago, Illinois

Contributors/Reviewers

Josephine Julianna Jones
Booker T. Washington High School
for the Performing and Visual Arts
Dallas, Texas

Johanna Stout
Art Teacher
New Caney High School
New Caney, Texas

Studio Lesson Consultants

Acknowledgments: The authors wish to express their gratitude to the following art coordinators and specialists who participated in the field test of the studio lessons.

Thomas Beacham, Telfair County High School, McRae, GA; Kellene Champlain, Fulton County Schools, Fulton, GA; Jane Dixon, Highlands Junior High School, Jacksonville, FL; Karen Roach Ford, Tecumseh Middle School, Lafayette, IN; Nadine Gordon, Scarsdale High School, Scarsdale, NY; Margie Ellen Greer, Ridgeway Junior/Senior High School, Memphis, TN; Barbara Grimm, Taylor Road Middle School, Alpharetta, GA; Ken Hatcher, Douglas Anderson School of the Arts, Jacksonville, FL; Annette Jones, Fletcher Junior High School, Jacksonville Beach, FL; Frances Kovacheff, Charles N. Scott Middle School, Hammond, IN; Geri Leigh, Stanton College Preparatory School, Jacksonville, FL; Nellie Lynch, Duval County Schools, Jacksonville, FL; Sandra Moore, John Sevier Middle School, Kingsport, TN; Bunyon Morris, Marvin Pittman Laboratory School, Statesboro, GA; Virginia Marshall Ramsey, Mabry Middle School, Marietta, GA; Joanne Rempell, Bradwell Institute High School, Hinesville, GA; Lahwana Reynolds, Glen Hills High School, Augusta, GA; Jane Rhoades, Georgia Southern College, Statesboro, GA; Julia Russell, Memphis City Schools, Memphis, TN; Barbara Shaw, Cobb County Schools, Cobb County, GA; Linda Smith, Millen Middle School, Millen, GA; Carolyn Sollman, Eminence School, Eminence, IN; Catherine Stalk, North Augusta High School, North Augusta, SC; Nancy Walker, Colonial Junior High, Creative & Performing Arts School, Memphis, TN; Betty Womack, William James Middle School, Statesboro, GA; Shirley Yokley, Tennessee Department of Education, Nashville, TN.

Photography Credits

Contents

Text

Illustrations

Maps

CONTENTS

CHAPTER 1

The Language of Art   1

Lesson 1 The Elements of Art   2
Lesson 2 Using the Elements of Art   6
• Examining Your Work   7
Lesson 3 The Principles of Art   8
Lesson 4 Using the Principles of Art   12
• Examining Your Work   13
• Safety Tip—Safety Labels   13

Chapter 1 Review   14
• Looking at the Details   15

CHAPTER 2

The Media of Art   17

Lesson 1 Drawing, Painting,
            and Printmaking   18
Lesson 2 Creating Mixed Media Art   22
• Examining Your Work   23
Lesson 3 Sculpture, Architecture,
            and Crafts Media   24
Lesson 4 Creating an Environmental Design   28
• Examining Your Work   29

Chapter 2 Review   30
• Looking at the Details   31

CHAPTER 3

*Art Criticism, Aesthetics,
and Art History*   33

Lesson 1 **Art Criticism and Aesthetics**   34
Lesson 2 **Painting an Expressive Scene**   38
• Examining Your Work   39
Lesson 3 **Art History**   40
Lesson 4 **Painting in the Cubist Style**   42
• Examining Your Work   43

Chapter 3 Review   44
• Looking at the Details   45

CHAPTER 4

Art of Earliest Times   47

Lesson 1 **Prehistoric Art**   48
• Studio Experience   51
Lesson 2 **Painting Using Earth Pigments**   52
• Examining Your Work   53
Lesson 3 **Art of Ancient Egypt**   54
• Map—Ancient Egypt   54
• Studio Experience   57
Lesson 4 **Ancient China, India,
              and Mesopotamia**   58
• Map—Ancient China, India, and Mesopotamia   58
Lesson 5 **Creating a Picture Story**   62
• Examining Your Work   63

Chapter 4 Review   64
• Looking at the Details   65

CHAPTER 5

Art of the Far East 67

Lesson 1 **The Art of China** 68
• Studio Experience 69
Lesson 2 **Making a Scroll** 70
• Examining Your Work 71
• Safety Tip—Water-Based Markers 71
Lesson 3 **The Art of Japan** 72
• Map—Japan 72
• Studio Experience 75
Lesson 4 **Creating a Time Capsule** 76
• Examining Your Work 77

Chapter 5 Review 78
• Looking at the Details 79

CHAPTER 6

The Art of Pre-Columbian America 81

Lesson 1 **Art of Mesoamerica** 82
• Map—Mesoamerica 82
Lesson 2 **Making a Clay Urn** 86
• Examining Your Work 87
Lesson 3 **Art of the Andes** 88
• Map—Andean Cultures 88
Lesson 4 **Making a Stylized Motif** 92
• Examining Your Work 93

Chapter 6 Review 94
• Looking at the Details 95

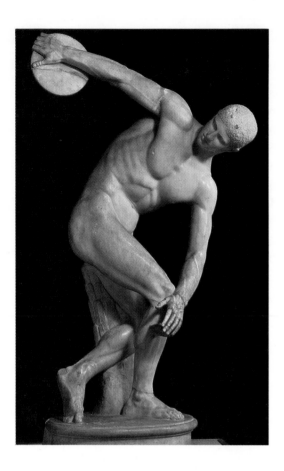

CHAPTER 7

Art of Greece and Rome   97

Lesson 1 **Art of Ancient Greece**   98
• Map—Aegean Civilization   98
• Studio Experience   101

Lesson 2 **Making a Painting for a Greek Vase**   102
• Safety Tip—Paints   102
• Examining Your Work   103

Lesson 3 **Art of Ancient Rome**   104
• Map—Ancient Rome   104
• Studio Experience   107

Lesson 4 **Making a Model of a Roman Triumphal Arch**   108
• Examining Your Work   109
• Safety Tip—Cutting Tools   109

Chapter 7 Review   110
• Looking at the Details   111

CHAPTER 8

Art of India and Islam   113

Lesson 1 **Art of India**   114
• Map—India   115
• Studio Experience   117

Lesson 2 **Making a Tempera Batik**   118
• Examining Your Work   119
• Safety Tip—Waterproof Ink   119

Lesson 3 **Art of Islam**   120
• Map—The Lands of Islam   120
• Studio Experience   123

Lesson 4 **Making of Collage in the Islamic Style**   124
• Examining Your Work   125

Chapter 8 Review   126
• Looking at the Details   127

CHAPTER 9

Art of Africa   129

Lesson 1   **The Figure Sculptures of Africa**   130
- Map—Africa   130
- Studio Experience   133

Lesson 2   **Abstract Self-Portrait Cutout**   134
- Examining Your Work   135

Lesson 3   **The Masks of Africa**   136
- Studio Experience   139

Lesson 4   **Making a Mood Mask Relief**   140
- Examining Your Work   141
- Safety Tip—Glue and Papier Mâché   141

Chapter 9 Review   142
- Looking at the Details   143

CHAPTER 10

Art of the Middle Ages   145

Lesson 1   **Art of the Romanesque Period**   146
- Studio Experience   149

Lesson 2   **Romanesque Castle Relief**   150
- Examining Your Work   151

Lesson 3   **Art of the Gothic Period**   152
- Studio Experience   155

Lesson 4   **Making a Gothic Gargoyle**   156
- Examining Your Work   157

Chapter 10 Review   158
- Looking at the Details   159

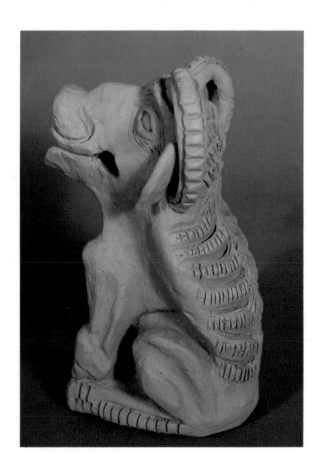

CHAPTER 11

Art of the Renaissance   161

Lesson 1   **Art of the Italian Renaissance**   162
- Map—Renaissance Italy   162
- Studio Experience   165

Lesson 2   **Drawing a Still Life**   166
- Examining Your Work   167

Lesson 3   **Art of the Northern Renaissance**   168
- Map—Renaissance Europe   168
- Studio Experience   171

Lesson 4   **Designing a Visual Symbol**   172
- Examining Your Work   173

Chapter 11 Review   174
- Looking at the Details   175

CHAPTER 12

European Art of the 1600s and 1700s   177

Lesson 1   **Art of the 1600s**   178

Lesson 2   **Drawing Expressive Hands**   182
- Examining Your Work   183

Lesson 3   **Art of the 1700s**   184
- Map—France   184
- Studio Experience   187

Lesson 4   **Constructing a Rococo Shoe**   188
- Examining Your Work   189

Chapter 12 Review   190
- Looking at the Details   191

CHAPTER 13

Native American Art   193

Lesson 1   **Native American Art of the Past**   194
- Map—Native American Cultures   194
- Studio Experience   197

Lesson 2   **Making a Round Weaving**   198
- Examining Your Work   199

Lesson 3   **Native American Art Today**   200

Lesson 4   **Inuit-Style Print**   204
- Examining Your Work   205

Chapter 13 Review   206
- Looking at the Details   207

CHAPTER 14

*European Art of the
Early 1800s*   209

Lesson 1   **Neoclassic and Romantic Art**   210
- Studio Experience   213

Lesson 2   **Designing a Neoclassic Stage Set**   214
- Examining Your Work   215

Lesson 3   **European Art—Late 1800s**   216
- Studio Experience   219

Lesson 4   **Painting an Impressionist
         Landscape**   220
- Examining Your Work   221

Chapter 14 Review   222
- Looking at the Details   223

CHAPTER 15

*Art of the Late
Nineteenth Century*   225

Lesson 1 **Art of the Post Impressionists**   226
• Studio Experience   229
Lesson 2 **Painting in the Style of
            Post-Impressionists**   230
• Safety Tip—Tempera Paints   230
• Examining Your Work   231
Lesson 3 **American Painting in the
            Late 1800s**   232
• Studio Experience   235
Lesson 4 **Making an Expressive
            Watercolor Painting**   236
• Examining Your Work   237

Chapter 15 Review   238
• Looking at the Details   239

CHAPTER 16

*Art of the Early Twentieth
Century*   241

Lesson 1 **Art of the Early Twentieth
            Century in Europe**   242
• Studio Experience   245
Lesson 2 **Making a Cubist Chalk Drawing**   246
• Examining Your Work   247
• Safety Tip—Chalk   247
Lesson 3 **Art of the Early Twentieth
            Century in America**   248
• Studio Experience   251
Lesson 4 **Making a Print of a
            Figure in Action**   252
• Examining Your Work   253

Chapter 16 Review   254
• Looking at the Details   255

CHAPTER 17

Art of Today   257

Lesson 1 **European Art Today**   258
• Studio Experience   261
Lesson 2 **Painting in the Surrealist Style**   262
• Examining Your Work   263
Lesson 3 **American Art Today**   264
• Studio Experience   267
Lesson 4 **Making a Hard-Edge
              Op Art Work**   268
• Examining Your Work   269
Lesson 5 **Art of the Next Frontier**   270
• Studio Experience   271

Chapter 17 Review   272
• Looking at the Details   273

Handbook

• Table of Contents   275
• Technique Tips   277
• Artist Profiles   289
• Career Spotlights   297
• Additional Studio Lessons   304
• World Map   314
• Artists and Their Works   316
• Glossary   319
• Index   322

LISTING OF STUDIO LESSONS BY MEDIA

Acrylics
Painting Using Earth Pigments   52

Chalk
Making a Cubist Chalk Drawing   246

Clay
Creating a Time Capsule   76
Making a Clay Urn   86
Making a Gothic Gargoyle   156
Coil Pot   306

Fibers
Making a Round Weaving   198

Mixed Media
Creating Mixed-Media Art   22
Creating an Environmental Design   28
Making a Collage in the
   Islamic Style   124

Paper
Making a Stylized Motif   92
Making a Model for a Roman
   Triumphal Arch   108
Abstract Self-Portrait Cutout   134
Making a Mood Mask Relief   140
Romanesque Castle Relief   150
Constructing a Rococo Shoe   188
False Face Mask   310

Pencil, Pen, Charcoal, and Markers
Using the Elements of Art   6
Making a Scroll   70
Drawing a Still Life   166
Drawing Expressive Hands   182
Making a Hard-Edge Op Art Work   268

Printmaking
Making a Tempera Batik   118
Inuit-Style Print   204
Making a Print of a Figure in Action   252

Tempera
Using the Principles of Art   12
Painting an Expressive Scene   38
Painting in the Cubist Style   42
Making a Painting for a Greek Vase   102
Designing a Visual Symbol   172
Painting an Impressionist Landscape   220
Painting in the Style of the
   Post-Impressionists   230
Painting in the Surrealist Style   262

Watercolor
Creating a Picture Story   62
Making an Expressive Watercolor
   Painting   236

Other
Designing a Neoclassic Stage Set   214
Computer-Type Drawing   304
Photo Essay   308
Space Colony   312

Understanding Art

▲ Gabriele Münter has made use of the elements of art to create a dramatic picture. Notice how she leads your eye from the foreground to the hills in the distance. How does her use of color make you feel?

Gabriele Münter. *Staffelsee in Autumn*. 1923. Oil on board. 34.9 x 48.9 cm (13¾ x 19¼"). National Museum of Women in the Arts, Washington D.C. Gift of Wallace and Wilhelmina Holladay.

The Language of Art

To learn how a watch works, you might take it apart and study the pieces. While the parts are spread out before you, however, the watch cannot run. Only when the parts are in place will the familiar ticking tell you the watch is working.

Like watches, works of art are made up of parts. When an artist skillfully puts the pieces of an art work together, it succeeds as art. That means that the parts work together to make a unified and visually pleasing whole. In this chapter you will learn about these parts and how they can be organized, as in the painting at the left, to make a pleasing whole.

OBJECTIVES

After completing this chapter, you will be able to:
- Define and recognize the elements of art.
- Make an abstract design, experimenting with the elements of art.
- Identify the principles of art.
- Use the elements of art and principles of art in a studio experience.

WORDS YOU WILL LEARN

balance	proportion
color	rhythm
emphasis	shape
form	space
harmony	texture
line	unity
movement	variety
non-objective art	

ARTISTS YOU WILL MEET

Marc Chagall	Richard Lindner
Charles Demuth	Gabriele Münter
William Harnett	Auguste Renoir
Grace Hartigan	Vincent van Gogh

The Elements of Art

Art is a powerful language. Through it, artists communicate thoughts, ideas, and feelings. Like most languages, the language of art has its own special vocabulary. Unlike other vocabularies, however, the vocabulary of art is not made up of words. Rather, it is made up of visual elements. The visual elements include color, line, shape, form, space, and texture.

COLOR

Have you ever noticed it is harder to see colors when the light is dim? Color relies on light. In fact, **color** is *what the eyes see when light is reflected off an object*.

Color has three properties, or traits. These are:

- **Hue**. Hue is the name of a color, such as red, blue, or yellow. Hues are arranged in a circular format on a color wheel. Red, yellow, and blue are the primary hues. They are equally spaced on the color wheel. (See Figure 1–1.) Look at the picture in Figure 1–2. How many different hues, or colors, can you find in this work? Which ones can you name?

- **Value**. Value is the lightness or darkness of a hue. The value of a hue can be changed by adding white or black. Can you point out different values of any one color in the picture in Figure 1–2?

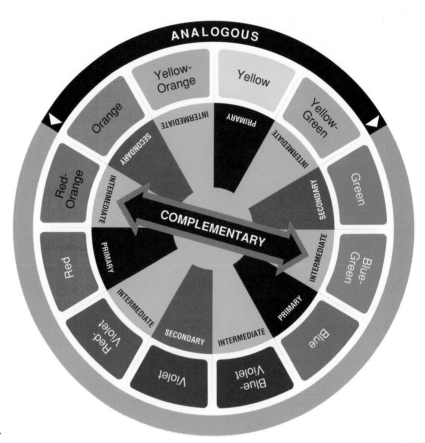

▶ **Figure 1–1   Color Wheel.**

- **Intensity**. Intensity is the brightness or dullness of a hue. Pure hues are high-intensity colors. Dull hues are low-intensity colors. Which objects in Figure 1–2 would you describe as high in intensity? Which would you describe as low in intensity?

Colors can be combined to produce many interesting and striking results. Artists make use of different types of color schemes to create different effects. Following are some of the color schemes that trained artists use:

- **Monochromatic** (mahn-uh-kroh-**mat**-ik) **color scheme**. This scheme uses different values of a single hue. For example, dark green, medium green, and light green make a monochromatic scheme.
- **Analogous** (uh-**nal**-uh-gus) **color scheme**. This scheme uses colors that are side by side on the color wheel and share a hue. Look at the color wheel in Figure 1–1. What colors share the hue red?
- **Warm or cool color scheme**. Warm color schemes—with red, yellow, and orange colors—remind us of the sun and warmth. Artists use blue, green, and violet—cool color schemes—to make us think of cool items such as ice or grass.

▲ **Figure 1–2** Notice how Harnett has captured a realistic scene using the elements of space, form, and texture. Would he have been as successful in showing depth if he had painted a lighter background?

William Michael Harnett. *Munich Still Life*. 1882. Oil on canvas. 62.5 x 76.8 cm (24⅝ x 30¼"). Dallas Museum of Art, Dallas, Texas.

LINE

An element of art that can be used to send different messages to viewers is a line. **Line** is defined as *the path of a moving point through space*. You can draw lines on paper or scratch a line in wet clay with a tool. Lines can be seen in your environment, such as the web of a spider or the railing on a stair.

There are five main kinds of lines:

- Horizontal lines, which run parallel to the ground, appear to be at rest.

- Vertical lines — lines that run up and down — seem to show dignity, formality, and strength.
- Diagonal, or slanting, lines signal action and excitement.
- Zigzag lines, which are made from combined diagonal lines, can create a feeling of confusion or suggest action.
- Curved lines express movement in a graceful, flowing way.

▶ Figure 1–3 Color, line and shape are successfully combined to create the appearance of a three-dimensional form. Why do you think Chagall has shown the violinist floating?

Marc Chagall. *Green Violinist.* 1923–1924. Oil on canvas. 198 x 108.6 cm (78 x 42¾"). Solomon R. Guggenheim Museum, New York, New York. Gift of Solomon R. Guggenheim.

Look again at Figure 1–2 on page **3**. How many different lines can you find? In what directions do these lines go?

In art, line quality and line variation influence the viewer's reaction to a work of art. Line quality is the unique character of the line. It can be affected by the tool or medium used to produce the mark or by the particular motion of the artist's hand. Line variation describes the thickness or thinness, lightness or darkness of a line.

SHAPE AND FORM

Every object — a cloud, a house, a pebble — has a shape. **Shape** is *an element of art that refers to an area clearly set off by one or more of the other elements of art*. Shapes are limited to two dimensions — length and width.

All shapes belong to one of two classes:

- **Geometric** (jee-uh-**meh**-trik). Geometric shapes look as though they were made with a ruler or drawing tool. The square, the circle, the triangle, the rectangle, and the oval are the five basic geometric shapes. Look at the painting in Figure 1–3. Can you find any geometric shapes?
- **Organic**. Also called free-form, organic shapes are not regular or even. Their outlines may be curved or angular, or they may be a combination of both, to make free-form shapes. Organic shapes, such as clouds and pebbles, are usually found in nature. Can you find any organic shapes in Figure 1–3?

Like shapes, forms have length and width. Forms also have a third dimension, depth. **Form** is *an element of art that refers to an object with three dimensions*. With the forms found in works of art, such as sculpture and architecture, you can actually experience the three dimensions by walking around or into the works.

SPACE

All objects take up space. **Space** is *an element of art that refers to the distance between, around, above, below, and within things*. Which objects in Figure 1–3 appear closest to you? Which seem to be farther back in space?

In both two- and three-dimensional works of art, the shapes or forms are called the positive area. The empty spaces between the shapes are called negative spaces. The relationship between the positive and negative space will affect how the art work is interpreted.

TEXTURE

Run your fingers over the top of your desk or work table. You are feeling the surface's texture. **Texture** is *an element of art that refers to the way things feel, or look as though they might feel, if touched*.

Imagine you could touch the objects in the picture in Figure 1–2 on page **3**. Which of them do you think would feel smooth? Do any look rough or uneven?

✔CHECK YOUR UNDERSTANDING

1. What are the three properties of color?
2. What message do vertical lines send to a viewer? What message do diagonal lines send?
3. What is the difference between shape and form?
4. What is the difference between the positive area and the negative area in a work of art?
5. Define *texture*.

Using the Elements of Art

Sometimes artists create **non-objective art**. These are *works in which no objects or subjects can be readily identified*. Figure 1–4 is such a work. This one is by Grace Hartigan. She has combined several elements of art in this work to create unusual effects.

WHAT YOU WILL LEARN

This is the first of many studio lessons. In these lessons you will use your creative skills and experiment with different media. You will create many works of art that may be displayed.

For this first studio experiment, you will create a non-objective design using all the elements of art. You will use pencil, felt-tip markers, colored pencils, and crayons. (See Figure 1–5.)

WHAT YOU WILL NEED

- Pencil and ruler
- Sheet of white drawing paper, 18 x 24 inches (46 x 61 cm)
- Colored markers, colored pencils, and crayons

WHAT YOU WILL DO

1. Using one continuous pencil line, make a design that fills the sheet of drawing paper. Allow your pencil to drift off the edge of the paper and return. Try to create a design that has both large and small shapes.
2. Using the ruler, divide your paper into eight equal rectangles. Each should measure 6 x 9 inches (15 x 23 cm). Number the eight boxed areas lightly in pencil. You may order the numbers any way you like (Figure 1–6).

▲ **Figure 1–4   Hartigan has painted a non-objective work that shows several elements of art combined to make a pleasing whole. What elements can you identify in this painting?**

Grace Hartigan. *The Faraway Places*. 1974. Oil on canvas. 228.6 x 166.4 cm (90 x 65½"). McNay Art Museum, San Antonio, Texas. Purchase made possible by a grant from the National Endowment for the Arts with matching funds, Marion Koogler.

3. Using primary *hues* of crayons, color the shapes in Area 1. (See the color wheel on page 2.)
4. Using light and dark *values* of colored pencils, color in the shapes in Area 2. Using bright and dull *intensities* of colored pencils, color in the shapes in Area 3.
5. Using the pencil, go over the *lines* in Area 4. Make some of the lines straight and others curved. Try pressing down on the pencil for some of the lines. This will give a thicker, darker result.

6. Using pencil, crayons, colored pencils, or markers, create three different *textures* in Area 5.
7. Using the markers, draw outlines around *shapes* in Area 6. Fill in some of the shapes with the markers. Leave the others white:
8. Use pencil to add a new shape that overlaps the existing shapes in Area 7 to show *space*. Add to this feeling of space by using colored pencil to color this shape in a bright hue. Color the other shapes in dull hues.
9. Using the pencil, shade the shapes in Area 8 little by little. Try to make these shapes look like rounded, three-dimensional *forms*. (For information on shading, see Technique Tip **6**, *Handbook* page **278**.)
10. Display your design. See if other members of your class can identify the different art elements found in each area.

▲ **Figure 1–5** Student work. Non-objective design.

EXAMINING YOUR WORK

- **Describe** Tell which element each area of your design highlights. Identify the media you used to create the different areas.
- **Judge** State whether your design clearly highlights each element of art. Tell which section of your design you think is the most successful. Explain your answer.

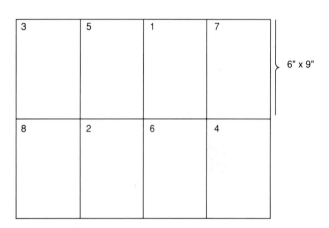

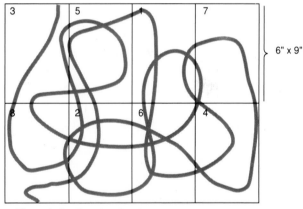

▲ **Figure 1–6** Drawing the elements of art.

OTHER STUDIO IDEAS

- On a sheet of white paper, create a second design using geometric shapes. Complete your design as before using only tempera paint as your medium.
- •• Draw a simple still life using *lines* to create each of the *shapes*. Overlap some shapes to add a feeling of *space*. Choose three hues to add *color* to your picture.

Gradual and sudden changes in value should be used to make some shapes look like three-dimensional *forms*. Create different rough and smooth *textures*. Exhibit your finished work in class. Identify and discuss each of the art elements used.

The Principles of Art

If you want to use a language, knowing the vocabulary is not enough. You must also know how the words go together. You must know the rules of grammar for that language.

The same is true of art. Instead of rules of grammar, the language of art has art principles. These principles, or guidelines, govern how artists organize the visual elements to create a work of art.

The principles of art include balance, variety, harmony, emphasis, proportion, movement, and rhythm.

▶ **Figure 1–7 This picture combines familiar images from our modern rock culture. What are some of the images? What do you think the artist is trying to say about this culture?**

Richard Lindner. *Rock-Rock*. 1966. Oil on canvas. 177.8 x 152.4 cm (70 x 60"). Dallas Museum of Art, Dallas, Texas. Gift of Mr. & Mrs. James H. Clark.

BALANCE

If you have ever carried a stack of dishes or books, you know the importance of balance. In art, balance is also important. **Balance** is *a principle of art concerned with arranging elements so no one part of a work overpowers, or seems heavier than, any other part*. In art, balance is seen or felt by the viewer.

In works of art, three kinds of balance are possible. They are formal balance, informal balance, and radial balance. In works of art with formal, or symmetrical (suh-**meh**-trih-kuhl), balance the two halves are mirror images. In works with informal, or asymmetrical (ay-suh-**meh**-trih-kuhl), balance two unlike elements seem to carry equal weight. For example, a small shape painted bright red will balance several larger items painted in duller reds.

Radial balance occurs when elements or objects in an art work are positioned around a central point. Study the art works in Figures 1–7, 1–8, and 1–9. Which uses formal balance? Which uses informal balance? Which uses radial balance?

▲ Figure 1–8   This painting creates a certain mood or feeling about the girl playing the guitar. How has Renoir combined the element of color and the principle of balance to create a pleasing portrait?

Auguste Renoir. *Young Spanish Woman with a Guitar.* 1898. Canvas. 55.6 x 65.2 cm (21⅞ x 25⅝"). National Gallery of Art, Washington, D.C. Ailsa Mellon Bruce Collection.

▲ **Figure 1–9** Van Gogh has blended many elements and principles of art in this work. Notice how he has used the elements of color and line to create a feeling of movement. How has he created balance?

Vincent van Gogh. *The Starry Night*. 1889. Oil on canvas. 73.7 x 92.1 cm (29 x 36¼"). Collection, The Museum of Modern Art, New York, New York. Acquired through the Lillie P. Bliss bequest.

VARIETY

The same routine day after day can become dull. The same color or shape repeated over and over in an art work can become equally dull. To avoid dullness, artists use the principle of variety in their works. **Variety** is *a principle of art concerned with combining one or more elements to create interest by adding slight changes*. By giving a work variety, the artist heightens the visual appeal of the work.

Look again at the picture in Figure 1–7. How does the artist's use of color add variety to the work? Which other elements are used to add variety?

HARMONY

If too little variety can become boring, too much variety can create chaos. Artists avoid chaos in their works by using the principle of harmony. **Harmony** is *a principle of art concerned with blending elements to create a more calm, restful appearance*.

Of the two paintings in Figures 1–7 and 1–8, which has greater harmony? Which elements does the artist use to introduce harmony to the work?

EMPHASIS

To attract a viewer's attention to important parts of a work, artists use the principle of emphasis. **Emphasis** is *making an element in a work stand out*. Emphasis can be created by contrast or by extreme changes in an element.

Look once more at Figure 1–8. What has been done to emphasize the face of the young woman?

PROPORTION

Have you ever tasted a food that was so salty you couldn't eat it? The problem was one of proportion. **Proportion** is *the principle of art concerned with the relationship of one part to another and to the whole*.

The principle of proportion is not limited to size. Elements such as color can be used in differing proportions to create emphasis. It is used this way in Figure 1–7. Which color is used in greatest proportion?

MOVEMENT

You may not have realized it, but when you look at a work of art your eye moves from part to part. Artists use the principle of movement to lead the viewer's eyes throughout the work. **Movement** is *the principle of art used to create the look and feeling of action and to guide a viewer's eye throughout the work of art*.

Study yet again the paintings in Figures 1–7, 1–8, and 1–9. How have the artists used line and shape to move your eyes throughout the works?

RHYTHM

Often artists seek to make their works seem active. When they do, they call upon the principle of rhythm. **Rhythm** is *the principle of art concerned with repeating an element to make a work seem active or to suggest vibration*. Sometimes to create rhythm, an artist will repeat not just elements but also the same exact objects over and over. When this is done, a pattern is formed.

Compare the works in Figures 1–7, 1–8, and 1–9. Which uses the principle of rhythm? What element is repeated?

UNITY IN ART

When you look at works of art, it may be difficult to determine where one part ends and the other begins. Instead, the piece of art works together as a whole. It has unity. **Unity** is *the arrangement of elements and principles with media to create a feeling of completeness or wholeness*. You will sense this unity as you look at works of art in which artists use the elements and principles with skill, imagination, and sensitivity.

✔ CHECK YOUR UNDERSTANDING

1. What are principles of art?
2. Name three kinds of balance. Describe each kind.
3. What principles do artists use to prevent works from being static?
4. How can emphasis be created in a work of art?
5. Define *movement*.

Using the Principles of Art

Artists use the language of art in different and often highly imaginative ways. Figure 1–10 gives us painter Charles Demuth's (duh-**mooth**) view of a fire engine racing through a rain-swept city at night.

Notice that the artist has not attempted to create a true-to-life picture. There are no clear images of trucks, wet streets, or darkened buildings. Rather, Demuth has captured the *idea* of those images. Look closely and you can almost hear the screaming of Engine Company 5's siren. You can almost see the red truck's lights flashing.

▲ **Figure 1–10   Charles Demuth creates amazing impact by using simple images. What do you notice first when you look at this picture?**

Charles Henry Demuth. *I Saw the Figure 5 in Gold.* 1928. Oil on composition board. 91.4 x 75.6 cm (36 x 29¾"). The Metropolitan Museum of Art, New York, New York. The Alfred Stieglitz Collection.

WHAT YOU WILL LEARN

You will create the "idea of your name." You will do this through a design made up of the letters of your name or nickname. All the principles of art will be used in your design. You will use watercolor paint and tempera paint in your work. (See Figure 1–11.)

WHAT YOU WILL NEED

- Sheets of scrap paper
- Pencil, ruler, and eraser
- Sheet of white drawing paper, 18 x 24 inches (46 x 61 cm)
- Watercolor paint and several brushes
- Tempera paint and mixing tray

WHAT YOU WILL DO

1. On scrap paper, practice making block letters of different sizes and shapes. Focus only on the letters in your name or nickname. Working lightly in pencil, create a design with the letters on the sheet of drawing paper. Arrange for some of the letters to overlap and some to go off the page. Fill the entire sheet of paper. (See Figure 1–12.)
2. Using the ruler, divide your paper into eight equal rectangles. Each should measure 6 x 9 inches (15 x 23 cm). Number the eight boxed areas lightly in pencil in any order you like.
3. Using the pencil and eraser, draw in or erase lines to rearrange the shapes in Area 1 so they have formal *balance*. Fill in some of the shapes with pencil.
4. Using a *variety* of hues of tempera, paint the shapes in Area 2.
5. Using no more than three hues, paint the shapes in Area 3. Repeat one of these colors over and over to add *harmony*.

6. Identify the most interesting shape in Area 4. Using the brightest hue, paint this area to give *emphasis* to this shape. Paint other shapes with dull hues.

7. Using the pencil and eraser, rearrange the shapes in Area 5 to create *rhythm*. Use watercolors to paint the shapes.

8. Using watercolors, paint the shapes in Area 6. Increase the *proportion* of one of the colors you use. Notice how doing this *emphasizes* that color.

9. Using the pencil and eraser, rearrange the shapes in Area 7 to create a sense of *movement* in any direction. Use watercolors to paint the shapes. Pick colors that will add to the feeling of movement.

10. Rearrange similar shapes in Area 8 to create a pattern. Pick one color of tempera to paint the shapes in Area 8. Paint the nearest shapes. Paint the other shapes, adding white to lighten the value of the hue. (For information on mixing paint to change value, see Technique Tip **12**, *Handbook* page **280**.) In this way the shapes will appear to create rhythm.

11. Display your design and identify the different principles of art found in each area.

EXAMINING YOUR WORK

- **Describe** Tell where the different letters of your name or nickname are found in your design. Identify the art media you used to create the different areas.
- **Analyze** Name the principle of art highlighted in each area of your design.
- **Judge** Tell whether your design clearly highlights each principle of art. Tell which section of your design you think is the most successful. Explain your answer.

SAFETY TIP

Remember to check paints for safety labels. The labels *AP* (for Approved Product) and *CP* (for Certified Product) mean the paint does not contain harmful amounts of poisonous substances. An *HL* label (for Health Label), on the other hand, warns that the paint contains poisonous ingredients and is dangerous to use.

▲ Figure 1–11 Student work. Design using your name.

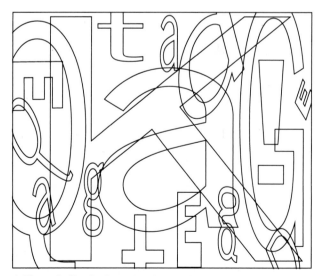

▲ Figure 1–12 Design using the principles of art.

OTHER STUDIO IDEAS

- On a sheet of white paper, create a second design. This work should be based on your initials. Focus on the part of your first design that you found most interesting.

CHAPTER 1 REVIEW

BUILDING VOCABULARY

Number a sheet of paper from 1 to 15. After each number, write the term from the box that best matches each description below.

balance	proportion
color	rhythm
emphasis	shape
form	space
harmony	texture
line	unity
movement	variety
non-objective art	

1. What the eyes see when light is reflected off an object.
2. Path of a moving point through space.
3. The way things feel, or look as though they might feel, if touched.
4. An area clearly set off by one or more of the other elements of art.
5. An object with three dimensions.
6. Arranging elements so no one part of a work overpowers, or seems heavier than, any other part.
7. Combining one or more elements to create interest by adding slight changes.
8. Blending elements to create a more calm, restful appearance.
9. Making an element in a work stand out.
10. The repeating of an element to make a work seem active or to suggest vibration.
11. The relationship of one part to another and to the whole.
12. The arrangement of elements and principles with media to create a feeling of completeness or wholeness.
13. The principle of art used to create the look and feeling of action and to guide a viewer's eye throughout the work.
14. Art works in which no objects or subjects can be readily identified.
15. The distance between, around, above, below, and within things.

REVIEWING ART FACTS

Number a sheet of paper from 16 to 20. Answer each question in a complete sentence.

16. What are the elements of art?
17. Which of the three properties of color refers to a color's name and place on a color wheel?
18. What are the two different kinds of shapes?
19. What is non-objective art?
20. What is symmetrical balance? What is asymmetrical balance?

THINKING ABOUT ART

On a sheet of paper, answer each question in a sentence or two.

1. **Extend.** What kind of lines would you use in creating a picture of an action-packed horse race? What kind of lines would you use in creating a calm, peaceful picture of a lake and trees? Explain your answers.
2. **Analyze.** Which type of shapes, geometric or organic, are you more likely to find in nature? Why do you suppose this to be the case?
3. **Compare and contrast.** What do the elements of shape and form have in common? In what ways are the two different?

MAKING ART CONNECTIONS

1. **Science.** Make a list of the elements of art you have learned about in this chapter. Choose an object from nature that shows examples of these elements. Beside each art element listed, write a one- or two-word description of the natural object you chose.
2. **Language Arts.** Writers use words to express ideas. Choose three words from the elements and principles of art and write a paragraph expressing these ideas.

LOOKING AT THE DETAILS

The detail shown below is from Gabrielle Münter's *Staffelsee in Autumn*. Study the detail and answer the questions below.

1. Give examples of types of shapes that you see in this work. Are they free-form or geometric shapes?
2. How is color used to create unity?

3. Where is the emphasis in this detail? Look at the entire work on page **xviii**. Has the emphasis changed? Explain your answer.
4. What does the artist's choice of color communicate about this scene?

Gabriele Münter. *Staffelsee in Autumn*. 1923. Oil on board. (Detail.) 34.9 x 48.9 cm (13¾ x 19¼"). National Museum of Women in the Arts, Washington, D.C. Gift of Wallace and Wilhelmina Holladay.

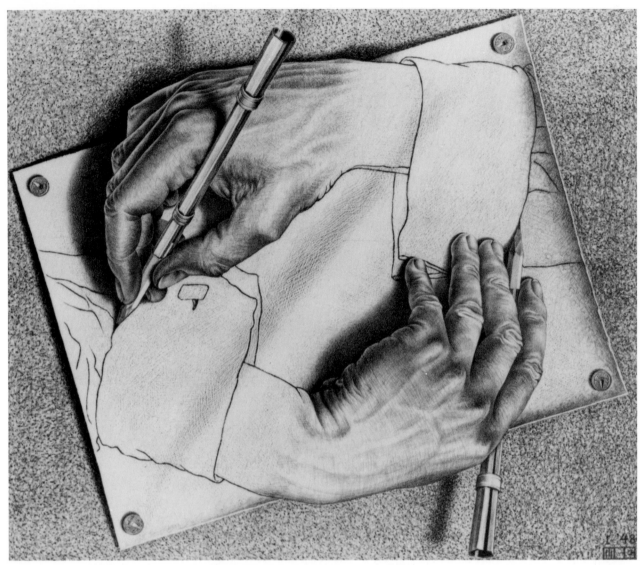

▲ **The artist was famous for creating "impossible" buildings and landscapes. In what way is this work impossible?**

M. C. Escher. *Drawing Hands*. Lithograph. M. C. Escher Heirs/Cordon Art. Baarn, Holland.

CHAPTER 2

The Media of Art

You may think of an artist as someone who paints. While it is true that many artists are painters, paint is just one material artists use. Some artists prefer to work with the tools and materials of sculpting. Others prefer to work with the tools and materials of architecture. Still others would rather work with the tools used to create the picture at the left.

In this chapter you will learn about the many different materials of the artist's profession.

OBJECTIVES

After completing this chapter, you will be able to:
- Name the ways in which drawing, painting, and printmaking media are used in art.
- Explain the basic methods of printmaking and sculpting.
- Explain the basic uses of architecture.
- Name and describe some important crafts.
- Create art work using different art media.

WORDS YOU WILL LEARN

architecture
binder
crafts
edition
freestanding
   sculpture

medium of art
mixed media
pigment
printmaking
relief sculpture
solvent

ARTISTS YOU WILL MEET

Barbara Aubin
Isabel Bishop
Mary Cassatt
Paul Cézanne
Abastenia St. Leger
   Eberle
M. C. Escher

Helen Frankenthaler
Antonio Gaudi
Vinnie Ream Hoxie
John Marin
Joan Miró
Gertrud and Otto
   Natzler

Drawing, Painting, and Printmaking

As you have read, when artists set out to create, they are faced with many choices. One of the most important is the decision of which medium to use. A **medium of art** is *a material used to create a work of art*. Paint, which you used in the studio lessons in Chapter 1, is one medium. Pencil and crayon, which you also used, are two others. When we speak of more than one medium at a time, we use the plural *media*.

▲ Figure 2–1 Works created with pastels sometimes seem like paintings. What does this work have in common with a painting? How is it different?

Mary Cassatt. *Sleepy Baby.* c. 1910. Pastel on paper. 64.7 x 52.0 cm (25½ x 20½"). Dallas Museum of Art, Dallas, Texas. Munger Fund.

When artists use several different media, such as pen and ink and watercolor, they create a mixed media work of art. **Mixed media** means *the use of more than one medium in a work of art*.

In this lesson you will learn about the media used in drawing, painting, and printmaking.

DRAWING

If you have ever scribbled with a pen or pencil, you have used drawing media. Pen, pencil, charcoal, and chalk are some of the media used to draw. The picture in Figure 2–1 was made using another medium, pastels. This is a soft, chalky medium. Notice how delicately the artist has used this medium to capture her subject.

The Purpose of Drawing

Artists use drawing for different purposes. One is to create finished works of art, such as the one you have just seen. Another use is to help plan projects. Artists often make studies, or sketches, for their works. Look at the drawing in Figure 2–2. This was done by French artist Paul Cézanne (say-**zahn**) as a study for the painting in Figure 2–3. Can you match up the figure in the drawing with one in the painting?

PAINTING

Like other artists, painters use a wide variety of media. Before a painter begins a work, he or she chooses a type of paint and an appropriate surface on which to work. Canvas, paper, or fabric are three surface materials that painters use.

▲ **Figure 2–2** Cézanne used pencil and watercolors for his study of a card player. Did he use all the detail captured in this sketch for his painted version?

Paul Cézanne. *The Card Player.* 1892. Pencil and watercolor. 53.4 x 36.4 cm (20¼ x 14⁹⁄₁₆"). Museum of Art, Rhode Island School of Design, Providence, Rhode Island. Gift of Mrs. Murray S. Danforth.

Regardless of the type of paint, all paint has three basic parts:

- **Pigment** (**pig**-muhnt) is *a finely ground, colored powder that gives every paint its color.*
- **Binder** is *a liquid that holds together the grains of pigment.* The binder is what makes the pigment stick to a surface.
- **Solvent** is *a material used to thin a paint's binder.* The thickness or thinness of a paint depends on the amount of solvent used. Turpentine is the solvent in oil paints. Water is the solvent in watercolors. Solvents are also used to clean brushes.

Painting Media

Every medium of painting has its own unmistakable look. Some of the most commonly used media are the following:

- **Oil paint.** Oil paint takes its name from its binder, linseed oil. Turpentine is its solvent. Because oil paint dries slowly, the artist is able to blend colors right on the canvas. The painting in Figure 2–3, which you have already examined, was painted with oils.

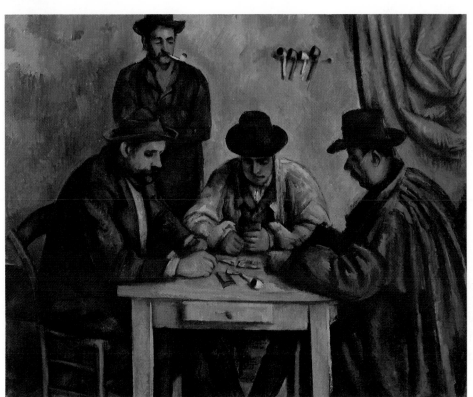

◀ **Figure 2–3** Did the medium make a difference in how Cézanne painted the figures in his oil painting? Compare the man in the sketch with the one in the final version.

Paul Cézanne. *The Card Players.* Oil on canvas. 65.4 x 81.9 cm (25¾ x 32¼"). The Metropolitan Museum of Art, New York, New York. Bequest of Stephen C. Clark.

► Figure 2–4   Study the painting on the right. Can you find spots in the picture where the artist seems to have used a lot of solvent? Do you remember what the solvent for watercolor is?

John Marin. *Sunset, Casco Bay.* 1936. Watercolor on paper. Wichita Art Museum, Wichita, Kansas. Ronald P. Murdock Collection.

- **Tempera** (**tem**-puh-ruh). Some of the earliest paintings on record were made with tempera. A mixture of pigment, egg yolk, and water, tempera is very hard to use. The school tempera you used in the studio lesson in Chapter 1 is a different type. It is also called poster paint.

- **Watercolor.** Watercolor is named for its solvent. Its binder, gum arabic, is a gummy plant matter. Watercolor gives paintings a light, misty quality. Look at the painting in Figure 2–4. Notice how the sun rays seem to "melt" into the sky and water.

- **Acrylic** (uh-**kril**-ik). A quick-drying water-based paint, acrylic is a very popular medium among painters today. Acrylics are synthetic, or manufactured, paints that were introduced in the 1950s. Because its solvent is water, acrylic is easy to use. More important, it offers the artist a wide range of pure, bold colors. Notice the lively splashes of color in the work in Figure 2–5.

▲ Figure 2–5   Do you think this artist was interested in painting a clear and real-looking subject? If not, what do you think she was interested in?

Helen Frankenthaler. *Interior Landscape.* 1964. Acrylic on canvas. 266.4 x 235.3 cm (104⅞ x 92⅝"). San Francisco Museum of Modern Art, San Francisco, California. Gift of The Women's Board.

PRINTMAKING BASICS

Over the centuries artists have searched for new ways to create art. Around 2,000 years ago the Chinese developed a form of art called **printmaking**. This is *a technique in which an inked image from a prepared surface is transferred onto another surface*, such as paper or fabric.

There are three basic steps in printmaking. First, the printmaker creates a printing plate by altering a surface to create an image. Next, ink is applied to the plate. Finally, the printmaker transfers the ink to the paper or cloth by pressing the plate against the surface to be printed and then pulling the paper or cloth off the plate.

These steps may be repeated many times for a given plate. *A series of identical prints made from a single plate* is called an **edition**.

Printmaking Methods

There are four main methods of making prints. These are:

- **Relief printing**. In relief printing, the image to be printed is raised from a background. A medium used often in relief printing is wood.
- **Intaglio** (in-**tal**-yoh). Intaglio may be thought of as the reverse of relief printing. In this method, the image to be printed is scratched or etched into a surface. (See Figure 2–6.) The plates for intaglio prints are often made of metal.
- **Lithography** (lith-**ahg**-ruh-fee). To make a lithograph, the artist draws the image to be printed on a limestone, zinc, or aluminum slab with a special greasy crayon. Lithography lets the artist blend, little by little, light and dark values of a hue. The art on page **16** is a lithograph.
- **Screen printing**. To make a screen print, the artist transfers the design through various processes on a silk screen. The areas not to be printed are blocked off so that a kind of stencil remains. Screen prints that are handmade by an artist are also known as serigraphs (**ser**-uh-grafs).

✔CHECK YOUR UNDERSTANDING

1. Define *medium of art*.
2. Name three media used in drawing.
3. What are the three basic parts, or ingredients, of paint?
4. Name three media used in painting.
5. Name and describe two printmaking methods.

◀ **Figure 2–6 Notice how the use of line and shapes can be effective in different media, as in this intaglio print.**

Isabel Bishop. *Men and Girls Walking*. 1969. Aquatint on paper. 21.3 x 29.2 cm (8⅜ x 11½″). National Museum of Women in the Arts, Washington, D.C. Gift of Mr. and Mrs. Edward P. Levy.

Creating Mixed-Media Art

Study the mixed-media work of art in Figure 2–7. Notice how the artist has united visual and verbal symbols. The letters are woven into the design so that their shapes are as important as their meanings. They are not written in neat rows that are easy to read, but are integrated into the surface of the work.

Some of the visual symbols are directly related to the words, while other symbols just fit the design. Some visual symbols have been drawn and painted by the artist, or have been printed with rubber stamps. Others are made with decals, lace, and stamps. Notice that some of the letters are written and printed by the artist. Stick-on letters or those cut from magazines and glued on are also used.

WHAT YOU WILL LEARN

You will create a mixed-media design uniting visual and verbal symbols in the manner of Aubin. Weave the letters into the design so that their shapes are as important as their meanings. Use the principle of rhythm to create a sense of visual movement in the work. Use harmony of shape, color, and texture to unify your work.

▲ **Figure 2–7**   The artist, Barbara Aubin, created a dream-like mood in this work. What other sources of inspiration do artists use in getting ideas for their art?

Barbara Aubin. *I Dreamed I Saw a Pink Flamingo in the Salle de Bain.* 1981. Mixed media on paper. (Detail.) 45.7 x 61 cm (18 x 24″).

WHAT YOU WILL NEED

- Pencil and sketch paper
- Found materials
- Magazines, scissors, and white glue
- Envelope
- Construction paper or lightweight poster board, 12 x 18 inches (30 x 46 cm), in a color of your choice
- Watercolor markers, thick and thin-tipped
- Crayons, colored pencils, and watercolor paints

WHAT YOU WILL DO

1. Select some lines from a favorite poem, song, story, or saying. The words may be your own or something you have read. Write the words on your sketch paper.
2. Make sketches of objects and scenes to go with your words.
3. Look through magazines and cut out interesting shapes, letters, or printed words for your work. Collect found materials that fit your ideas. Keep all the small cutouts in an envelope. Select a color for your background.
4. Notice how Aubin has used the letters as design elements. They are not written in neat rows that are easy to read, but are woven into the composition as shapes. Make some rough sketches to plan your design on your sketch paper. Repeat shapes to create movement that makes the viewer's eyes move through the work. Plan for harmony by using monochromatic or analogous colors as well as related shapes and textures. Select your best idea, and sketch it lightly on your construction paper or poster board.

EXAMINING YOUR WORK

- **Describe**   Identify the media you used. Read the phrase you chose, and explain why you chose it. Describe the visual images you chose to go with the words.
- **Analyze**   What shapes did you repeat to create rhythmic movement? How did you use color, shape, and texture to create harmony?
- **Judge**   Did you create a unified design? Are the verbal symbols and visual images equally important? If not, how could the unity of the work be improved?

5. Place the found objects and cutouts on your design. Do not glue them down. Take time to arrange and rearrange your words and images until you are satisfied. Then glue them down.
6. Use a variety of media to draw and paint the remaining images and words. For example, use paints to fill large spaces, and use fine-line markers to draw thin lines.
7. Place your work on display with that of your classmates. Look for works in which the words and pictures are unified.

OTHER STUDIO IDEAS

- Select one key word from current events. Cut out the word itself and photographs illustrating that word from newspapers and magazines. Create a mixed-media work in the same manner as described in this lesson.

- ● Make another mixed-media work combining art media with recyclable found materials. You may integrate words cut from recyclable newspaper, but do not let the words dominate your work.

Sculpture, Architecture, and Crafts Media

Drawings, paintings, and prints created as two-dimensional works often appear to have roundness and depth. Some works of art have *real* roundness and depth. These works, which have height, width, and depth, are known as three-dimensional works.

In this lesson you will learn about three areas of art—sculpture, architecture, and crafts—in which three-dimensional works are created. You will learn about the media used in making such works.

SCULPTURE

Sculpture is art that is made to stand out in space. All sculpture is of one of two types, freestanding or relief. Also called sculpture "in the round," **freestanding sculpture** is *sculpture surrounded on all sides by space.* It is meant to be seen from all sides. The work in Figure 2–8 is an example of freestanding sculpture.

Relief sculpture, on the other hand, is *sculpture only partly enclosed by space.* It is flat along the back and is meant to be viewed only from the front. The work in Figure 2–9 is an example of relief sculpture.

Sculpting Methods

Sculptors use four basic methods or techniques in their work. These are:

- **Carving.** Carving is cutting or chipping a form from a mass. Often stone and other hard materials are used in carving. The sculpture in Figure 2–8 was carved from a block of marble.

▲ Figure 2–8 Hoxie used a very hard medium and was still able to portray fabric falling in soft folds. How does the light help?

Vinnie Ream Hoxie. *Abraham Lincoln.* 1870. Marble. 210.8 cm (6'11") high. United States Capitol Art Collection.

▲ **Figure 2–9** Notice how the horses seem to be galloping in this relief sculpture. This frieze circles the top of a famous Greek temple known as the Parthenon.

Horsemen Riding at a Gallop. Parthenon. British Museum.

- **Casting**. In casting, a melted-down metal or other liquid substance is poured into a mold to harden. Bronze is a material often used in casting. (See Figure 2–10.)
- **Modeling**. In modeling, a soft or workable material is built up and shaped. Clay is the material used most often in this sculpting method.
- **Assembling**. Assembling is gathering and joining different kinds of materials. Wood, wire, glue, and nails are a few of the materials used in assembling. The figure on page **28** is an example of assembling.

▶ **Figure 2–10** How did the sculptor show movement in this figure? Would you have needed the title to tell you the wind was blowing?

Abastenia St. Leger Eberle. *The Windy Doorstep.* 1910. Bronze. 34.5 x 24.4 x 16 cm (13⅝ x 9⅝ x 6⅜"). Worcester Art Museum, Worcester, Massachusetts.

▶ **Figure 2–11** This is a unique example of architecture. Notice how the architect repeated the pointed arch shape in the towers, emphasizing the height of the structure.

Antonio Gaudi. *Church of the Sacred Family.* Barcelona, Spain.

ARCHITECTURE

All art is made to be seen. Some art is made to be used as well as seen. Works of art known as architecture fit into this second category. **Architecture** is *the planning and creating of buildings.* The success of a work of architecture is measured partly by how well it does the job it was meant to do and partly by its appearance.

The Uses of Architecture

Since earliest times, a chief form of architecture has been the creation of dwelling places. This has by no means been the only type, however. Two other examples have been the artistic creation of the following kinds of buildings:

- **Structures for prayer.** The building of temples, churches, and other houses of worship dates to the dawn of history. The unusual house of prayer shown in Figure 2–11 was begun in the late 1800s. It is still under construction. Notice how this unique building seems almost to be reaching toward the sky.

- **Structures for business.** With the spread of civilization in ancient times came the need for places to carry on business. In our own time that need is often met by vertical creations such as skyscrapers.

CRAFTS

In ages past, artists worked not only out of a desire to create but also out of a need to provide items required for everyday use. Clothing, cooking pots, and whatever other goods people needed were handmade.

Artistic craftspeople still make functional items that are often considered aesthetically pleasing works of art. The useful and decorative goods these artists make, and *the different areas of applied art in which craftspeople work* are called **crafts**.

Craft Areas

Craftspeople today, like those long ago, work in a number of special areas. Some of these are:

- **Pottery**. This is the making of objects from clay. Before objects of pottery can be used, they must be hardened by heat, or fired. This takes place in a special oven called a kiln. Ceramics is the name of objects made in this fashion. The vase shown in Figure 2–12 is an example of modern American ceramics.
- **Weaving**. This is the interlocking of fiber strands to create objects. Fibers such as wool, cotton, plant materials, and synthetic materials are used in weaving. Weaving is done on a special machine called a loom, which holds the threads in place as they are woven together. The weaving in Figure 2–13 was done by twentieth-century Spanish artist Joan Miró (zhoh-**ahn** mee-**roh**).
- **Glassblowing**. This is the shaping of melted glass into objects. Glassblowers work by forcing air through a tube into globs of melted glass.

▲ **Figure 2–13   This weaving shows large areas of color against a textured background. Can you see a woman in the tapestry?**

Joan Miró, Josep Royo. *Woman*. 1977. Dyed New Zealand Wool. 105.3 x 604.3 cm (415 x 238″). National Gallery of Art, Washington, D.C. Gift of the Collectors Committee and George L. Erion.

▲ **Figure 2–12   The Natzlers are famous for their glazes. They called this a crater glaze.**

Gertrud Natzler/Otto Natzler. *Pilgrim Bottle*. c. 1956. Earthenware. 33 x 43 cm (17 x 13″). Los Angeles County Museum of Art, Los Angeles, California. Gift of Howard and Gwen Laurie Smits.

✔ CHECK YOUR UNDERSTANDING

1. What are the two main types of sculpture?
2. What are the four basic sculpting methods?
3. Define *architecture*. How is the success of a work of architecture measured?
4. Define *crafts*. Name three areas in which craftspeople work.

Creating an Environmental Design

Today we are all concerned about our environment. Some people have invented a way to recycle used tires by building playgrounds with them. (See Figure 2–14.) These areas are fun, and they are also visually pleasing. They have visual unity.

WHAT YOU WILL DO

Working in teams of three to five, you will design and construct models of playground equipment using found materials. You will organize this equipment on a heavy cardboard base that represents the ground. The forms you create must invite children to crawl through, jump over, climb up, and balance upon. You must also consider space in this plan. Consider how children will move around the area. Place equipment pieces with space for the children to move around the area.

▶ Figure 2–14 Recycled tires provide safe and inviting playground equipment. What other products might be given a second life in parks and playgrounds?

WHAT YOU WILL NEED

- Found materials
- White glue, transparent tape, pins, and scissors
- Markers, school acrylics, paint brushes, and construction paper
- Piece of heavy cardboard, 18 x 18 inches (46 x 46 cm) or larger

WHAT YOU WILL DO

1. Collect a large assortment of found materials such as corks, wood scraps, and plastic containers.
2. Brainstorm with your class for ideas about things young children would like to play on in a playground.
3. Divide into small groups of three to five students. Work together as a team to solve problems. Look over the found materials you have collected. Experiment with the forms. Try different ways to combine objects until they look like something to climb up, crawl through, swing on, balance upon, or jump over. When you are satisfied with the forms, glue them together. Since white glue takes time to dry, you might want to secure some pieces with pins or tape until the glue dries.
4. You may decorate some pieces with markers, paint, or construction paper.
5. Get out the cardboard base, and arrange your model equipment on the base. Remember to consider the necessary space between different pieces of equipment. When you are satisfied with the arrangement, glue the equipment to the base.
6. Decorate the base by painting it or gluing sand to it to make it look like earth. You might turn twigs into trees by adding

EXAMINING YOUR WORK

- **Describe** Identify the found materials you collected, and point to the ones you used. Explain how the brainstorming session helped in the planning stages. Tell how your group worked together. Describe the equipment you constructed. What can a child do on each piece?
- **Analyze** Explain how you decided to arrange the space for each piece.
- **Interpret** What did you name your playground? Why?
- **Judge** Tell whether your design was successful.

green paper leaves. You may even make some cutouts of people to play on the playground. (See Figure 2–15.)
7. Give your playground a name, and put it on a sign. Place your work on display with the other model playgrounds. Which ones invite you to play?

▲ **Figure 2–15 Student work. Environmental design.**

OTHER STUDIO IDEAS

- Create a playground using paper sculpture techniques to create the forms. (See Technique Tip **21**, *Handbook* page **284**.)

- • Use found materials to create a model of a shelter for travelers who have been stranded on a desert island.

BUILDING VOCABULARY

Number a sheet of paper from 1 to 11. After each number, write the term from the box that best matches each description below.

architecture	medium of art
binder	mixed media
crafts	pigment
edition	printmaking
freestanding	relief sculpture
sculpture	solvent

1. A material used to create a work of art.
2. A finely ground powder that gives every paint its color.
3. A liquid that holds together the grains of pigment in paint.
4. A material used to thin a paint's binder.
5. A technique in which an inked image from a prepared surface is transferred onto another surface.
6. A series of identical prints made from a single plate.
7. Sculpture surrounded on all sides by space.
8. Sculpture partly enclosed by space.
9. The planning and creating of buildings.
10. The different areas of applied art in which craftspeople work.
11. The use of more than one medium in a work of art.

REVIEWING ART FACTS

Number a sheet of paper from 12 to 17. Answer each question in a complete sentence.

12. What are the two main ways in which artists use drawing?
13. Describe the steps in printmaking.
14. What is a lithograph? What is a serigraph? What is a woodcut?
15. What is "in the round" a substitute term for?
16. In what method of sculpting is a melted-down metal poured into a mold?
17. What are three types of architecture?

THINKING ABOUT ART

On a sheet of paper, answer each question in a sentence or two.

1. **Compare and contrast**. Some paints, as you learned, dry slowly and others dry quickly. What would be some of the advantages and disadvantages of each type?
2. **Extend**. In attempting to define *art* over the centuries, scholars have often noted that an art work is a one-of-a-kind creation. Does accepting this view rule out prints as a form of art? Explain your answer.
3. **Analyze**. Which of the methods of sculpting you learned about would be best for making a sand castle? Explain your choice.
4. **Extend**. Name two kinds of structures not mentioned in this chapter that architects create. Look through books and magazines and bring examples to class.

MAKING ART CONNECTIONS

1. **Social Studies.** Many people today create crafts as a leisure activity. Try to find an individual you know who is interested in a craft. Interview him or her and make a report for your class. Tell how the craft affects the life of the person.
2. **Science.** Find out how the study of anatomy contributes to the work of a sculptor. Compare an anatomical drawing from a science book to a freestanding sculpture of the same subject. What similarities and differences do you see?

LOOKING AT THE DETAILS

The detail shown below is from M. C. Escher's *Drawing Hands*. Study the detail and answer the following questions.

1. What did the artist accomplish by combining a highly detailed hand with the unfinished sketch of a cuff?
2. Would it have been possible for Escher to show as much realistic detail if he had used oil paints?

3. Which parts of the drawing depict three-dimensional form and which show only shape? Why?
4. Look at the entire work on page **16**. What is lost by looking at only the detail?
5. Looking at the entire work, which element of art does the artist emphasize and how?
6. What is it about this work that appears to be "impossible"?

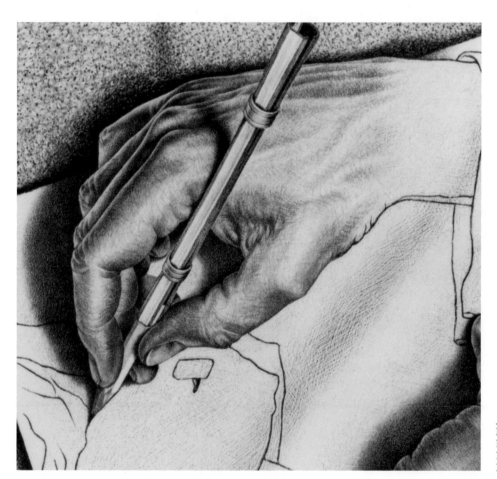

M. C. Escher. *Drawing Hands.*
Lithograph. (Detail.) M. C.
Escher Heirs/Cordon Art. Baarn,
Holland.

▲ Early in his career Georges Rouault worked for a maker of stained glass. What makes this painting look like a stained-glass window?

Georges Rouault. *Christ Mocked by Soldiers*. 1932. Oil on canvas. 92.1 x 72.4 cm (36¼ x 28½").
Museum of Modern Art, New York, New York. Given anonymously.

CHAPTER 3

Art Criticism, Aesthetics, and Art History

Imagine you were visiting the museum where the painting on the left is hung. What questions might you ask as you look at the painting? You might ask:

- With what media and how was the painting made?
- What elements and principles of art are used?
- How does the painting make me feel?
- Who is the artist, and when and where was the art work made?

What other questions might you ask? In this chapter you will learn how to find your own answers to the questions about works of art.

OBJECTIVES

After completing this chapter, you will be able to:
- Describe the four steps used in art criticism.
- Identify three aesthetic views.
- Explain the four steps used by art historians.
- Create paintings based on art criticism and art history.

WORDS YOU WILL LEARN

aesthetic view
art criticism
art history
composition

content
style
subject

ARTISTS YOU WILL MEET

James Brooks
Edward Hopper
Pablo Picasso

Georges Rouault
Jan Steen
Beatrice Whitney
van Ness

Art Criticism and Aesthetics

You have heard the saying "Don't judge a book by its cover." What this saying means is that to judge something fairly, you need to have all the facts. It is not enough to look at the surface of the object. You need to dig beneath the surface — to understand as much as you can about the object.

In this lesson you will learn ways of looking at art that will help increase your understanding and appreciation of it.

ART CRITICISM

Have you ever looked at a work of art and wondered if there was more to the painting than you understood? You may have asked yourself this question when you looked at Figure 3–1. Works of art are sometimes like mysteries. Solving art mysteries is one of the jobs of people in the field called art criticism. **Art criticism** is *studying, understanding, and judging works of art*.

In carrying out their work, art critics often use a four-step system. The four steps are describing, analyzing, interpreting, and judging.

▶ **Figure 3–1   In describing this art work, what element would you choose to discuss first? What do you think the artist was most interested in as he created this oil painting?**

James Brooks. *Rasalus*. 1959. Oil on canvas. 167.6 x 202.6 cm (66 x 79¾"). Whitney Museum of American Art, New York, New York.

Describing an Art Work

In describing an art work, the critic notes certain key facts. These include the following:

- **The size of the work, the medium, and the process used.** The credit line gives the viewer information about the size of the work and the medium used. It also lists the process, such as serigraph or woodcut.
- **The subject, object, and details.** The **subject** is *the image viewers can easily identify in an art work*. The subject answers the question "What do I see when I look at this work?" The subject in Figure 3–2 is a group of people, probably a family, at a holiday gathering. What other objects and details might the art critic mention? What subject, object, and details would be described in Figure 3–3 on page **36**?

- **The elements used in the work.** Look again at Figure 3–2. Line and color are two of the elements of art that play an important part in this work. Can you identify the other art elements? What elements can you point out in Figure 3–3?

Notice that while every work of art uses elements, not all have subjects. Figure 3–1 is a painting without a recognized subject. Because such works are not "about" something, some viewers are uncertain how to describe them. These viewers should learn to focus attention on the elements of art. This is what the critic—or anyone else—will see in this work. This is called describing the formal aspects of the work.

◀ **Figure 3–2   Notice the title of the work. What American holiday is similar to the one being celebrated in this picture? What do you think the man at the right is pointing to?**

Jan Steen. *Eve of St. Nicholas.* c. 1667. Canvas. 81.9 x 70.5 cm (32¼ x 27¾"). Rijksmuseum, Amsterdam.

▲ Figure 3–3   Is this work successful because it looks lifelike or because it expresses an idea or mood? Why is it necessary to use more than one aesthetic view when judging works of art?

Beatrice Whitney van Ness. *Summer Sunlight.* c. 1936. Oil on canvas. 99.1 x 124.5 cm (39 x 49"). National Museum of Women in the Arts, Washington, D.C. Gift of Wallace and Wilhelmina Holladay.

Analyzing an Art Work

In analyzing an art work, the critic focuses on the work's composition. **Composition** is *the way the art principles are used to organize the art elements of color, line, shape, form, space, and texture.* Look once again at the painting in Figure 3–2 on page **35**. Find the long loaf of bread in the lower left and the chair in the lower right. Notice how the diagonal lines of these and other objects lead your eye to the center of the picture. There you find a small child grinning and looking out at you. The child is one of the most important figures in the work. How are the elements organized in the painting in Figure 3–3?

Interpreting an Art Work

In interpreting an art work, the critic focuses on the work's **content**. This is *the message, idea, or feeling expressed by an art work.* Each art critic may interpret an art work differently, according to individual feelings. Your interpretation of an art work will be based on your personal opinions and experiences.

Look once more at Figure 3–2. Notice that the grinning child is pointing at another child, who is crying. It appears that this second boy has received no presents. His smiling sister holds his wooden shoe in which his gifts were to be placed. But the shoe holds only a hickory stick instead of presents. Maybe the artist's message to children of all ages is that gifts come only to those who behave. What mood or feeling does the painting in Figure 3–3 communicate to you?

Judging an Art Work

In judging an art work, the critic tells whether the work succeeds. He or she answers the question "Is this a successful work of art?"

How, exactly, the critic answers this question depends on his or her particular aesthetic (ess-**thet**-ik) view. An **aesthetic view** is *an idea, or school of thought, on what is important in a work of art*. Such views help critics better understand and explain the meaning of art to others.

AESTHETICS AND ART

Through the ages, scholars have put forth many different aesthetic views. The following are three common ones:

- **The subject view.** In this aesthetic view, a successful work of art is one with a lifelike subject. Look yet again at the picture in Figure 3–2. The members of the family are painted to look like real people. Critics holding this aesthetic view would praise this work for being true to life. How do you think these same critics would react to the painting in Figure 3–3? How would they judge the painting in Figure 3–1?
- **The composition view.** In this view, what is most important in an art work is its composition. Notice how light and dark

values of hue in Figure 3–2 create a feeling of depth. Critics taking this view would praise the artist's use of the elements and principles of art to create a visually pleasing design. How do you suppose these same critics would respond to the work in Figure 3–3? How might they react to the picture in Figure 3–1?
- **The content view.** In this view, what counts most is the content, or the mood or feeling, an art work communicates. Critics supporting this view would praise the work in Figure 3–2 for the joyous holiday mood it captures. What do you imagine these critics would have to say about the painting in Figure 3–3? What might their response be to the painting in Figure 3–1?

Keep in mind that few critics limit themselves to a single aesthetic view. Most feel that learning as much as possible from an art work requires keeping an open mind. How might a critic accepting all three views above react to the painting that opened this chapter on page **32**?

✔ CHECK YOUR UNDERSTANDING

1. What is art criticism? Name the four steps used by art critics.
2. What are subject, composition, and content?
3. What is an aesthetic view?
4. Describe the three commonly held aesthetic views detailed in this lesson.

Painting an Expressive Scene

Study the painting in Figure 3–4. The work is by American painter Edward Hopper. How do you think an art critic would react to this painting? What is the work's subject? What elements are emphasized? What principles are used to organize the elements? What mood or feeling does the work express? Does the work succeed? Why, or why not? One last question: How do you think the painting would look if the artist had extended its left boundary?

WHAT YOU WILL LEARN

You will create a painting that continues the row of empty shops in Figure 3–4. You will use the same hues, values, and intensities in your work. You will create harmony by repeating the same vertical and horizontal lines. You will add variety by placing a circular shape somewhere in your work. Finally, you will try to capture the same feeling of loneliness. (See Figure 3–5.)

WHAT YOU WILL NEED

- Pencil, sketch paper, and eraser
- Sheet of white drawing paper, 8 x 13 inches (20 x 33 cm)
- Tempera paint and several brushes
- Mixing tray

WHAT YOU WILL DO

1. Imagine the scene in Figure 3–4 as it might appear if the artist had continued it on the left side. Make several pencil sketches of possibilities you imagine. Use horizontal and vertical lines like the ones in the painting to outline shapes. For variety, include somewhere in each sketch an object with a circular shape. (Did you discover the circular shape in Hopper's painting when you examined its elements?) Let your imagination guide you.

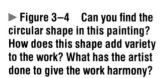

▶ **Figure 3–4** Can you find the circular shape in this painting? How does this shape add variety to the work? What has the artist done to give the work harmony?

Edward Hopper. *Early Sunday Morning*. 1930. Oil on canvas. 88.9 x 152.4 cm (35 x 60"). Whitney Museum of American Art, New York, New York. Gertrude Vanderbilt Whitney Funds.

2. Place the sheet of drawing paper alongside the photograph of Figure 3–4. Line up the paper so that it touches the left edge of the photograph. Starting at the edge of the paper, carefully continue the horizontal lines of the buildings and sidewalk. Working lightly in pencil, draw details from the best of your sketches.
3. Mix tempera colors to match the hues, values, and intensities of Figure 3–4. Use a brush to fill in the shapes of your drawing with color. (For information on using a brush see Technique Tip **4**, *Handbook* page **277**.)
4. Allow time for your painting to dry. Display the finished work alongside those created by other members of your class. Discuss your works using the steps in art criticism.

▲ Figure 3–5   Student work. Expressive scene.

EXAMINING YOUR WORK

- **Describe**   Point out the row of buildings and empty streets in your picture. Explain how they resemble the buildings and streets in Figure 3–4. Identify the hues, values, and intensities in your work. Show where these same elements are found in Figure 3–4.
- **Analyze**   Explain how you used the principles of harmony and variety. Point to places in Figure 3–4 where these same principles have been used.
- **Interpret**   Ask other students to describe the mood expressed by your picture. See if they are able to identify a mood of loneliness.
- **Judge**   Tell whether your picture looks like the one in Figure 3–4. State whether it uses many of the same elements and principles. Tell whether your work is successful in expressing the same mood of loneliness.

OTHER STUDIO IDEAS

- Imagine you live in the apartment above the barbershop in the work in Figure 3–4. Complete a perspective drawing of things you might see looking out the window of your apartment. Before you begin your drawing, think about the feeling your work will express.

- ●● Complete another painting of the same street scene, this one titled *Late Saturday Night*. Show how the scene might come alive on a Saturday night. Include people, cars, and other objects. Change the hues, values, and intensities of color to create a mood of excitement.

Art History

Look briefly again at the painting in Figure 3–4 on page **38**. Having created an "extension" to the work, you now have a better understanding of its composition and content. What do you know about its artist, Edward Hopper? When and where did he live? Did

his other paintings look like the one in Figure 3–6? Is he thought to be an important artist?

Answering these and similar questions is the goal of art history. In this lesson you will learn ways of answering these questions.

▲ **Figure 3–6**   **What makes this work more than just a realistic picture of two people in a room? How do these people behave toward each other? How do their actions make you feel?**

Edward Hopper. *Room in New York.* 1932. Oil on canvas. 71.1 x 91.4 cm (28 x 36"). Sheldon Memorial Art Gallery, University of Nebraska, Lincoln, Nebraska. F. M. Hall Collection.

ART HISTORY AND YOU

To understand an art work completely, you need to do more than just look at it. You need to look beyond it. You need to know when and where the work was done. You need to know something about the artist who created it. Searching of this sort is the job of people in the field of art history. **Art history** is *the study of art from past to present*.

When they study art, art historians often use the same four steps art critics use: they describe, analyze, interpret, and judge. Unlike art critics, however, art historians do not use these steps to learn *from* art. They use them to learn *about* art.

Describing an Art Work

In describing an art work, art historians answer the questions "Who?" "Where?" and "When?" In other words, "Who painted the work, and when and where was it painted?" Look at the painting in Figure 3–6. Acting as an art historian, you can answer the first two of these questions by reading the credit line. The "who" is, again, Edward Hopper. The "when" is 1932. A visit to your school or local library will give you more information about the artist. There you will find that Hopper was an American painter who lived from 1882 to 1967.

Analyzing an Art Work

In analyzing an art work, the historian focuses on questions of style. **Style** is *an artist's personal way of using the elements and principles of art and expressing feelings and ideas in art*. Two typical questions the historian asks when analyzing a work are the following:

- What style did the artist use?
- Did the artist use the same style in other works?

Look again at the painting in Figure 3–6. An art historian would describe the style of this work as realistic. Compare this work with Figure 3–4 on page **38**. Would you say that both are done in a realistic style? Do you sense the same feeling of quiet loneliness in each?

Interpreting an Art Work

In interpreting an art work, the historian tries to determine how time and place may have affected the artist's style. Usually, this requires some research on the art historian's part. A trip to the library would reveal that:

- The painting in Figure 3–6 was completed during a period called the Great Depression.
- The Depression was a time during the 1930s when many people were out of work and money was scarce.
- To many people living through the Depression, the future looked hopeless.

In this work, Hopper captures the loneliness many people felt during that bleak time. The painting shows two people in a room. Notice that they do not face one another. Each, in fact, seems to be ignoring the other. A large door seems further to separate them. The people share the room but little else. Each is neglected and alone.

Judging an Art Work

In judging an art work, the historian notes its place in all art history. The historian decides whether the work and its artist make an important contribution to art. One way in which an artist can make a contribution is by introducing new materials or perfecting a style. Hopper is noted for developing a style that captured the mood of the times more effectively than most artists of that period.

✔CHECK YOUR UNDERSTANDING

1. What is art history?
2. Explain *describing, analyzing, interpreting,* and *judging* as the terms are used by art historians.
3. Define *style*.

Painting in the Cubist Style

Study the painting in Figure 3–7. Think about how an art historian would react to this work. Begin by describing the work. Who is the artist? When was the painting done? The style, Cubism (**kyoob**-izm), grew out of a wish to show objects from many different angles at once. Would you guess that Cubist works like this changed the course of art history? Why, or why not?

WHAT YOU WILL LEARN

Using tempera, you will enlarge and re-create a section of the painting in Figure 3–7 or of another Cubist painting. You will use the same colors, lines, shapes, and textures in your work that were used in the original. You will use the principles of variety, harmony, and rhythm to organize these elements. Your section will be added to those completed by your classmates to form a large version of Figure 3–7. (See Figure 3–8.)

WHAT YOU WILL NEED

- Tracing paper, pencil, and ruler
- Sheet of white drawing paper, 8 x 24 inches (20 x 61 cm)
- Tempera paint and several brushes
- Mixing tray

▶ **Figure 3–7** Why do you think this artist is among the best known in the history of art? Which aesthetic view would you use when judging this work of art?

Pablo Picasso. *First Steps*. 1943. Oil on canvas. 130.2 x 97.1 cm (51¼ x 38¼"). Yale University, New Haven, Connecticut. Gift of Stephen C. Clark.

WHAT YOU WILL DO

1. Lay a sheet of tracing paper over the painting in Figure 3–7. Using pencil, lightly and carefully trace the lines and shapes of the picture.
2. Using a ruler, divide your drawing into sections measuring 3 x 1 inches (8 x 3 cm). Your teacher will assign you one of the sections. Enlarge and draw freehand the lines and shapes of your section onto the sheet of drawing paper. Stay as close as you can to the original work.
3. Mix tempera colors to match the hues used in Figure 3–7. (For information on mixing paints, see Technique Tip **12**, *Handbook* page **280**). As you work, try also to use the same lines, textures, and shapes found in the original painting.
4. When your section is dry, add it to those completed by other members of your class. Compare your class effort with the original work. Decide whether it is made up of the same features as the original.

EXAMINING YOUR WORK

- **Describe**   Identify the objects in your section of the class painting. Show where these same objects are found in the matching section of the original art. Point out the colors, lines, textures, and shapes in your section. Show where these same elements are found in the matching section of the original.
- **Analyze**   Explain how you used the principles of harmony, variety, and rhythm. Point out places in the matching section of the original where these same principles have been used.
- **Judge**   Tell whether your section of the painting blends in with those completed by classmates. If it does not, explain why. Tell whether the class effort as a whole succeeds. Explain your answer.

▶ **Figure 3–8**   Student work. Cubist style painting using another Cubist work.

OTHER STUDIO IDEAS

- Make another painting of your section of Figure 3–7. This time limit yourself to different values of a single hue. Be prepared to discuss in what ways this new version is different from the original.
- •• Pick another painting from this chapter. Using tracing paper, copy a section of the work measuring 2 x 2 inches (5 x 5 cm). Enlarge the drawing to fit a larger square sheet of drawing paper. Paint the section using tempera. See if classmates can identify the original work of art and the section of the work you used.

BUILDING VOCABULARY

Number a sheet of paper from 1 to 7. After each number, write the term from the box that best matches each description below.

aesthetic view	content
art criticism	style
art history	subject
composition	

1. Studying, understanding, and judging works of art.
2. The image viewers can easily identify in an art work.
3. The way the art principles are used to organize the elements of art in an art work.
4. The idea, feeling, mood, or message expressed by an art work.
5. An idea, or school of thought, on what is important in a work of art.
6. The study of art from past to present.
7. An artist's personal way of using the elements and principles of art and expressing feelings and ideas in art.

REVIEWING ART FACTS

Number a sheet of paper from 8 to 17. Answer each question in a complete sentence.

8. What is *describing*, as the term is defined by art critics? What are two key facts a critic would note when describing a work?
9. What is *analyzing*, as the term is defined by art critics?
10. What is *interpreting*, as the term is defined by art critics?
11. What question is asked by art critics when judging a work?
12. Summarize the three aesthetic views discussed in the chapter.
13. What are three questions an art historian would answer when describing a work?

14. What are two typical questions an art historian would ask when analyzing a work?
15. What is *interpreting*, as the term is defined by art historians?
16. What questions do art historians ask when interpreting an art work?
17. What do art historians decide during the judging stage?

THINKING ABOUT ART

On a sheet of paper, answer each question in a sentence or two.

1. **Interpret.** Could two art critics using the four-step system of art criticism come up with different judgments of a work? Explain your answer.
2. **Interpret.** Is any one step in art criticism more or less important than any other step? Which step? Explain your answer.
3. **Extend.** Art, it is often said, is not created in a vacuum. To which lesson in this chapter does this statement apply? Explain your answer.
4. **Analyze.** Give an example of events taking place in the world right now that could affect an artist's style.
5. **Compare and contrast.** In what ways is the judging of art similar for art critics and art historians? In what ways is the task different?

MAKING ART CONNECTIONS

1. **Social Studies.** Visit the library and learn what you can about the artist of the sculpture in Figure 2–8 on page **24**. How would an art historian say that time and place affected the artist's work?
2. **Language Arts.** Pretend you are an art critic. Write an article you could submit to a magazine judging the work in Figure 3–4 by Edward Hopper.

LOOKING AT THE DETAILS

The detail shown below is from Georges Rouault's *Christ Mocked by Soldiers*. Study the detail and answer the following questions.

1. What mood do you sense in this work? What elements of art are used to convey this mood?
2. Which aesthetic view would you use in judging this work? Give reasons to support your answer.
3. What would an art historian discuss when analyzing this painting?
4. Compare Rouault's style in this painting with Jan Steen's style in Figure 3–2 on page 35. What differences do you see?

Georges Rouault. *Christ Mocked by Soldiers*. 1932. Oil on canvas. (Detail.) 92.1 x 72.4 cm (36¼ x 28½"). Museum of Modern Art, New York, New York. Given anonymously.

▲ Ancient Egyptians portrayed figures' faces in profile, following strict artistic rules.

Funerary Feast, Stele of Nefertiabet. Old Kingdom, 4th Dynasty. Painted limestone. The Louvre, Paris, France.

CHAPTER 4

Art of Earliest Times

You have heard the saying "a picture is worth a thousand words." This saying holds true especially for pictures like the one at the left. This is a photograph of an art object from the ancient world. Such pictures, and the objects themselves, are like windows on life at the dawn of civilization. Ancient art tells us, often in ways that words cannot, about how people lived and what they believed.

In this chapter you will study and learn about art from the distant past.

OBJECTIVES

After completing this chapter, you will be able to:

- Define the term *culture*.
- Describe life during ancient times.
- Tell what kinds of art were created during ancient times.
- Create art works with media in the art styles of early civilizations.

WORDS YOU WILL LEARN

culture	stele
hieroglyphic	urban planning
megaliths	ziggurat
post and lintel system	

Prehistoric Art

As long as there have been people, there has been art. The need to create has always been a driving force among people. In this lesson you will look at prehistoric art. This is art dating back to the time before people kept written records. By studying this art, you will find out about the civilizations of early times. You will learn about their **culture**, or *ideas, beliefs, and living customs.*

ART OF THE OLD STONE AGE

The earliest art works modern experts have uncovered date back to the Old Stone Age. Also known as the Paleolithic (pay-lee-uh-**lith**-ik) period, the Old Stone Age lasted from around 30,000 until about 10,000 B.C.

The lives of people during the Old Stone Age were filled with danger, hunger, and fear. Each day meant a new struggle just to survive. In the winter they searched for shelter against the snow and cold. In the summer they battled the heat and the sudden rains that flooded their caves. Those lucky enough to survive were old by age 40. Few lived past their fiftieth year.

Painting

Many of the Old Stone age art works that have lasted into recent times are paintings. The animal painting in Figure 4–1 is one such work. It was discovered on the wall of a cave in France. Others like it have been found in Spain and elsewhere in western Europe. Examples of cave art have been found on every continent, from the Sahara desert to the Arctic. Notice also how lifelike the animals look.

No one knows the real reason behind the creation of paintings like this one. Such works have always been found deep within caves, far from entrances and daylight. Their

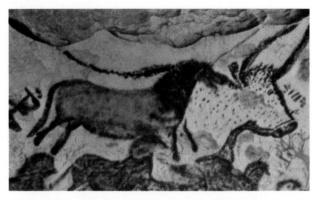

▲ **Figure 4–1** The cave which houses this painting was discovered by two boys playing ball. What do you suppose was their first reaction to this painting?

Cave painting. c. 15,000–10,000 B.C. Lascaux, Dordogne, France.

location has led experts to think they were not created merely as decoration. Some think the paintings played a part in hunting rituals. Many have imagined scenes like the following . . .

The evening meal over, the men of the tribe stood. The boy—now a man—stood with them. One by one, they moved away from the warm cooking fires and into the cool, shadowy depths of the cave. Suddenly the boy felt himself being shoved to his knees. As he groped forward, he found himself crawling through a narrow passageway.

By and by, the path widened again. In the distance ahead, the boy could see the glow of a fire. Soon he found himself in a great hall lighted by torches. On one wall was a huge bison. In the flickering light, the beast seemed to be charging toward him. The boy's heart raced.

As the boy watched with wide eyes, an artist began creating a second bison. With a sharp-ended stick, the artist scratched the outlines of the animal into the wall. Using clumps of fur and moss, he filled in the body with a variety of reds and browns. Using a bit of coal, he added a single fierce eye.

▲ **Figure 4–2** These figures were found in a chamber one mile underground. In what ways did their location help preserve them?

Clay Bison from Le Tuc d'Audoubert Cave, France. c. 17,000 B.C. Archeological Museum, Madrid, Spain.

At last the second beast was finished. The men, now excited about the promise of tomorrow's hunt, began to chant. The boy chanted with them. He picked up the spear his father had carved for him. With his fellow hunters, he attacked the "spirit" of the bison up on the wall, just as he would attack the real bison during the hunt.

Sculpture and Crafts

Old Stone Age artists were skilled not only at painting, but equally talented at sculpture and crafts. Notice the attention to detail in the bison shown in Figure 4–2. These remarkable sculptures, which are thought to date to around 15,000 B.C., were modeled out of clay.

The necklace in Figure 4–3 was found in an ancient grave. It is made of animal teeth and shells. Stone, ivory, and bone were some other media used by early sculptors and craftspeople.

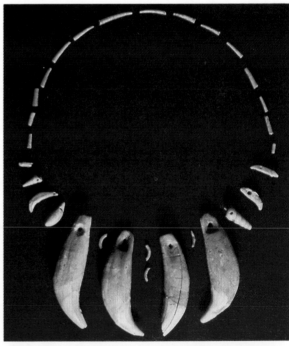

▲ **Figure 4–3** During prehistoric times, there were many animals to hunt. Bear and lion teeth such as those in this necklace were easy to find.

Bear-tooth necklace. c. 13,000 B.C. Private collection.

ART OF THE NEW STONE AGE

People gradually began to change as civilizations moved into the New Stone Age. Prehistoric peoples stopped wandering and formed villages. They learned to raise livestock and started growing their own food. Ways of making art changed, too.

Crafts

In the area of crafts, people learned to spin fibers, weave, and make pottery. Figure 4–4 shows a vase made about 6000 B.C. Note the potter's use of formal balance in this piece. Notice how the geometric design and balance combine to give the work a sense of unity.

▲ **Figure 4–4   What steps did the maker of this work take to obtain harmony? How was variety achieved?**

Neolithic pottery. Vase with flat base. Ceramique armoricaine. St. Germainen Lays.

▲ **Figure 4–5   Some scholars believe this circle of stone was built as an accurate calendar. What other purpose might it have served?**

Stonehenge. Salisbury Plain, Wiltshire, England.

Architecture

The New Stone Age, or Neolithic (nee-uh-**lith**-ik) period, also saw the first attempts at architecture. One kind of early building took the form of *large stone monuments* called **megaliths** (**meg**-uh-liths). The most famous of these is Stonehenge in England (Figure 4–5). This style of construction demonstrated the **post and lintel system**. This is *an approach to building in which a crossbeam is placed above two uprights*. As with the early cave paintings, the reason behind the creation of Stonehenge is unknown. As much a mystery is how the stones, many of which weigh 50 tons, were set in place. To this day, we can only guess and wonder.

▲ **Figure 4–6   Student work. Image on natural object.**

STUDIO EXPERIENCE

Bring a stone, piece of driftwood, seashell, or a hard chunk of clay to class. Look at it from every point of view until the natural form of the object suggests an image to you. You may see something related to your own environment such as a car, a skateboard, a football, or a house. When you have found the hidden image of your object do something to make it more visible to others. Use a sharp tool to scratch around the form, or use crayons, markers, or paint to make the found form stand out. (See Figure 4–6.) When you have completed your imaginary object, present it to your class.

✔ CHECK YOUR UNDERSTANDING

1. Define the term *culture*?
2. Describe life during the Old Stone Age.
3. What is a possible explanation for the creation of the cave paintings?
4. What changes in the way people lived took place in the New Stone Age?
5. What is a megalith? What is the name of the most famous megalith? Where is it found?

Painting Using Earth Pigments

When prehistoric artists created their cave paintings, they weren't able simply to open paint jars. They made use of natural sources of pigment around them. For reds, browns, and golds, they mixed ground-up earth minerals in animal fat, vegetable juices, and egg whites. For black they used charcoal from burned firewood. Minerals like these do not fade over time as other materials do. Notice how the painting in Figure 4–7 has kept its brilliant color for 15,000 years.

WHAT YOU WILL LEARN

You will create a painting about your environment using earth pigment paints that you have made from local earth minerals. At least half the paint you use in your work will be made from natural earth pigments. Use thin and built-up layers of this paint to obtain different textures that will add variety to your painting. For the remaining paint, you will use two hues of school acrylics plus black and white. (See Figure 4–8.)

WHAT YOU WILL NEED

- Pencil and sheets of sketch paper
- Yellow chalk
- Sheet of white paper, 12 x 18 inches (30 x 46 cm)
- Natural pigments
- School acrylic paint, several brushes, and palette
- Diluted white glue and a small jar
- Painting knife
- Water and paper towels

▶ **Figure 4–7 This horse is often called the Chinese horse. It resembles work done a few centuries ago.**

Horse from Cave Painting. Lascaux, Dordogne, France.

WHAT YOU WILL DO

1. Collect and grind your own earth pigment. (See Technique Tip **11**, *Handbook* page **280**.)
2. Make several sketches of scenes from your environment that would make good use of these colors. White sand would be good for a beach scene. Gray dirt could be used to show city sidewalks. Reddish-brown colors would work well for brick walls. Look at the colors you have, and let the colors give you ideas.
3. Select your best sketch. Using yellow chalk, draw the outline shapes of your sketch on the sheet of white paper.
4. Choose the colors of paint you will use. Remember to limit yourself to two hues of school acrylic, plus black and white. Prepare the earth pigment paints. Take care to mix no more than what you will use in a single day.
5. Paint your scene. Experiment with different ways of using the earth pigments. For a thin smooth area, use only the liquid part of the paint. For a built-up, textured area, make a thick binder using extra glue and add plenty of powder. Apply the thick paint with the painting knife.
6. Display your work when it is dry. Look for ways in which your work is similar to and different from those of your classmates. Take note of any unusual effects created using the earth pigments.

- **Describe** Tell what scene from your environment you chose to make. Identify the different earth colors you used. Name the hues of school acrylic paint you used.
- **Analyze** Point out areas in which you used thick and thin layers of paint to create different textures. Explain how these different textures add variety to your picture.
- **Interpret** Explain why this scene represents your environment.
- **Judge** Tell whether you feel your work succeeds. Explain your answer.

▲ **Figure 4–8** **Student work. Earth pigments.**

OTHER STUDIO IDEAS

- Create a small non-objective design using earth pigment and white school acrylic.

- ●● Using white glue from the bottle, squeeze out a design on a sheet of paper. Sprinkle powdered pigment onto the lines to create a form of sand painting. Shake off excess powder.

LESSON 3

Art of Ancient Egypt

During prehistoric times the chief enemy of the human race was nature. Unfriendly weather and fierce beasts of prey kept early humans always on their guard. By the time people began keeping written records, they had a new enemy. That enemy was other people.

As tribes learned to herd animals and grow crops, they also learned to live in harmony with their surroundings. This peaceful balance was upset by population growth. Small tribes began to fight over grazing land and soil suitable for growing crops. They were forced to band together into more organized groups for protection and also to be able to produce more food. By around 3000 B.C. four major civilizations had developed at different points on the globe. The ancient civilizations of Egypt, China, India, and Mesopotamia (mes-uh-puh-**tay**-mee-uh) emerged at this time.

In this lesson you will learn about the culture and art of ancient Egypt.

ANCIENT EGYPTIAN CULTURE

Ancient Egypt developed along the banks of the Nile before 3000 B.C. Find this area on the map in Figure 4–9. This civilization lasted for almost 3000 years. The arts of ancient Egypt reflect the endurance and solid foundation of that culture.

Egypt was ruled by a leader called a pharaoh (**fehr**-oh). The pharaoh was not merely a king in the eyes of the Egyptian people, he was also a god. After death he was believed to join other gods, whom the Egyptians identified with forces of nature. The afterlife of the pharaoh and other important people is a theme running through much of ancient Egyptian art.

Architecture

There can be little doubt that ancient Egypt's greatest achievement in art was in architecture. Figure 4–10 shows the civilization's most remarkable achievement of all, the great pyramids. These magnificent structures were built as tombs for the pharaohs. Thousands upon thousands of workers toiled for decades to build a single pyramid. Today the pyramids remain among the true wonders of the world.

Proof of the genius of later Egyptian architects is found in temples like the one in Figure 4–11. This temple is named in honor of the Egyptian sun god, Re (**Ray**). Apart from their beauty, temples like this were among the first buildings ever to use the post and lintel system. What structure of the New Stone Age that you studied also used posts and lintels?

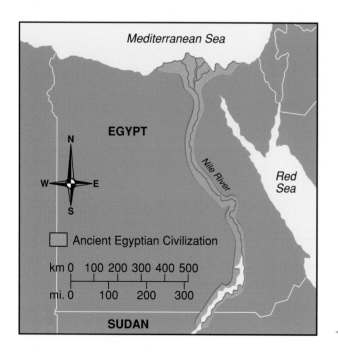

◄ **Figure 4–9 Ancient Egypt.**

◄ **Figure 4–10** In ancient times, these pyramids were each covered with a layer of polished white limestone. What do you suppose happened to this outer layer?

Sphinx and Pyramid of Khafre. c. 2600 B.C. Giza.

▲ **Figure 4–11** It is thought that the post and lintel system dates back to prehistoric times. Trees and bundles of stalks may have served as the first posts and lintels.

Built by Amenophis III. *Temple of Luxor.* Pylon and Hypostyle Hall. Egypt.

▲ **Figure 4–12   Much of the information we have about daily life in Egypt comes from paintings on walls and coffins found in tombs.**

Egyptian. *Fishing Scene: Attendants with harpoons and string of fish.* 1436–1411 B.C. Wall painting from the Tomb of Kenamun. 43.5 x 53 cm (17 x 21"). Egyptian Expedition of The Metropolitan Museum of Art, New York, New York. Rogers Fund.

Sculpture

In Egypt it became customary to decorate the tombs of rich or important people. Often this was done with painted relief sculptures. An example of this type of art appears in the relief that opened this chapter (page **46**). This is a **stele** (**stee**-lee), *a carved upright stone slab used as a monument*. Each frame shows a different part of a person's life or preoccupation for the afterlife. The frame closest to the top shows the subject seated at his own funeral banquet.

Painting

The wall paintings found in the tombs of royalty and the wealthy tell us about the daily life of the Egyptians. Figure 4–12 shows a typical Egyptian painting. Scenes from the buried person's life were painted on the walls. Notice that some body parts are painted as they would appear from the side. The head, arms, and legs are three such parts. Other parts appear as they would if we were seeing the people head-on. The single eye and shoulders demonstrate this. These views show the strict rules that artists of ancient Egypt followed. One of these was to show every body part from its most visible angle.

STUDIO EXPERIENCE

Look once again at the stele on page **46**. Notice the rows and columns of small birds and other shapes. Experts today know these to be examples of **hieroglyphic** (hy-ruh-**glif**-ik), *an early form of picture writing*. In this writing system, shapes stand not for sounds, as in our modern alphabet, but for ideas. (A heart shape, for instance, might be used to mean "love.") Here the symbols provide a written record of the achievements of the stele's subject.

Imagine that you are a citizen of a future civilization who has been called upon to create a new writing system. As you begin to work on this task, remember that you know nothing of modern alphabets. Think about what ideas you will need to express in your culture. Create a shape for each idea. When your system is complete, write a sentence in it. See if anyone in your class can read the message.

✔ CHECK YOUR UNDERSTANDING

1. When did ancient Egypt come into being? How long did the civilization survive?
2. Who were the pharaohs? What part did they play in the art of ancient Egypt?
3. Name two achievements in ancient Egyptian architecture.
4. What is a stele?
5. How did Egyptian artists show the human figure in their work? What was their reason for doing this?

Ancient China, India, and Mesopotamia

Like Egypt, the ancient civilizations of China, India, and Mesopotamia each developed in a river valley. Like Egypt, each had a king and a religion that was based on nature.

Yet, despite some similarities, each civilization had its own separate culture and ways of making art. In this lesson you will learn about the culture and art of these civilizations.

ANCIENT CHINESE CULTURE

The first Egyptian pyramids were built around 2600 B.C. Around that time another new civilization was emerging a continent away, in the Yellow River valley. Can you find the Yellow River on the map in Figure 4–13? This civilization, China, is still alive today. It boasts the oldest continuous culture in the history of the world.

The history of China, until modern times, is divided into periods known as dynasties. Dynasties are named for ruling families of emperors. The first of these, the Shang dynasty, began around 1766 B.C. The last of them, the Ch'ing, ended in fairly recent times. Like the history of China itself, the art of China is grouped by dynasties.

ANCIENT CHINESE ART

The ancient Chinese were skilled in all areas of art. Legends show that Chinese artists were creating pictures as early as 2200 B.C. The works we have today were made in bronze and on stone and pottery instead of silk or paper, which has not survived. The architecture of this early period has also vanished, though large building foundations have been unearthed.

Sculpture and Crafts

The single greatest achievement of early Chinese artists was their work in bronze. A bronze pitcher dating from the Shang Dynasty is shown in Figure 4–14. Like most art of the time, the work is covered with motifs and squared spirals. Experts today believe the spirals to stand for clouds, rain, or water. What do these images seem to say about the ancient Chinese view of nature?

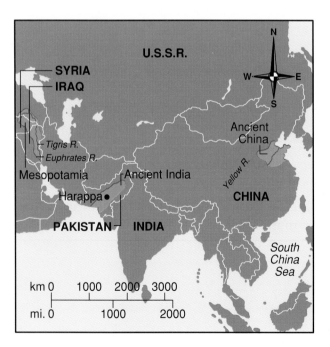

◀ Figure 4–13 Ancient China, India, and Mesopotamia.

ANCIENT INDIAN CULTURE

Like that of the Shang dynasty, the culture of ancient India remained a legend until modern times. In 1856 railroad workers laying track in the Indus River valley made a discovery. Near the city of Harappa (huh-**rap**-uh), they found a hill of crumbling fired clay bricks. These bricks date to between 2500 and 1500 B.C. Can you find the city of Harappa on the map in Figure 4–13? In what modern country is it located?

In addition to bricks, the railroad workers found a number of small relief carvings in soapstone. One of these is shown in Figure 4–15. These carvings are the oldest examples of Indian art.

Did you notice the odd lines and shapes above the animal form? These are known to be letters from an ancient system of writing. Scholars have yet to decipher the Harappan language.

◀ **Figure 4–14   Would you describe the images shown on this pitcher as realistic? If not, how would you describe them?**

Chinese. Ritual Wine Vessel, with Spout. Shang Dynasty, 14th Century B.C. Bronze. 21.6 cm (8½"). The Metropolitan Museum of Art, New York, New York. Gift of Ernest Erickson Foundation, Inc.

◀ **Figure 4–15   Soapstone seals may have been used as personal adornment. Could the symbols have identified the owner?**

Soapstone seal from Mohenjo-daro showing a Brahmani bull. Harappan culture. c. 2300–1750 B.C. 3.5 cm (18½"). British Museum, London, England.

▲ Figure 4–16   Perhaps the most famous ziggurat of all is the one recorded in the Bible. It is the tower of Babylon.

Ziggurat at Ur, Iraq.

Architecture

In 1922 a second ancient city was found in the area of Harappa. Its name is Mohenjo-Daro (moh-hen-joh-**dahr**-oh), which means "Hill of the Dead." The city is believed to have had a population of 35,000.

Mohenjo-Daro is an early example of the art of **urban planning**. This is *arranging the construction and services of a city to best meet its people's needs*. The ancient city had wide, open streets dividing it into large blocks about the size of four football fields. There were homes, shops, and large buildings thought to be houses of worship.

MESOPOTAMIAN CULTURE

The culture of Mesopotamia was more the culture of a region than of a people. The region was the fertile crescent of land between the Tigris (**ty**-gruhs) and Euphrates (yoo-**frayt**-eez) Rivers. This land is shared today by Syria and Iraq. (See Figure 4–13.) The people of Mesopotamia lived in city states that each had their own king. Sometimes these city states fought with each other and one would become more powerful.

The first important group to live in Mesopotamia was the Sumerians (soo-**mehr**-ee-uhns). Where the Sumerians came from is unclear. There is evidence that they learned to control the floods that were common in the fertile crescent. They also built strong walled cities, each with its own king.

The Sumerians were the first people to have a system of writing. Called cuneiform (kyoo-**nee**-uh-form), the system was made up of wedge-shaped characters. The Sumerians did not have paper so they wrote the cuneiform upon clay tablets.

Other city states that later became important were Babylon and Assyria.

Architecture

At the center of the Sumerian city, and of their form of art, was the **ziggurat** (**zig**-uh-rat). This was *a stepped mountain made of brick-covered earth*. A temple honoring the god of the city was placed at the top of the ziggurat. Figure 4–16 shows a ziggurat dating from 2100 B.C. What other ancient building does the ziggurat resemble?

Sculpture

As with other ancient cultures, the tribes of Mesopotamia often expressed their religious beliefs in their art. Study the sculpture in Figure 4–17. This marble figure stands for a Sumerian goddess or worshipper. This work has been dated from between 2700 and 2600 B.C. What other art that you studied in this chapter was completed around the same time? How does the style of that work compare with this?

▲ Figure 4–17   This figure is typical of Sumerian sculpture. Notice the large eyes and the hands clasped in prayer.

Statua di Donna. The Iraq Museum, Baghdad, Iraq.

✔ CHECK YOUR UNDERSTANDING

1. What are dynasties? How do they relate to the art of China?
2. How was the Harappan culture of ancient India discovered?
3. Why is the ancient city of Mohenjo-Daro important?
4. What is a ziggurat? In what culture were ziggurats built?

Creating a Picture Story

Egyptian artists, as you have read, followed strict rules when they worked. One rule required that they show human body parts from their most familiar angle. Another required artists to make the most important people in a work the largest. Both these rules are followed in the wall painting in Figure 4–18. The important man and woman at the left are observing a hunting and fishing scene. The smaller figures are the servants. The painting tells a story.

WHAT YOU WILL LEARN

You will paint a picture story about the important events in your life. You will use the rules of Egyptian art shown in Figure 4–18. (For example, make your proportions larger to emphasize your importance.) Select lines and shapes to look stiff and dignified. Use contrasting colors to draw attention to the center of interest. Do *not* show depth of space in your painting. Instead, give it the same flat look as an Egyptian work. (See Figure 4–19.)

▲ **Figure 4–18**   **Notice that little shading was used. The pictures look flat, as though they are cut from paper.**

Wall painting from the Tomb of Nakht. *Nakht and his Wife.* Egypt. c. 1425 B.C. The Metropolitan Museum of Art, New York, New York.

WHAT YOU WILL NEED

- Pencil, sheets of sketch paper, and an eraser
- Watercolor paints and several watercolor brushes, some thick and some thin
- Sheet of white paper, 18 x 24 inches (46 x 61 cm)
- Paper towels

WHAT YOU WILL DO

1. Brainstorm with your class about ideas for your story painting. Some possibilities might be a birthday party, a school dance, a ride on your bike, a family get-together, passing an important test, and taking part in a class play or athletic event. You may want to pick more than one event for your work.
2. Study the figures in Figure 4–18. Make some rough pencil sketches that show figures in the same way. These should help you plan not only the story but also the size, location, and proportion of figures. The pictures do not have to read across the paper like the lines in a story. Rather, you may, if you like, place the most important scene in the center. Let your imagination guide you.
3. Choose your best plan. Working lightly in pencil, sketch it on the sheet of white paper.
4. Use your watercolors to paint the scene. Using your brushes, paint the areas. Take care not to smear any areas of paint. (For information on using watercolors, see Technique Tip **14**, *Handbook* page **281**.)
5. When your work has dried, display it. See if any of your classmates can "read" your picture story.

EXAMINING YOUR WORK

- **Describe** Describe the events in your painting. Tell how you used size to emphasize the most important person — you.
- **Analyze** Tell whether your lines and shapes give a feeling of stiffness. Explain how you used contrasting color to create a center of interest. Tell how you used proportion to emphasize yourself.
- **Interpret** State whether a viewer will be able to "read" your picture story and identify the important events in your life. Give your work a title.
- **Judge** Tell whether you feel your work succeeds. Explain your answer.

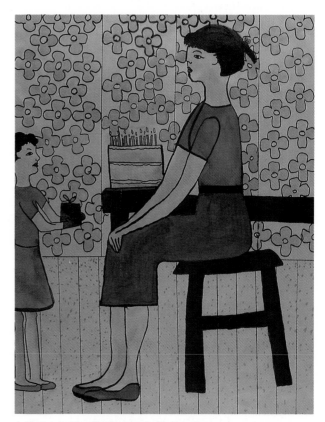

▲ Figure 4–19 Student work. Picture story.

OTHER STUDIO IDEAS

- Create a second story painting. This time, tell your story in a straight line using a rectangular strip of paper.
- •• Work in small groups to create a story painting mural. Choose events that relate to a famous leader. Use school acrylic paint to color your mural.

BUILDING VOCABULARY

Number a sheet of paper from 1 to 7. After each number, write the term from the box that best matches each description below.

culture	stele
hieroglyphic	urban planning
megaliths	ziggurat
post and lintel system	

1. The ideas, beliefs, and living customs of a people.
2. Large stone monuments, such as Stonehenge in England.
3. Approach to building in which a crossbeam is placed above two uprights.
4. Carved upright stone slab used as a monument.
5. An early form of picture writing
6. Arranging the construction and services of a city to best meet its people's needs.
7. Stepped mountain made of brick-covered earth.

REVIEWING ART FACTS

Number a sheet of paper from 8 to 15. Answer each question in a complete sentence.

8. What is another term for the Paleolithic period and when did it begin?
9. What fact about the cave paintings has led experts to suspect they were not created for decoration alone?
10. Name three media used by sculptors and craftspeople during the Old Stone Age.
11. How did the style of art change by the time of the Neolithic period?
12. What are two mysteries surrounding Stonehenge?
13. How did ancient Egyptian artists show the human body in their works? Why?
14. Name two ways in which ancient China, India, and Mesopotamia were like ancient Egypt.
15. What was the greatest achievement of early China?

THINKING ABOUT ART

On a sheet of paper, answer each question in a sentence or two.

1. **Summarize.** From a historical standpoint, why are the soapstone carvings of the Harappan culture important?
2. **Extend.** Suppose you learned of the discovery of a new civilization dating to 3000 B.C. Based on your reading of this chapter, what themes might you expect to find running through its art?
3. **Compare and contrast.** Some art scholars, you will recall, believe a successful art work is one with a realistic subject. Which of the ancient periods and civilizations you studied would appeal most to such a person? Which would appeal least? Explain your answers.

MAKING ART CONNECTIONS

1. **Mathematics.** Construction of the ancient pyramids was based on specific mathematical formulas. This is one reason why they have existed so long. Look up *pyramid* in an encyclopedia. Explain how math was involved in designing these architectural structures.
2. **Social Studies.** Choose a personality from current events. Imagine this person living in an ancient culture. Plan an appropriate monument to honor this figure.

LOOKING AT THE DETAILS

The detail shown below is from the Stele of Nefertiabet, *Funerary Feast*. Study the detail and answer the following questions using complete sentences.

1. What are some universally recognizable images in this work?
2. This painting is from an ancient culture. Can you guess what is being shown here?

3. How does art history help you to understand this work?
4. How might this work of art help you understand ancient Egyptian figure drawing styles?

Funerary Feast, Stele of Nefertiabet. Old Kingdom, 4th Dynasty. Painted limestone. (Detail.) The Louvre, Paris, France.

▲ **Why do you think the artist chose to show so much sky in the painting? Describe everything you see in this work. Does the picture show only natural objects?**

Unknown. Fan Mounted as an Album Leaf. *Evening in Spring Hills*. Southern Sung Dynasty. 1127–1278. Ink and color on silk. 24.8 x 26.1 cm (9¾ x 10¼"). The Metropolitan Museum of Art, New York, New York. Gift of John M. Crawford, Jr., in honor of Alfreda Murck.

Art of the Far East

"East is East and West is West, and never the twain shall meet." These words, penned a century ago by a well-known British poet, express a view still sometimes heard. In truth, the twain — or two — opposite sides of our planet — hold much in common. They both express their feelings about their culture in paintings and through art.

Can you read the message in the Chinese silk painting at the left? In the pages ahead you will learn about the art of China and Japan.

OBJECTIVES

After completing this chapter, you will be able to:

- Describe the role of religion in the art of China and Japan.
- Identify key developments in Chinese painting, sculpture, and crafts.
- Identify key developments in Japanese architecture, sculpture, painting, and printmaking.
- Create art objects that record experiences or events in your world.

WORDS YOU WILL LEARN

glaze
pagoda
perceive
porcelain
screen

scroll
Ukiyo-e
woodblock printing
Yamato-e

ARTISTS YOU WILL MEET

Chao Meng-fu

Kiyotada

The Art of China

The Chinese have a long history of being highly creative. Two thousand years before the invention of the seismograph, they were recording earthquakes. Long before the first Texas oil wells were drilled, they were drilling holes 2000 feet deep. The compass and kite are two other early Chinese inventions.

Added proof of the Chinese gift for creating can be found in their art. In this lesson you will learn about the important contributions they have made.

MODERN CHINESE CULTURE

The "modern" period of Chinese civilization is thought to have begun with the Han dynasty. This dynasty lasted from 206 B.C. to A.D. 220. To this day, the Chinese still refer to themselves as the "Han people."

During this period a new religion came to China, called Buddhism (**boo**-diz-uhm), which stressed the oneness of humans with nature. An important part of Buddhism is meditation, focusing one's thoughts on a single object or idea. This experience allows the person to know the inner beauty of the object or idea. Chinese art of the last 2000 years has been greatly influenced by Buddhism and meditation.

Scroll Painting

The Chinese were the first people to think of "picture painting" as honorable work. This was because many artists were also scholars. They wrote with brushes that could make thick and thin lines. They used the same brush and line technique to paint pictures. They painted fans, pages of books, and scrolls. A **scroll** is *a long roll of illustrated parchment or silk.* Some scrolls were meant to hang on walls. Other scrolls were made of long rolls of silk or paper. They were meant to be unrolled a little at a time and read like a book.

Like other Chinese artists, scroll painters began a work only after a long period of meditation. The work itself was an attempt to capture a feeling, not an image. Shapes and figures were limited to the barest essentials. The artist included only those lines and shapes needed to capture the mood of the scene. (See Figure 5–3 on page **70**.)

Landscape Painting

The earliest Chinese paintings were filled with images of people illustrating the beliefs that people should live together peacefully and be respectful of their elders. With the influence of a new religion, the focus of painting began shifting away from humans and toward nature. By around A.D. 1100, the landscape was the main theme of Chinese painting.

The work that opened this chapter on page **66** is a landscape painting. Look closely at the work. Can you find a covered deck, or pavilion (puh-**vil**-yuhn), nestled within the hills? Studying the painting more closely still, do you see two small shapes inside the pavilion? These are meant to be seen as the heads of people. What statement is the artist making about the place of humans in nature?

Sculpture

For many centuries important people in China were buried in tombs with objects they could use in the afterworld. These figures were made from clay. Many, like the horses in Figure 5–1 were of animals. Notice how the artist uses line and movement to create the feeling of action.

After the collapse of the Han dynasty, China fell into chaos. It remained this way until the mighty T'ang (**tahng**) dynasty rose to power some 400 years later. It was during this new dynasty that Chinese sculpture flourished.

▲ Figure 5–1   Both the ladies and horses are shown in action in this work. Centuries ago they played similar games to what we do today.

Four Ladies of the Court Playing Polo. Tang Dynasty. A.D. 618–906. Painted terra cotta. Nelson-Atkins Museum of Art, Kansas City, Missouri.

Crafts

The T'ang dynasty was followed in A.D. 960 by another powerful dynasty, the Sung (**soong**). Landscape painting soared to new heights during the Sung dynasty. So did the making of **porcelain** (**pore**-suh-luhn), *a fine-grained, high-quality form of pottery*. Porcelain is made from a fine and fairly hard-to-find white clay called kaolin (**kay**-uh-luhn).

Work in porcelain reached its highest point ever during the Ming dynasty (1368–1644).

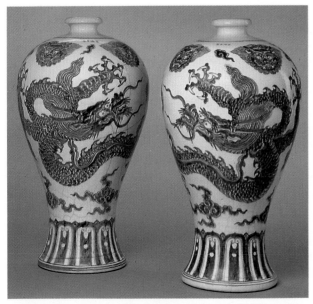

▲ Figure 5–2   The blue pigment came from Persia. Unless the timing was precise, the blue could turn black or brown during the firing.

Pair of Vases, Meiping. Reign of Xuande. Ming Dynasty. 1426–1435. Porcelain with underglaze blue decoration. Nelson-Atkins Museum of Art, Kansas City, Missouri.

The remarkable matched vases shown in Figure 5–2 date from this period. The painted dragon designs are protected by a *glass-like finish*, or **glaze**, on these Ming porcelains. What kind of balance does each of the vases have? What kind of balance do they have as a matched set?

✔CHECK YOUR UNDERSTANDING

1. Name two inventions credited to the early Chinese.
2. What religion was introduced to China during the Han dynasty?
3. What is meditation? What has been its role in Chinese art of the last 2000 years?
4. What are scrolls?
5. What art form flourished during the T'ang dynasty and during the Sung dynasty?
6. What art form reached its highest point during the Ming dynasty?

Making a Scroll

Look at the Chinese scroll painting in Figure 5–3. The work is by Chao Meng-fu (chow meng-foo), a leading scroll painter of the Yuan dynasty. Though the artist trained himself to paint quickly, his work was meant to be viewed slowly. The viewer was meant to meditate on each scene as the artist did before creating it.

WHAT YOU WILL LEARN

You will create a scroll recording the events of a nature walk in the manner of the Chinese painter. Record scenes of your walk on a long strip of paper, using pencils and markers. Leave large areas of negative space around the shapes. Shapes to be emphasized will be filled with color. (See Figure 5–4.)

WHAT YOU WILL NEED

- Sheet of white paper, 1 x 6 feet (30 cm x 2 m)
- Pencil, watercolor markers, and transparent tape
- 2 dowels, 14 inches (36 cm)
- Piece of ribbon, 24 inches (61 cm)

WHAT YOU WILL DO

1. Set aside time to walk slowly through your school and around the school grounds. Gaze at objects and scenes as though you are seeing them for the first time. Stop as necessary to perceive the visual impression of the texture of a bush or the color of a flower. Try to focus on the feeling or mood each scene communicates. This feeling may come to you in a small detail, such as the texture of a wall or the line of the path you walk.

▲ **Figure 5–3** How is space treated differently here than in Western paintings?

Chao Meng-fu. Handscroll: *Twin Pines, Level Distance*. Yuan Dynasty. Early 1300s. Ink on paper. (Detail.) 25.4 x 127.3 cm (10 x 42½"). The Metropolitan Museum of Art, New York, New York. Gift of the Dillon Fund.

2. Roll the large sheet of paper into a scroll. Close your eyes and try to picture one of the scenes and the mood attached to it. Keep the lines, shapes, colors, and textures uppermost in your mind. Unroll 10 inches (25 cm) of your scroll and, using pencil, very lightly draw the scene. The scene should not fill the section of paper. You should, in other words, have plenty of negative space around shapes and objects.

3. Using markers, trace over the pencil lines. Make sure no pencil marks are left showing. Fill in the shapes you want to emphasize with color. Do not color everything in the scene.

4. When you are satisfied with your work, unroll another 10 inches (25 cm) of scroll. Close your eyes again and try to picture another scene. Again record the scene in pencil and trace over the lines with markers. Continue to work in this fashion until you have used up all your paper.

5. Using tape, fasten each end of your scroll to a dowel. Roll up the scroll and tie it with the ribbon.

6. Exchange scrolls with a friend. Study the works slowly and silently. See if you can identify the scenes in the other person's work.

EXAMINING YOUR WORK

- **Describe** Tell what scenes you chose to show. State whether your work has any pencil lines showing.
- **Analyze** Point to the places where you used negative space in your scroll. Point to places where you used color for emphasis. Identify other elements you used.
- **Interpret** Show features in your work that would help a viewer understand how it captures a mood. Identify the different moods of the scenes.
- **Judge** Tell whether you feel your work succeeds. Explain your answer.

▲ Figure 5–4   Student work. Scroll painting.

OTHER STUDIO IDEAS

- Using a brush and one hue of watercolor, paint the scenes in your scroll.
- •• Create a vertical scroll. Start with the scene at ground level in front of your feet. Shift your eyes upward little by little. The last scene in your scroll should be the sky. At each level, search for and include details that capture the mood of the scene.

LESSON 3

The Art of Japan

The history of Japanese art began around 5000 B.C. In the years that followed, art influenced every aspect of Japanese life. In this lesson you will learn about the one-of-a-kind culture and art of the "floating world" called Japan.

JAPANESE CULTURE

Japan makes its home on an island group in the South Pacific. Find Japan on the map in Figure 5–5.

In most civilizations, art follows culture. In a sense, the reverse is true of Japan. In A.D. 552 the ruler of a kingdom in nearby Korea sent the Emperor of Japan a gift. The gift was a piece of art. More specifically, it was a bronze figure of the Buddha (**bood**-uh), the founder of Buddhism. Along with the sculpture came priests to spread Buddhist teachings. Eventually the people of Japan came to accept this new religion. They also learned

about different ways of making art. For the next 250 years Japanese art would show strong traces of Korean, Chinese, and other Asian styles.

Architecture

Before the arrival of the bronze Buddha, the only Japanese art worth noting was prehistoric. Clay objects created by artists of the ancient Jomon (**joh**-muhn) culture are thought to date as early as 3000 B.C.

The first important Japanese art of "modern" times began being created in A.D. 594. These were magnificent Buddhist temples like the one shown in Figure 5–6. These temples were designed by Chinese or Chinese-trained architects and show a strong Chinese influence. Since the islands have little usable rock, wood was the main building material, except for the roofs which were made from tile. One of the most interesting features of early Japanese temples was the **pagoda** (puh-**gohd**-uh). This is *a tower several stories high with roofs curving slightly upward at the edges.* Figure 5–7 shows a pagoda from one of the greatest temples of the day. It is exactly like the first pagoda built at this temple. What does this fact reveal about the design of the building and how the Japanese feel about the past?

◄ Figure 5–5 Japan.

▲ **Figure 5–6** At least 10,000 pieces of the art of the period have been stored at this temple for over a thousand years.

Nara Todai-Ji Temple. c. A.D. 600. Japan.

Sculpture

The Japanese of this early period modeled small sculptures out of clay. They also carved images of wood and cast them in bronze. Most, like the one in Figure 5–8, featured the figure of the Buddha. As a new emperor came into power he would order a new Buddha to be cast. Each emperor would order his Buddha to be made larger than before to emphasize the emperor's own importance.

▲ **Figure 5–8** Why do you think sculptures like this are found outdoors?

Bronze Buddha of Todai-Ji. Japan.

▲ **Figure 5–7** Structures like these were used to store religious items.

Nara Horyu-Ji Temple Pagoda. A.D. 700. Japan.

Painting

In 784 Japan entered its golden age of art. During this period, which lasted some 400 years, countless new temples were built. The period also witnessed, around 898, the birth of a new painting style. Its name, **Yamato-e** (yah-**mah**-toh-ay), means *pictures in the Japanese manner*. Paintings done in this style were the first true examples of pure Japanese art.

Figure 5–9 shows a Yamato-e painting. The work is a scroll. What scene is shown in this painting? In what ways is the work different from a Chinese scroll painting? In what ways is it similar?

Another important form of painting was the decoration of screens. A **screen** is *a partition used as a wall to divide a room*. The use of screens made it easy to rearrange a house and use space efficiently. Most screens were painted with Chinese subjects.

Printmaking

The outbreak of civil war brought the golden age to an end in 1185. Japan remained in a state of political unrest for the next 430 years. The art of these stormy times focused both on the harsh realities of war and on escaping those realities. When peace came at last, another new style of art came with it. This style was called **Ukiyo-e** (oo-**kee**-yoh-ay), meaning *pictures of the floating world*. These pictures show different ways the Japanese enjoyed life.

The demand for art works in the new style was great. To meet this demand, artists used the technique of **woodblock printing**. This is *making prints by carving images in blocks of wood*. The prints, or woodcuts, were made by a team of artists and craftspeople. Figure 5–10 shows a woodcut in the Ukiyo-e style. Notice the artist's use of strong lines and flat areas of color. Both were typical of such works. Equally typical was the balance shown here. What kind of balance has the artist of this print used?

▲ **Figure 5–9**   This scroll shows an important person of the day, an ambassador, on a journey. Which figure do you think is the ambassador? Explain your answer.

Unknown. Illustrated Handscroll of *Minister Kibi's Trip to China* (Kibi diajin nitto emaki). 12th Century. Ink and color on paper. 32.2 x 244.2 cm (12⅞ x 96⅛"). Museum of Fine Arts, Boston, Massachusetts. William Sturgis Bigelow Collection.

▲ **Figure 5–10** Can you find the figure's feet? Can you find the artist's signature?

Torii Kiyotada. *An Actor of the Ichikawa Clan.* Woodcut, hand colored. 28.6 x 15.2 cm (11¼ x 6"). The Metropolitan Museum of Art, New York, New York. Harris Brisbane Dick Fund.

STUDIO EXPERIENCE

The print in Figure 5–10 is of a Kabuki (kuh-**boo**-kee) actor. Kabuki is a form of popular Japanese theater. Notice the richly decorated costume. Another Japanese stage tradition with even more spectular costumes is the Nō (**noh**) drama. Figure 5–11 shows the type of headbands worn by a Nō actor. Notice the highly decorative pattern in the headband. Design a decorative pattern related to an important activity in your life. If, for example, you are in the school band, the pattern might be made up of musical notes. If you are in the math club, the pattern could be made up of mathematical symbols. Using school acrylic paint, transfer the pattern to a headband made of paper or cloth.

✔CHECK YOUR UNDERSTANDING

1. What important event in the history of Japanese art happened in A.D. 552?
2. What is a pagoda?
3. When did the golden age of Japanese art begin? What painting style came into being during that period?
4. What is Ukiyo-e? What technique was most commonly used for Ukiyo-e art works?

◄**Figure 5–11** What do you think the purpose of these headbands might have been? What is the purpose of headbands today?

Headbands for Nō costumes. Japanese. Edo Period. 1615–1867. Embroidered in silk on satin., 40 x 3.2 cm (15¾ x 1¾"). The Metropolitan Museum of Art, New York, New York. Gift of Mr. and Mrs. Teigi Ito.

Creating a Time Capsule

Look at the object in Figure 5–12. This clay sculpture of a horse is from the ancient culture of Japan. Studying objects like these, you have learned, teaches us about past civilizations.

Imagine that students of your school have been asked by community leaders to create clay objects. These are to be buried in a time capsule to tell future cultures about our own. Working in small groups, you will create a clay model of a teenager's room. You may use your own room at home or you may invent the room of your dreams. In the room you will include objects that represent the lifestyle of your group.

▲ Figure 5–12   Would you describe this horse as realistic? Do you think the surface would feel rough or smooth to the touch? Does the work communicate any particular feeling?

Horse sculpture. Japanese. A.D. 200–500. Terra cotta. 59.7 x 66 cm (23½ x 26"). The Cleveland Museum of Art, Cleveland, Ohio. Gift of Mrs. Henry Norweb.

WHAT YOU WILL LEARN

You will make and join together clay slabs to create a teen's room. Your model will have a floor and three walls. Furniture and other details will be modeled from clay. In designing your room you must consider the elements of space, shape, form, and texture. Use the principles of proportion and variety to organize the elements. (See Figure 5–13.)

WHAT YOU WILL NEED

- Pencil, notepad, and sheets of sketch paper
- 2 guide sticks, each about 1/2 inch (13 mm) thick
- Newspaper
- Clay
- Rolling pin, needle tool, modeling tools, and ruler
- Sheet of plastic
- Slip (a mixture of water and clay used for joining clay pieces) and container of water
- Scissors and scrap of fabric

WHAT YOU WILL DO

1. On the notepad, list the furniture, objects, and details your room will have. Note also the different shapes, forms, and textures you will use. Make pencil sketches of the room and its contents.

2. Set up the guide sticks 10 inches (25 cm) apart on the sheet of newspaper. Using the slab method, place the clay between these two guide sticks. Flatten the lump with the heel of your hand. Resting a rolling pin on the guide sticks, roll out the clay. This will help keep the thickness of the slab even. Using a ruler and knife or other sharp object, make four rectangles, each measuring 10 x 10 inches (25 x 25 cm). Cover the slabs loosely with the sheet of plastic. Leave them out overnight to firm up to the leather hard stage. This is the stage where clay is still damp but too hard to model.

3. The next day, score one of the slabs along three of its edges. This slab is to be the floor. Working a slab at a time, score each of the other slabs along its bottom. Use slip to join the walls to the floor. (For information on joining clay slabs and pieces, see Technique Tip **17**, *Handbook* page **281**.)

4. Model the furniture and other objects and details. Use proper joining methods for such tasks as adding legs to chairs. Using slip, attach the furniture and other objects to the floor.

5. When the clay is totally dry, fire the work. Complete your room by adding details — window coverings and a bedspread, for example — cut from the fabric.

6. Display your finished work. Look for similarities and differences between your work and that of other students.

EXAMINING YOUR WORK

- **Describe** Point to the floor and walls of your room. Describe the furniture and details you chose to include. Tell whether you followed the rules for making clay slabs and joining pieces.
- **Analyze** Show where you used the elements of space, shape, form, and texture. Explain how you used the principles of proportion and variety. Point out examples of each.
- **Interpret** Show what features in your work would help a viewer of the future understand this to be a teenager's room.
- **Judge** Tell whether you feel your work succeeds. Explain your answer.

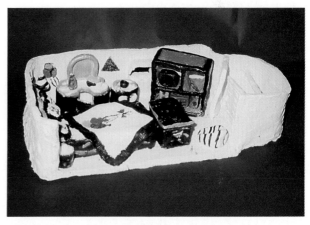

▲ **Figure 5–13** Student work. Model of teen's room.

OTHER STUDIO IDEAS

- Choose a room in your school. Some possibilities are the gym, the cafeteria, or the art room. Think about what furniture and other objects you find in that room. Make a clay model of the room.

- ●● Make a clay model of a whole single-story building. You might base your work on an actual building in your town or city, or you might invent your own. Think about what furniture and other objects you would find in each of the rooms. Add these details to your work.

CHAPTER 5 REVIEW

BUILDING VOCABULARY

Number a sheet of paper from 1 to 9. After each number, write the term from the box that best matches each description below.

glaze	scroll
pagoda	Ukiyo-e
perceive	woodblock
porcelain	printing
screen	Yamato-e

1. A long roll of illustrated parchment or silk.
2. A fine-grained, high-quality form of pottery.
3. A glass-like finish on pottery.
4. Look deeply at a subject.
5. A tower several stories high with roofs curving slightly upward at the edges.
6. An art style which means "pictures in the Japanese manner."
7. An art style which means "pictures of the floating world."
8. Making prints by carving images in blocks of wood.
9. A partition used as a wall to divide a room.

REVIEWING ART FACTS

Number a sheet of paper from 10 to 15. Answer each question in a complete sentence.

10. With what dynasty is the "modern" period of Chinese civilization sometimes connected?
11. What was the goal of Chinese scroll painting?
12. During which dynasty did work in porcelain reach its highest point?
13. Who sent the Emperor of Japan a gift in 552? What was the gift?
14. What date is associated with the earliest Jomon examples of Japanese art?

15. What culture strongly influenced the design of the first Buddhist temples in Japan? Where did the architects who designed these temples come from?

THINKING ABOUT ART

On a sheet of paper, answer each question in a sentence or two.

1. **Interpret.** Review the three aesthetic views that you studied in Chapter 3 (see page **37**). Tell how art critics of the three different views would each react to the painting that opened the chapter (see page **66**).
2. **Analyze.** It has been said that no artist works in a vacuum. Name three events or happenings you read about in this chapter that support this statement. Explain your choices.
3. **Analyze.** Look at the scroll painting in Figure 5–3. Review the four stages of work in the art historian's job (see page **41**). Then describe the scroll painting.

MAKING ART CONNECTIONS

1. **Language Arts.** A type of Japanese poetry called haiku is influenced by meditation on subjects in nature. Look in the library for some examples of haiku. Find out the style and form of a haiku poem. Try to create some haiku of your own.
2. **Social Studies.** Look in the encyclopedia or history books to learn about the Great Wall of China. Find out when it was constructed and why. Prepare a short oral report for your class. Explain some of the features of the Great Wall, such as how and where it was constructed.

LOOKING AT THE DETAILS

The detail shown below is from the Chinese painting *Evening In Spring Hills*. Study the detail and answer the following questions using complete sentences.

1. Do you think that the time period in which the artist lived influenced the subject matter of this work? Explain your answer.
2. How do you think Buddhism influenced this artist's choice of color?

3. In what way does negative space reveal something about the beliefs of this artist and his/her culture?
4. Look at the entire work on page 66. Notice how the proportion of the negative space compared to the objects in the painting provides balance. What type of balance is this called?

Unknown. Fan Mounted as an Album Leaf. *Evening in Spring Hills*. Southern Sung Dynasty. 1127–1278. Ink and color on silk. (Detail.) 24.8 x 26.1 cm (9¾ x 10¼"). The Metropolitan Museum of Art, New York, New York. Gift of John M. Crawford, Jr., in honor of Alfreda Murck.

▲ The headdress on this figure stands for an ancient goddess. What kind of balance was used in creating this work?

Mexican (Zapotec) from Monte Alban. *Funerary Urn.* A.D. 500–700. Terra cotta with traces of polychrome. Nelson-Atkins Museum of Art, Kansas City, Missouri.

Art of Pre-Columbian America

Can you name an important event that took place in the year 1492? If you said this was the year Columbus discovered the New World, you were *almost* right. In 1492 Christopher Columbus did explore the lands in the western hemisphere. Long before Columbus's arrival, however, civilizations were developing in this part of the globe. Many tribes and peoples were already living there. All were part of a rich heritage or culture, and all created art, such as the work shown at the left. In this chapter you will learn about these peoples and their art.

OBJECTIVES

After completing this chapter, you will be able to:

● Name and describe four major Pre-Columbian cultures.
● Identify the contributions the various Pre-Columbian cultures made to the art world.
● Work in the art styles of early Mesoamerican peoples.

WORDS YOU WILL LEARN

adobe	genre pieces
artifacts	monolith
effigy	motif
funerary urn	stylized

Art of Mesoamerica

You can probably guess the meaning of the word *Pre-Columbian*. This term means "before Columbus." However, art historians use the term in a special way. They use it to refer to the art of early Mexico, Central America, and South America. Less is known about the cultures of these regions than about most others you have studied so far. This is because scientists have only recently begun to find and examine evidence of them.

In this lesson you will read about four major cultures of ancient Mexico and Central America. These are the Olmec, West Mexican, Mayan, and Aztec cultures.

OLMEC CULTURE

The Olmec (**ol**-mek) people lived on the Gulf of Mexico nearly 3000 years ago. Find the center of their civilization on the map in Figure 6–1. Olmec culture is often called the "mother culture" of Mexico. This is because the **artifacts**, or *simple handmade tools or objects*, found in the region where the Olmecs lived are the most ancient. The artifacts left by the Olmecs had an influence on all the civilizations that were to follow.

Like other Pre-Columbian civilizations, the Olmecs were not a prehistoric race. They had a very important culture and a very accurate calendar. They also left behind a number of interesting works of art.

Sculpture

Among the most interesting of the Olmec creations are four huge human heads carved from rock. These were discovered at La Venta, a center for religious ceremonies. One of these sculptures is shown in Figure 6–2. Notice the childlike features on this giant face. The full lips, which seem almost to be pouting, are typical of the Olmec style.

WEST MEXICAN CULTURE

After the Olmecs, the next oldest civilization seems to have been that of West Mexico. The center of West Mexican culture was the city of Colima (koh-**leem**-uh). Find Colima on the map in Figure 6–1. For many years scientists ignored this region. Much of what we know of West Mexican culture was discovered when scientists studied the artifacts accidentally turned up by grave diggers.

Sculpture

Among the West Mexican art that has surfaced are many small clay sculptures of dogs. One of these is shown in Figure 6–3. Study the figure. Would you describe the work as realistic?

▲ Figure 6–1 Mesoamerica.

At one time these sculptures were thought to be **genre** (**zhahn**-ruh) **pieces**. These are *art works that focus on a subject or scene from everyday life.* It is now known that ancient Mexicans viewed dogs as having special powers. Specifically, the animals were believed to serve the dead. A sculpture of this type is called an **effigy** (**eff**-uh-jee), *an image that stands for ideas or beliefs.*

MAYAN CULTURE

The first great Pre-Columbian civilization was that of the Mayas (**my**-uhs). By around A.D. 800 their empire covered the Yucatán (yoo-kuh-**tahn**) peninsula, modern Belize (buh-**leez**), Guatemala, and Honduras. Find these places on the map in Figure 6–1. The Mayas were gifted mathematicians. They had the most accurate calendar of any people in history. They were also great builders. The Mayas erected huge temples and cities with tools of wood, stone, and bone.

▲ Figure 6–3 This is a hollow clay form. The swollen lower body is typical of Colima figures.

Effigy Vessel. c. A.D. 250. Ceramic. Fowler Museum of Cultural History, UCLA, Los Angeles, California.

▶ Figure 6–4   The project to dig up this ancient city is one of the biggest in history. Why do you think scientists spend so much time and effort digging up lost civilizations?

Mayan-Tikal Site. Jaguar Temple. C. A.D. 800. Peten, Guatemala.

Architecture

In the late 1800s scientists digging in northern Guatemala made an important discovery. They found traces of an ancient city. Today this Mayan city, Tikal (tih-**kahl**), is known to have covered an area of 50 square miles (130 sq km). That is roughly the size of Boston. The city is thought to have been home to some 55,000 people. Figure 6–4 shows a view of the site.

Mayan architects not only built outward but they also built upward. Look again at Figure 6–4. The pyramid in the foreground has a temple on top of it. It is typical of many temples built throughout the Mayan civilization. Two others have been discovered at Tikal alone. How many tops of them can you find above the trees in this picture? Amazing structures like these rose at times to heights of 175 feet (53 m). What kind of balance did Mayan architects use in designing these impressive temples?

Sculpture

Most of the Mayan sculpture that has lasted is relief carvings on buildings and monuments. In the early stages of the Mayan civilization, these carvings were mostly simple and realistic. In some later temples a more complex, geometric style came to be the rule. Study the relief sculpture in Figure 6–5. This is a staircase dating to around A.D. 755. Notice the symbols and writings that fill the background. These artists have not left any negative space.

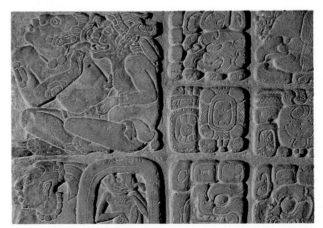

▲ Figure 6–5   This relief carving is from a stairway that was 50 feet (15 m) wide and had 72 steps. Each step was 18 inches (45 cm) high. Since a collapse in 1800, only 32 of the stairs remain.

Mexico Chiapas. Mayan Palenque Glyphs. A.D. 600–900.

AZTEC CULTURE

The largest of the cultures of ancient Mexico and Central America was the Aztec. This civilization emerged sometime between A.D. 1200 and 1325. The Aztecs were a small, warlike tribe. Like other Pre-Columbian peoples, they were very religious. When their god told them to leave their comfortable homeland and settle where they saw an eagle perched on a cactus, they did. A swampy island, which they called Tenochtitlán (tay-noch-tee-**tlahn**), became the center of their great empire. By the time Spanish conquerors arrived in 1519, their island city covered over 25 square miles (66 sq km). Today we know the city, which is no longer on an island, as Mexico City. Find Mexico City on the map in Figure 6–1.

Sculpture

The Aztecs adopted many of the ways of making art used by the people they conquered. They carved huge ceremonial sculptures like the one shown in Figure 6–6. This sculpture is one of 1600 gods and goddesses in the Aztec religion.

One unusual piece of Aztec art is the calendar stone, shown in Figure 6–7. The work is so called because its rim is decorated with signs for the 20 days of the Aztec month. The stone measures 12 feet (3.6 m) in diameter and weighs over 24 tons (22,000 kg).

✔CHECK YOUR UNDERSTANDING

1. Which culture is the mother culture of Mexico?
2. What is a genre piece? What is an effigy?
3. What was the first great Pre-Columbian civilization? What huge structures did the people of this civilization build?
4. What is the calendar stone? What Pre-Columbian civilization created the calendar stone?

▲ **Figure 6–6** This sculpture and its base are decorated with a number of designs. Can you see any that look like flowers?

Xochipilli, Lord of the Flowers. Aztec. National Museum of Anthropology, Mexico City, Mexico.

▲ **Figure 6–7** The stone was more than a calendar. It told the story of the universe. It stated when the Aztec world began and predicted when it would end.

The Aztec Calendar Stone. c. 1500. Tenochtitlán National Museum of Anthropology, Mexico City, Mexico.

Making A Clay Urn

Look again at the work that opened this chapter on page **80**. It is a **funerary (fyoo-nuh-rehr-ee) urn**, *a decorative vase or vessel found at burial sites.* Compare it with the clay vessel in Figure 6–8. The works were created by different Pre-Columbian cultures, but they have much in common. Both use formal balance and are covered with a repeated motif (moh-**teef**). A **motif** is *part of a design that is repeated over and over in a pattern or visual rhythm.* Finally, both works are rich with symbols that had special meaning for members of their cultures.

WHAT YOU WILL LEARN

You will make a cylinder-shaped container at least 6 inches (15 cm) high using the clay slab method. You will decorate your container with a figure wearing symbols that represent your life. You will use formal balance and repeating patterns in your work. The pattern will be in the style of an ancient Mexican culture. You may paint your figure using school acrylics, or you may glaze it. (See Figure 6–9.)

WHAT YOU WILL NEED

- Pencil and sheets of sketch paper
- 2 guide sticks, each about 1/2 inch (13 mm) thick
- Newspaper
- Clay
- Rolling pin, ruler, needle tool, paper towel, and modeling tools
- Slip (a mixture of water and clay used for joining clay pieces), and container of water
- Plastic bag
- *Optional:* Glaze or school acrylics

WHAT YOU WILL DO

1. Brainstorm with your classmates for ideas for personal symbols to be used to decorate your figure. For example, if you play football, the figure could be wearing a helmet. You could decorate the helmet with a pattern of footballs for a headdress. If your major interest is math, the headdress might be covered with numbers. The hands might hold pencils and a notebook to symbolize the student. Make pencil sketches of the figure and the different decorations you will use.

▲ **Figure 6–8** What relationship do you suppose existed between the figure of the clay vessel and what it was used for?

Pottery jar with removable head. Teotihuacan, Mexico. American Museum of Natural History, New York, New York.

2. Set up the guide sticks 6 inches (15 cm) apart on the sheet of newspaper. Using the slab method, make a rectangle, 6 x 12 inches (15 x 30 cm). Keep the unused clay damp by covering it with a lightly moistened towel. Score the short edges of your rectangle. Carefully bend your slab into a cylinder. Apply slip to the scored surfaces and press them together. Smooth both the inside and outside surfaces of the cylinder along the seams.

3. Using a portion of the remaining clay, roll out a slab measuring 10 inches square (65 sq cm). Stand the cylinder on top of the square. Using the needle tool, lightly trace around the cylinder. Score the surface of the circle you have created and the edges of the cylinder. Apply slip, and press the two surfaces together. Add a thin coil of clay inside your cylinder along the bottom. Press it gently into the seam to make the cylinder stronger. Cut off the excess clay from around the base of the cylinder.

4. Model the head, arms, legs, and headdress for your figure. Attach them using scoring and slip. With modeling tools add patterned markings to create rhythm to your work. Note that you may need to support the head and headdress as the work dries. Prop these in place using an object of the right height.

5. When your clay container is bone dry, fire it in a kiln.

6. *Optional*: Glaze or paint the fired container using acrylics.

7. Place the finished work on display. See if your friends can guess what the decorations on your work stand for.

EXAMINING YOUR WORK

- **Describe** Show that your container is at least 6 inches (15 cm) high. Show that the parts are properly joined. Describe the figure and symbols you used to decorate your container. Identify the hues used to color your figure.
- **Analyze** Describe the kind of balance you used. Identify the repeating rhythmic pattern in your work.
- **Interpret** Identify the features of your work that are similar to those of the ancient Mexican culture you used as a model. Explain how the symbols represent your life.
- **Judge** Tell whether you feel your work succeeds. Explain your answer.

▲ **Figure 6–9   Student work. Clay urn.**

OTHER STUDIO IDEAS

- Make a second container, this time using the medium of paper. (For information on making paper sculptures, see Technique Tip **21**, *Handbook* page **284**.)

- ●● Using construction paper or poster board, design and make a piece of jewelry in the style of the Mesoamerican cultures.

LESSON 3

Art of the Andes

Taken together, the four major cultures of Mesoamerica spanned a period of several thousand years. While these civilizations were developing, parallel developments were taking place in the Andes (**an**-deez) Mountains of South America.

In this lesson you will read about the culture and art of the Chavín, Moche, Tiahuanaco, and Inca Tribes.

CHAVÍN CULTURE

The earliest of the Andes civilizations, the Chavín (chuh-**veen**), made their home in the highlands of present-day Peru. The discovery of artifacts places the beginning of Chavín civilization at around 1000 B.C. Their name is taken from their ceremonial center, Chavín de Huántar (**hwahn**-tahr). Today stone pyramids and stone sculpture can still be found at that site. Find this place on the map in Figure 6–10.

Crafts

Like other Andean cultures, the Chavín held the jaguar to be sacred. Images of the cat turn up in much of their art.

One area of art in which the Chavín were especially skilled was crafts. The clay jaguar pitcher in Figure 6–11 is an example of one of their works. Notice the unusual stirrup-shaped spout. This design feature, used by later Andean cultures, was typical of Chavín pottery.

▲ **Figure 6–11** **This hollow vase is decorated with relief designs. Why do you think the Chavín developed the stirrup spout?**

Peru. Stirrup-Spout Vessel, Feline. 700–500 B.C. Ceramic. 23.5 x 14.1 x 20.9 cm (9⅛ x 5⅝ x 8⅛"). The Metropolitan Museum of Art, New York, New York. Michael C. Rockefeller Memorial Collection.

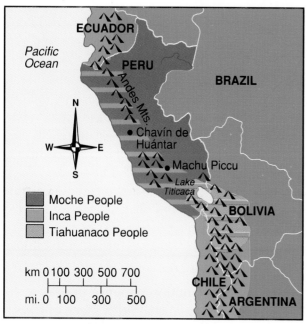

▲ **Figure 6–10** **Andean Cultures.**

▲ **Figure 6–12** The figure is the size of a thumb. It wears a movable nosepiece and carries a movable war club.

Earring. National Geographic Society, Washington, D.C.

Another way in which this object is typical is in the stylized look of its subject. **Stylized** means *simplified or exaggerated to fit a specific set of rules of design*. Did you notice the circles on the head and body? These were meant to stand for the jaguar's spots.

MOCHE CULTURE

West Mexican culture developed roughly between A.D. 100 and 700. Approximately these same years, interestingly, mark the rise and fall of Moche (**moh**-chay) culture. The Mochica (moh-**cheek**-uh), as these people were called, lived on the northern coast of what is now Peru. Find this area on the map in Figure 6–10.

The Mochica were farmers who irrigated the strips of desert between the Andes and the Pacific Coast. They grew corn, beans, squash, and peanuts. They built great pyramids and platforms with **adobe** (uh-**doh**-bee), or *sun-dried clay*. Here they buried their nobles.

▲ **Figure 6–13** This stirrup-spout vessel represents a deer. It shows two figures having a conversation. One has the head of a frog.

Peru, Moche. Stirrup-Spout Vessel in the Form of a Seated Deer. A.D. 200–500. Ceramic. 27.9 cm (11"). The Metropolitan Museum of Art, New York, New York. Gift of Nathan Cummings.

Crafts

The Mochica buried fine works of gold and pottery with their dead. One of these, a gold and turquoise earring, is shown in Figure 6–12. The object was found in 1987 in a tomb near Sipan (see-**pahn**), Peru. The tomb is one of few untouched by thieves that scientists have located. In it, they discovered the remains of a warrior-priest, several servants, and a dog. Did you notice the headdress and necklace worn by the human figure on the earring? One of the skeletons in the tomb was dressed in much the same way.

In the design of their pottery, the Mochica borrowed from the Chavín. A Mochica stirrup-spout pitcher is shown in Figure 6–13. Compare this object with the jaguar pitcher in Figure 6–11. Which spout do you find more graceful? Which of the two ways of showing figures do you find the more stylized?

TIAHUANACO CULTURE

The Tiahuanaco (tee-uh-wahn-**ahk**-oh) civilization developed around the time the Mayas were coming to power. The Tiahuanaco made their home in the Andes highlands of modern Bolivia, just below Lake Titicaca (tee-tee-**kahk**-uh). Find Lake Titicaca on the map in Figure 6–10.

Architecture

Like the Mayas, the Tiahuanaco were master builders. They built a great ceremonial center using stones of the region. The crowning jewel of this center was a stone gateway rich with relief carvings. The impressive work was a **monolith**, *a structure created from a single stone slab.* A detail of the gateway is shown in Figure 6–14. The large figure at the upper right is a winged god. Who do you imagine the smaller figures in the left half of the work are? What do you think they are doing?

Crafts

The unusually dry climate of the Andes highlands has helped preserve another side of Tiahuanaco art. That is the civilization's work in weaving. Figure 6–15 shows a detail from a shirt of the culture. Notice how many colors the weaver used. Would you describe the shapes in this design as organic or geometric?

INCAN CULTURE

About 1450 the Incas conquered the other Andean tribes. The Incan empire stretched more than 2500 miles (4023 km) from north to south. It included present-day Peru plus parts of Ecuador, Chile, Argentina, and Bolivia. Find these countries on the map in Figure 6–10. Each tribe the Incas conquered was forced to learn their language, Quechuan (**kech**-wahn). Today 6 million people speak this language.

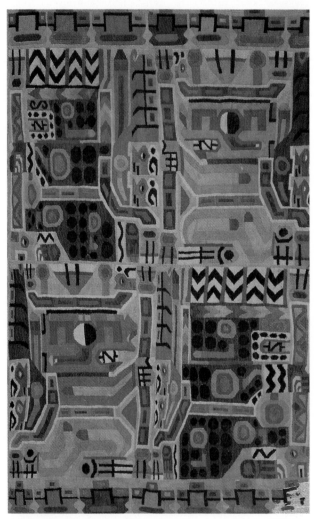

▲ Figure 6–15 Can you find a crowned cat carrying a staff in its paw? Notice how the details change slightly in each creature.

Peru, Coastal Huari-Tiahuanaco. Shirt Section. A.D. 600–1000. Wool, cotton. 53.5 cm (21"). The Metropolitan Museum of Art, New York, New York. Michael C. Rockefeller Memorial Collection.

▲ Figure 6–14 What kind of design has the artist used in this pattern — geometric or organic?

Tiahuanaco. Gate of Sun Creator-God Virachocha. (Detail.) Pre-Colombian. A.D. 600. Aymara Culture. Bolivia.

▲ **Figure 6–16** This town was built quickly. Yet it stood up to all invaders. What does this reveal about the skill of its builders?

Machu-Picchu, Peru.

▲ **Figure 6–17** Some of the feathers in this work are from tropical birds that lived far from the Incan capital of Cuzco. Some experts believe that this demonstrates that the Inca may have carried on trade with other civilizations.

Peru, South Coast. Pre-Inca period. A.D. 800–1300. Tunic. Feathers on canvas. 75.9 x 59.1 cm (29⅞ x 23¼"). The Metropolitan Museum of Art, New York, New York. Fletcher Fund.

The Incas never developed a true writing system. They did, however, develop a method for counting called quipu (**kee**-poo). In quipu, knotted strings were used to stand for numbers. These knots were also used as memory aids in reciting Incan history. The Incas' abilities with numbers is reflected in their art. Incan artifacts were made with great mathematical precision.

Architecture

The Incas were masters of shaping and fitting stone. They were also highly skilled urban planners. Proof of both talents can be found in the walled city of Machu Picchu (**mahch**-oo **peek**-choo). Figure 6–16 provides a view of this ancient city. Built on a mountainside to discourage would-be attackers, the city has withstood five centuries of earthquakes. The stones of its buildings were so carefully matched a knife blade cannot be slipped between any two.

Crafts

Like the Tiahuanaco, the Incas were also gifted weavers. Figure 6–17 shows a woven panel covered with feathers. The colors in the work are the natural ones found in the feathers. Why do you think the Incas chose feathers to decorate their works?

✔CHECK YOUR UNDERSTANDING

1. Which Andean tribe was the earliest? When did it come into being?
2. What is the meaning of *stylized*? What art works did you study in this lesson that were stylized?
3. For what types of art work are the Tiahuanaco best known?
4. The Incas were masters of what type of skills?

Making a Stylized Motif

Animals, as you have seen, play an important role in Pre-Columbian art. Look at Figure 6–18. The artist has used a stylized pairing of a man and animal as a motif. Notice how the man in the motif is holding a torch. Notice also how the motif is repeated through the use of shapes and colors.

WHAT YOU WILL LEARN

You will pick two related objects that are important in modern life. You will stylize and combine these into a motif that could be used in a design for fabric or wallpaper. Pick colors that add harmony to your design and carry over shapes from one object to the other to create a feeling of unity in your design. (See Figure 6–19.)

▲ Figure 6–18 Motifs may be simple or complex. Which word would you use to describe the motif in this shirt? Can you find motifs in any of the items of clothing you are wearing right now?

Peru. Textile fragments. Late Chimu. c. A.D. 1000. Cotton, wool. The Metropolitan Museum of Art, New York, New York. Gift of Henry G. Marquand.

WHAT YOU WILL NEED

- Pencil and sketch paper
- Sheet of white paper, 6 x 9 inches (15 x 23 cm)
- Sheets of construction paper in assorted colors, 12 x 18 inches (30 x 46 cm)
- Ruler, scissors, and white glue

WHAT YOU WILL DO

1. Brainstorm with members of your class to identify objects associated with late twentieth-century living. Some possibilities are cars, telephones, computers, and radios. Pick one object that holds particular importance for you. Then think of a second object that in some way is related to it. A car, for example, might be paired with a gasoline pump; a telephone might be paired with a teenager.

2. Make rough pencil sketches for a motif that combines the objects you picked. Connect the two in some manner. The curly wire of a telephone, for instance, could become the hair of a teenager. Draw one of the objects larger than the other. If possible, simplify some of the larger shapes or forms to geometric ones. Carry one or more shapes from one object over to the other. (Notice how the diamond shapes appearing as eyes on the animal in Figure 6–18 also appear on the man.) This will help lend a feeling of unity to your design.

3. Pick your best motif. Transfer it to the sheet of white paper. Draw the design large enough to fill most of the paper. Cut it out. This is your motif pattern.

4. Pick hues of construction paper that suit the mood of your design. Use one of these colors to serve as a background for

your work. Using the ruler and working lightly in pencil, divide a sheet in this color into four equal boxes.

5. Trace your motif pattern onto your remaining sheets of construction paper. You will need four copies in all. You may use the same color for each motif or use a different color for each. (See Figure 6–20.) Using scissors, carefully cut out the motifs you have drawn.

6. Experiment with arranging your motifs in the four boxes on your background sheet. Try turning two of the motifs upside down. When you have found an arrangement that satisfies you, glue the motifs in place.

7. Use leftover scraps of construction paper to make designs for your motif. Whatever designs you add to one must appear on all others.

8. Place your work on display. Can you identify the stylized objects in your classmates' works?

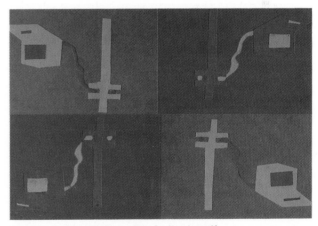

▲ Figure 6–20   Student work. Stylized motif.

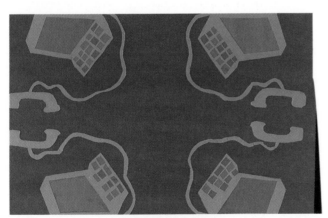

▲ Figure 6–19   Student work. Stylized motif.

OTHER STUDIO IDEAS

- Create another motif that might be used as your personal letterhead. The motif should sum up who you are. Avoid using initials or other letters.

- ●● Use the same motif and use tempera to paint it.

CHAPTER 6 REVIEW

BUILDING VOCABULARY

Number a sheet of paper from 1 to 8. After each number, write the term from the box that best matches each description below.

adobe	genre pieces
artifacts	monolith
effigy	motif
funerary urn	stylized

1. Simple handmade tools or objects.
2. Art works that focus on a subject or scene from everyday life.
3. An image that stands for ideas or beliefs.
4. A decorative vase or vessel found at burial sites.
5. Simplified or exaggerated to fit a specific set of rules of design.
6. Sun-dried clay.
7. A structure created from a single stone slab.
8. Part of a design that is repeated over and over in a pattern or visual rhythm.

REVIEWING ART FACTS

Number a sheet of paper from 9 to 17. Answer each question in a complete sentence.

9. What does the term *Pre-Columbian* mean? How do art historians use the term?
10. What is an artifact?
11. Why is the Olmec culture often called the "mother culture" of Mexico?
12. What city was the center of West Mexican culture?
13. What ancient city did scientists discover in northern Guatemala in the late 1800s? To what culture did this city belong?
14. What was the largest civilization of ancient Mexico and Central America?
15. What animal did the Chavín hold to be sacred?
16. What design feature did the Chavín create in their works that was later used by other cultures?
17. Why was Machu Picchu built on a mountainside? What evidence can be used to support the claim that the builders were talented architects?

THINKING ABOUT ART

On a sheet of paper, answer each question in a sentence or two.

1. **Summarize.** Tell how developments taking place throughout Pre-Columbian America were expressed through the art of the following time periods: 1000 B.C. to A.D. 100; A.D. 300 to 1000; A.D. 1000 to 1500.
2. **Compare and contrast.** Which of the two cultures of Mesoamerica that you read about were most alike? Which were the least alike? Support your answers with information from the chapter.
3. **Compare and contrast.** Review what you learned about the great Egyptian pyramids in Chapter 4. Which of the Pre-Columbian cultures built pyramids for the same reason? Which built pyramids for other reasons?

MAKING ART CONNECTIONS

1. **Language Arts.** Imagine you are touring the parts of present-day South America you studied in this chapter. Write a letter to a friend back home expressing your reactions to the art of ancient peoples of the region. Use the descriptions and pictures from this chapter as a starting point.
2. **Social Studies.** Research interesting facts and traditions of the Incan or Aztec cultures. Report your findings to the class.

LOOKING AT THE DETAILS

The detail below is of a Mexican funerary urn. Study the detail and answer the following questions using complete sentences.

1. Describe how the elements of line and texture are used in this sculptural piece.
2. What type of balance occurs in this detail? Compare the detail to the chapter opening on page 80. What type of balance would you use to describe the entire sculptural piece?
3. Identify a pattern that is repeated in the headdress.
4. What sculpting methods do you think were used in creating this work?

Mexican (Zapotec) from Monte Alban. Funerary Urn. A.D. 500–700. Terra cotta with traces of polychrome. (Detail.) Nelson-Atkins Museum of Art, Kansas City, Missouri.

▲ This temple was once used as a Christian church and then as a mosque. Later it was used
to store ammunition. It was partly destroyed when an artillery shell exploded in its center.

The Parthenon. Temple of Athena. 5th Century B.C. Acropolis, Athens, Greece.

CHAPTER 7

Art of Greece and Rome

Look up Greece in an almanac, and you will learn it has a population of about 10 million. Look up Rome, and the information will be similar.

Facts like these, while useful, do not begin to tell the story. They tell nothing of the mighty powers that Greece and Rome once were. They tell nothing of their contributions to art. One of these contributions is shown at the left. Do you know its name?

In this chapter you will learn about Greece and Rome and study some of the art works created by ancient artists.

OBJECTIVES

After completing this chapter, you will be able to:
- Identify the contributions of the ancient Greeks and Romans to the history of art.
- Name some important works by ancient Greek and Roman artists.
- Paint in the style of Greek and Roman artists.
- Model in the architectural style of ancient Greece and Rome.

WORDS YOU WILL LEARN

amphora   frieze
aqueduct   round arch
concrete   triumphal arch

ARTISTS YOU WILL MEET

Myron   Phidias

LESSON 1

Art of Ancient Greece

Why study events that happened over 3000 years ago in a country the size of Arizona? Why bother learning the names of artists whose works no longer exist? The reason in both cases is that the country — Greece — was the birthplace of Western civilization. The influences of ancient Greek culture and art can still be felt and seen today.

In this lesson you will learn about that culture and art.

THE BEGINNING OF GREEK CULTURE

The story of ancient Greece begins around 1500 B.C. It was around this time that different groups from the north settled in the region bordering the Aegean (ih-**jee**-uhn) Sea. Find the Aegean on the map in Figure 7–1.

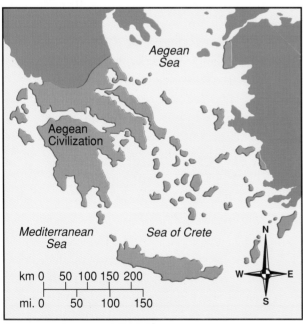

▲ Figure 7–1 Aegean Civilization.

Greece never became a nation. Instead, the tribes that formed it remained small, separately ruled powers called city-states.

Part of the reason for this was geography. High, rocky mountains and miles of sea divided the different city-states. Two other, and more important, factors were self-pride and jealousy. It was loyalty to their own and distrust of others that prevented the city-states from banding together to form a nation.

One of the largest and most powerful of the city-states was Athens. Athens was also the most important in the history of art.

Architecture

The artists of Greece valued above all else grace, harmony, and precision. These qualities are present in the work that opened this chapter on page **96**. This famous building is the Parthenon. The Parthenon was a temple built in honor of the Greek goddess Athena (uh-**thee**-nuh). It stood along with other temples on a sacred hill known as the Acropolis (uh-**krop**-uh-luhs). (See Figure 7–2.) The word *acropolis* means "high city."

The Parthenon is thought to be the most perfect building ever created. Take a moment to study this art treasure. Like other works of Greek architecture, it uses the post and lintel system. Do you remember learning about this system of building in Chapter 4? Can you find the posts in the Parthenon? Can you find the lintels?

▲ **Figure 7–2** The Acropolis rises 500 feet (150 m) above Athens. It was once filled with magnificent buildings.

Acropolis, Athens, Greece.

Sculpture

Sculpture was another of the outstanding achievements of ancient Greek art. At first sculptures were stiff and awkward. In time, however, as Greek sculptors gained skill and confidence, they began creating works that were remarkably lifelike and natural. Figure 7–3 shows one such work. Notice the attention to detail. Even the veins in the arm have been made to stand out in sharp relief. Carved in marble, sculptures like this looked even more realistic because sometimes their surfaces were painted.

Another example of Greek sculpture can be found in Figure 2–9 on page **25**. This long horizontal relief carving is a frieze (**freez**) from the Parthenon. A **frieze** is *a decorative band running across the upper part of a wall*. See how the horses almost seem to gallop across the work. The carving of this frieze was over-

seen by a sculptor named Phidias (**fid-ee-uhs**). Art historians agree that Phidias was among the greatest of all Greek sculptors. One of his most famous works was a magnificent statue of the goddess Athena created for the Parthenon. Made of gold and ivory, the statue rose 40 feet (12 m) to the ceiling. Sadly, this statue and almost all of Phidias's other individual works have been lost. The only knowledge we have of them comes through ancient written descriptions.

Painting and Crafts

Even more famous than the sculptors of ancient Greece were its painters. Like the sculptors, the painters sought to make their pictures as realistic as possible. None of the works of the great Greek painters have survived, however. As with the sculpture of Phidias, these works exist for us only in the words of ancient writers.

Some examples of ancient Greek painting do exist, however, in the pictures found on surviving pottery. The earliest Greek vases were decorated with bands of geometric patterns. One of these objects is shown in Figure 7–4. Found in a cemetery in Athens, this **amphora** (**am**-fuh-ruh), or *twin-handled vase*, was used as a grave marker. The small scene toward the center shows a burial ceremony.

Human figures were later added to the decorations on vases. At first these were little more than stick figures. Later they became more realistic and lively. Often the subjects were gods and goddesses or popular heroes. Scenes from sports and battles were also popular. The amphora in Figure 7–5 shows runners in a race. Notice how the repeated pattern of running figures adds a sense of movement. The curved surface of the vase adds to this feeling. Vases like this were sometimes used as prizes at the games held each summer in Athens. They were filled with olive oil from sacred groves and presented to victorious athletes.

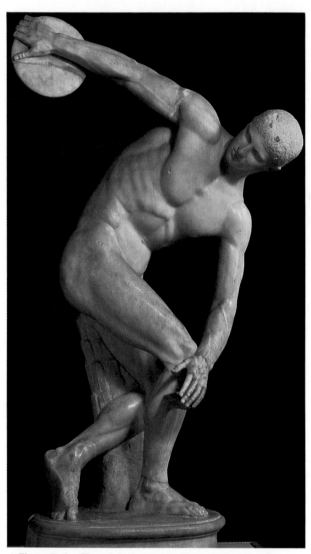

▲ Figure 7–3   The original statue by Myron is known only through descriptions and reconstructed copies. Notice how the sculptor used balance and rhythm to show harmonious form.

Myron. *The Discus Thrower*. Roman copy of a bronze original of c. 450 B.C. Life-size. Museo Nazionale Romano, Rome, Italy.

▲ Figure 7–4   Notice the geometric patterning. Does this design remind you of those created by any cultures you have read about? If so, which ones? This vase was used as a grave marker in much the same way tombstones are used today.

Amphora. Geometric Style. Athens National Museum, Athens, Greece.

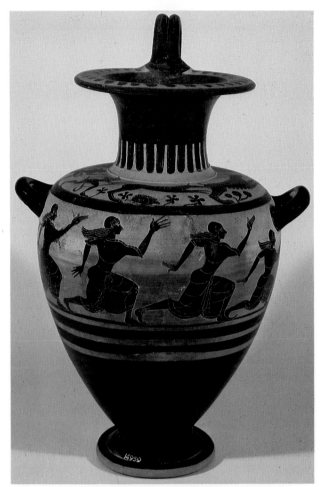

▲ Figure 7–5   The surface of the vase is curved. In what way does this add to the lively scene in the painting?

Amphora. *Runners in a Race*. Etruscan. Vatican Museum.

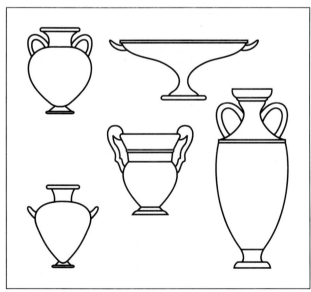

▲ Figure 7–6   Examples of Greek vase shapes.

STUDIO EXPERIENCE

Greek craftspeople designed their pottery for many different purposes. They created large jars for storage and delicate cups for drinking. Examples of these and other vase shapes are shown in Figure 7–6.

Fold a large rectangular sheet of white paper in half. Pick one of the vase shapes in Figure 7–6. Place the point of your pencil at the folded edge of the paper. Draw *one half* of the vase as accurately as you can. Make sure your drawing ends at the crease. Leaving the paper folded, cut your vase shape out along the line you have drawn. When the paper is unfolded, you will have a symmetrical cutout of the vase.

✔ CHECK YOUR UNDERSTANDING

1. Why did the city-states of ancient Greece never join together to form a nation?
2. What three qualities did the artists of Greece value most?
3. What was the Parthenon? On what sacred hill is it found?
4. What is a frieze? What famous artist oversaw the work on the Parthenon's frieze? What other contribution to the Parthenon did he make?
5. What sorts of designs were painted on early Greek vases? What was painted on later Greek vases?

Making a Painting for a Greek Vase

Art critics, you will recall, judge works in terms of different aesthetic views. Look carefully at the Greek amphora pictured in Figure 7–7. How might a critic stressing the importance of the subject of a work react to this vase? Do the figures on the vase look real? Are their actions lifelike?

Think next about how a critic emphasizing composition might respond to the work. Can you find the X made of real and imaginary lines? Do you notice how these lines link the warriors to each other and to the amphora's handles? Note, finally, how a critic stressing content might react to this vase. Did you notice the two women at either side of the work? Could these be the mothers of the two warriors? Could it be they are weeping and pleading for their sons to stop fighting?

A measure of this amphora's greatness is that it succeeds in terms of all three aesthetic views.

WHAT YOU WILL LEARN

You will use tempera to paint one of the following: a scene of warriors in battle, a wedding, an athletic event. Your picture will have at least two figures. Make these figures as realistic as you can. Use the principle of movement to organize the lines and shapes. Finally, your scene will communicate a meaning, mood, or feeling. Paint your scene on a vase cutout like the one you made for the Studio Experience in Lesson 1. (See Figure 7–8.)

WHAT YOU WILL NEED

- Pencil and sheets of sketch paper
- Scissors
- Sheet of white paper, 18 x 24 inches (45 x 61 cm)
- Black tempera paint, several brushes, and mixing tray

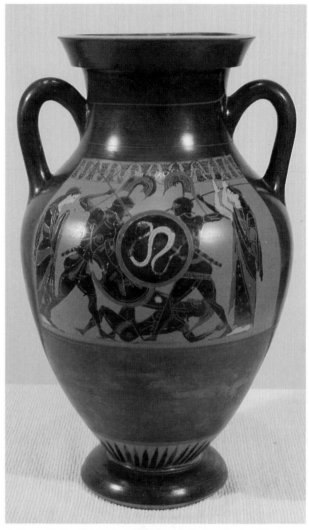

▲ Figure 7–7   This is one of two scenes of combat painted on this vase. Both show warriors of the Trojan war. Have you ever heard of that war? Do you know which sides fought in it?

Black Figured Panel Amphora. Painter of the Medea Group, Greek. 520–510 B.C. Terra cotta, glazed. Lip 19.7 x Base 16.4 x Height 46.4 x Diameter 27.9 cm (Lip 7¾ x Base 6⁷⁄₁₆ x Height 18¼ x Diameter 11″.) Dallas Art Museum, Dallas, Texas. Munger Fund.

SAFETY TIP

When a project calls for paints, use watercolors, liquid tempera, or school acrylics. If you must use powdered tempera, wear a dust mask. Try also to work away from other class members.

WHAT YOU WILL DO

1. Pick one of the three themes for your painting. Make several pencil sketches of scenes that have this theme. Use the vase painting in Figure 7–7 as a model. In your design, create real and imaginary lines that add a sense of movement to it. Keep your design simple. Make sure to emphasize the figures in it. Choose your best sketch.

2. Review the vase shapes in Figure 7–6 on page **101**. Decide which of the shapes would be best suited to your sketch. Using scissors, create this shape out of the large sheet of white paper. Follow the instructions given in the Studio Experience on page **101**.

3. Transfer your sketch to the cutout. Using a fine-pointed brush and black tempera, trace over the outlines of your figures. Carefully paint around lines that are to appear within figures. These lines will appear white in the finished painting.

4. Decorate and paint the rest of your vase using black only. (*Hint*: The neck, handles, and foot of the vase are well suited to decorations.)

5. When your vase painting is dry, display it. Note ways in which it is similar to and different from those created by your classmates.

- **Describe**   Tell which of the three scenes you picked for your work. Describe the shape of amphora you chose. Tell whether the figures in your work look lifelike.
- **Analyze**   Tell whether you used the principle of movement to organize the lines and shapes in your picture. Tell whether the shape of the vase is well suited to the picture you created.
- **Interpret**   State whether your picture communicates a meaning, mood, or feeling. Note whether your classmates are able to identify this mood or feeling.
- **Judge**   Tell whether you feel your work succeeds. Explain your answer.

▶ **Figure 7–8   Student work. Greek vase painting.**

OTHER STUDIO IDEAS

- Create a myth or legend about the event shown in your painting. Write it on an index card to be placed alongside your vase.

- ●● Create a second vase painting using two hues of tempera. Use one hue for the figures and a contrasting earth-toned hue, such as burnt orange, for the background.

Art of Ancient Rome

The Greek city-states were not only unable to band together to form a nation, they were also unable to keep the peace among themselves for long. Frequent outbreaks of fighting over a 1300–year period weakened the country. It made Greece helpless against attack from outside forces. Finally in 146 B.C., Greece fell to the Romans.

Although the Greek empire was defeated, Greek influence continued. The Romans were influenced by Greek ideas about art and used them in their own works.

In this lesson you will learn about some of those works.

ANCIENT ROMAN CULTURE

By the time of its takeover of Greece, Rome was the greatest power in the civilized world. At its peak, the city had a population of over one million people. Find this city on the map in Figure 7–9.

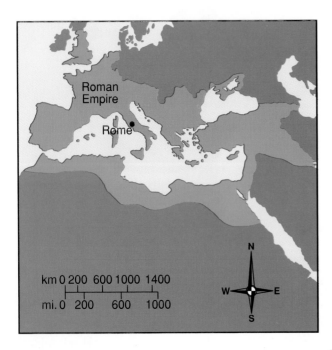

Rome was a city of contrasts. There were magnificent public buildings, baths, and parks, but there were also narrow streets crammed with shabby dwellings.

The Romans were a practical-minded people. They were more interested in such things as engineering, law, and government than in art. Romans did, however, make some very important contributions to the world of art.

Architecture

Rome's greatest contributions were in the field of architecture. Among its accomplishments were:

- **Concrete.** This *mixture of powdered minerals and small stones* was used to create buildings with great domes and ceilings. One such building is shown in Figures 7–10 and 7–11. This is the Pantheon. It was a temple built to honor all the Roman gods. Concrete made it possible for Roman architects to build a huge dome over this temple. The Pantheon is the largest domed building from ancient times still standing.
- **The round arch.** This *curved arrangement of stones over an open space* opened up new building possibilities. A series of round arches could be used to build bridges and other structures.

◀ Figure 7–9   Ancient Rome.

◀ Figure 7–10   Greek temples were built to be "used" only by their gods. Roman temples like this one were built to be used by the people for prayer. The building is large enough to hold 3000 people.

Restored by Hadrian. Pantheon Facade and Piazza della Rotunda. A.D. 118–125. Rome, Italy.

◀ Figure 7–11   The dome of the Pantheon soars to a height of 144 feet (44 m). The hole at its center is the building's only source of light. Though the hole looks small, it is actually 30 feet (9 m) across.

Restored by Hadrian. Pantheon Interior. A.D. 118–125. Rome, Italy.

▲ **Figure 7–12** Aqueducts like this one sloped ever so slightly. This allowed gravity to carry the water on its way.

Pont du Gard. 20–16 B.C. Near Nimes, France.

▲ **Figure 7–13** Would you describe the design of this work as simple or complicated? What elements of art were used in the work? What principles were used?

Arch of Constantine. A.D. 312–15. Rome, Italy.

- **The aqueduct (ak**-wuh-duhkt**).** This *network of channels, meant to carry water to a city,* was another type of structure that used round arches. The aqueduct in Figure 7–12 was built to carry water over a valley 600 yards (548 m) wide. This impressive structure is 160 feet (48 m) high. Note how the arches are placed side by side. This allowed them to support each other and carry the weight to the ground.
- **The triumphal (try-uhm**-fuhl**) arch.** This was *a monument built to celebrate great army victories.* The largest ever built was the Arch of Constantine, shown in Figure 7–13. The round arch was used here by the ancient Romans for purely decorative reasons. Notice how the structure uses three round arches. The emperor and his officers would ride chariots or horses through the large center one. Foot soldiers would march through the smaller side arches as the people of Rome cheered.

Sculpture

Like the Greeks before them, the Romans aimed for realism in their sculpture. A number of the works that remain are portrait sculptures. One of these is pictured in Figure 7–14. Study this work. Notice the care the sculptor has taken to capture not just lifelike detail but also the features of a specific individual. The eyes look as though they might blink at any moment. What mood or feeling does this sculpture communicate?

The Romans also excelled at relief sculpture. The ones shown in Figure 7–15 are from the Arch of Constantine. These reliefs tell of the deeds of the emperor in battle. What events seem to be taking place in the section of the story shown?

▲ **Figure 7–14   What is there about this face that makes it look like someone you might see on the street?**

Bust of Philip the Arab dressed in a toga. A.D. 244–249. Marble. Vatican Museum, Rome, Italy.

◀ **Figure 7–15   Many of the relief carvings on this arch were taken from earlier monuments. Some of the figures on them were changed so they would look more like the emperor Constantine.**

Arch of Constantine. A.D. 312–15. (Detail.) Rome, Italy.

STUDIO EXPERIENCE

Suppose one of your school's sports teams has just scored an important victory. You have been asked to design a triumphal arch to be built in the school gym.

Study the Roman arch in Figure 7–13, noticing the different features. Then, working in pencil, design your arch using the same features. Make sure your work has three rounded arches and columns. Draw in some freestanding sculpture of the coach and star players. Then sketch relief carvings on the arches that focus on highlights of the winning game.

✔CHECK YOUR UNDERSTANDING

1. What led to the downfall of Greece? When was Greece finally conquered?
2. What were Rome's three main contributions to the history of architecture?
3. What was the Pantheon?
4. What is an aqueduct? What is a triumphal arch? What was the triumphal arch used for?
5. What was a key aim of Roman sculpture?

Making a Model of a Roman Triumphal Arch

Art critics often approach their study of architecture just as they do the study of paintings or sculptures. They begin by describing what they see, and then they analyze the ways the principles have been used to organize the elements. After that they interpret the meanings, moods, and feelings the work communicates. Finally, they judge whether the work succeeds and explain why. Doing this helps the critic understand and appreciate a work of architecture.

Look at the triumphal arch pictured in Figure 7–16. What do you think an art critic would say about this arch during each of the four steps of art criticism? How would you, as an art critic, describe, analyze, interpret, and judge it?

▲ Figure 7–16   What type of balance do you see in this triumphal arch? How is proportion used?

Arch of Septimus, Roman Forum.

WHAT YOU WILL LEARN

You will build a model of a triumphal arch out of cardboard and construction paper. Your arch will have all the features outlined in the Studio Experience in Lesson 3. You will use a variety of different shapes and forms. Some of these will be repeated to add harmony. Your work will have formal balance. (See Figure 7–17.)

WHAT YOU WILL NEED

- Empty cardboard soap or cereal box, taped shut
- Large sheets of colored construction paper, including gray and black
- Pencil, scissors, and white glue
- Assortment of magazines featuring sports illustrations
- Scraps of heavy cardboard

WHAT YOU WILL DO

1. Place the cardboard box down flat on a sheet of gray construction paper. With the pencil, trace around the box. Hold a second sheet of gray construction paper firmly against the first. Using scissors, carefully cut through both sheets along the line you drew. Glue the sheets to the front and back of the box. Cover the top and side panels of the box with gray construction paper.
2. Look back at the drawing you made for the Studio Experience in Lesson 3. Doubling two sheets of black construction paper, cut out two large rounded arches and four smaller ones. Glue these arches in place on the front and back of the box. Use your drawing as a guide.

3. Use construction paper to create columns and other decorations. Glue these in place.
4. Look through the sports magazines. Locate black-and-white photographs showing scenes of the sport you chose for your design drawing. Look for action shots that focus on athletes. Cut these out and trim them to fit on your arch. Glue those that are to work as reliefs directly to the arch. Glue those that are to work as free-standing sculpture to small scraps of heavy cardboard before gluing them in place on the arch. This will make them seem to project outward in space.
5. When the glue has dried, display your arch. Compare your work with that of your classmates.

SAFETY TIP

Be very careful when using cutting tools such as scissors and knives. Pick these up only by the handle, never by the blade. Make sure also to offer the handle when you are handing the tool to another person.

EXAMINING YOUR WORK

- **Describe** Point out the round arches on the front and back of your arch. Point out the columns. Point out the two different types of sculpture.
- **Analyze** Tell whether your arch has formal balance. Identify the variety of shapes and forms you used. Tell whether these add harmony to the work.
- **Interpret** State whether your arch tells the story of an important team win. Tell whether it communicates pride in this victory.
- **Judge** Tell whether you feel your work succeeds. Explain your answer.

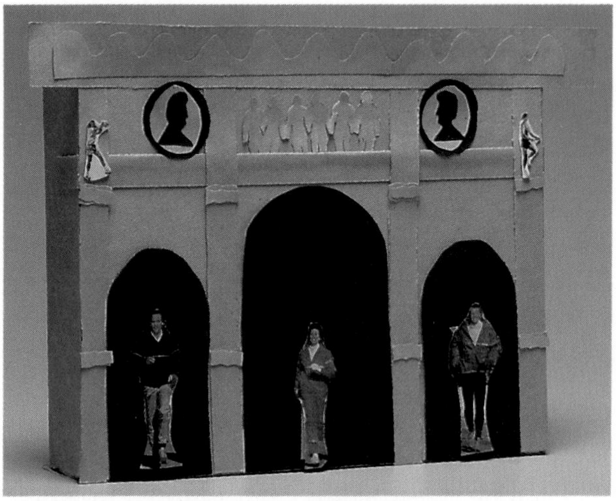

▲ **Figure 7–17 Student work. Triumphal arch.**

OTHER STUDIO IDEAS

- On a large sheet of poster board, draw the outline of a triumphal arch using a black felt-tipped marker. Decorate the arch with magazine cutouts standing for a personal victory. Possibilities include learning to play a musical instrument, making one of the school's athletic teams, or being accepted to a school club.
- •• Create another triumphal arch, this time out of clay. Use the clay slab method. Be sure to use proper joining techniques. Use a clay tool to carve decorations and relief sculptures on your arch.

BUILDING VOCABULARY

Number a sheet of paper from 1 to 6. After each number, write the term from the box that best matches each description below.

amphora	frieze
aqueduct	round arch
concrete	triumphal arch

1. A decorative band running across the upper part of a wall.
2. A twin-handled vase.
3. A mixture of powdered minerals and small stones used in building.
4. A curved arrangement of stones over an open space.
5. A network of channels meant to carry water to a city.
6. A monument built to celebrate great army victories.

REVIEWING ART FACTS

Number a sheet of paper from 7 to 15. Answer each question in a complete sentence.

7. What are two reasons why the Greek city-states never banded together?
8. Which was the largest and most powerful of the Greek city-states?
9. What is the Acropolis? What does the word *acropolis* mean?
10. What goddess was the Parthenon built to honor?
11. To make their sculptures appear even more realistic, what did the Greeks do?
12. Who was Phidias? Name two contributions he made to the Parthenon.
13. In what area of art did the Romans make their greatest contribution?
14. What made possible the building of the dome on the Pantheon?
15. Name two structures in which the Romans used the round arch.

THINKING ABOUT ART

On a sheet of paper, answer each question in a sentence or two.

1. **Interpret.** Look again at the sculpture in Figure 7–3 on page **100**. Tell what you think this figure is doing. Decide what word you would use to describe his feelings at this moment. Explain your answer.
2. **Compare and contrast.** Using the Parthenon and Pantheon as models, list the similarities and differences between Greek and Roman temples.
3. **Analyze.** Examine the aqueduct shown in Figure 7–12 on page **106**. What art elements can you identify in this structure? What principles of art have been used to organize the elements?
4. **Extend.** The Romans, you read, were influenced by Greek ideas about art and used them in their own works. In which area of art do you find this influence to be most evident? Support your answer with facts and examples of specific works from the chapter.

MAKING ART CONNECTIONS

1. **Social Studies.** In this chapter you learned that the Romans were very interested in law and government. In an encyclopedia or other library resource, read about these areas. Search for ties between Rome's system of government and its architecture. Write a short report on your findings.
2. **Language Arts.** Ancient Greece and Rome had rich traditions in mythology. Often, myths were formed to explain events like the origin of man or the change of seasons. Create a myth expressing your own ideas about a natural event.

LOOKING AT THE DETAILS

The detail shown below is of the Parthenon, Temple of Athena. Study the detail and answer the following questions using complete sentences.

1. Which elements of art are used to create harmony in this structure?
2. Compare this detail with Figure 7–12 on page **106**. What similarities as well as differences do you see in the architect's use of the elements and principles of art?
3. What architectural form is used to provide rhythm in this structure?
4. What two purposes did the architect have in mind in his use of the columns?

The Parthenon. Temple of Athena. 5th Century B.C. (Detail.) Acropolis, Athens, Greece.

▲ This miniature painting celebrates the discovery of fire by an early king. Only the skin coats give a clue that this is a scene from the Stone Age. Notice how every space in this miniature is filled with objects and patterns.

Sultan Muhammad. *The Feast of Sadeh*. c. 1520–1522. Colors, ink, silver and gold on paper. 27.4 x 23 cm (9½ x 9 1/16"). The Metropolitan Museum of Art, New York, New York. Gift of Arthur A. Houghton, Jr.

CHAPTER 8

Art of India and Islam

In a way, the frame around a work of art is like a window. The miniature painting on the left does not always stay within the limits of its frame. Notice which parts break free, and which parts stay inside the frame.

This is from a book that illustrates the legends of Iran and its leaders. The artist used intricate details and rich colors to enhance this story. What do you think the curved lines at the bottom of the painting represent?

You will learn to interpret images like this one in the pages to come.

OBJECTIVES

After completing this chapter, you will be able to:

- Identify the major Indian contributions to architecture and sculpture.
- Explain how Islamic culture began.
- Identify the major Islamic contributions to painting, architecture, and crafts.
- Create a design in the Hindu style.
- Make an art work in the Islamic style.

WORDS YOU WILL LEARN

arabesques	mihrab
batik	minaret
calligraphy	mosque
collage	stupas

ARTISTS YOU WILL MEET

'Abd Allah Musawwir	Tamil Nadu
Sultan Muhammad	

Art of India

India is a land of opposites. It is a country of snow-capped peaks and tropical lowlands, of parched deserts and rain-soaked valleys.

Yet, for all its differences, India is a land joined by the strong religious beliefs of its people. These beliefs have in large measure shaped Indian art since the dawn of civilization. In this lesson you will learn about the religion and art of India.

THE RELIGIONS OF INDIA

Indian culture has long been guided by two religions. One of these, Buddhism, you read about in Chapter 5. The other, and older, of India's religions, Hinduism (**hin**-doo-iz-uhm), has its roots in prehistoric times. It was as an outgrowth of Hinduism that Buddhism emerged around 500 B.C.

Unlike Buddhism, Hinduism is not based on the teachings of a single leader. Rather, it is the collected ideas and beliefs of many peoples and cultures over thousands of years. A key belief of Hinduism is that the individual can come to know the powers of the universe through worship. Another is that the soul never dies. Instead, it is reincarnated (ree-uhn-**kahr**-nayt-uhd), or reborn, into a lower or higher life form depending on a person's behavior during his or her previous life.

Hinduism and Buddhism—sometimes together, sometimes separately—have influenced Indian art over the last 2500 years.

Architecture

Among the earliest, and most important, examples of modern Indian architecture are **stupas** (**stoop**-uhs), which are *beehive-shaped domed places of worship*. These were built by Buddhist architects to honor their religion's founder and other important leaders. Each stupa was reached through four gates covered with relief sculptures. Figure 8–1 shows the Great Stupa at Sanchi (san-**chee**). Find Sanchi on the map in Figure 8–2. Completed before A.D. 1, this impressive structure rises to 50 feet (15 m) at its highest point. Notice the contrast between the dome's smooth surface and the detailed carvings of the gate.

▶ Figure 8–1 Believers would pass through one of the gates, then slowly walk around the dome. All the while they would meditate. Do you recall what meditation is?

The Great Stupa. c. A.D. 1. Sanchi, India.

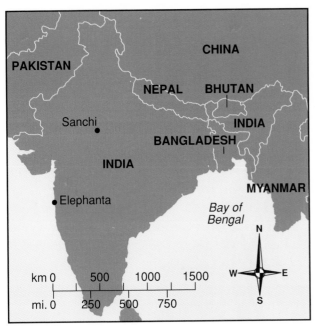

No less impressive were the great temples Hindu architects created some 600 years later. One of the most striking facts about these temples is how some of them were built. They were cut directly into solid natural rock formations.

Figure 8–3 shows an important achievement of Hindu temple building. This amazing structure was cut from a hilltop by many craftspeople. Its hall, almost 100 feet (30 m) square, is decorated with deeply carved religious panels. Yet, like other early Hindu temples, it was made to be viewed mainly from the outside. To the Hindus, a temple was as much sculpture as it was architecture.

▲ Figure 8–3   On entering the hall, visitors would come upon three gigantic heads. Standing for important Hindu religious figures, these heads were each nearly 14 feet (4 m) high.

Rock Cut Temple, India.

▲ **Figure 8–4** Some of the Buddhas created during this period had an unmistakably Greek look. This was the result of a conquest of parts of India in 327 B.C. by Alexander the Great, a powerful general who admired Greek art.

Gautama Buddha in Contemplation. India, Gandharan. 1st-3rd Century A.D. Black schist. 73 cm (28¾"). Yale University Art Gallery, New Haven, Connecticut. Anonymous gift through Alfred R. Bellinger.

Sculpture

Many sculptures, such as the work in Figure 8–4, show the Buddha seated in meditation. Look closely at this sculpture. Notice the dot on the forehead, the seated pose, and the unusually long earlobes of the figure. All are standard features of the Buddha image, each having its own special meaning. The earlobes, for instance, are a reminder of the heavy earrings the Buddha, who was born an Indian prince, wore before he gave up worldly possessions.

In sharp contrast to the weighty stone Buddha figures are the light, open sculptures of cast metal created later by Hindu sculptors. One of these works, the *Tree of Life and Knowledge*, is pictured in Figure 8–5. This sculpture expresses the Hindu belief in the creative force of the universe. Many animals were sacred to the Hindus, especially the cow. Can you find the cows in this work? What other creatures and birds do you notice? What kind of balance has the sculptor used?

STUDIO EXPERIENCE

Look once again at Figure 8–5. Each animal in the work plays a special part in the Hindu view of life. The goose at the end of each branch, for example, stands for the soul's ability to "take flight." The five-headed serpent at the center is a sign of evil and danger.

With a pencil and fine-tipped markers, create your own tree of life. Use the same kind of balance noted in the *Tree of Life and Knowledge*. Fill the branches of your tree with objects that play a part in your personal happiness. Some possibilities are pets, signs of favorite pastimes (a tennis racquet, for example), or good-luck charms. Create decorative patterns of repeated objects similar to the patterns in Figure 8–5. See whether classmates can guess the importance of objects based upon where they appear on your tree.

Figure 8–5 The "tree of life" ties in with the Hindu belief in reincarnation. Since Hinduism teaches that animals have souls, they too can be reborn into higher or lower forms.

Tree of Life and Knowledge. Southern India, Late 1500–1600 A.D. Bronze. Nelson-Atkins Museum of Art, Kansas City, Missouri. Given anonymously.

CHECK YOUR UNDERSTANDING

1. What are two key beliefs of Hinduism?
2. What is a stupa?
3. How was the temple shown in Figure 8–3 created?
4. Name three standard features of early Indian Buddhist sculptures.

Making a Tempera Batik

Hindu art is full of contrasts. Study the sculpture in Figure 8–6. This is Shiva (**shee-vuh**), one of three main gods of the Hindu religion. Notice the contrast between the vertical calm of Shiva's head and the diagonal movement of his arms, legs, and body. His pose captures the feeling of Hindu dance.

WHAT YOU WILL LEARN

You will create a painting of a dancing figure based on the style of the Hindu sculpture. You will use the contrast of vertical calm and diagonal movement. You will use the principle of rhythmic repetition to make your work decorative. You will add contrast and unusual effects to your work using a tempera batik (buh-**teek**) method. **Batik** is *a method of designing on fabric using wax and dyes.* (See Figure 8–7.) Your finished batik will express a mood of excitement.

WHAT YOU WILL NEED

- Pencil and sketchbook
- Yellow chalk and facial tissue
- Sheet of heavy white paper, 12 x 18 inches (30 x 45 cm)
- Thick, creamy liquid tempera paint in a variety of bright hues
- Thick and thin watercolor brushes
- Waterproof black ink
- Tray or pan measuring at least 12 x 18 inches (30 x 45 cm)
- Thick pads of newspaper
- Polymer gloss medium

WHAT YOU WILL DO

1. Study the sculpture of Shiva. Notice the placement of the arms and legs. Make rough sketches creating your own design for a dancer moving in the Hindu style.
2. Using yellow chalk, lightly draw your best dancing figure to fill your paper. Use rhythmic repetition to decorate the figure.
3. Go over your lines to make them wider. Trace over all your lines heavily with a layer of chalk.

◄ **Figure 8–6** Every part of this sculpture has a meaning. The arch and its three-tongued flames stand for the universe and its destruction by fire. The drum in the figure's "upper right" hand stands for the sound of the bang beginning the universe.

Tamil Nadu. *Shiva, King of the Dancers* (Nataraja). Chole Dynasty, 10th Century. Bronze. 76.2 x 57.1 x 17.8 cm (30 x 22½ x 7"). Los Angeles County Museum of Art, Los Angeles, California. Given anonymously.

4. Paint all the shapes, both positive and negative, with bright hues and light values. Do not paint over the chalk lines. Instead carefully paint up to them, but do not cover them. Put down a thick layer of paint. If necessary go over all the colors a second time. Set your work aside to dry at least 24 hours.

5. Gently rub off the thick layer of chalk with the facial tissue. Using a thick, soft brush cover the whole painting with one layer of black waterproof ink. Move the brush across the surface in one direction only. Rubbing it back and forth may dissolve the paint. When you have finished, dab any spots you missed with a brush loaded with ink. Allow the work to dry again 24 hours or longer if possible.

6. When the paper is dry, place it, ink side up, in the tray. Gently pour water over your work to cover it. After several minutes, pour off the water by tilting the tray. Add more water. Repeat this process until the ink has worn off in spots, leaving a crackling effect like you see in batik fabric.

7. Pick up your paper very carefully by two corners. Set it down flat on a thick pad of newspaper to dry.

8. *Optional:* Coat your work with a layer of clear, glossy polymer medium. This will make the colors look richer and it will protect the ink from flaking off.

SAFETY TIP

Wear a smock or protective apron when using waterproof ink. This ink will leave permanent stains on clothing.

EXAMINING YOUR WORK

- **Describe**   Identify the figure in your design. Did you follow all the technique directions?
- **Analyze**   Explain how your figure shows movement. Explain how you used contrast of line and value. Tell whether you have created a decorative quality by using rhythmic repetition.
- **Interpret**   Describe the mood of this work. Explain how this mood is shown. Give your work a title.
- **Judge**   Tell whether you feel your work succeeds. Explain your answer.

▲ **Figure 8–7   Student work. Tempera batik.**

OTHER STUDIO IDEAS

- Do a second version of your Hindu pattern, this time using a monochromatic color scheme with tempera paint. Describe in what ways this design differs from your original.

- ●● Draw the figure and cover it with a chalk line pattern. Paint between the lines and paint the negative space.

LESSON 3

Art of Islam

Around A.D. 600 Hinduism, which had lost favor in India with the rise of Buddhism, began making a comeback. During this same period another religion was taking shape 2000 miles (3220 km) to the east. This new religion would grow into one of the world's largest, with some half billion followers. Its name is Islam (**iz**-lahm).

THE GROWTH OF ISLAM

The birthplace of Islam is the city of Mecca (**mek**-uh), located on the Arabian peninsula. Can you find Mecca on the map in Figure 8–8? There in A.D. 613 a merchant named Muhammad (moh-**ham**-uhd) began preaching a faith centering on one god. This god, called Allah, had revealed himself to Muhammad during meditation. People who came to share Muhammad's beliefs recognized him as Allah's holy messenger. They, themselves, were called Muslims (**muhz**-luhms).

Muhammad's lifelong dream was a world united under Islam. By the early 700s, his followers had spread his message to the Middle East, North Africa, Europe, and Asia.

Painting

The Koran (kuh-**ran**) is the bible of Islam, recording the beliefs of Muhammad. A page from the Koran is shown in Figure 8–9. Some of the finest examples of early calligraphy (kuh-**ligg**-ruh-fee) are found in this book. **Calligraphy** is *a method of beautiful handwriting sometimes using a brush*. Notice the circular gold decorations among the flowing letters. **Arabesques** (ar-uh-**besks**) are the *swirling geometric patterns of plant life used as decorations*. These became a popular decoration because the early Muslim teachings forbade picturing humans or animals.

Architecture

Muhammad taught that dying in battle for the faith guaranteed Muslims entrance into Paradise. As a result, Islam was often spread through force rather than preaching. Each new conquest was celebrated by the building of a **mosque**, *a Muslim house of worship*. By the 800s the Muslim capital of Córdoba (**kord**-uh-vuh), Spain, alone was reported to have 300 mosques.

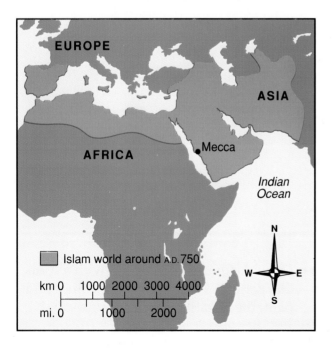

◀ **Figure 8–8   The lands of Islam.**

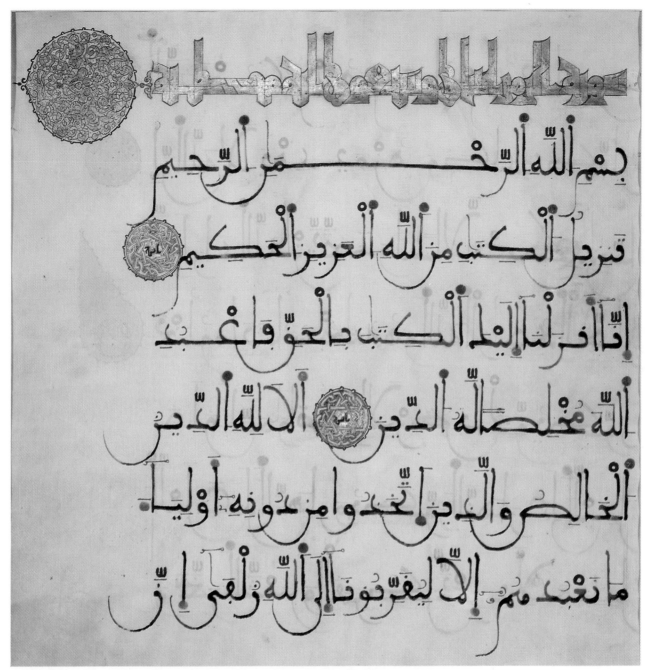

▲ **Figure 8–9** Calligraphy means "beautiful writing." The work that opened this chapter on page 112 also makes use of calligraphy. Can you find it in among the figures?

Leaf from Qur'an (Koran), in Maghribi Script. Islamic, North African. c. 1300. Ink, colors and gold on parchment. 53.3 x 55.8 cm (21 x 22"). The Metropolitan Museum of Art, New York, New York. Rogers Fund.

Figures 8–10 and 8–11 show two views of a Spanish mosque begun in the 700s. In Figure 8–10 you can see a **mihrab** (**mee**-ruhb), which is *a highly decorated nook found in a mosque.* Covered with calligraphic inscriptions from the Koran, the mihrab is found on the wall closest to the holy city of Mecca. The origin and purpose of the mihrab is still a mystery. Some scholars feel it may honor the place where Muhammad stood in his own house when he led his followers in prayer. It became a standard feature of all mosques. Rising above the outside of such mosques are found one or more minarets (min-uh-**rets**). A **minaret** is a *slender tower from which Muslims are called to prayer* five times a day. Can you

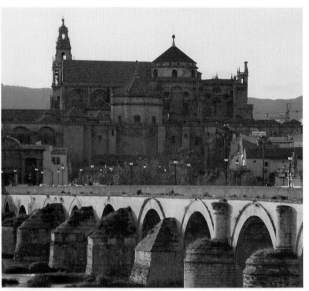

▲ Figure 8–11   What feeling does this seemingly endless row of columns and arches communicate?

The Great Mosque and Roman Bridge. Cordoba, Spain.

▲ Figure 8–10   Muslims always turn toward Mecca while praying. The mihrab, placed inside a mosque, is a pointer to this holy city.

The Great Mosque of Abd ar-Rahman. 8-12th Century. Moorish. Mihrab with arched dome. Cordoba, Spain.

▶ Figure 8–12   This work was built by a Muslim leader as a memorial to his wife. Notice the perfect symmetry of the building and all that surrounds it.

Taj Mahal, garden and pools. c. 1650. Agra, India.

find the minarets in the famous structure in Figure 8–12? Do you know the name and location of this famous building?

Crafts

One of the most outstanding contributions of Islamic art is the knotted-pile, or Persian, rug. Persian knots in this type of rug are so close together that when the pile (raised loops of yarn) is all worn away the colors of the design are still visible. Figure 8–13 shows a Persian rug dating from 1550. This object uses 18 different shades of wool. Notice the care the weaver has used in balancing the complex design. Can you name the type of pattern running through this carpet?

▲ **Figure 8–13   A single rug would take one craftsperson many years to complete.**

Iranian. Prayer rug. 16th Century. Wool, cotton, silk. 161.3 x 108 cm (63½ x 42½"). The Metropolitan Museum of Art, New York, New York. Mr. and Mrs. Isaac D. Fletcher Collection. Bequest of Isaac D. Fletcher.

▲ **Figure 8–14   Persian knot diagram.**

✔CHECK YOUR UNDERSTANDING

1. Who was Muhammad? When and where did he begin preaching his new faith?
2. What are followers of Muhammad called?
3. What is the Koran? What is calligraphy?
4. What is an arabesque? Why did arabesques become popular?
5. What is a mosque? What are two standard features of mosques?
6. What kind of rugs are Islamic artists famous for?

Making a Collage in the Islamic Style

Look at the Islamic miniature painting in Figure 8–15. Everything seems to be flat on the picture plane. The colors are intensely bright. How many different scenes or images do you see? Notice how the artist presents many points of view in the same work of art. A variety of patterns are used to fill the background spaces. Shapes, colors, and patterns are emphasized. By doing so, the illusion of depth is not felt.

WHAT YOU WILL LEARN

In this lesson you will create a **collage**, *an art work made up of bits and pieces of two-dimensional materials pasted to a surface*. Your collage will focus on several scenes related to a current event or activity. The work will be organized, however, in the manner of a flat, patterned Islamic miniature painting. You will use bright colors, decorative patterns, and flat shapes as in Figure 8–15. You will create the background shapes using patterned fabrics and papers. People and other objects can be made by drawing and painting them on white paper. See Figure 8–16.

WHAT YOU WILL NEED

- Pencil, sketch paper, ruler, scissors
- Sheet of white paper or poster board, 22 x 28 inches (56 x 71 cm)
- A variety of patterned fabrics and papers
- White glue, colored pencils
- Small pieces of white drawing paper

◄ Figure 8–15 **This is a page of a book meant to be held in the hand and studied closely. Notice the patterns, rhythmic designs, and bright colors. Some of the pigments for the work were made by grinding precious metals such as gold and silver.**

'Abd Allah Musawwir. *The Meeting of the Theologians.* c. 1540–1549. Colors on paper. Bokhara. Nelson-Atkins Museum of Fine Arts, Kansas City, Missouri.

WHAT YOU WILL DO

1. Brainstorm with classmates for ideas that could best be explained by showing several different scenes. For example, to show a football game you might have one scene of a huddle, one of a tackle, and one of the ball being kicked. Pick an event, such as a school dance, a parade, or a wedding. Make pencil sketches of different objects and scenes from the event you picked.
2. Make a plan to arrange your best ideas within rectangles of different sizes. Using the ruler and pencil, lightly draw these rectangles on the poster board.
3. Measure each shape and cut out patterned fabric or paper to fit each shape. As you select each pattern for the background, consider how one will look next to another. Look for contrast in the fabric so that you can see the distinction between each shape. If you wish, you may draw and color patterns in some of the spaces. Glue the pieces of fabric and paper to the poster board.
4. Draw and color figures and objects to place in each scene. Measure first to be sure that the figure will fit inside its area. Cut out the drawn objects and glue them onto the design.
5. When the glue is dry display your work. See whether classmates can guess what event your collage celebrates.

EXAMINING YOUR WORK

- **Describe**   Identify the different scenes and objects related to your events. Explain why you placed each scene or object where you did.
- **Analyze**   Show where you used contrast in your design. Identify how you used the element of space. Explain how the many different patterned areas made your work look different from other art works you have created.
- **Interpret**   State what feeling or mood your work communicates to viewers.
- **Judge**   Tell whether you feel your work succeeds. Explain your answer.

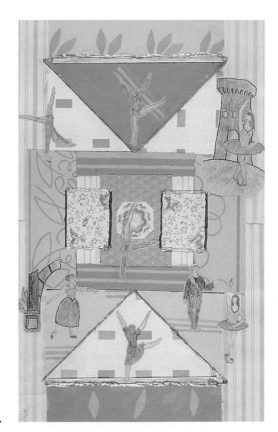

▶ Figure 8–16   Student work. Collage in the Islamic style.

OTHER STUDIO IDEAS

- Working as part of a group of four students, make another collage. This time use a larger sheet of poster board.

- ●● Pick an American legend or hero, such as Paul Bunyan, Daniel Boone, or Betsy Ross. Organize the events of the person's life in a second collage.

BUILDING VOCABULARY

Number a sheet of paper from 1 to 8. After each number, write the term from the box that best matches each description below.

arabesques	mihrab
batik	minaret
calligraphy	mosque
collage	stupas

1. Beehive-shaped domed places of worship.
2. A method of designing on fabric using wax and dyes.
3. A method of beautiful handwriting sometimes using a brush.
4. Swirling geometric patterns of plant life used as decorations.
5. A Muslim house of worship.
6. A highly decorated nook found in a mosque.
7. A slender tower from which Muslims are called to prayer.
8. An art work made up of bits and pieces of two-dimensional materials pasted to a surface.

REVIEWING ART FACTS

Number a sheet of paper from 9 to 16. Answer each question in a complete sentence.

9. What two religions have played a major role in the art of India over the last 2500 years?
10. How were Hindu temples like the one shown in Figure 8–3 created?
11. What is the explanation for the unusually long earlobes found on Buddha sculptures?
12. What Hindu belief is revealed in the *Tree of Life and Knowledge* sculpture?
13. What is the name of the god of Islam? How did Muhammad come to know this god?
14. In what book central to the Islam faith was calligraphy used?
15. What buildings did Muslim conquerors raise after each new conquest?
16. What can you see in Persian rugs that reveals the special weaving method with which they were made?

THINKING ABOUT ART

On a sheet of paper, answer each question in a sentence or two.

1. **Interpret.** Read the following statement: "To appreciate fully a work of religious art you must be a member of the religion." Tell whether you agree or disagree. Defend your position with information and examples from this and other chapters.
2. **Compare and contrast.** What common features can you find between Buddhist and Hindu temples? What differences between the two can you note?
3. **Analyze.** Pick one art work from the chapter. Note how the elements of art and principles of art were used in the work. Identify the way they were used.
4. **Extend.** Look once more at the inside view of the mosque in Figure 8–10. How would the experience of walking through this building differ from the experience of seeing it in a photograph? What does this difference reveal to you about ways of looking at art?

MAKING ART CONNECTIONS

1. **Social Studies.** Like Islam, Buddhism spread far from its birthplace. Compare the Japanese sculpture of Buddha you studied in Chapter 5 on page **73** with Figure 8–4. List the ways the two works are alike and different. Note standard style features of each. Identify the influences of culture that led to these similarities and differences.
2. **Language Arts.** Create a verse for a greeting card. Write your poem using a calligraphy style.

LOOKING AT THE DETAILS

The detail shown below is from Sultan Mu-hammad's *The Feast of Sadeh*. Study the detail and answer the following questions using complete sentences.

1. Can you see evidence of a renowned Islamic craft in this painting?
2. If you were not aware of the origin of this painting and a credit line was not available, what clues do you see that might tell you that it is an Islamic work of art?
3. How would you describe the mood of the top figure? Is the same mood expressed by the lower figure? Explain your answer.
4. Look at the entire work on page **112**. Do you think this painting is meant to be "read" in a clockwise or counter clock-wise direction? Explain your answer.

Sultan Muhammed. *The Feast of Sadeh*. c. 1520–1522. Colors, ink, silver and gold on paper. 27.4 x 23 cm (9½ x 9⅟₁₆"). The Metropolitan Museum of Art, New York, New York. Gift of Arthur A. Houghton, Jr.

▲ This headdress was to be worn as a sign of magical power. The section over the cap stands for a tribal altar. The birds signal the presence of ghosts.

Africa, Nigeria, Ibo Tribe. Dance Headdress. Wood, paint, metal, fiber. 47 x 32.7 x 27.7 cm (18½ x 12⅞ x 10⅞"). Dallas Museum of Art, Dallas, Texas. The Eugene & Margaret McDermott Fund.

CHAPTER 9

Art of Africa

Africa's past is shrouded in mystery. Until recent times there were no written documents and contacts with peoples from other lands were limited. Even the wood figures and masks of the past no longer exist. They were destroyed by the damp climate and wood-eating insects.

Most of the African art you see in museums today was made within the past 100 years. Works like the one pictured at the left are more than a tribute to the imagination and skill of recent African artists. They are our only clues to the works of generations of artists who came before.

OBJECTIVES

After completing this chapter, you will be able to:

- Describe the figures in wood and bronze made by African tribal sculptors.
- Name the three kinds of masks made by African tribal sculptors.
- Work with different media to create abstract and imaginative art objects.

WORDS YOU WILL LEARN

abstract work
face mask
headpieces

papier-mâché
shoulder masks

The Figure Sculptures of Africa

Africa is the second largest continent in the world. It is more than three times the size of the United States. Yet, until Portuguese explorers came in the late 1400s, little about Africa was known. To this day the continent's distant past remains cloaked in mystery.

THE CULTURES OF AFRICA

The peoples of Africa below the Sahara live in many different tribes and kingdoms. The location of the larger of these tribes is shown on the map in Figure 9–1. Each tribe has its own language, customs, and religion.

Each tribe has also made its own unique contribution to the world of art. Many of these contributions have taken the form of sculpted human figures and masks. In this lesson you will read about the human figure sculptures created by African artists.

Carved Wood Figures

A favored medium of the African tribal sculptor was wood. Most carvings were made from a single log. The original shape of the log was often suggested in the finished work. Many were rubbed with natural oils to heighten the beauty of the work. This was also thought to add to the carving's magical powers.

Figure 9–2 shows a carving by an artist of a west African tribe. Like all African wood figures, the work is boldly carved. It is also typically abstract. An **abstract work** is *a work in which the artist uses a recognizable subject but portrays it in an unrealistic manner*.

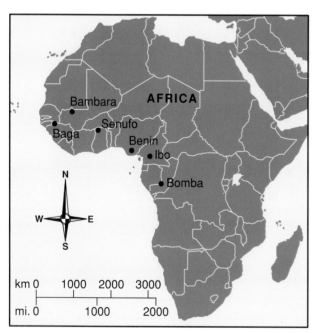

▲ Figure 9–1 Africa.

▲ Figure 9–2 Carvings like this were not done to please their owners. They were done for the sake of the spirit who lived inside the carving.

Africa, Ivory Coast, Senufo Tribe. Bird. 19th-20th Century. Wood. 121.2 cm (47½"). The Metropolitan Museum of Art, New York, New York. The Michael C. Rockefeller Memorial Collection. Gift of Nelson A. Rockefeller.

Figure 9–3 shows a Senufo carving. This one appears to be a man on a horse. Actually, it is much more than that. Legend has it that the rider is a magician. His powers allow him to travel between the spirit world and the real world. Notice how this carving seems almost to reveal the artist at work. You can almost picture the artist's knife slashing the forms of horse and rider from the log. The finished work captures the dignity and pride of the rider with his shoulders back and his chest and chin thrust forward.

◀ Figure 9–3 In creating figures like this, the artist would perform certain rituals. One was making an offering to the tree the wood was taken from.

Africa, Ivory Coast, Senufo Tribe. Equestrian Figure. 19-20th Century. Wood, patination. 32.5 x 7.3 x 22.3 cm (12¾ x 3 x 8¾"). Dallas Museum of Art, Dallas, Texas. Gustave and Franyo Schindler Collection. Gift of the McDermott Foundation.

▲ **Figure 9–4** The sculptor effectively shows mood through the use of texture and composition in this work.

Africa, Nigeria. Court of Benin, Bini Tribe. *Mounted King and Attendants.* c. 1550–1680. Bronze. 49.5 x 41.9 x 11.3 cm (19½ x 16½ x 4½"). The Metropolitan Museum of Art, New York, New York. The Michael C. Rockefeller Memorial Collection. Gift of Nelson A. Rockefeller.

Cast Bronze Figures

In the spring of 1897 a shipload of bronze sculptures arrived in England. The works showed a skill at casting equal to that of any sculptor of the day. Imagine the excitement of the art community upon discovering these marvelous bronzes.

These sculptures were made by artists of the Benin (buh-**neen**) Empire. Among the most remarkable of the works were reliefs used to decorate the wooden pillars of the palace. One of these appears in Figure 9–4. It shows the powerful king of the tribe on horseback. Two servants protect him from the sun with their shields. Two others support him with their hands, while still another supports the king's feet with his head. Notice the sculptor has made the figure of the king larger than those of the servants. This was done to emphasize the king's importance. What ancient culture that you read about had a similar practice?

Not all bronze castings by African artists are reliefs. Some, like the sculpture in Figure 9–5, are freestanding. Bronze heads like this one were placed on an altar as memorials to the king's ancestors. Notice the lifelike quality of this sculpture. What kind of balance has the artist used?

✔ CHECK YOUR UNDERSTANDING

1. Explain why the art of each African tribe has been a unique contribution to the art world.
2. What is the meaning of abstract work?
3. In what year did the bronze sculptures from Africa reach Europe? How did the Europeans react upon seeing these works?

◀ **Figure 9–5   Bronze sculptures like this show the skill of the tribal artist. Notice the varied patterns on this sculpture.**

Africa, Nigeria. Court of Benin, Bini Tribe. Head. c. 1550. Bronze. 23.5 x 22 x 22.9 cm (9¼ x 8⅝ x 9"). The Metropolitan Museum of Art, New York, New York. Bequest of Nelson A. Rockefeller.

Abstract Self-Portrait Cutout

The African figure sculptures you studied in Lesson 1 were made to honor past tribe members. They were also made to hold the spirits of past tribe members. Figure 9–6 shows another of these figure sculptures. Notice that, like other African standing figures, it is highly abstract. This work goes a step further, however. The artist here has simplified the human figure into a series of flat shapes and simple forms. You may be able to see how this abstract style had an effect on the later development of cubism in European art.

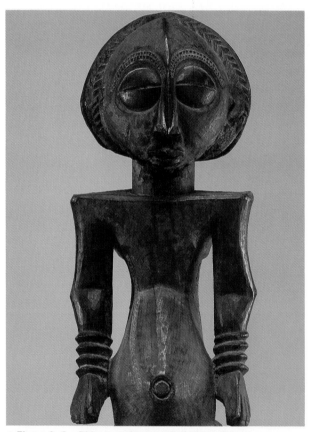

▲ **Figure 9–6** Did you notice how the features have been stylized? What has been done to simplify the figure?

Africa, Zaire. Buye style. 19th-20th Century. Wood, kaolin. (Detail.) 77.5 x 28.9 x 21.6 (30½ x 11⅜ x 8½"). The Metropolitan Museum of Art, New York, New York. The Michael C. Rockefeller Memorial Collection. Gift of Nelson A. Rockefeller.

WHAT YOU WILL LEARN

You will create an abstract cardboard cutout self-portrait as seen from the front. Show yourself in a posture or activity that tells something about your personality. You will use flat shapes and simple forms for body parts and features. You will give the work a three-dimensional look by painting certain parts of the figure in black and white. You will add harmony by using only sharp-angled shapes and forms. (See Figure 9–7.)

WHAT YOU WILL NEED

- Pencil and sheets of sketch paper
- Piece of cardboard, 6 x 12 inches (15 x 30 cm)
- Ruler and scissors
- Black and white tempera paint
- Brushes and polymer gloss medium
- Scrap of heavy cardboard and transparent tape

WHAT YOU WILL DO

1. Look back at the drawing you made for the Studio Experience in Lesson 1. Do another drawing, this time replacing all curved lines with straight ones. Simplify the facial expression, but make sure your new version still shows a pose or expression that tells viewers about the kind of person you are. Make several sketches.
2. Draw the best of your sketches on the piece of cardboard. Use the ruler to make sure all the lines in your drawing are straight. Take care also to create shapes that are flat and angled.

3. Using the scissors, cut out your shape. Add more straight lines *within* the shapes on your cutout. These should suggest flat surfaces at different angles to each other. This will make the shapes seem more like three-dimensional forms.
4. Study the carving in Figure 9–6. Decide which shapes in your work could be painted either black or white to give it a sense of depth. Paint the cutout with black and white tempera.
5. When the paint has dried, apply a coat of polymer gloss to your cutout. Cut a wedge shape from the scrap of heavy cardboard. Using tape, attach the wedge to the back of your cutout. This will allow you to stand the cutout for display.

▲ Figure 9–7   Student work. Abstract self-portrait.

EXAMINING YOUR WORK

- **Describe**   Tell how you created your cutout to be a standing figure as seen from the front. Tell whether your work is abstract. Explain why your work is considered an abstract piece.
- **Analyze**   Point out the flat shapes and simple forms in your work. Identify the places where you used black or white paint to add a three-dimensional look to the work. Explain why the use of angled shapes and forms throughout adds harmony to the work.
- **Interpret**   Show what features in your work would help a viewer understand what kind of person you are.
- **Judge**   Identify what is most successful about your cutout. Explain whether the work succeeds because of its abstract look. Tell whether its success arises out of your use of art elements and principles. State, finally, whether its most successful feature is the message it communicates about you as a person.

OTHER STUDIO IDEAS

- On a sheet of white paper, make a pencil drawing of another standing figure. The subject this time should be a friend or relative you admire. Decide what qualities you admire most in the person. Decide how best to show these qualities in your work.

- ● Make another cardboard cutout, this time of a figure on horseback. Your figure should exhibit an emotion or feeling, such as pride, humility, or anger. Use the sculpture in Figure 9–3 on page **131** as your model. Again, simplify each of the figures into a series of flat shapes and forms. Paint your cutout with two complementary colors.

The Masks of Africa

African tribespeople had several ways of relating to the spirit world through art. One, which you read about in Lesson 1, was through figure sculptures. Another was through masks. Like the figure sculptures, the masks made by African tribal artists were richly carved. They are among the finest and most remarkable art forms of Africa. The masks also had great magical importance attached to them.

The artists of Africa created three different types of masks. These were the face mask; the headpiece, or headdress; and the shoulder mask.

▲ **Figure 9–8** How do you think a dancer wearing this mask would appear to onlooking tribespeople?

Africa, Chumbanndu, Buluba. Face Mask. American Museum of Natural History, New York, New York.

THE FACE MASK

The **face mask** was *a mask worn to hide the identity of the wearer*. The wearer even changed his or her voice so as not to be recognized. An example of a face mask is shown in Figure 9–8. Animal furs, feathers, and shells are included in its decoration.

The face mask was used in a number of different tribal ceremonies. Sometimes these ceremonies were held to protect the tribe from the unknown forces of nature. Others were intended to ensure a good harvest. Once the ceremony began, the tribespeople wearing masks would dance to rhythmic music. Seen by flickering firelight, these masked dancers were sometimes frightening and sometimes amusing. Always they were exciting.

THE HEADPIECE

Not all African masks were made to hide the wearer's identity. The headpieces created by artists of the Bambara tribe of west Africa were made with an abstract animal design. **Headpieces** were *masks carved of wood and worn on the head like a cap*. In Bambara culture the antelope is a symbol for a rich harvest and appeared as the model for their headpieces. Figure 9–9 shows examples of these headpieces.

Bambara headpieces were used in a ritual performed when a new field was readied for planting. This ritual honored Tyi Wara, a mysterious being who was credited with having taught the Bambara how to plant and grow crops. The design of the headpiece was meant to blend the speed and grace of the antelope with the powerful spirit of Tyi Wara. Study the headpiece in Figure 9–9. What element in the work is used to capture a feeling of grace? What art element is used to capture a feeling of power?

▲ **Figure 9–9** **The antelope on the right is male. Notice its beautiful, flowing mane. The female carries a baby on her back.**

Africa, Mali, Bamana Tribe. Two Antelope Headpieces. 19th-20th Century. Wood, metal bands. Left: 71.2 x 30.9 x 5.4 cm (28 x 12⅛ x 2⅛″). Right: 90.7 x 40 x 8.5 cm (35¾ x 15¾ x 3⅜″). The Metropolitan Museum of Art, New York, New York. The Michael C. Rockefeller Memorial Collection. Gift of Nelson A. Rockefeller.

THE SHOULDER MASK

Face masks were meant to cover the face of the wearer. Headpieces were meant to cover the wearer's head. The third kind of African mask, shoulder masks, were meant to do both. **Shoulder masks** were *large, carved masks made to rest on the shoulders of the wearer.*

They are sometimes called helmet masks. A shoulder mask of the Baga tribe is shown in Figure 9–10. It was used during a dance performed as part of a ceremony to guarantee a successful harvest. Notice how the face in this work is highly stylized.

▲ **Figure 9–10** **Masks are meant to be seen in motion. They were thought to have great magical powers.**

Africa, Guinea, Baga Tribe. Headdress. 19th-20th Century. Wood. 122.6 x 40.9 x 70.3 cm (48¼ x 16⅛ x 27⅝"). Dallas Museum of Art, Dallas, Texas. The Gustave and Franyo Schindler Collection. Gift of the McDermott Foundation in honor of Eugene McDermott.

The wearer of a shoulder mask peered out through holes cut in the chest. Like face masks and headpieces, shoulder masks were part of a complete costume. Long strips of fiber were used to cover the body of the wearer. Unlike the other masks, shoulder masks were quite heavy, often weighing 75 pounds (34 kg) or more. When the mask was in place, the wearer stood over 8 feet (243 cm) tall. Wearing such a mask called for very strong performers. Even so, they could perform in rituals for only a short time.

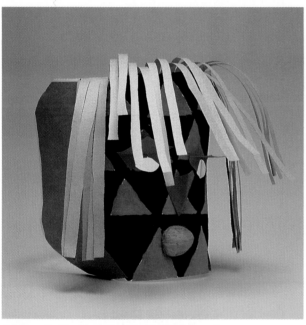

▲ Figure 9–11   Student work. Cardboard mask.

✔CHECK YOUR UNDERSTANDING

1. What are face masks? What were face masks used for?
2. What role did the antelope play in Bambara culture? Who or what was Tyi Wara?
3. In what way were shoulder masks different from face masks and headpieces?

Making a Mood Mask Relief

The goal of African artists was to make expressive art. Masks were meant to communicate a mood or feeling to the viewer. Study the helmet mask shown in Figure 9–12. It is known as the "Firespitter." What mood does this half-animal, half-human mask communicate?

WHAT YOU WILL LEARN

You will create a mask relief that communicates a particular feeling or mood. You will model your mask out of papier-mâché (pap-yay-muh-**shay**). **Papier-mâché** is *a sculpting technique using newspaper and liquid paste*. You will use a variety of different shapes, forms, and textures. You will exaggerate the proportions of the shapes and forms used for the face features. Your shapes and forms will be organized into patterns to decorate the whole mask. (See Figure 9–13.)

WHAT YOU WILL NEED

- Pencil and sheets of sketch paper
- Heavy-duty aluminum foil and newspaper
- Masking tape and a large sheet of cardboard
- Non-toxic commercially prepared papier-mâché paste or white glue
- Plastic mixing bowl and water
- Newspaper torn into strips about 1/2 inch x 1 1/2 inches (13 x 39 mm)
- Fine-grain sandpaper
- Scissors or other sharp cutting tool
- Tempera paint and brushes
- Yarn, cloth, and cotton for decoration
- Polymer gloss medium

WHAT YOU WILL DO

1. Pretend that you belong to a tribe that has been having a series of misfortunes. The crops are dying and the water supply is low. Create a mask to be used in a ceremony your tribe might perform to restore your tribe's good fortune.
2. Do sketches for a mood mask expressing joy and happiness to attract the spirit of good fortune. Exaggerate the proportions of the features of the face. Use lines and shapes to create decorative patterns.

◄ **Figure 9–12** Notice the care with which this work was designed. Real and imaginary lines of the horns, tusks, and mouth are used to unify the work.

Africa, Ivory Coast, Senufo Tribe. Helmet Mask. 19th-20th Century. Wood. 94 cm (35⅝"). The Metropolitan Museum of Art, New York, New York. The Michael C. Rockefeller Memorial Collection. Gift of Nelson A. Rockefeller.

3. Cut a sheet of heavy-duty aluminum foil large enough to cover your face. Using your fingers, gently press the foil around your eyes, nose, and mouth.

4. Place the foil mask on the cardboard and stuff wads of newspaper under it. This will help it keep its shape when the papier-mâché is applied. Using masking tape, fasten the stuffed foil to the cardboard.

5. Follow the instructions for applying papier mâché in Technique Tip **20**, *Handbook* page **283**. As you work, take care not to press too hard on the foil. If you do, the raised areas may collapse. Set the mask aside overnight to dry.

6. The next day sand your mask lightly with the fine-grain sandpaper. Trim the edges with scissors and carefully cut holes or slits for eyes. If you do not wish to wear your mask you might want to paint the eyes on your mask instead.

7. Look back at your sketches. Working in pencil, transfer the other face features and decorative patterns from your best sketch.

8. Pick colors of tempera paint for your mask. Your color choices should emphasize the joyous mood of the work. Paint your mask and add yarn, cloth, or cotton to create texture. Apply a coat of polymer gloss to add sheen to the mask.

SAFETY TIP

Avoid using wallpaper paste and similar glues for your work in papier-mâché. These glues have poisons in them that can enter the body through the skin.

EXAMINING YOUR WORK

- **Describe**   Point to the different face features of your mask.
- **Analyze**   Identify where your mask has a variety of different shapes, forms, and textures. Explain how shapes and forms are organized into decorative patterns. Point out the exaggerated proportions of shapes and forms in the face features of your mask.
- **Interpret**   Point to the features in your work that would help a viewer understand its joyous mood. Explain how exaggeration helped communicate this mood.
- **Judge**   Tell whether you feel your work succeeds. Identify the best features of your mask.

▲ **Figure 9–13   Student work. Mood mask.**

OTHER STUDIO IDEAS

- Create a ritual to go with your mask. Invent a tribe name and an aspect of nature or of an animal that the mask honors. Share this information with your class in an oral demonstration.

- •• Design another mask for another tribal ceremony. Perhaps the ceremony is intended to ensure a successful hunt or to frighten away evil spirits. Exhibit your mask in class. Ask if anyone can name the kind of ceremony in which it would be used.

BUILDING VOCABULARY

Number a sheet of paper from 1 to 5. After each number, write the term from the box that best matches each description below.

abstract work	papier-mâché
face mask	shoulder masks
headpieces	

1. A work in which the artist uses a recognizable subject but portrays it in an unrealistic manner.
2. A mask worn to hide the identity of the wearer.
3. Masks carved of wood and worn on the head like a cap.
4. Large, carved masks made to rest on the shoulders of the wearer.
5. A sculpting technique using newspaper and liquid paste.

REVIEWING ART FACTS

Number a sheet of paper from 6 to 13. Answer each question in a complete sentence.

6. When did Portuguese explorers first come to Africa?
7. What is the favored medium among African tribal sculptors?
8. What two reasons did African sculptors have for rubbing their wood carvings with oil?
9. Which African tribe created the remarkable bronze sculptures that arrived in Europe in 1897?
10. What three kinds of masks were created by African artists?
11. Name two ceremonies in which face masks were used. In what ceremonies were Bambara headpieces used?
12. What mysterious being did the Bambara credit with having taught them about planting?
13. Why did rituals calling for shoulder masks require strong tribe members?

THINKING ABOUT ART

On a sheet of paper, answer each question in a sentence or two.

1. **Extend.** You read in this chapter that the antelope has a special meaning among the Bambara of Africa. In what other cultures that you read about were animals important?
2. **Analyze.** Which of the works in this chapter do you find the most stylized? The least stylized? Explain your answer.
3. **Compare and contrast.** Look back at the works in Figures 9–3 and 9–12. Both were created by artists of the Senufo tribe. Make a list of the similarities and differences between the two objects.
4. **Interpret.** Select three words that you think best describe African art. Write these on a sheet of paper. Compare your choices with those made by other members of the class. Which words were used most often?

MAKING ART CONNECTIONS

1. **Social Studies.** You read in this chapter that the different African tribes each have their own religion. Look up Africa in an encyclopedia in the school library. Learn what you can about African tribal religions and about the role of religion in art. Share your findings with the class in the form of a brief oral report.
2. **Science.** Artists all over Africa were able to choose from a large variety of wildlife for inspiration. List some animal forms unique to the continent of Africa. Choose an animal that interests you and research its habitat and lifestyle. Write a one-page report on your animal.

LOOKING AT THE DETAILS

The detail shown below is from the sculpture *Dance Headdress*. Study the detail and answer the following questions using complete sentences.

1. What is the visual texture of this work?
2. What mood is the artist communicating in this sculpture? What elements and principles of art help to create this mood?

3. Note the expression on the figure's face, and the title of the work. What does this sculpture tell you about how this culture feels about dance?
4. What elements of art are combined to create harmony?

Africa, Nigeria, Ibo Tribe. Dance Headdress. Wood, paint, metal, fiber. (Detail.) 47 x 32.7 x 27.7 cm (18½ x 12⅞ x 10⅞"). Dallas Museum of Art, Dallas, Texas. The Eugene & Margaret McDermott Fund.

▲ **Notice how the vertical lines of this church act as arrows pointing upward toward heaven.**

Cathedral of Leon. Leon, Spain.

Art of the Middle Ages

The period of history beginning about A.D. 500 is known by several names. One is the Middle Ages. Another is Medieval (mid-**ee**-vuhl) times. A third name sometimes given to these years is the Dark Ages. In the world of art, however, the times were anything but dark. Sculpture and painting were used to express ideas of the times. Architecture found expression in magnificent churches. Sculpture and stained glass were used to add splendor to these buildings. Do you know what structures like the one at the left are called?

OBJECTIVES

After completing this chapter, you will be able to:

- Tell how life in Romanesque times affected the art of the period.
- Identify the role of Romanesque sculpture and illuminations.
- Describe the contributions of Gothic artists to architecture and painting.
- Work with Romanesque and Gothic styles of architecture and sculpture.

WORDS YOU WILL LEARN

buttress	gargoyle
castles	illuminations
cathedral	pointed arch
fresco	stained glass

ARTIST YOU WILL MEET

Giotto di Bondone

Art of the Romanesque Period

History teaches many meaningful lessons. One is that even the most powerful empires, in time, weaken and crumble. Rome was no exception. The Roman Empire fell to invading armies around A.D. 400. Both the style of life as well as the art of this period were affected by these historical changes. Temples and palaces were torn down and the stone was used to build fortresses to keep out the invaders.

Shortly before Rome fell, the practice of Christianity became widely accepted. The Catholic Church stood as the single most important influence in western Europe. Its influence on people and events was widespread throughout the span of history now called the Middle Ages. The art and architecture at the end of the Middle Ages is divided into two periods: the Romanesque (roh-muh-**nesk**), from around 1050 to around 1150, and the Gothic from around 1150 to about 1500. In this lesson you will learn about the art of the Romanesque period.

LIFE IN ROMANESQUE TIMES

Warfare was common during the Romanesque period. Since land was the main source of power and wealth, kings and rich landowners were forever fighting among themselves to protect or add to their holdings.

Architecture

To protect themselves, the rich lived in **castles**, or *fortlike dwellings with high walls and towers*. These castles were often protected further by a moat and drawbridge. One of these structures is pictured in Figure 10–1. Notice how sturdy the castle looks even now, some 600 to 700 years after it was built. The structure has few windows. Why do you suppose this is so? Do you think the builder was more interested in constructing a structure that was comfortable or well fortified?

▶ Figure 10–1 Early castles like this were massive and strong. They were also dark and drafty. Instead of windows, narrow slits were cut into the walls. These helped those inside detect, and attack, intruders.

La Calahorra Castle. Andalucia, Spain. 16th Century.

▲ **Figure 10–2** High, thick walls and towers protected those living in this city. Only a few well-protected gates allowed people to enter or leave the city.

Walled City of Carcassone. c. 1100. Southern France.

The leaders and rulers lived in the castles during the Middle Ages. Communities of people living outside the castles were left open to attack. For this reason, whole towns and cities were surrounded by walls for protection. At first these walls were made of wood. In the 1100s and 1200s stone began to be used. One of the most impressive of these walled cities is shown in Figure 10–2. Today this city looks much as it did during the Middle Ages.

During this time the Catholic Church also had a great influence on the architecture. As early as A.D. 400 churches were springing up in towns and villages across Europe. All, like the one shown in Figures 10–3 and 10–4, were low and thick-walled. Windows, which might weaken the walls and bring the heavy stone roof crashing down, were avoided. As a result, these churches were dark and somber inside.

▲ **Figure 10–3 (Left) and Figure 10–4 (Right)** Thick walls and lack of windows made these churches look like forts, or fortresses. This may be the origin of the phrase "fortresses of God," used to describe these churches.

Anersall-Romanesque Church.

Sculpture

The Church was also responsible for the development of sculpture during this period. Since most people were unable to read, sculpture was used to teach religion. The exteriors of churches were covered with reliefs and statues like the ones in Figure 10–5. These sculptures portrayed the same Bible teachings that were taught verbally. Look closely at Figure 10–5. Notice the detailed figures shown in the half-round space above the doorway.

▶ **Figure 10–5   Sculptures on the outside of churches were meant to remind people to lead good lives.**

Santa Maria la Real Church. 13th Century. Sanguesa, near Pamplona, Spain.

Painting

In addition to being portrayed in sculpture, the teachings of the Church were spread through hand-lettered books, which contained illuminations. **Illuminations** are *hand-painted book illustrations*. For nearly a thousand years, these illustrations were the most important paintings created in Europe. Figure 10–6 shows an illumination from a prayer book. The work shows a scene from the life of Moses. In the illustration, Moses is looking up to receive the word of the Lord. His upturned face and outstretched arms suggest his willingness to accept the teachings for his people. Would you describe the work as realistic? What do you suppose was the artist's main goal in creating this illumination? Which aesthetic view would you use if someone asked you to judge this work?

▲ **Figure 10–6** The story in this work was told simply so it could be understood by anyone who knew the Bible. The picture does not look real because the story was more important to the artist than was a lifelike subject.

Illuminated Page of the Bible. *The Tablets of the Law.* 13th Century. Psalter of Ingeburg of Denmark. France.

STUDIO EXPERIENCE

The story illustrated in Figure 10–6 is from the Old Testament. Notice how the artist in portraying this story includes only those details needed in its telling.

Working in pencil, draw an illustration of a scene from a favorite story from literature or a movie. As in the illumination, leave out all unnecessary details. Keep your figures flat, and outline them with a variety of thick and thin black lines. Add bright colors to your picture with oil pastels. Share your finished work with classmates. See if anyone can identify the scene or story you have illustrated.

✔ CHECK YOUR UNDERSTANDING

1. In what century did Rome fall? What became the single most important influence in western Europe after its collapse?
2. When did the Romanesque period begin? When did it end?
3. What fact of life in the Middle Ages led to the building of castles?
4. Why were Romanesque churches thick-walled and without windows?
5. What was the purpose of sculpture during the Romanesque period? What other art form had the same purpose?

Romanesque Castle Relief

Castles, as you have read, were common in Europe during the Romanesque period. Two more of these structures are shown in Figures 10–7 and 10–8. The ridged geometric pattern along the top of each is called a battlement. Can you guess what battlements were used for? Can you identify any other features in these castles?

WHAT YOU WILL LEARN

You will design a castle of your own. You will create a relief of your castle using heavy cord and aluminum foil. Focus on the use of line to highlight the different features of your castle. Use the element of line to add harmony to your design. (See Figure 10–9.) Your castle should look strong and safe.

WHAT YOU WILL NEED

- Pencil and notepad
- Sheets of sketch paper
- Sheet of cardboard, 12 x 18 inches (30 x 45 cm)
- Scissors, tape, and heavy wrapping cord
- White glue
- Sheet of aluminum foil, 16 x 20 inches (41 x 50 cm)

WHAT YOU WILL DO

1. Begin by studying the castles in Figures 10–1 (on page **146**), 10–7, and 10–8. On your notepad, list the features common to these buildings. One common feature

▲ Figure 10–7   How many features can you find that helped make these castles safe?

Castle at Penafiel, Spain. c. 14th Century.

▲ Figure 10–8   See caption for Figure 10–7.

Gothic Castle on Rio Esla, south of Leon, Spain. 15th Century.

in the castles shown here, for example, is the battlement. On a sheet of sketch paper, make several drawings of an original castle. Show the building as it appears from the front. Draw all the features included on your list.

2. Choose your best design. Make a line drawing of this sketch on the sheet of cardboard. Fill the surface of the cardboard with your drawing.

3. Glue cord along the lines in your drawing. To do this, squeeze a thin band of glue along the line. Press the piece of cord into place. Repeat this process until all lines are covered.

4. Small pieces of cardboard can be glued to your castle design to give it more detail.

5. Cover your design with the sheet of aluminum foil. Wrap the foil around the ends and sides of the cardboard. Using tape, fasten the foil to the cardboard along the back.

6. Using the end of your pencil, carefully but firmly press down on the foil along the cord lines and around the cardboard shapes. Display your finished work to your class. Note ways in which your castle relief is similar to and different from those of other class artists.

- **Describe**   Point out the features of your castle listed on your notepad.
- **Analyze**   Tell whether the use of line adds harmony to your design.
- **Interpret**   State whether your castle communicates the ideas of strength and safety. Tell whether the castle shown would succeed in protecting those inside from attackers.
- **Judge**   Tell whether you feel your work succeeds. Explain your answer.

▲ **Figure 10–9   Student work in progress. Castle relief.**

OTHER STUDIO IDEAS

- Spray your castle with black paint. When the paint is dry, lightly rub the relief with steel wool. This will remove the paint from the raised surfaces, creating an interesting effect.

●● Create another castle relief, this time out of a continuous piece of 14-gauge steel wire. Show each feature in your castle by bending and twisting the wire until it has the right shape.

Art of the Gothic Period

Throughout history an important part of creating art has been solving problems. A key problem facing artists of the Romanesque period was mentioned in Lesson 1. This was figuring out how to build walls that could both contain windows and support a heavy roof.

Romanesque builders never solved this problem. Architects of the Gothic period did, however. In this lesson you will learn about this and other contributions of artists of the Gothic period.

▲ Figure 10–10   The hundreds of sculptures lining this huge cathedral were meant to be seen up close. To this day, visitors can climb up to the roof and walk among the many carvings.

Milan Cathedral. Begun 1386. Milan, Italy.

LIFE IN GOTHIC TIMES

Toward the end of the Romanesque period, Europe began to change. With the growth of trade, money replaced land as the measure of wealth. Castles became unpopular as cities grew and thrived. Many of these cities developed into large population centers by the year 1200.

The Church continued to have a great effect on the people as well as on the art of these new European cities.

Architecture

One structure that exists as a great contribution of Gothic artists is the cathedral. A **cathedral** is *a large, complex church created as a seat of office for a bishop*. The bishop would have several parishes, or congregations, under his leadership. An example of one of these huge structures opened this chapter (page **144**). Another is shown in Figure 10–10. Notice the openness of both these buildings. Notice how both seem to soar upward. Magnificent works of architecture like these were possible thanks to two improvements made by Gothic French architects. These were:

- **The pointed arch.** The **pointed arch** is *a curved arrangement of stones reaching up to a central point*. Gothic architects found that the vertical shape of this design feature allowed it to carry weight downward. Examine the inside view of a cathedral in Figure 10–11 and find the pointed arches.
- **The flying buttress.** A **buttress** (buh-truhs) is *a brace or support placed on the outside of a building*. Such supports are said to "fly" when they arch out over other parts of a building. In Gothic cathedrals, flying buttresses took on some of the load of the heavy roof. Which structures in Figure 10–12 are flying buttresses?

◄ Figure 10–11 The weight of the roof is carried by the pointed arches and transferred to columns inside the building. Can you find the pointed arches in this church?

Avila Cathedral. Avila, Spain.

► Figure 10–12 Flying buttresses like these helped make thick solid walls unnecessary in Gothic cathedrals. What replaced these walls?

Notre Dame Cathedral. Paris, France.

Crafts

The pointed arch and flying buttress did away with the need for solid walls. They also opened up the possibility of having many windows in churches and cathedrals. This created yet another outlet for expression by artists and craftspeople of the day. Brilliantly colored stained glass windows like those in Figure 10–13 began gracing the walls of cathedrals. **Stained glass** is made of *colored glass pieces held in place with lead strips*. These windows filled the cathedrals with softly tinted light. The pictures in these windows, focusing on religious figures and events, also helped teach the Bible. Do you recall which art forms of the Romanesque period showed Bible stories?

▲ Figure 10–13   The lead strips appear as dark lines in the finished design. Do you feel these lines add to or take away from the beauty of the work? Explain your answer.

Stained Glass from Cathedral of Leon — *Head of a Prophet*. Leon, Spain.

► Figure 10–14   What has the artist done to make the people in this work look lifelike? What has he done to emphasize the woman, child, and donkey?

Giotto. *The Flight Into Egypt*. c. 1305–06. Fresco. Arena Chapel, Padua, Italy.

Painting

The Gothic style of building cathedrals never fully caught on in Italy. There churches continued to be built in the Romanesque manner with large, unbroken walls. Instead of stained glass, religious decoration was added with a form of painting known as fresco. **Fresco** (fres-koh) is *a painting created when pigment is applied to a section of wall spread with fresh plaster. Fresco* is the Italian word for "fresh." This technique required the artist to work quickly before the plaster dried. The pigment was absorbed and the painting was permanently preserved.

The work in Figure 10–14 is a fresco. It is one of a series found on the walls of a chapel in Padua, Italy. All were done by a gifted artist named Giotto (**jah**-toh). Take a moment to study this work. In creating this and other frescoes, Giotto wished to do more than tell Bible stories. His goal was to make the people in his pictures come alive. His genius was such that a century would pass before an artist of equal skill would appear.

▲ Figure 10–15   Student work. Rose window design.

STUDIO EXPERIENCE

Make a pencil sketch based on a rose window design. Rose windows sometimes appear on the front of a church or cathedral. They are round, so your design should have either symmetrical or radial balance. Leave out all unnecessary details in your work. Transfer your sketch to a sheet of black construction paper. Go over all the lines with white chalk. Make some of the lines thicker than others.

Using scissors, cut out all the spaces between the chalk lines. Cut out patches of tissue paper in the shape of the spaces, only slightly larger. Pick different colors of paper for different spaces. Using white glue, attach these patches to the construction paper along their edges. *Optional:* You may want to use two thicknesses of black construction paper and sandwich pieces of tissue paper between the outlined areas. Turn your work over to reveal your own stained glass window. (See Figure 10–15.)

✔ CHECK YOUR UNDERSTANDING

1. What problem faced architects of the Romanesque period? What two improvements allowed Gothic architects to solve this problem?
2. What is a cathedral?
3. What is stained glass? For what purpose did Gothic artists use stained glass?
4. What is a fresco? How was it done?
5. Who was Giotto? What was his goal?

Making a Gothic Gargoyle

If you look up to the highest point of a Gothic cathedral, you will see creatures known as gargoyles. Look at Figure 10–16. A **gargoyle** is *a projecting ornament on a building carved in the shape of a fantastic animal or grotesque creature*. Gargoyles were made of carved stone and metal. They were meant to look like spirits fleeing, or being driven, from the holy building. However, these strange creations actually served a very practical purpose. They are really rain spouts that carried rainwater from the roof of the cathedral.

Creating these fascinating, sometimes frightening creatures required a great deal of imagination. In this lesson you will have an opportunity to design a gargoyle like the ones that appeared on Gothic cathedrals. (See Figure 10–17.)

WHAT YOU WILL LEARN

You will use clay to model and carve a gargoyle that will have imaginary rather than realistic proportions. Surface patterns will be created with a variety of textures to suggest fur, hair, scales, or feathers. Your model will be a freestanding sculpture.

WHAT YOU WILL NEED

- Pencil and sketchbook
- Slips of paper and small box
- Clay and clay modeling tools
- Burlap or cloth cut into sections, 14 x 14 inches, (36 x 36 cm)

▶ **Figure 10–16   How do you suppose someone of Gothic times would have felt to look up and find these odd-looking figures overhead?**

Gargoyles at Narbonne, France.

WHAT YOU WILL DO

1. Find examples of gargoyles in books from the library. Make a list of the animals or parts of animals used in these gargoyles.
2. On three separate slips of paper, write the name of a different animal. Place these slips of paper, along with those completed by other students, in a box.
3. Pass the box around the room. Without looking, pick out two slips.
4. Complete several pencil sketches in which you combine the animals named on your slips of paper to create a gargoyle design. Use your imagination to draw a creature unlike anything seen in real life. Add details such as hair, fur, scales, and feathers.
5. Complete a three-dimensional version of your gargoyle in clay. Begin by modeling the basic form of the gargoyle. Add details using both modeling and carving techniques.
6. Add interesting textures and surface patterns with modeling tools. These can be made to look like hair, fur, scales, feathers, or a combination of these.
7. Hollow out your model so it will dry more quickly and thoroughly. Work from the back to create a channel through the sculpture that exits through the open mouth. This channel can represent the passage through which rainwater would flow in a real gargoyle.
8. Fire your sculpture.
9. *Optional:* You may wish to add color by glazing in one or several colors. After glazing, fire the gargoyle again.

- **Describe**   Show how your gargoyle combines more than one animal. Does it have fantastic proportions?
- **Analyze**   Did you use a variety of actual textures to create an interesting surface pattern?
- **Interpret**   Does your gargoyle resemble any animal seen in real life? How does it make you feel?
- **Judge**   Does your sculpture look as though it belongs as a decoration of a Gothic cathedral?

▲ **Figure 10–17   Student work. Gargoyle.**

OTHER STUDIO IDEAS

- If you choose not to glaze your gargoyle, shoe polish may be applied to the fired piece and rubbed to a shine with a soft cloth.

- ●● Make another gargoyle, this time as a relief sculpture. Use the slab method. Trace your design onto the soft clay with a pencil. Use modeling tools to carve your picture out of the clay. Add textures to the surface of your relief.

CHAPTER 10 REVIEW

BUILDING VOCABULARY

Number a sheet of paper from 1 to 8. After each number, write the term from the box that best matches each description below.

buttress	gargoyle
castles	illuminations
cathedral	pointed arch
fresco	stained glass

1. Fortlike dwellings with high walls and towers.
2. Hand-painted book illustrations.
3. A large, complex church created as a seat of office for a bishop.
4. A curved arrangement of stones reaching up to a central point.
5. A brace or support placed on the outside of a building.
6. Colored glass pieces held in place with lead strips.
7. A painting created when pigment is applied to a section of wall spread with fresh plaster.
8. A projecting ornament on a building carved in the shape of a fantastic animal or grotesque creature.

REVIEWING ART FACTS

Number a sheet of paper from 9 to 13. Answer each question in a complete sentence.

9. Name three common features of a Romanesque castle.
10. What was the purpose of the sculptures found on the outside of Romanesque churches?
11. Where were illuminations found? What were they used for?
12. Under what circumstances can a buttress be said to "fly"?
13. What subjects appeared in the stained glass windows of Gothic cathedrals?

THINKING ABOUT ART

On a sheet of paper, answer each question in a sentence or two.

1. **Analyze.** Look back at the picture of a castle in Figure 10–1. What changes in society would have had to take place in order for this building's architects to add more windows?
2. **Compare and contrast.** What are the most important differences between Romanesque churches and Gothic cathedrals?
3. **Extend.** Imagine yourself walking through one of the Gothic cathedrals pictured in this chapter. What feature do you think would impress you most?

MAKING ART CONNECTIONS

1. **Language Arts.** Acting as an art critic, describe, analyze, interpret, and judge the illumination in Figure 10–6 on page **149**. Use these questions to guide you: Do the people in the picture look lifelike? Why, or why not? Which elements of art are important in this picture? What clues tell you this is a religious work? In judging the work, tell whether your reaction is based on subject, composition, or content.
2. **History.** Find the term *fresco* in an encyclopedia or art history book in your library. Learn as much as you can about how frescoes are made and what difficulties fresco painters experienced. If you can, make photocopies of several different frescoes showing the range of possibilities within the medium. Share your findings with your class in an audiovisual presentation.

LOOKING AT THE DETAILS

The detail shown below is from the Cathedral of Leon, Spain. Study the detail and answer the following questions using complete sentences.

1. What direction do the lines of the cathedral take the viewer's eye? Do you think this is effective for a cathedral? Explain your answer.
2. Compare the visual texture of this structure with the one in Figure 10–1 on page **146**. How do they differ?

3. Is there another art form besides architecture used in this structure?
4. If you were not aware of the period in which this cathedral was built, what clues would you use to estimate when it was built?

Cathedral of Leon. (Detail.) Leon, Spain.

▲ Notice how the change little by little from light to dark values makes this face seem three-dimensional. By using a three-quarter view the artist makes the face seem to project out toward the viewer.

Andrea del Castagno. *Portrait of a Man.* c. 1450. Oil on wood. 54 x 40.5 cm (21¼ x 15⅞").
National Gallery of Art, Washington, D.C. Andrew W. Mellon Collection.

CHAPTER 11

Art of the Renaissance

The years following the Middle Ages in Europe were a time of great growth and discovery. Trade spread, and so did knowledge. New discoveries were made in every field, including science and geography. One of the most startling was the discovery of the New World by Christopher Columbus.

The period also saw great discoveries in art. Among the most important were exciting new ways of adding realism to works. The painting at the left makes use of one of these techniques. In the pages to come, you will learn about others.

OBJECTIVES

After completing this chapter, you will be able to:

- Identify artists of the Italian Renaissance and describe their contributions.
- Identify the contributions of artists working in northern Europe during the Renaissance.
- Use details and symbolism in studio experiences.

WORDS YOU WILL LEARN

linear perspective
Madonna
oil paint
Pietà
Renaissance
symbolism

ARTISTS YOU WILL MEET

Andrea del Castagno
Jan van Eyck
Masaccio
Michelangelo
    Buonarroti
Raphael
Leonardo da Vinci
Rogier van der
    Weyden

Art of the Italian Renaissance

During the Middle Ages the teachings of the Catholic Church were the focus of much of the art work. By the beginning of the 1400s, however, artists gradually began to change their style. After centuries of creating religious works, artists began to paint pictures to look as realistic as possible. The emphasis was not always on religious subjects. This time is known as the **Renaissance** (ren-uh-sahns), *a period of great awakening*. The word renaissance means "rebirth."

THE RENAISSANCE IN ITALY

The shift in interests that took place during the Renaissance was especially noticeable in Italy. There, a number of cities grew into trading and business centers. One of these, Florence, became the capital of Europe's cloth trade and home to its richest bank. Find Florence on the map in Figure 11–1.

Florence also became a center for art during the Renaissance. In this lesson you will read about the contributions of its artists.

Painting

Among the people living in Florence during the early 1400s was a young artist named Masaccio (muh-**zahch**-ee-oh). Masaccio continued where Giotto had left off a century earlier. He made the figures in his works seem solid and real. (See Figure 11–2.)

Masaccio also sought to add a true-to-life, three-dimensional quality using a technique called linear perspective (puhr-**spek**-tiv). **Linear perspective** is *the use of slanted lines to make objects appear to extend back into space.* (See Figure 11–3.) The technique was discovered by an architect and friend of Masaccio named Filippo Brunelleschi (fi-**leep**-oh broon-uhl-**ess**-kee).

The artist adds to this realistic appearance by giving the subject an expression of genuine grief. This combination of three-dimensional form and emotion became a trademark of Renaissance art.

Masaccio died suddenly at the age of 27. Some believe he may have been poisoned by a jealous rival. Luckily, there were other artists with the talent to build upon Masaccio's discoveries. One of these was a man whose talents were not limited to art. He was also skilled in science, literature, and music. The name of this gifted man was Leonardo da Vinci (lee-uh-**nard**-oh duh **vin**-chee).

◀ Figure 11–1 Renaissance Italy.

162   Lesson 1   *Art of the Italian Renaissance*

◄ **Figure 11–2** Look at this painting and identify where Masaccio has used slanted lines to produce a three-dimensional quality.

Masaccio. *The Holy Trinity.* c. 1428. Fresco. Church of Santa Maria Novella, Florence, Italy.

▼ **Figure 11–3** Diagram showing linear perspective. Linear perspective is based on a trick the eyes play on us. This trick causes the sides of a highway, for example, to seem to come together in the distance. The point at which such lines appear to meet at the horizon is called the vanishing point.

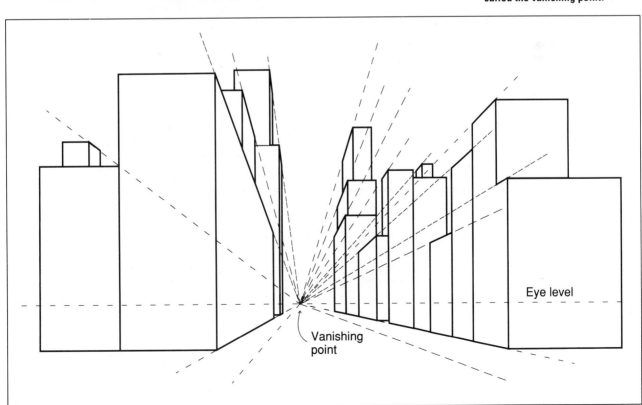

Eye level

Vanishing point

Leonardo's most famous work is a portrait, the *Mona Lisa*. Figure 11–4 shows another of his haunting portraits. In this painting Leonardo uses light and dark values in the manner developed by Giotto and Masaccio. The blending is so precise, however, that it is impossible to tell where one value ends and the next begins. Notice how these gently changing values help make the sad face seem three-dimensional. Notice how the figure of the woman stands out dramatically against the dark background.

Leonardo was recognized as a great artist even in his own day. Artists from all over flocked to Florence in the hopes of learning from him. One of these was a young painter named Raphael (**raf**-ee-el). Figure 11–5 is one of over 300 Madonnas that Raphael painted. A **Madonna** is *a work showing the Virgin Mary with the Christ Child*. In this one, Leonardo's influence can be seen in the soft change from light to dark values. Notice the expressions of the faces of the different people. How would you describe each one?

Sculpture

Like Leonardo, Michelangelo Buonarroti (my-kuh-**lan**-juh-loh bwon-nar-**roe**-tee) excelled in many fields, including poetry, painting, and architecture. As an artist, however, he thought of himself as a sculptor first. One of Michelangelo's greatest and best-known works is his *Pietà* (pee-ay-**tah**), pictured in Figure 11–6. A **Pietà** is *a work showing Mary mourning over the body of Christ*. Michelangelo carved his *Pietà* when he was 24 years old.

Study this work. Can you find anything unusual about the proportion of the two figures? Did you notice that Mary is much larger than her son, a full-grown man? In fact, if the figure were to stand, she would be nearly 9 feet (3 m) tall! Michelangelo purposely planned the sculpture this way. He wanted the viewer to focus on the work's mood—not on Mary's struggle to support the weight of Jesus' body. How would you describe the mood of Michelangelo's *Pietà*?

▲ **Figure 11–4** Who is this woman, and why is she so sad? Some historians claim she was the daughter of a rich banker abandoned by the man she loved.

Leonardo da Vinci. *Ginevra de 'Benci.* c. 1474. Wood. 38.8 x 36.7 cm (15¼ x 14½"). National Gallery of Art, Washington, D.C. Ailsa Mellon Bruce Fund.

▲ **Figure 11–5** Where has the artist used linear perspective? How has the use of linear perspective added to this painting?

Raphael. *Madonna and Child Enthroned with Saints.* Tempera on wood. 169.2 x 169.5 cm (66⅝ x 66¾"). The Metropolitan Museum of Art, New York, New York. Gift of J. Pierpont Morgan.

▲ **Figure 11–6** Notice that the two figures — one horizontal, the other vertical — seem almost to form a pyramid. Can you trace the lines of that pyramid with your finger?

Michelangelo. *Pietà*. c. 1501. Marble. St. Peter's Basilica, Rome, Italy.

▲ **Figure 11–7** Triangles and pyramids used for balance.

STUDIO EXPERIENCE

Many Renaissance artists followed a triangular or pyramid plan to balance their work. This was used to organize the main figures in their works. This triangle plan can be found in the *Pietà*. (See Figure 11–7.) Can you find a similar plan in any other works seen in this lesson?

Using pencil and ruler, draw a large triangle on a sheet of white paper. Within this shape, fit one or more of the letters that make up your initials. Fill as much of the space inside the triangle as you can. Use only straight, ruled lines for your letters.

Now continue some of the lines beyond the triangle to the edge of the paper. This will divide the rest of your composition into various shapes. Paint the shapes within the triangle with different values of a single hue. Paint the outside shapes with different values of the complementary hue.

✔CHECK YOUR UNDERSTANDING

1. How did the art in Europe at the beginning of the 1400s differ from that of the Middle Ages?
2. What was the Renaissance? What city was its center in Italy?
3. What is linear perspective? Who discovered it? Who was one of the first artists to use it in a painting?
4. What is remarkable about the portraits painted by Leonardo da Vinci?
5. What is a Madonna? What Renaissance artist was influenced by Leonardo in his painting of Madonnas?
6. What is a Pietà? What is unusual about the use of proportion in Michelangelo's *Pietà*?

Drawing a Still Life

Many artists use sketch pads to record sights and ideas that interest them. In his lifetime Leonardo da Vinci filled some 100 sketchbooks with drawings on many subjects. Some of these were of storm clouds. Some were of rock formations and the action of waves. Some — like the one in Figure 11–8 — were of the human body. What sets Leonardo's drawings apart was how precisely he captured every detail of an object. Clearly, this Renaissance master had remarkable powers of concentration.

WHAT YOU WILL LEARN

You will make a pencil drawing of a still life, using your powers of concentration to make the drawing as accurate as possible. Gradual and sudden changes of value will be used to suggest rounded and angular forms. Space will be shown by overlapping these forms. Differences in texture will be emphasized. (See Figure 11–9.)

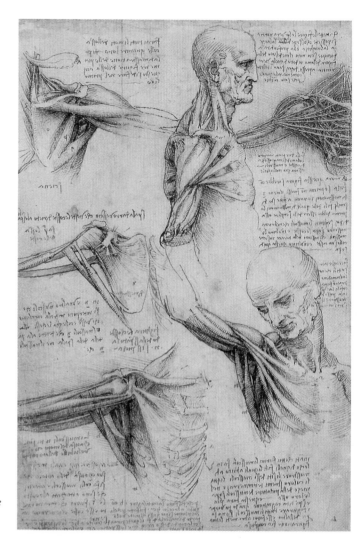

▶ **Figure 11–8** **Leonardo was left handed. He wrote the notes you see backward to keep his ideas private. A mirror was needed to read them.**

Leonardo da Vinci. *Studies of Male Shoulder.* Royal Library, Windsor Castle, England.

WHAT YOU WILL NEED

- Pencil and sheets of sketch paper
- Sheet of white drawing paper, 12 x 18 inches (30 x 46 cm)

WHAT YOU WILL DO

1. Bring an unusual found object to class, something that is broken or in some other way altered. Possibilities are a crushed can, a broken toy, or an old hand tool.
2. Set your object on a table in front of you. Place the point of your pencil on a sheet of sketch paper. Without taking your eyes off the object, begin to draw it. Attempt to feel the lines of the object with your pencil as you draw. Concentrate on and draw each object in accurate detail. Make several more drawings on the same sheet until your work looks like your object.
3. Working with four other students, arrange your five objects in an interesting way. Some of the objects should overlap others. Make a drawing of the arrangement. Concentrate on overlapping objects to create an illusion of space. (See Technique Tip 2, *Handbook* page **277**.)
4. Carefully draw the key lines of your sketch onto the large sheet of drawing paper. Include in this finished version as many details as you can, including differences in texture. Use your pencil to add gradual and sudden changes of value to show rounded and angular forms.
5. Display your work along with those of your classmates. Discuss how this drawing has helped you to better see details.

EXAMINING YOUR WORK

- **Describe** Tell what objects you sketched. Point to the features of your drawing that would help others identify the objects.
- **Analyze** Point to the objects in your still life that overlap others. Explain whether this overlapping adds a feeling of space to the work. Tell how gradual and sudden changes of value suggest rounded and angular forms. Show the different textures you have emphasized.
- **Interpret** Give a name to your work that reflects the feelings you experienced while doing it.
- **Judge** Tell whether you feel your work as a whole succeeds as an accurate still life. Point to the most successful parts of your drawing. Explain why you think these parts are successful.

▲ **Figure 11–9** **Student work. Still life.**

OTHER STUDIO IDEAS

- Do a still life drawing of a familiar object, such as your shoe, to fill an entire sheet of paper. Select a single color of tempera and add white and black to create gradual changes of value to show rounded forms. Use abrupt changes of value to show angular forms.

- ●● Color in another still life with pastels. Vary the pressure with which you apply the pastel to your paper. This will create differences in value and add to the three-dimensional look of the forms. Use color also to further emphasize the textures of forms.

Art of the Northern Renaissance

The shift from a Gothic to a Renaissance art style happened in northern Europe later than in Italy. The changes were also slower to develop and found different forms of expression.

In this lesson you will read about the contributions of Renaissance artists of northern Europe.

THE RENAISSANCE IN THE NORTH

The Northern Renaissance was concentrated in the area of Europe known as Flanders. It had as its center the modern Belgian capital of Brussels. Find Flanders and the city of Brussels on the map in Figure 11–10.

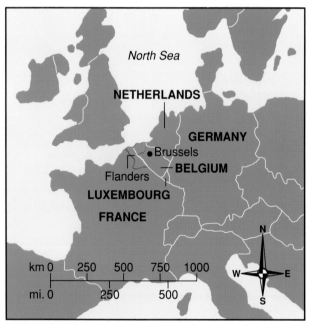

▲ Figure 11–10   Renaissance Europe.

The art of the Northern Renaissance continued to make use of several Gothic techniques and features. One of these was symbolism. **Symbolism** is *the use of an image to stand for a quality or an idea*. A dog, for example, was a symbol of loyalty; a lily could mean purity.

In other ways Northern Renaissance artists experimented with new ideas. This was especially true in the area of painting.

Painting

The most important contribution of the Northern Renaissance was a new painting technique. Artists discovered that **oil paint**, *a mixture of pigment, linseed oil, and turpentine*, gave them a slow-drying paint. This oil-based paint was far easier to use than tempera. It allowed the artist to work more slowly and add more details. Colors, moreover, could be mixed right on the canvas.

Jan van Eyck

The person often credited with discovering the oil painting technique was a Flemish artist named Jan van Eyck (**yahn** van **ike**). Like painters working in Italy, those in the North were fascinated with precision. Van Eyck was no exception. He would spend hours using the smallest brushes he could find to paint patterns of bark on a tree or the blades of grass in a meadow. Notice the attention to detail in the brilliantly colored work in Figure 11–11. Look especially at the textures of the robe and jeweled crown on the figure at the left. The paint is applied so skillfully that not a single brush stroke can be seen. Do you know what Bible story this work illustrates? Do you recall where you saw this event before?

◀ **Figure 11–11** **The work is rich with symbolism. The tiles on the floor show scenes from the Old Testament telling of the coming of the Messiah. A dove, symbol of the Holy Spirit, follows a path of light streaming through an open window. The light stands for Christ.**

Jan van Eyck. *The Annunciation.* 1434–1436. Oil on wood transferred to canvas. 90.2 x 34.1 cm (35⅜ x 13⅞"). National Gallery of Art, Washington, D.C. Andrew W. Mellon Collection.

▲ Figure 11–12 How is the artist's treatment of the Crucifixion different from how an artist of the Romanesque period would have treated it?

Rogier van der Weyden. *Descent from the Cross.* c. 1435. Museo del Prado, Madrid, Spain.

Rogier van der Weyden

Another important Northern Renaissance painter is Rogier van der Weyden (roh-**jehr** van duhr **vyd**-uhn). Van der Weyden was greatly influenced by van Eyck. Like van Eyck, he was able to reproduce each hair, each stitch in his paintings. Unlike van Eyck, whose pictures are calm and quiet, van der Weyden painted powerful, emotional scenes.

One of these is shown in Figure 11–12. In this picture, 10 life-size figures are placed in a shallow nook. The nook is just wide enough to hold them. The wall behind pushes the figures forward, bringing them closer to the viewer. In this way the artist forces the viewer to look at and experience this emotional scene from the Bible. Notice how the different people are reacting to the death of Christ. What has just happened to the woman in the blue dress in the foreground?

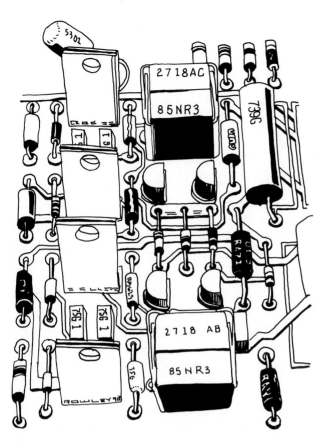

▲ Figure 11–13   Student work. Detail drawing.

STUDIO EXPERIENCE

Look again at the paintings by van Eyck and van der Weyden in Figures 11–11 and 11–12. Notice how every last detail is captured in sharp focus.

Using your imagination, do a detailed drawing of a new, complicated electronic gadget. The item might be a new type of hand-held computer, a compact disc player, or other device. In your drawing include all the features and parts, such as dials and speakers. These should be drawn in sharp focus. Fill a whole sheet of paper with your drawing. (See Figure 11–13.)

✔CHECK YOUR UNDERSTANDING

1. What area became the center of the Northern Renaissance?
2. What Gothic feature continued to be used by Northern Renaissance artists?
3. What was a major contribution of artists of the Northern Renaissance? Who is credited with having discovered it?
4. In what ways were the religious paintings of Jan van Eyck and Rogier van der Weyden similar? In what ways were they different?

Designing a Visual Symbol

Symbolism, as you have read, was an important feature of Northern Renaissance art. Its importance can be seen in the picture by Jan van Eyck in Figure 11–14. The painting, which shows a wedding ceremony, is heavy with symbols. The dog stands for the loyalty the marriage partners have promised each other. The single burning candle in the chandelier symbolizes the presence of God at the event. Even the shoes on the floor have meaning. They have been removed to show that the couple is standing on ground made holy by the exchange of vows.

Symbolism is as popular today as it was over 500 years ago. Think of all the symbols you see every day for cars, fast-food chains, and brands of clothing. Can you think of other products in our culture that use symbols? What symbols do these products use?

Imagine you have been asked to design a symbol for a shoe company. The design is to be colorful, detailed, and easy to recognize. It is also to be strictly visual—without any lettering.

WHAT YOU WILL LEARN

You will create a visual symbol for a shoe company. You will use repeated flat shapes to give harmony to your design. Variety will be obtained by making the shapes in different sizes. Use color to emphasize the most important shoe in your design. (See Figure 11–15.)

WHAT YOU WILL NEED

- Pencil and sheets of sketch paper
- Ruler and scissors
- Shoe box lid
- Sheet of white paper, 12 x 18 inches (30 x 46 cm)
- Tempera paint and several brushes
- White glue

WHAT YOU WILL DO

1. Look at the table of shoes that your teacher has arranged.
2. Make several pencil sketches of the shoe pile. Use only lines in your sketches. Do not fill in any of the shapes with shading.

▲ **Figure 11–14** The translation of the words above the mirror is: "Jan van Eyck was here." Experts have put forth the idea that this painting might have been an official wedding document. If it was, what importance would these words have?

Jan van Eyck. *Giovanni Arnolfini and His Bride.* 1434. National Gallery, London, England.

3. Choose the best of your sketches and study it. Using the ruler, draw a rectangle around the part of your sketch that seems most interesting. This is to be your design.
4. Using the ruler, measure the length and width of the shoe box lid. Rule off a rectangle with the same measurements on the sheet of white paper. With scissors, cut out the rectangle.
5. Draw your design sketch on the rectangle, filling the space. Keep the shapes flat to give your design harmony. Make some of the shapes larger than others to add variety. Pick out one shoe that you would like to emphasize. Add details to this shoe.
6. Paint your design using tempera. Paint the different shoes so they look flat. Use a contrasting hue for the shoe you want to emphasize.
7. When the paint is dry, glue your painting to the shoe box lid. Display your finished work along with those of your classmates. Include some professionally designed shoe box lids in the display. Discuss which of the designs works best as a symbol for a shoe company. Try to identify the reasons for your opinions.

▲ **Figure 11–15**   Student work. Design of a visual symbol.

OTHER STUDIO IDEAS

- Think of a brand name for the shoes your design symbolizes. From a contrasting color of construction paper, cut letters that spell out this name. Glue the letters to the shoe box lid so that they fit the overall design.

- ● With pencil, transfer your shoe design to a sheet of white paper. Go over all the pencil lines with India ink. Fill in the shapes of your design with as many textures as possible using only closely spaced ink lines.

BUILDING VOCABULARY

Number a sheet of paper from 1 to 6. After each number, write the term from the box that best matches each description below.

linear perspective	Pietà
Madonna	Renaissance
oil paint	symbolism

1. A period of great awakening.
2. The use of slanted lines to make objects appear to extend back into space.
3. A work showing the Virgin Mary with the Christ Child.
4. A work showing Mary mourning over the body of Christ.
5. The use of an image to stand for a quality or an idea.
6. A mixture of pigment, linseed oil, and turpentine.

REVIEWING ART FACTS

Number a sheet of paper from 7 to 14. Answer each question in a complete sentence.

7. Name three things the city of Florence was noted for in the 1400s.
8. Who was Masaccio? What is he remembered for?
9. Name two areas besides art in which Leonardo da Vinci was skilled.
10. In what way can Leonardo's influence be seen in the works of Raphael?
11. What is unusual about the proportions of the two figures in Michelangelo's *Pietà*?
12. What geometric shape did Renaissance artists use as a way of planning their works?
13. What feature of Gothic art did Northern Renaissance artists continue to use in their works?
14. What Northern Renaissance painter is credited for discovering oil paint?

THINKING ABOUT ART

On a sheet of paper, answer each question in a sentence or two.

1. **Interpret.** Read the following statement: "Art of the present would not be possible without art of the past." Describe three facts about artists or events of the Renaissance that you would use to support this statement.
2. **Analyze.** Look once again at the two paintings by Jan van Eyck (Figures 11–11 and 11–14). Which has the most lifelike details? Which particular details struck you as looking most like a photograph?
3. **Compare and contrast.** In what ways were the art styles of the Renaissance in Italy and in the North similar? In what ways were they different?

MAKING ART CONNECTIONS

1. **Language Arts.** Artists of the Renaissance were greatly influenced by the art of ancient Greece and Rome. Pick a painting or sculpture that you studied in Chapter 7. Choose another from the present chapter. Write a short report noting where Greek or Roman influences were strongest in Renaissance art. Discuss how breakthroughs during the Renaissance allowed artists to expand their horizons still further.
2. **Social Studies.** Michelangelo, as you read in this chapter, was gifted in many fields. Two of these were painting and architecture. In an art history book or encyclopedia, read about his contributions in these two areas. Note names of specific projects and, if possible, make photocopies of pictures of the works. In addition, gather details of Michelangelo's life. Combine your findings with information on his sculpture into a book.

LOOKING AT THE DETAILS

The detail shown below is from Andrea del Castagno's *Portrait of a Man.* Study the detail and answering the following questions using complete sentences.

1. How does color affect the mood in this painting?
2. What details has the artist used to contribute to a mood of wealth and authority?
3. How do you, as a viewer, feel in the presence of this work?
4. Do you think Castagno involves the viewer in this work of art? Explain your answer.

Andrea del Castagno. *Portrait of a Man.* c. 1450. Oil on wood. (Detail.) 54 x 40.5 cm (21¼ x 15⅞"). National Gallery of Art, Washington, D.C. Andrew W. Mellon Collection.

▲ Notice the striking use of light in this work. Notice also the work's size: it is over 6 feet (2 m) high. That the figures are larger than life adds to the impression the painting makes on its viewer.

Artemisia Gentileschi. *Judith and Maidservant with the Head of Holofernes*. c. 1625. Oil on canvas. Detroit Institute of Art, Detroit, Michigan.

CHAPTER 12

European Art of the 1600s and 1700s

"What goes around comes around." Have you ever heard this saying? The truth behind it is clear from events in Europe following the Renaissance. There, in the 1500s, a religious revolution took place — only to be followed a century later by another.

This second revolution resulted in a new peaceful atmosphere. It also resulted in a new wave of artists and new ways of making art. The picture at the left was done in a style of the age. Can you identify any of its features? You will soon be able to recognize them.

OBJECTIVES

After completing this chapter, you will be able to:

- Explain what new ways of creating art were brought about by the Counter-Reformation.
- Identify features of the Baroque style and name important artists who practiced it.
- Describe features of the Rococo style and identify important artists of the period.
- Create art works in the expressive style of Rembrandt.
- Experiment with art in the Rococo style.

WORDS YOU WILL LEARN

Baroque	portrait
etching	Rococo
facade	

ARTISTS YOU WILL MEET

Francesco Borromini	Rembrandt van Rijn
Michelangelo Merisi	Peter Paul Rubens
da Caravaggio	Louis Le Vau and Jules
Jean-Baptiste Siméon	Hardouin-Mansart
Chardin	Diego Velázquez
Artemisia Gentileschi	Élisabeth Vigée-
Francisco Goya	Lebrun
Judith Leyster	Antoine Watteau

Art of the 1600s

When Rome collapsed, you will recall, the Catholic Church became more influential. It remained this way until the early 1500s, when the Church's power began to slip. A group of Christians led by a man named Martin Luther splintered off from the Church in revolt to form their own religion.

▲ **Figure 12–1** Study the changing light and dark values on the surface of this church. What principles are used to organize these different values?

Francesco Borromini. San Carlo alle Quattro Fontane. c. 1665–1676. Rome, Italy.

The Protestant Reformation, as this movement was called, drew many people away from the Catholic Church. In an effort to win them back, the Church started its own reform movement in the 1600s. This movement, which began in Italy, is known as the Counter-Reformation.

Art was an important part of the Counter-Reformation. Artists were called upon to create works that would renew religious spirit. A sense of flowing movement is one feature of a new art style of the day, **Baroque** (buh-**rohk**), or *an art style emphasizing movement, contrast, and variety.*

ARCHITECTURE AND PAINTING

In architecture the call to renew religious spirit was answered by, among others, an artist named Francesco Borromini (fran-**ches**-koh bor-uh-**meen**-ee). The church pictured in Figure 12–1 won Borromini great fame. He created the **facade** (fuh-**sahd**), *the outside front of a building*, to express his art. Do you notice how the surface seems to flow — first in, then out, then in again? Notice how the structure looks almost as though it were modeled from soft clay. This helps create a pattern of light and dark values across the whole facade. The Baroque emphasis on movement is also seen in painting of the period. Although the style originated in Italy, it spread to Spain and northern Europe.

Italy

The leader of the Baroque style in Italy was a young painter named Michelangelo Merisi da Caravaggio (kar-uh-**vahj**-yo). One of his key contributions was the use of light in a daring new way. This ability is combined with the artist's skill as a storyteller in the picture in Figure 12–2. Take a moment to study the work, which pictures the burial of

Christ. It is as if a spotlight has been shone on real actors on a stage. Find the man holding Christ's legs. This man, whose eyes meet yours, draws you into the painting. Notice the puzzled expression on his face. He seems about to ask you to identify yourself. Perhaps he will also ask if you intend to merely watch or to help in laying Christ in his tomb. In this way, Caravaggio makes you feel that you are a part of the drama.

Caravaggio's style influenced the work of many other Italian painters of the day. Among them was a woman named Artemisia Gentileschi (ahr-tuh-**meez**-ee-uh jent-uhl-**ess**-kee). Like Caravaggio, Gentileschi used light and shadow to add excitement to her paintings. One of these opens this chapter (page **176**). The work shows the Bible hero Judith in the tension-filled moments after she has slain an enemy of her people. A servant is seen placing the victim's severed head in a sack. Suddenly Judith, still clutching her sword, raises a hand in warning. Have the two been discovered? They wait silently, afraid to move. The light from a single flickering candle creates the only movement in the hushed tent. It reveals the anxious faces of the two women staring into the darkness.

Spain

Not all Baroque paintings showed such tense, dramatic movement. Movement of another sort is found in the works of Spanish painter Diego Velázquez (dee-**ay**-goh vuh-**las**-kuhs). One of these, a simple painting of a woman sewing, is pictured in Figure 12–3. Examine this painting. Note how the fingers of both hands are blurred. This helps show that her fingers are moving rapidly as she sews.

▲ **Figure 12–2** Light is used to emphasize the most important details of this picture. These details are shown in shocking realism. Notice that even the soles of Christ's feet are painted to look dirty.

Caravaggio. *The Deposition*. 1604. Vatican Museum, Pinacoteca, Rome, Italy.

▲ **Figure 12–3** The young woman in this picture may be the artist's daughter. She is known to have married one of his pupils.

Diego Velázquez. *The Needlewoman*. c. 1640–1650. Oil on canvas. 74 x 60 cm (29⅛ x 23⅝"). National Gallery of Art, Washington, D.C. Andrew W. Mellon Collection.

▲ Figure 12–4   Nothing seems to stand still in this painting. You are made to feel as though you are witnessing a moment in time.

Sir Peter Paul Rubens. *The Assumption of the Virgin*. c. 1626. Wood. 125.4 x 94.2 cm (49⅜ x 37⅛"). National Gallery of Art, Washington, D.C. Samuel H. Kress Collection.

Northern Europe

The major talents in Northern Europe, you will remember, developed during the Renaissance. This trend continued into the 1600s, led by a Flemish painter named Peter Paul Rubens. No other Baroque artist came close to Rubens in capturing the action and feeling of the new style. Notice his use of line in the work in Figure 12–4. The picture shows the Virgin Mary rising toward heaven. Can you find the line—partly real, partly imaginary—beginning in the raised arm of the figure at the left? Where does this line lead? What kind of line is it? Notice how the line pulls the viewer into the work, making him or her feel present.

In neighboring Holland, which remained a Protestant stronghold, a new subject matter for paintings was busily being explored. Genre pictures showing simple scenes from daily life were preferred over religious paintings. Another type of painting being introduced was the **portrait**, *a painting of a person*. A gifted young painter named Judith Leyster (**lye**-stuhr) specialized in portraits, using quick, dazzling brush strokes. This allowed her to catch the fleeting expressions on the faces of her subjects. Figure 12–5 shows a portrait she did of herself. Note how she seems to smile out of the picture at the viewer. Could she be eager for the viewer's reaction to the painting she is working on?

▲ **Figure 12–5   By the time she was 17, the artist was already gaining fame as a painter. Later in life, as a married woman with three children, she painted less. She died when she was only 50.**

Judith Leyster. *Self Portrait.* c. 1635. Canvas. 72.3 x 65.3 cm (29⅜ x 25⅝"). National Gallery of Art, Washington, D.C. Gift of Mr. & Mrs. Robert Woods Bliss.

✔CHECK YOUR UNDERSTANDING

1. What was the Protestant Reformation? Who was its leader?
2. What was the Counter-Reformation?
3. What new art style arose during the period of the Counter-Reformation? What are the main features of this style?
4. What was a main contribution of Caravaggio?
5. Name a major Baroque painter of northern Europe.
6. What is a portrait? What artist that you read about specialized in painting portraits?

Drawing Expressive Hands

The leading Dutch painter of the 1600s is a man named Rembrandt van Rijn (**ryn**). Figure 12–6 shows a portrait by this master. The artist uses a soft light to highlight the main parts of the picture. The subject, you will notice, is not beautiful. She seems, however, not to care about this. She is not bothered by the fact that others may be more attractive. If anything, she appears to be at peace with the world and her place in it. Notice how even her hands mirror this gentle calm. The artist has managed to make them look totally relaxed and at rest.

WHAT YOU WILL LEARN

You will make a drawing of your hand on black construction paper. Draw the hand to express a particular feeling. White crayon will be used to emphasize the three-dimensional form of the hand. (See Figure 12–7.)

WHAT YOU WILL NEED

- Pencil and sheets of sketch paper
- Sheet of black construction paper, 9 x 12 inches (23 x 30 cm)
- White crayon

▶ **Figure 12–6** The artist uses a straight horizontal line in the center of this picture. He separates the linen scarf from the lady's clothing. Do you remember what kind of mood a straight line like this calls to mind?

Rembrandt van Rijn. *Portrait of a Lady with an Ostrich-Feather Fan.* c. 1660. Canvas. 99.5 x 83 cm (39¼ x 32⅝"). National Gallery of Art, Washington, D.C. Widener Collection.

WHAT YOU WILL DO

1. Brainstorm with your classmates on ways hands can show different moods and feelings. Some possibilities for discussion are surprise, anger, sadness, joy, and nervousness. Choose one of these moods or feelings. Do not tell anyone in your class which one you have picked.
2. Pose the hand you do not use to draw with in a way that shows the mood you have selected. It might be relaxed, clenched, or distorted in some way. With your drawing hand, make pencil sketches of the posed hand. Make your drawings as accurate as you can.
3. Still using pencil, draw the best of your sketches on the sheet of black paper. Make the drawing large enough to fill the sheet.
4. Switching to white crayon, add highlights to your drawing. Begin by coloring lightly. Gently blend the crayon around the fingers and other hand parts to make them look three-dimensional and lifelike. (For information on shading techniques, see Technique Tip **6**, *Handbook* page **278**.) Press lightly when coloring shadowed areas. Press harder on the crayon when coloring the most highly lighted areas.
5. Place your finished drawing on display with those of other students. Decide which of the drawings are most lifelike. Are your classmates able to guess the feeling or mood your hand drawing expresses?

EXAMINING YOUR WORK

- **Describe**   Tell whether your drawing looks like your hand. Identify its most realistic features.
- **Analyze**   Show where you used white crayon to highlight your drawing. State whether the light and dark values emphasize the three-dimensional form of the hand.
- **Interpret**   Tell whether your drawing expresses a particular mood or feeling. Tell whether viewers were able to identify this feeling.
- **Judge**   Identify the best feature of your drawing. Tell whether it is the realistic appearance of your work, the use of light and dark to give a sense of roundness, or the expressive content of your drawing.

▲ **Figure 12–7   Student work. Expressive hands.**

OTHER STUDIO IDEAS

- Make another drawing of an expressive hand, this time using charcoal on white paper. Use the charcoal as you did the chalk, both for drawing and shading.

- ●● Blending values of a single hue of tempera, paint a large picture of your hand. Create a range of values from very dark (for shading) to very light (for the most lighted areas).

Art of the 1700s

Just as events of the 1500s brought in the Baroque style, so events of the 1600s brought about its end. The most important of these was the crowning of one of history's most colorful, pleasure-loving rulers. Because this king chose the sun as his emblem, he became known as the Sun King.

In this lesson you will learn about this king, the period in which he lived, and the new art style that he helped inspire.

EUROPE IN THE LATE 1600s

During the 1600s France emerged as Europe's strongest and wealthiest nation. Its capital, Paris, became the center of art. Find this city on the map shown in Figure 12–8.

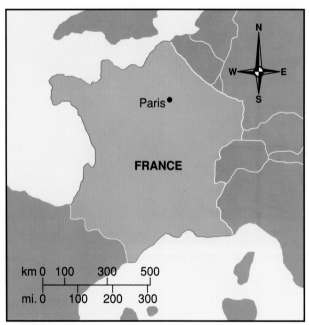

▲ Figure 12–8   France.

The force behind these changes was a powerful king with very rich tastes. He was Louis XIV, who ruled France for over 70 years. Louis' tastes were to help chart the course Western art would follow over the next 100 years.

Architecture

The beginnings of the new art style were put into motion in 1661. That year Louis ordered architects to build him the biggest, most elaborate palace in the world. It was built at Versailles (vuhr-**sye**), a short distance from Paris (Figure 12–9).

No photograph can begin to do the Palace of Versailles justice. The building covers 15 acres and contains enough rooms to house 10,000 people. The landscaped gardens around the palace cover another 250 acres. In Louis' time, 4 million flower bulbs were brought in each year from Holland to fill these gardens with the flowers the king loved.

Painting

Life for the king and his friends at Versailles was happy and carefree. This mood gave rise to a new style of art in the early 1700s. This style, which has come to be called **Rococo** (ruh-**koh**-koh), is *an art style stressing free, graceful movement; a playful use of line; and bright colors*.

The first artist to create works in the Rococo style was a painter named Antoine Watteau (an-**twahn** wah-**toh**). Watteau's pictures show a make-believe world peopled by untroubled members of France's ruling class. The painting in Figure 12–10 is one such picture. Like the figures in Watteau's other works, the people in this one appear to have not a care in the world. They are shown in a parklike garden listening to music. Notice

▲ **Figure 12–9** The gardens at Versailles also included a small zoo with unusual animals and birds. Louis XIV spent nearly three-fourths of all taxes collected to pay for this and other luxuries of his palace.

Louis Le Vau and Jules Hardouin-Mansart. Palace at Versailles, France.

◀ **Figure 12–10** Watteau's paintings are meant not only to be seen but also to be heard. With a little imagination you can hear the soft strumming of a guitar and the breezes rustling the leaves on trees.

Antoine Watteau. *The Vista*. 1716. Oil on canvas. 47 x 56 cm (18½ x 22"). Museum of Fine Arts, Boston, Massachusetts. Maria Antoinette Evans Fund.

▲ Figure 12–11   The artist lived to be 87. When she died, her will called for a relief carving of a painter's palette and brush on her tombstone.

Élisabeth Vigée-Lebrun. *Portrait of a Lady.* 1789. Wood. 107 x 83 cm (42⅛ x 32¾"). National Gallery of Art, Washington, D.C. Samuel H. Kress Collection.

▲ Figure 12–12   Chardin painted many scenes like the one in this work. Each treats familiar scenes and ordinary objects with respect and affection.

Jean-Baptiste-Siméon Chardin. *The Kitchen Maid.* 1738. Canvas. 46.2 x 37.5 cm (18⅛ x 14¾"). National Gallery of Art, Washington, D.C. Samuel H. Kress Collection.

that the viewer seems to be looking at this scene from far off. What reason might the artist have had for removing us—and himself—from the events in the painting?

The members of the French ruling class enjoyed having their portraits painted. An artist who met this demand was Élisabeth Vigée-Lebrun (ay-**lee**-zah-bet vee-**zhay**-luh-**bruhn**). Before she was 20, Vigée-Lebrun had painted many important nobles. By the time she was 25, she was named the queen's personal portrait painter. Vigée-Lebrun's portraits often put the subject in a very favorable light. She also reveals, in works like the one in Figure 12–11, how successful a simple pose can be. Notice how the young woman appears to be watching and listening *to you*. How flattering this is. No doubt this attention adds to a warm feeling about her.

Another side of French life was shown in the Rococo paintings done by Jean-Baptiste Siméon Chardin (**zhahn**-bah-**teest** see-may-**ohnh** shahr-**danh**). His genre pictures take the viewer into the simple homes of everyday people. One of these works, Figure 12–12, shows a woman preparing a meal. She seems to be lost in dreamy thought as she works. Everyone has had similar experiences when a sound or image sets the mind wandering for a few moments. Notice how the artist blends mellow colors and carefully painted still-life objects to communicate a quiet mood. The world of Chardin's art is one where time stands still and nothing disturbs the peacefulness. The viewer is able to observe simple domestic scenes treated with respect and affection.

ROCOCO ART IN SPAIN

The Rococo style in painting was not limited to France. In Spain the style was picked up by a free-thinking artist named Francisco Goya (fran-**sis**-koh **goy**-uh). Through his early forties, Goya painted softly lighted portraits of people from Spanish high society. A glimpse of the horrors and suffering of war, however, changed all that.

In 1808 French troops attacked Spain. The bloody scenes Goya witnessed prompted a series of etchings. An **etching** is *an intaglio print made by scratching an image onto a specially treated copper plate*. The etching in Figure 12–13 shows a French firing squad taking aim at a captured war prisoner. The figures and weapons stand out against a darkened sky. Goya's view of war is stripped of brave warriors and glorious victories. It is a shocking vision of death and destruction.

▲ **Figure 12–13   How do you suppose viewers in the 1800s reacted to the manner in which Goya chose to express scenes like this in his work?**

Francisco de Goya. *Cornered (From the Disasters of War).* Barbares, Paris, France. Bibliotheque Nationale.

STUDIO EXPERIENCE

Look once again at the painting in Figure 12–12 by Jean-Baptiste Siméon Chardin. The artist, it might be said, changes the ordinary into the extraordinary. With a little imagination, you can do the same.

Find a small ordinary object. Focus your search on something you would not usually think of in connection with a painting. Some examples are a clothespin, a nail, or a safety pin. Study the object carefully, and then draw it on a sheet of white paper. The drawing should totally fill the page. It should also be as accurate as you can make it. Use tempera to add color. Work at capturing the color, form, and texture of the object. Paint the background a dark color so the object will stand out boldly.

✔ CHECK YOUR UNDERSTANDING

1. What country became the center of art in the late 1600s? What king helped bring about the change?
2. What new art style grew out of the carefree life of the ruling class at Versailles? What are the main features of works done in this style?
3. What kinds of paintings were created by Antoine Watteau? What kind of paintings were done by Élisabeth Vigée-Lebrun and by Jean-Baptiste Siméon Chardin?
4. What are etchings? What events prompted Goya's etchings of war-related scenes? What do these etchings tell about Goya's view of war?

Constructing a Rococo Shoe

The 1700s were, above all else, a period of high fashion. It was said that if a woman left Paris on a short vacation, she would return to find all her clothes outdated. Hairdos grew taller and taller, and so did the heels on shoes — men's as well as women's. Architects began raising doors higher so people could pass through. Paintings by Antoine Watteau, like the one in Figure 12–14, mirror this concern for fashion. The figures in this painting look almost like fashion dolls.

Imagine that the president of a modern-day shoe company has decided to stage a contest. Designers are to come up with ideas for a shoe. It is to be of a type that might be found on the foot of a figure in a Watteau painting.

WHAT YOU WILL LEARN

You will design and create a Rococo shoe using cardboard and scrap materials. Use a variety of colors, shapes, and textures to create a highly decorative pattern. Your finished shoe will be a three-dimensional form. (See Figure 12–15.)

WHAT YOU WILL NEED

- Pencil and sheets of sketch paper
- Sheets of lightweight cardboard
- Scissors, heavy cardboard scraps, white glue, and stapler
- Pieces of brightly colored, richly patterned cloth
- Scrap materials, such as buckles, laces, bows, and sequins

▶ **Figure 12–14   This painting shows a group of aristocrats about to leave the legendary island of romance. Notice the delicate figures, rich costumes, and dreamlike setting. These, along with the soft colors, are typical of Watteau's Rococo style.**

Antoine Watteau. *Embarkation from Cythera*. 1717–1719. Charlottemburg Museo, The Louvre, Paris, France.

WHAT YOU WILL DO

1. Make several pencil sketches of a shoe as seen from the side. Make your design as elaborate and unusual as you can. Use exaggerated heels, soles, laces, and decorative features. Let your imagination guide you.
2. Choose your best sketch. Draw the outline of the shoe on a sheet of cardboard. Make the shoe lifesize. Carefully cut out the shoe.
3. Place your cutout on a second piece of cardboard. Holding it firmly in place, carefully cut around it, creating a second identical shoe.
4. Glue strips of heavy cardboard between the two shoe cutouts. These will be hidden inside, and will give you the basic form of a shoe.
5. Using pieces of cloth in different colors and patterns, cover the shoe form. Curve the cloth pieces around the heel of the shoe and across the top and the toe. Staple the cloth in place. (*Hint:* Cutting the cloth scraps small will help add to the decorative look of the shoe.) Glue buckles, bows, laces, and other scrap items in place as added decoration.
6. When the glue is dry, place your shoe on display. Compare your finished shoe with those of your classmates.

- **Describe** Tell whether your finished object can be recognized as a shoe. State whether it has a heel, sole, and other shoe parts. Explain how your shoe is a three-dimensional form.
- **Analyze** Point out the variety of colors, shapes, and textures in your work.
- **Interpret** Identify the kind of person who would wear the shoe you designed. State whether you could imagine the shoe on the foot of a subject in Figure 12–14.
- **Judge** Tell whether you feel you have succeeded in creating a Rococo shoe. State whether you feel it would win the shoe company contest. Explain why.

▲ Figure 12–15 Student work. Rococo shoe.

OTHER STUDIO IDEAS

- Create a shoe box with a design in the same Rococo style as your shoe. Follow the instructions given in Lesson 4 of Chapter 11.
- •• How would an ancient Egyptian, Greek, or Roman shoe differ from your Rococo shoe? Select a period you have read about, and design a shoe that reflects that period in a humorous way. Do this as a painting using tempera colors. Display your work, and ask if anyone can identify the period you selected.

BUILDING VOCABULARY

Number a sheet of paper from 1 to 5. After each number, write the term from the box that best matches each description below.

Baroque	portrait
etching	Rococo
facade	

1. The outside front of a building.
2. An art style emphasizing movement, contrast, and variety.
3. A painting of a person.
4. An art style stressing free, graceful movement; a playful use of line; and bright colors.
5. An intaglio print made by scratching an image onto a specially treated copper plate.

REVIEWING ART FACTS

Number a sheet of paper from 6 to 14. Answer each question in a complete sentence.

6. What architectural art style was practiced by Francesco Borromini?
7. What was a key contribution of Caravaggio to the art of the 1600s?
8. What artist's style most influenced the work of Artemisia Gentileschi?
9. What kinds of paintings were in demand in Holland during the 1600s?
10. What kinds of paintings were the specialty of Judith Leyster?
11. Who was the first artist to create Rococo paintings?
12. To what post was Élisabeth Vigée-Lebrun named as a young woman?
13. What side of French life of the 1700s is revealed in the paintings of Jean-Baptiste Siméon Chardin?
14. What sorts of paintings did Francisco Goya create through his early forties?

THINKING ABOUT ART

On a sheet of paper, answer each question in a sentence or two.

1. **Analyze.** Turn again to Caravaggio's painting of Christ's burial (Figure 12–2). Notice the artist's use of texture to add variety to the work. How many different textures can you find? On what objects in the work are these textures found?
2. **Compare and contrast.** Look once again at the portraits by Judith Leyster (Figure 12–5) and Élisabeth Vigée-Lebrun (Figure 12–11). Tell in what ways the two works are alike. Explain how they are different. Which of these two artists' works do you find most successful? Explain your decision by referring to one or more aesthetic views.

MAKING ART CONNECTIONS

1. **Music.** The Baroque style was not limited to art. It is also found in music of the period. Working as part of a team of students, (1) find and tape-record a musical composition by the famous Baroque composer Johann Sebastian Bach (**yo-hahn suh-bast-ee-uhn bahk**), and (2) find and photocopy other works by several Baroque artists you learned about in this chapter. Stage a sound-and-sight presentation before your class.
2. **Social Studies.** Several of the painters you read about in this chapter created genre, rather than religious, works. Rembrandt, during the 1600s, was one. Chardin, during the 1700s, was another. Find a third genre artist from either of the two periods. Imagine that this person were living today. Based on what you know of the artist, describe what a twentieth-century work by him or her might look like. Give details about both the subject and style of the work.

LOOKING AT THE DETAILS

The detail shown below is from Artemisia Gentileschi's *Judith and the Maid Servant with the Head of Holofernes*. Study the detail and answer the following questions using complete sentences.

1. How does the artist pull the viewer into the drama of the scene?
2. How is light used to affect the mood of this work of art?
3. Compare this detail with Figure 12–2 on page **179**. How is the use of light similar? How is it different?

4. Compare this work with Figure 12–14 on page **188**. What differences do you see in the use of the elements of space and texture?
5. Look at the entire work on page **176**. If the artist had shown more of the room and placed the women farther into the scene, how do you think this would have changed the mood of the work? Explain your answer.

Artemisia Gentileschi. *Judith and Maidservant with the Head of Holofernes*. c. 1625. Oil on canvas. (Detail.) Detroit Institute of Art, Detroit, Michigan.

▲ The artist is a teacher of sculpture. His advice to students is to go out and find their own styles.

Allan Houser. *Sacred Rain Arrow*. 1988. Bronze. 249 x 99 x 78.7 cm (98 x 39 x 31"). Glenn Green Galleries, Phoenix, Arizona.

CHAPTER 13

Native American Art

In history books the part of the globe we live in is called the New World. To the people who have dwelled in this region since earliest times, there is nothing new about it. Some of these groups—from Central and South America—you learned about in Chapter 6.

In this chapter you will read about the first people of North America. You will learn about their culture. You will learn, finally, about the proud traditions that have led to the making of art works like the one shown on the left.

OBJECTIVES

After completing this chapter, you will be able to:

- Name and describe five major groups of Native Americans.
- Identify the contributions to art the different Native American cultures have made.
- Identify Native American artists working today.
- Create art in the style developed by the Native Americans.

WORDS YOU WILL LEARN

coiled pot
cradle board
Kachina doll
loom
petroglyphs
polychrome
pueblos
sand painting
tepee
totem pole
warp
weft

ARTISTS YOU WILL MEET

T. C. Cannon
Tony Dallas
Allan Houser
Oscar Howe
Kenojuak
Lucy Lewis
Dan Namingha
Margaret Tafoya

Native American Art of the Past

When Christopher Columbus reached North America in 1492, he thought his ships had landed on the east coast of India. He referred to the natives he found living there as Indians. Today these first settlers of the United States and Canada are called Native Americans.

In this lesson you will study four of the major Native American groups: the Pueblo, Northwest Coast Indians, Plains Indians, and Woodlands Indians. You will look at the art they produced hundreds of years ago and see how their contributions influence Native American art today.

PUEBLO CULTURE

In prehistoric times the Pueblo (poo-**eb**-loh) people settled in what is now known as the Four Corners region of the United States. Find this region on the map in Figure 13–1. Like other Native American groups, the Pueblo are believed to have come from Asia.

Scientific records show they probably came by way of the Bering Sea some 20,000 to 30,000 years ago.

"The People," as the early Pueblo called themselves, were farmers. They wore clothes woven from cotton, had a democratic form of government, and traded with other cultures.

Crafts

It was through trade with Mexico around A.D. 400 that the Pueblo learned to make pottery. The earliest kind of pot, called a **coiled pot**, was *a pot formed by coiling long ropes of clay in a spiral*. An example of such a pot is shown in Figure 13–2. The careful pinching together of the coils was meant to be both decorative and useful. In what ways is this type of pot similar to the ones made by the Chavín of South America? (See Figure 6–11 on page **88**). In what ways is it different?

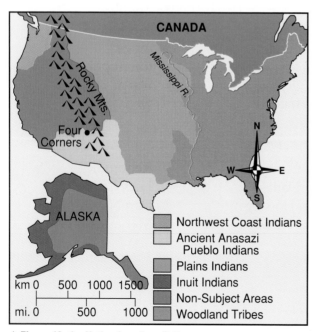

▲ Figure 13–1 Native American Cultures.

CANADA

Rocky Mts.

Mississippi R.

Four Corners

ALASKA

km 0   500 1000 1500
mi. 0   500   1000

Northwest Coast Indians
Ancient Anasazi Pueblo Indians
Plains Indians
Inuit Indians
Non-Subject Areas
Woodland Tribes

▲ Figure 13–2 Pots like this had to be able to hold water, which was precious in the dry hot southwestern desert. The pots were also used to store food and were buried with the dead to help them in the afterlife.

Coil pot. Pueblo. A.D. 1050–1200. Exterior: coiled neck; pinched coil underbody and base; lug handles on each side of neck; smoothed interior. 27.9 x 26.7 cm (11 x 10½"). Courtesy of the School of American Research, Indian Arts Research Center, Santa Fe, New Mexico. Gift of Maria Chabot, Albuquerque, New Mexico.

Petroglyphs

Although they were farmers, the early Pueblo also hunted for food. To ensure a good hunt, they made **petroglyphs** (peh-truh-glifs), or *rock carvings and paintings*, of their prey. This, they believed, would allow them to capture the animal's spirit. Can you think of another culture you learned about that shared this belief?

Examine the petroglyph of a bighorn sheep in Figure 13–3. Would you describe the work as realistic? Would you say it is stylized?

Architecture

The early inhabitants of the southwestern United States lived in round pit houses dug into the earth and covered with branches. Over the years the Indians learned to build with adobe, mud, and straw. When the Spanish arrived in the Southwest in 1540, they found *stacked, many-family dwellings made of adobe*. The Spaniards called these **pueblos**, after the Spanish word for "village." The same word was also used to refer to the Native American builders of these dwellings. Study the pueblo in Figure 13–4 on page **196**. Notice how the structure seems to grow out of the earth. What modern form of dwelling in our own culture has a purpose similar to the pueblo?

NORTHWEST COAST INDIAN CULTURE

The coastal sections of British Columbia and the states of Washington, Oregon, and northern California are rich with plant and animal life. Rain for growing crops is plentiful, and cooling sea breezes keep temperatures mild. It is no doubt these features appealed to several groups of people heading south before 7000 B.C.

Today the collected groups of the region are known by the name of Northwest Coast Indians. Find the area settled by these early cultures on the map in Figure 13–1.

Like the Pueblos, the Northwest Coast Indians made use of the resources around them. They used the tall trees of the area to make boats and logs for houses. They also used the trees to make art.

Sculpture

No art form is more unmistakably Native American than the totem pole. A **totem pole** is *an upright log carving picturing stories of different families or clans*. The word *totem* means "spirit or guardian." Figure 13–5 on page **196** shows a totem pole carved by an artist of a Northwest Coast tribe. Typically, this pole is meant to be read from top to bottom. The top figure identifies the clan to which the pole belongs. Notice how the facial features have been stylized to fit the available space.

PLAINS INDIAN CULTURE

Not all peoples who arrived here in Pre-Columbian times set up permanent villages. Some were wanderers who moved from place to place as the food supply dwindled. One such group was the people known as the Plains Indians.

◄ **Figure 13–3** Petroglyphs like these have survived for many centuries.

Petroglyph: Bighorn Sheep. A.D. 900–1100. Three Rivers Site, New Mexico.

▲ Figure 13–4   Most Pueblo people live in ordinary houses today. Some still return to a family pueblo, however, for holidays.

Pueblo Dwellings. c. 1100. Taos, New Mexico.

The Plains Indians made their home in the large area bounded by the Mississippi River and the Rocky Mountains. Find these boundaries on the map in Figure 13–1. The Plains Indians hunted the bison. As the herds moved, so did the Plains people, dragging their possessions behind them on their custom-made sleds.

Architecture

Among the belongings the Plains people carried with them was the tepee. A **tepee** (**tee**-pee) was *a portable house*. As a rule, the tepee was cone-shaped and made of rawhide patches stretched over poles. The hides were covered with designs symbolizing the forces of nature.

At its base a tepee could range anywhere from 12 to 30 feet (4 to 9 m) in diameter. A large tepee contained about as much space as a standard living room of today. How many people do you think could live comfortably in such a space?

Crafts

Like the tepee, the crafts created by the Plains people were made to be easily carried. An example is the object pictured in Figure 13–6. This is a **cradle board**, *a harness worn on the shoulders and used to carry a small child.*

▲ Figure 13–5   Totem poles like this can symbolize a marriage, a birth, or a death. Sometimes a great chief was buried inside a totem pole.

Northwest Coast Totem Pole. Kwakiutl. c. 1900. Channing, Dale, Throckmorton Gallery, Santa Fe, New Mexico.

Notice the care that went into the woven design. What kinds of shapes—organic or geometric—has the artist used in this design? What natural materials are used to decorate the cradle board?

WOODLANDS CULTURE

The Woodlands made up the largest cultural group of Native Americans. They settled in North America east of the Mississippi River. The Woodlands people combined hunting and gathering with primitive farming. The Iroquois, made up of six different Woodlands groups, combined to form the highly organized Iroquois nation. Their most spectacular art works were wooden False Face masks, carved from living trees, and believed to hold live spirits. (See Studio Lesson 4, *Handbook* pages **310–311**.)

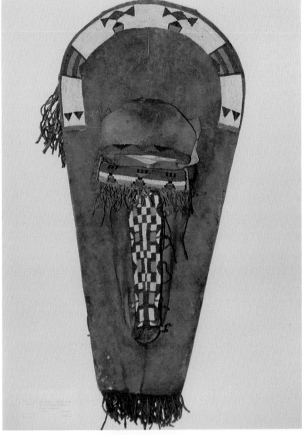

▲ **Figure 13–6** Even though their life was hard, the Plains Indians took great pride in their art. What features of this work reveal this pride?

Ute Cradle Board. c. 1870. Buffalo hide, trade beads. Channing, Dale, Throckmorton Gallery, Santa Fe, New Mexico.

STUDIO EXPERIENCE

Plains Indians painted tales of their battles on skins. An example of one such work is shown in Figure 13–7. Notice that the artist has used a bird's-eye view in telling this tale.

Look through a newspaper or magazine for coverage of an important event in your city or in the world. On a sheet of paper, sketch the story behind this event. Use the Plains style illustrated in Figure 13–7. Carefully outline each object in your design. Color the work using watercolor markers. Compare your finished work with those of classmates. Which picture tells its story most clearly? Which is closest in style to the work in Figure 13–7?

✔ CHECK YOUR UNDERSTANDING

1. In what region did the Pueblo settle? Where are they and other Native American groups believed to have come from?
2. What are coiled pots? What are petroglyphs?
3. What form of architecture gave one Native American group its name? Why was this word chosen?
4. For what unmistakably Native American form of art are the Northwest Coast Indians known?
5. What are tepees? Why did the Plains Indians have a need for tepees?

◄ **Figure 13–7** This hide tells stories from the artist's own life. Can you tell what is taking place in this scene?

Exploits of a Sioux Leader. c. 1870–1875. Hide Painting. Phillbrook Museum of Art, Tulsa, Oklahoma. Gift of Kills Eagle.

Making a Round Weaving

Some Native American craft styles and techniques are borrowed from other cultures. One you have learned about is Pueblo pottery, which came from artists in Mexico. Another craft, which also became an important art medium to many Native American cultures, is weaving. Woven materials were used for clothing and blankets. They were often highly decorated and expressed the artists' beliefs, customs, and traditions. Study the decorative weaving shown in Figure 13–8. It was created on a **loom**, or *frame holding a set of crisscrossing threads*. The loom holds two sets of threads. The **warp** threads are *threads running vertically and attached to the loom's frame*. The **weft** threads are those *threads passed horizontally over and under the warp*. The weaver of the object in Figure 13–8 was able to change colors and patterns by using different weaving techniques. This weaving was created on a circular loom.

▲ **Figure 13–8**   Student work. Round weaving.

WHAT YOU WILL LEARN

You will make a round weaving on a loom made from wire coat hangers. Plan a color scheme for your weaving, and use weaving techniques to change colors in your design. Use a complementary, monochromatic, or analogous color scheme.

WHAT YOU WILL NEED

- 2 wire coat hangers
- Masking tape
- Assorted fibers
- 2 or more blunt tapestry needles

WHAT YOU WILL DO

1. Make a frame for your loom by putting two wire coat hangers together and bending them to form a flat circle. Connect the hangers in two places around the circle with masking tape. Bend the hook on one of the hangers into a loop. This will be used to hang your completed work.
2. Pick the colors of fiber you will use in your weaving. Choose a complementary, monochromatic, or analogous color scheme. Set the fibers aside.
3. Tie a long strand of fiber to your frame using an overhand knot. Wrap the fiber strand completely around the frame using half-hitch knots. (See Figure 13–9.) Thread the end of your fiber strand through a needle. Pull it through several of the knot loops to keep the fiber from coming undone. Cut off any extra fiber.

4. Create a warp by attaching a single long strand of fiber to the frame. Pass this across the circle at different points. Make sure each pass of the warp fiber crosses the center of the loom. (See Figure 13–10.) After six passes, begin a seventh. This time, take the warp strand only as far as the center. Tie all passes at this point.
5. Working from the center out, begin the weft using a tabby (over and under) weave. After several circuits, switch to one of the other techniques detailed in Figure 13–10. Experiment to create different color shapes or designs. You may leave some open spaces where the warp is not covered.
6. Display your weaving along with those done by classmates. See if you can identify the weaving techniques used in different works.

EXAMINING YOUR WORK

- **Describe**   Explain how you created a loom using two wire coat hangers. Identify the different color shapes you created by switching weaves.
- **Analyze**   Describe the shape of your loom. Tell what kind of color scheme you picked. Name the colors you used. Tell how you used weaving techniques to change the colors in your design.
- **Interpret**   Explain how the colors you chose help communicate a certain mood to viewers. Give your work a title.
- **Judge**   Tell whether your work succeeds. State what you might do differently in a second attempt at the assignment.

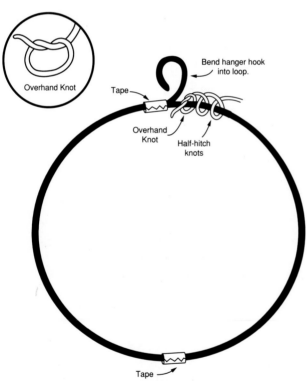

▲ Figure 13–9   Making the wire loom.

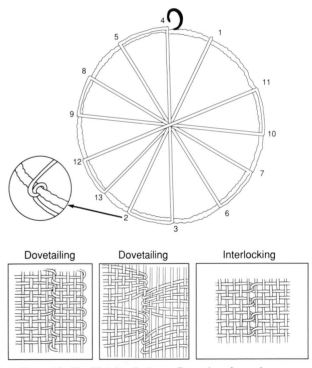

▲ Figure 13–10   Warping the loom. Examples of weaving techniques are detailed.

OTHER STUDIO IDEAS

- Make a second weaving, this time picking a different type of color scheme. Emphasize texture by using different fibers.

- ●● Use a heavy-duty paper plate as a loom. Make an uneven number of notches around the edge. Warp it following the instructions in the lesson. Create a second weaving.

Native American Art Today

During the 1700s and 1800s America was explored and settled by newcomers from Europe. Native Americans fought to keep the lands they had lived on for generations. Their efforts were unsuccessful. As the land was developed by Europeans, the Native American population dwindled. Those who remained were eventually forced to live in limited areas called reservations.

Although the original Native American way of life has been lost, their art lives on. Many Native American artists working today continue the traditions of earlier artists.

TRADITIONAL NATIVE AMERICAN ART

Traditional art is art based on past forms and ideas. Some designs and techniques used by traditional artists today date from over a thousand years ago.

Crafts

Pueblo legend tells of supernatural spirits called Kachina (kuh-**chee**-nuh) who once lived among the people. The Kachina taught the Pueblo how to live in harmony with nature. This legend gave rise long ago to the making of Kachina dolls. A **Kachina doll** was *a hand-carved statuette used to teach children about Pueblo rituals*. Figure 13–11 shows a Kachina doll created in this century. Like the dolls of old, this object uses formal balance. What toys of our own culture does this remind you of? What idea or mood does it communicate to the viewer?

Another tradition carried forward by craftspeople today is pottery. The **polychrome**, or *many-colored*, pots in Figure 13–12 are by Lucy Lewis, a leading twentieth-century Native American potter. Lewis cre-

ated these pots using the same skills she learned as a child watching her elders. Each step was carefully done by hand, from digging the clay to grinding the minerals for the paints she used. She worked without the aid of a potter's wheel. Look closely at these works. The patterns on the surface are adaptations of prehistoric designs. What images do you see in these abstract decorations?

▲ **Figure 13–11**   The Pueblo believe there are between 300 and 400 Kachinas. Can you think of another culture you learned about that believed in a great many spirits?

Tony Dallas. *Koshare Clown*. Kachina Doll. Joan Cawley Gallery, Santa Fe, New Mexico.

▲ **Figure 13–12** The artist learned to make pots from an aunt. What other skills besides art are learned through tradition?

Lucy Lewis. Polychrome Pots. Lewis Family. c. 1989/90. Acoma, New Mexico.

▲ **Figure 13–13** In what ways is this water jar similar to the ones by Lucy Lewis? How are they different?

Margaret Tafoya. Jar. 1965. Blackware. 43 x 33 cm (17 x 13"). National Museum of Women in the Arts. Gift of Wallace & Wilhelmina Holladay.

Margaret Tafoya is another Native American artist who has also preserved the traditional methods with modern experimental techniques. She has created the pottery water jar shown in Figure 13–13 using a method of intaglio molding and carving. Her jar is decorated with an ancient water-serpent design.

Painting

Some ancient art techniques still practiced today are associated with health and well-being. One of these, sand painting, is part of a healing ritual. **Sand painting** is *the pouring of different colors of powdered rock on a flat section of earth to create an image or design.* Examine the sand painting pictured in Figure 13–14. As with all creations of this type, this one is abstract in design.

▲ **Figure 13–14** Works like this are temporary; a new one is made from scratch for each ritual.

Sand Painting. Medicine men placing feathers. American Museum of Natural History, New York, New York.

MODERN NATIVE AMERICAN ART

Not all Native American artists of the twentieth century have been content to follow tradition. Some have struck out in new directions, using new media and techniques.

Sculpture

One of the most influential Native American artists at work today is Allan Houser (**ha**-oo-zohr). A Chiricahua Apache (chir-uh-**kah**-wuh uh-**pach**-ee), Houser was born in Oklahoma in 1914. As a child, he listened intently to stories about his people. After studying art, he went on to retell — usually in stone or bronze — the stories he had heard. Study the sculpture by Houser that opened this chapter, on page **192**. Can you imagine a story about this young warrior? How has Houser used line to move your eyes around the statue?

Painting

Portrait and landscape paintings are not parts of Native American art tradition. However, both played major roles in the brief life and career of twentieth-century painter T. C. Cannon. Cannon, a member of the Kiowa (**ky**-uh-waw) tribe, was born in 1946. A student of Allan Houser, he painted traditional subjects in brightly colored modern-day settings. Typical of his work is the portrait in Figure 13–15. Note the strong sense of design. What kind of detail has the artist shown in the man's clothing?

▶ **Figure 13–15** The subject of this painting seems to exist in two worlds. How does the artist show this?

T. C. Cannon. *Turn of the Century Dandy.* 1976. Acrylic on canvas. 152.4 x 132.1 cm (60 x 52″). Aberbach Fine Arts, New York, New York. Private Collection.

In the painting shown in Figure 13–16, another artist, Oscar Howe, breaks with painting traditions imposed upon Native Americans by European teachers. Traditionally, Indians did not use a realistic style. They believed that they could not depict nature as well as the Creator had made it. They depicted the spirit of animals and plants in symbolic, stylized designs. Howe uses line, shape, and color to show excitement. He expresses the powerful energy of the spirit of victory.

The painting by Dan Naminga, Figure 13–17, is yet another example of the blending of contemporary subject and traditional styles. This time the artist paints modern dwellings in a rich, colorful landscape.

▲ **Figure 13–17** The work is an interpretation of modern times, yet it reveals strong feelings on the artist's part for the land and nature. What aesthetic view would you take in judging this work? Why?

Dan Namingha. *Hopi Dwelling.* Acrylic on canvas. 102 x 102 cm (40 x 40").

✔ CHECK YOUR UNDERSTANDING

1. What is traditional art?
2. What is a Kachina doll?
3. What is sand painting? For what is sand painting used?
4. In what area of art does Allan Houser specialize?
5. What was the art specialty of T. C. Cannon?

▲ **Figure 13–16** What story do you imagine this dancer is telling?

Oscar Howe. *Victory Dance.* Philbrook Museum of Art, Tulsa, Oklahoma.

Inuit-Style Print

Another Native American group that has been around since earliest times is the Inuit (**in**-yuh-wuht). You probably know these people of Canada and Alaska better as Eskimos. The name "Eskimo" was used by explorers from other lands. The people from this group call themselves the Inuit. The Inuit have a tradition of carving bone, ivory, or stone to create abstract views of images from nature. This tradition is being upheld by artists working today. The print in Figure 13–18 is by a leading Inuit artist named Kenojuak (kuh-**noh**-joo-ak). Like all Native American artists, she combines nature, religion, and her own imagination.

WHAT YOU WILL LEARN

You will design a print based on your school mascot or some other school symbol. Your print will be abstract in design and should use line and shape to express your feelings about the animal. You will make an edition of three prints. (See Figure 13–19.)

WHAT YOU WILL NEED

- Pencil, eraser, and sheets of sketch paper
- 2 pieces of corrugated cardboard, 8 x 10 inches (20 x 25 cm)
- Paper-cutting knife and white glue
- Water-based printing ink
- Shallow pan and soft brayer
- Paper for printing
- Tablespoon

▶ **Figure 13–18 What kind of balance has the artist used? Is the subject in the work readily identifiable?**

Kenojuak. *Owls, Ravens and Dogs.* Courtesy of Dorset Fine Arts, Toronto, Ontario, Canada.

WHAT YOU WILL DO

1. On sketch paper, do a drawing of the animal you chose. On a second sheet of sketch paper, create an abstract design based on your first sketch. Leave out all unneeded details. Use line and shape to express feelings. Round shapes can express gentleness, diagonal lines can show danger or quick movement.

2. Transfer your design to a piece of corrugated cardboard. Using the paper-cutting knife, carefully cut out the design. Glue it to the second piece of cardboard to form a printing plate.

3. Squeeze out a small amount of ink into the pan. Roll the brayer back and forth in the ink to coat it evenly. Roll the brayer lightly over your printing plate. If you press down too hard, you might collapse the relief.

4. Place a clean sheet of paper on your plate. Gently rub the paper with the back of the spoon or your fingertips. Work quickly. Carefully remove the print. Set it aside to dry. Repeat the process twice more to make an edition of three prints. When all the prints are dry, sign and number them.

5. Display your finished prints alongside those of classmates. Decide which design you feel best captures the appearance and the spirit of your school mascot.

EXAMINING YOUR WORK

- **Describe**   Identify the sources of your ideas for abstraction. Identify the unnecessary details you eliminated to create an abstract design.
- **Analyze**   Tell which elements stand out most in your design.
- **Interpret**   State what feelings toward your mascot your print expresses. Identify the features that help communicate those feelings.
- **Judge**   Tell whether you feel your work succeeds. If you could redo your work, tell what changes, if any, you would make.

▲ **Figure 13–19   Student work. Inuit-style print.**

OTHER STUDIO IDEAS

- Make another print, this time using a darker-colored ink. Explain how this changes the mood of the work.

- ●● Work with three or four classmates. On a large sheet of paper, create a repeated pattern incorporating all your plates.

BUILDING VOCABULARY

Number a sheet of paper from 1 to 12. After each number, write the term from the box that best matches each description below.

coiled pot	pueblos
cradle board	sand painting
Kachina doll	tepee
loom	totem pole
petroglyphs	warp
polychrome	weft

1. A pot formed by coiling long ropes of clay in a spiral.
2. Rock carvings and paintings.
3. Stacked, many-family dwellings made of adobe.
4. An upright log carving picturing stories of different families or clans.
5. A portable house.
6. A harness worn on the shoulders and used to carry a small child.
7. A hand-carved statuette used to teach children about Pueblo rituals.
8. The pouring of different colors of powdered rock on a flat section of earth to create an image or design.
9. Having many colors.
10. A frame holding a set of crisscrossing threads.
11. Threads running vertically and attached to the loom's frame.
12. Threads passed horizontally over and under the warp.

REVIEWING ART FACTS

Number a sheet of paper from 13 to 19. Answer each question in a complete sentence.

13. In what areas did the early Pueblo settle?
14. When did the Northwest Coast Indians reach the region they settled? What convinced them to remain in this region?
15. Which group of Woodlands people became organized as one large nation?
16. Which group of Native Americans is famous for its totem poles?
17. What were the Kachina?
18. What Native American artist was famous for his portraits and landscapes?
19. Where do the Inuit live?

THINKING ABOUT ART

On a sheet of paper, answer each question in a sentence or two.

1. **Analyze**. One of the three aesthetic views holds that the most important feature of a work of art is its composition. Tell how an art critic accepting this view would react to the sculpture that opened this chapter (page **192**). Explain why you believe the critic would have this reaction.
2. **Extend**. Explain how the part of the world the Inuit live in is a factor in their artists' choice of media.

MAKING ART CONNECTIONS

1. **Science**. Find all the works in this chapter that make use of geometric patterns. Identify the number and kind of motifs that appear in each one. See if you can make any general statements about the use of patterns from nature used in Native American design.
2. **Social Studies**. In the encyclopedia or another library reference book, read about (a) the Seminole Native Americans of Florida, or (b) the Iroquois Native Americans of New York State. Find out when the people arrived in the region they settled. Learn about the customs and art of the group. Share your findings with the class in the form of an interesting audio-visual presentation.

LOOKING AT THE DETAILS

The detail shown below is from Allan Houser's *Sacred Rain Arrow.* Study the detail and answer the following questions using complete sentences.

1. How has the artist depicted strength in this sculpture?
2. Look at the credit line. In what year was this sculpture created? Does this information give you more insight into the values of the artist and his culture?
3. How has Houser created the impression of anticipated movement?
4. Explain how the element of line is used to show contrast in this work.

Alan Houser. *Sacred Rain Arrow.* 1988. Bronze. (Detail.) 249 x 99 x 78.7 cm (98 x 39 x 31"). Glenn Green Galleries, Phoenix, Arizona.

▲ The artist once stated that his desire was to paint pictures that were happy and pretty. Do you suppose this is one of them? Explain your answer.

Auguste Renoir. *Oarsmen at Chatou*. 1879. Canvas. 81.3 x 100.3 cm (32 x 39½"). National Gallery of Art, Washington, D.C. Gift of Sam A. Lewisohn.

CHAPTER 14

European Art of the Early 1800s

The 1600s, you have learned, was the age of Baroque art; the 1700s, of Rococo. The 1800s can be thought of as an age of change. No single art style dominated. One art style was hardly in place before it was challenged and replaced by another.

The century began with artists looking to the past for ideas. By mid-century they were roaming the countryside, painting every-day scenes with dabs of paint. One work done in this manner is shown at the left. In this chapter you will learn about such works and the artists who created them.

OBJECTIVES

After completing this chapter, you will be able to:
- Describe the Neoclassic, Romantic, and Impressionist styles of art.
- Discuss the importance of the Salon to artists of the day.
- Create art work in the Neoclassic and Impressionist style.

WORDS YOU WILL LEARN

art movement
Impressionism
landscape

Neoclassic
Romanticism
Salon

ARTISTS YOU WILL MEET

Jacques Louis David
Eugène Delacroix
Claude Monet
Berthe Morisot

Auguste Renoir
Auguste Rodin
Joseph M. W. Turner

LESSON 1

Neoclassic and Romantic Art

The late 1700s and early 1800s were stormy times in France. Outraged by the shameless greed of the wealthy ruling class, the poor people rose up in revolt. This uprising, known as the French Revolution, began with a bloody reign of terror. Thousands lost their heads on the guillotine. The following 20 years, marked by war and struggle, were no less bitter. Finally, the troubled French government was turned over to a popular young general. His name was Napoléon Bonaparte (nuh-**pol**-yuhn **boh**-nuh-part).

▲ **Figure 14–1** Notice how the artist arranged the three groups of figures. Do the arches and columns help unify the groups?

Jacques Louis David. *The Oath of the Horatii.* 1786. Toledo Museum of Art, Toledo, Ohio.

NEOCLASSIC ART

Artists of the day believed these events were equal in importance to the rise and fall of ancient Greece and Rome. They even chose to show the events using an updated version of the styles of ancient Greece and Rome. As a result, their work became known as **Neoclassic** (nee-oh-**klas**-ik), meaning "new classic," *an art style that borrowed from the early classical period of ancient Greece and Rome.*

One of the most successful of the Neoclassic artists was Jacques Louis David (**zhahk** loo-**ee** dah-**veed**). Even though he later took part in the revolt against the French king, David was Louis XVI's painter. It was the king who asked David to paint what would become one of his most famous pictures. The painting, shown in Figure 14–1, shows two families living in neighboring ancient Roman cities. The families are related by marriage but divided by a war between their cities. A father and three sons of one family are shown pledging to fight to the death. All know their relatives will be among those they must battle. The women, helpless to prevent the tragedy, weep.

The picture is made up of three groups of figures. These are arranged across the canvas as though it were a stage. Notice David's skillful use of the background arches and columns to separate and frame these groups. The artist's careful painting of details—the swords, the helmets—adds to the picture's realism. His use of light adds drama to the picture.

ROMANTIC ART

As the 1800s wore on, people became weary of the political unrest and fighting. They looked for things that would take their minds off the upsetting events around them. Some artists shared this same desire. These artists were responsible for developing a new style of art called **Romanticism** (roh-**mant**-uh-siz-uhm). This is *a style of art that found its subjects in the world of the dramatic and exotic.*

France

To Romanticists, nothing stirred the imagination better than far-off places and colorful, action-filled adventures. The two are combined in the paintings of Eugène Delacroix (oo-**zhen** del-uh-**kwah**), a leader of the Romantic school. One of his paintings is pictured in Figure 14–2. In this work, Delacroix refused to allow his taste for action to interfere with his sense of design. He planned his painting so the viewer would miss none of its exciting details.

Study this work. Find the diagonal line beginning in the horse and rider at the lower left. This line leads your eye upward to the figures at the right. From there the gunsmoke pulls your gaze across the picture to the far-off figures and fortress.

England

Another artist who turned to his imagination for ideas was the English painter Joseph M. W. Turner. Unlike other Romanticists, however, Turner expected his viewers to use their imaginations as well. His glowing colors and blurred images free viewers to interpret his pictures in their own ways.

Turner spent his life painting landscapes. A **landscape** is *a drawing or painting focusing on mountains, trees, or other natural scenery.* He was fascinated in particular by sunlight and its shimmering reflection on water. This fascination can be seen in the painting in Figure 14–3. The work excites the viewer's curiosity with its dazzling sky and shimmering waters. There are ships in the center of the painting, and a church is visible on the right. With the use of light on the structures, the artist leads the viewer's eye down the canal and out to sea. As in all of Turner's best works, the real subjects are light and color.

▲ **Figure 14–2   Delacroix often painted pictures that included action and adventure. Look at the figures in the foreground. Notice how they help to lead the viewer's eyes around the painting.**

Eugène Delacroix. *Arabs Skirmishing in the Mountains.* 1863. Canvas. 92.5 x 74.6 cm (36⅜ x 29⅜"). National Gallery of Art, Washington, D.C. Chester Dale Fund.

✔ CHECK YOUR UNDERSTANDING

1. Describe events in France in the late 1700s and early 1800s.
2. What is Neoclassic art? What led artists to begin creating art in this style?
3. What is Romantic art? What led artists to begin creating art in this style?

▲ **Figure 14–3** Earlier in his career the artist painted pictures with more realistic subjects. What do you like about the way he painted this one?

Joseph M. W. Turner. *The Grand Canal, Venice.* 1835. Canvas. 91.4 x 122.2 cm (36 x 48⅛"). The Metropolitan Museum of Art, New York, New York. Bequest of Cornelius Vanderbilt, 1899.

Designing a Neoclassic Stage Set

Look at the painting in Figure 14–4. It is by Jacques Louis David. As in the other work by this foremost Neoclassicist you studied (Figure 14–1), the figures appear almost as actors. The setting is like a stage.

Imagine for a moment that the stone dungeon in this work *is* part of a stage set. Imagine that just beyond the rightmost figure in the painting are wings—the area in a theater leading backstage. Imagine that to the left of the shadowed archway the set continues. What lies beyond the left edge of this painting? In this lesson you will invent a continuation of this scene.

WHAT YOU WILL LEARN

Design and build a three-dimensional model for a stage set. Your model will extend the stage in Figure 14–4. Match as closely as possible the colors, textures, and patterns of the walls and floor. Make two pieces of furniture to place in your model. These will emphasize the real space in the model. Your stage set will have the same feeling or mood suggested by David's painting.

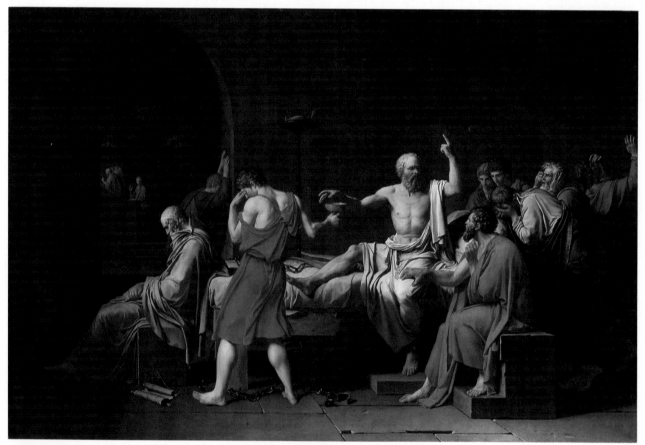

▲ Figure 14–4   Socrates, a great Greek philosopher, is shown in prison. He has been placed here after falsely being accused of denying the existence of Greek gods. His punishment is to drink poison.

Jacques Louis David. *The Death of Socrates*. 1787. Oil on canvas. 129.5 x 196.2 cm (51 x 77¼"). The Metropolitan Museum of Art, New York, New York. Catherine Lorillard Wolfe Collection.

WHAT YOU WILL NEED

- Pencil and sheets of sketch paper
- Mixing tray, tempera paint, and 2 brushes—one wide, one fine-tipped
- Shoe box and 2 sheets of mat board
- Scissors and white glue

WHAT YOU WILL DO

1. Brainstorm with your classmates for possible answers to the question "What lies beyond the left border of this painting?" Then working by yourself, sketch several ideas for extending the stage. Create windows, doorways, stairs, arches, and other design features you like. Let your imagination and David's painting guide you. Choose your best sketch and set it aside.

2. Mix hues of tempera paint to match the lighted portions of the walls and the floor in David's painting. Create darker values of the same hue to match the shaded portions. Using the thick brush, paint the back, sides, and bottom of the shoe box. Using the fine-tipped brush, add the thin lines between stone blocks.

3. With scissors, cut from mat board doors, arches, and other design features appearing in your sketch. Make sure all added features match the colors, patterns, and textures found in the painting. Glue these features in place in your model.

4. Make furniture, such as a table, bench, or bed, to complete your design.

- **Describe** Tell whether the walls, floor, and other features of your model look real. Point out the features that help viewers identify your model as an extension of David's painting.
- **Analyze** State whether the colors and textures in your work match those in David's painting. Point out similarities between the patterns on the walls and floor in your model and those in the painting. Show ways in which you used real space in your model.
- **Interpret** Tell whether your stage set has the same mood or feeling as the one David's painting communicates. Decide what words you would use to describe that mood or feeling.
- **Judge** Decide in what way your model most succeeds. Tell whether it succeeds because of its realistic appearance, its composition, or its content.

5. When dry, display your model. Compare it with the stage set in the painting and with other student models. Decide which were most successful in matching the look of David's painting.

OTHER STUDIO IDEAS

- Look through a magazine to find figures to cut out and use as actors for your stage. Glue cardboard backings to your figures so they will stand. Pose them in your model so they appear to be relating to one another.

- • Imagine the words each of your actors is speaking. Write these on pieces of white paper cut to look like the dialogue balloons in comic strips. Glue these to each actor so the words seem to be coming from his or her mouth.

European Art — Late 1800s

Each age has its customs and fashions. One custom common in Paris and London during the 1800s was a yearly art show. The **Salon** (suh-**lahn**), *an annual exhibition of art*, was a major social event. An artist's reputation often depended upon whether or not his or her work was selected for showing at the Salon.

In this lesson you will read how the Salon led to the formation of an **art movement**, *a trend formed when a group of artists band together to create works of a single style*.

▲ Figure 14–5 Cool colors — blues and greens — seem to move back in space. Warm colors — reds and yellows — seem to come forward. How has the artist used warm and cool colors in this work? Why do you think he made these choices?

Claude Monet. *Banks of the Seine, Vetheuil.* 1880. Canvas. 73.4 x 100.5 cm (28⅞ x 39⅝"). National Gallery of Art, Washington, D.C. Chester Dale Collection.

IMPRESSIONIST PAINTING

In 1874 a group of discouraged artists decided to hold an exhibition of their own. They found an empty studio in Paris. There they hung pictures that had been rejected by the Salon. The people who came to view the exhibition reacted in different ways. Some were confused. Others laughed. Still others were angry. On one point most viewers were agreed: the paintings looked more like quick sketches than like finished art works. One angry critic, after viewing a painting titled *Impression: Sunrise*, referred to all the paintings as "impressionistic." The name stuck and continued to be used to identify paintings done in this new style.

This style, **Impressionism**, is *a style that attempted to capture the rapidly changing effects of light on objects*. Members of the Impressionist movement left their studios to paint outdoors. They looked at life around them and found subjects everywhere they looked. They painted landscapes and street scenes; they even set up their easels in cafes.

Claude Monet

The painting that gave Impressionism its name was the work of one of the movement's founders, Claude Monet (**klohd** moh-**nay**). Imagine Monet as he prepares to paint the landscape in Figure 14–5. He notes how the sunlight flickers on the gently swaying flowers. He notices how it reflects on rippling waters and glows through gray clouds. He observes, too, how the strongest sunlight blurs forms and blots out details. Now, taking brush in hand, he applies small dabs and dashes of paint to his canvas. He works quickly, trying to capture the effect of sunlight on every object. Each stroke of paint is a little different from the next in hue, value, and intensity. Monet knows the yellows and blues he is using will play against each other in the viewer's eye. They will give the painting a sparkle and brilliance to match that of the sun. Where does the artist use different values of yellow in the work? Where does he use different values of blue?

Auguste Renoir

One of the most productive of the Impressionists was a man named Pierre Auguste Renoir (pee-**ehr** oh-**goost** ren-**wahr**). Another of the movement's founders, Renoir painted right up to the day he died.

An area of painting Renoir explored using the Impressionist style was portraits. He was especially attracted to the eyes of his subject and often made these the focus of attention. Look at the portrait in Figure 14–6. The eyes, you will notice, are painted in sharp focus. The rest of the figure, meanwhile, is blurred. Renoir knew that when we look at a person or object, not all parts appear in focus at once. Only the part where our eyes rest at a given moment is seen sharply. Everything else appears fuzzy and slightly out of focus.

▲ **Figure 14–6** The eyes in this work look right out at you. Even when you glance at other parts of the painting, your attention is always attracted back to the eyes.

Auguste Renoir. *Madame Henriot.* c. 1876. Canvas. 65.9 x 49.8 cm (26 x 19⅝"). National Gallery of Art, Washington, D.C. Gift of Adele R. Levy Fund, Inc.

▶ **Figure 14–7** The artist has painted her sister. How might it be harder to paint a portrait of someone you know? In what ways might it be easier?

Berthe Morisot. *The Artist's Sister at a Window.* 1869. Canvas. 54.8 x 46.3 cm (21⅝ x 18¼"). National Gallery of Art, Washington, D.C. Ailsa Mellon Bruce Collection.

Berthe Morisot

Another important member of the Impressionist movement, Berthe Morisot (**behrt** maw-ree-**zoh**), had strong family ties to art. Her great-grandfather, Jean Honoré Fragonard (**zhahnh** oh-nor-**ay** frah-goh-**nahrh**), was an important painter of the Rococo period. Her parents solidly supported her decision to follow a career as an artist. Like Renoir, Morisot chose portraits as a main avenue of expression for her work. One of these is pictured in Figure 14–7. Notice how the artist uses rapidly applied dabs of paint to capture her subject's expression. What mood does the artist communicate in this painting?

SCULPTURE

A sculptor working during the same time as the Impressionist movement was a man named Auguste Rodin (oh-**goost** roh-**dan**). Rodin used bits of wax or clay in his creations. Their rough, bumpy surfaces make his sculptures appear as though in a flickering light. Examine Rodin's work in Figure 14–8. Note how the sculpture looks as if it were created in an instant.

▲ Figure 14–8   This is a sculpture of a painter from the seventeenth century named Claude Lorrain. How has Rodin shown the artist at work here?

Auguste Rodin. *Claude Lorrain*. Musee Rodin. Paris, France.

▲ Figure 14–9   Student work. Object painted in Impressionist style.

STUDIO EXPERIENCE

Pick a familiar object. Working lightly in pencil, draw the object large enough to fill a sheet of paper 9 x 12 inches (23 x 30 cm). Decide what part of the drawing is to be the center of interest. Add more detail to this area. Use short strokes of crayon, chalk, or paint to add color to the drawing. Make the center of interest stand out by coloring it carefully using your brightest hues. Make the colors duller the farther you get from the center of interest. (See Figure 14–9.)

✔ **CHECK YOUR UNDERSTANDING**

1. What was the Salon? How was the Salon tied to the beginning of the Impressionist movement?
2. What are some of the ways people reacted at the first showing of Impressionist works in 1874?
3. What did the Impressionists try to capture in their pictures? Where did they go to find subjects for their work?
4. What sorts of paintings did Auguste Renoir and Berthe Morisot specialize in?
5. In what area of art did Auguste Rodin work? How did he give his works the look and feel of Impressionist paintings?

Painting an Impressionist Landscape

Impressionist artists, you have learned, were interested in painting everyday scenes they saw around them. To Claude Monet, in particular, it made little difference whether he was painting a haystack, a few ordinary trees, or—as in Figure 14–10—a bridge. What mattered was how best to show the colors reflected from these subjects. Study the painting in Figure 14–10. Up close the picture appears to be little more than dabs of color.

WHAT YOU WILL LEARN

Use tempera to paint a summer landscape. You will use a variety of colors, values, and intensities, applying these as dots of paint.

Warm colors—yellows, reds, oranges—will be used to paint foreground objects. Cool colors—blues, purples, greens—will be used for background objects. Together these colors will be used to create an illusion of space. (See Figure 14–11.)

WHAT YOU WILL NEED

- Pencil and sheets of sketch paper
- Sheet of white paper, 9 x 12 inches (23 x 30 cm)
- Several brushes, tempera paint, and mixing tray

▶ Figure 14–10 Monet painted 16 separate views of this bridge. The scenes show the bridge at all different times of day. Some, moreover, show the bridge during rain or heavy fog. What reason might the artist have had for making so many paintings of the same scene?

Claude Monet. *Waterloo Bridge.* 1903. Oil on canvas. 65.4 x 92.9 cm (25⅝ x 36½"). Worcester Art Museum, Worcester, Massachusetts.

WHAT YOU WILL DO

1. On a sheet of paper, list the different items that might be found in a landscape painting, such as a tree, stream, and valley. Pick three items from this list. Combine them in simple pencil sketches of warm, sunlit landscapes. Use the space technique of size to place some of the objects near to the viewer. Place others farther back. Draw only very light outlines or indications of your shapes.
2. Choose the best of your sketches. Draw it on the sheet of white paper. Fill the whole sheet with your drawing.
3. Without mixing colors, load a medium-pointed brush with a cool color of paint. Use dots and dabs of the brush to apply the paint to a background object. Pick a second cool hue that, when seen from a distance, will blend with the first to create a new hue. For example, dots of green placed next to dots of blue would create blue-green. Dots of complementary colors can be added to lessen or increase the intensity of the colors.
4. Use warm colors for foreground objects, applying paint in the same fashion. Stand back from your work from time to time. This will help you make sure the colors selected are blending as you expect them to.
5. When the paint is dry, display your work. View all the works, first from a distance, then close up.

▲ Figure 14–11 Student work. Impressionist landscape.

OTHER STUDIO IDEAS

- Using colored markers, create a winter landscape in the Impressionist style. Again, make a list of objects. This time, however, include those you might see on a winter's day. Think how you might go about showing the effects of sunlight on snow.

- • Using watercolors, paint a view of the bridge in Figure 14–10 as it might appear at night. Begin by sketching the lines of the bridge. Think about what might serve as a source of light in your painting. Be sure to apply your paint as dots and dashes of color.

BUILDING VOCABULARY

Number a sheet of paper from 1 to 6. After each number, write the term from the box that best matches each description below.

art movement	Neoclassic
Impressionism	Romanticism
landscape	Salon

1. An art style that borrowed from the early classical period of ancient Greece and Rome.
2. A style of art that found its subjects in the world of the dramatic and exotic.
3. A drawing or painting focusing on mountains, trees, or other natural scenery.
4. An annual exhibition of art.
5. A trend formed when a group of artists band together to create works of a single style.
6. A style that attempted to capture the rapidly changing effects of light on objects.

REVIEWING ART FACTS

Number a sheet of paper from 7 to 14. Answer each question in a complete sentence.

7. How did the French Revolution help give rise to a new art style? What was the name of this style?
8. Name an important painter of the Neoclassic school.
9. What events helped bring about the Romantic movement?
10. What sorts of themes are found in the paintings of Eugène Delacroix?
11. Why did Joseph M. W. Turner use glowing colors and blurred images in his works?
12. Name two artists whose works were turned down by the Salon. Tell what movement they went on to develop.
13. To what school of art did Berthe Morisot belong?
14. What is Auguste Rodin's special contribution to art?

THINKING ABOUT ART

On a sheet of paper, answer each question in a sentence or two.

1. **Analyze.** Imagine you lived in France during the 1800s. Which of the three art styles you learned about in this chapter would best fit your view of life? Explain your answer using information from the chapter.
2. **Compare and Contrast.** Look at the landscape paintings by Joseph M. W. Turner (Figure 14–3) and Claude Monet (Figure 14–5). In what ways are the two works alike in subject matter, composition, and content? In what ways are they different in these three areas?
3. **Summarize.** What prompted the Impressionists to decide to hold their own art show in 1874?
4. **Extend.** Berthe Morisot's paintings were ignored by critics during her lifetime. Why do you think this was so? How did her fellow Impressionists regard her?

MAKING ART CONNECTIONS

1. **Social Studies.** You are looking at the painting by Eugène Delacroix (Figure 14–2) with two friends. One notes that some of the figures seem to be in awkward poses. The other remarks that the artist "probably had problems drawing these figures." How would you reply?
2. **History.** Another art movement that took shape in the 1800s is one called Realism. In an encyclopedia or other library resource, learn about this movement. Find the names of key artists and what they were trying to show in their works. Share your findings with the class.

LOOKING AT THE DETAILS

The detail shown below is from Auguste Renoir's *Oarsmen at Chatou*. Study the detail and answer the following questions using complete sentences.

1. What gives this painting the "impression" of realism? What defines it as a painting done in the Impressionist style?
2. Look at the credit line. In what year was it painted? How would you describe clothing styles of this period?

3. Compare this detail to the complete work on page **208**. Does this look like the type of everyday scenes that Impressionist painters preferred? Explain your answer.
4. What time of the day do you think is shown in the painting? How is this effect created?

Auguste Renoir. *Oarsmen at Chatou*. 1879. Canvas. (Detail.) 81.3 x 100.3 cm (32 x 39½"). National Gallery of Art, Washington, D.C. Gift of Sam A. Lewisohn.

▲ **How do you think composition and content affect the mood of this painting by Degas? Do you think that the artist has expressed a sense of realism in this work?**

Edgar Degas. *Dancers Practicing at the Bar.* Date Unknown. Oil colors, mixed with turpentine, on canvas. 75.6 x 81.3 cm (29¾ x 32"). Metropolitan Museum of Art, New York, New York. H. O. Havemeyer Collection.

Art of the Late Nineteenth Century

To some artists working toward the end of the 1800s, Impressionism was the perfect means of self-expression. To others, the new style raised as many questions as it answered. These artists, who had been working as Impressionists, felt that something was missing from their pictures. Their own works struck them, for one reason or another, as "unfinished."

In time, this dissatisfaction led to still newer forms of expression. One is showcased in the work at the left. In this chapter you will learn about such efforts and the pioneers behind them.

OBJECTIVES

After completing this chapter, you will be able to:
- Identify the artists who became known as the Post-Impressionists.
- Describe different ways the Post-Impressionists tried to solve the problems of Impressionism.
- Name artists who affected the development of American art of the 1800s.
- Create art works in the style of the Post-Impressionists.

WORDS YOU WILL LEARN

arbitrary colors
optical colors
Pointillism

Post-Impressionism
Realism

ARTISTS YOU WILL MEET

Mary Cassatt
Paul Cézanne
Edgar Degas
Thomas Eakins
Paul Gauguin

Vincent van Gogh
Winslow Homer
Albert Pinkham Ryder
Georges Seurat
Henry O. Tanner

Art of the Post-Impressionists

Have you ever created something that pleased you at first but didn't seem right later? This was the case with several artists working toward the close of the 1800s. These artists worked as Impressionists but came to feel that there were problems with this style. The more they studied their art, the more dissatisfied they became. Art, they believed, should do more than just show the changing effects of light on objects. **Post-Impressionism** is *the name given to an art movement that appeared after the Impressionist movement.* The word *post* means "after."

▲ Figure 15–1   The artist repeated colors throughout this work to give it a sense of harmony. Can you find places where colors have been repeated?

Paul Cézanne. *Mont Sainte-Victoire.* 1902–04. Oil on canvas. 69.8 x 89.5 cm (27½ x 35¼").
Philadelphia Museum of Art, Philadelphia, Pennsylvania. George W. Elkins Collection.

In this lesson you will learn about the key artists of the Post-Impressionist movement. You will also look at the important contributions they made to the history of art.

POST-IMPRESSIONIST ART

While the Post-Impressionists agreed that there were problems with Impressionism, their solutions to these problems differed. Some argued that art should be more carefully designed — that composition should not be forgotten. Others claimed feelings and emotions should be emphasized — that content deserved its rightful place. Still others championed design and mood — both composition *and* content — as important features.

Composition

One of the Post-Impressionists was also, interestingly, an original member of the Impressionist movement. This artist's name was Paul Cézanne (say-**zan**). Cézanne objected to the loss of composition arising from the Impressionist blurring of shapes. His solution was to use patches of color. These he joined together like pieces of a puzzle to create solid-looking forms.

The painting in Figure 15–1 illustrates Cézanne's technique. This mountain near the artist's home in southern France was one of his favorite subjects. He painted it more than 60 times and from nearly every angle.

◀ **Figure 15–2 Besides their bright colors, van Gogh's paintings are known for their rich textures. He often squeezed his colors from the tubes right onto the canvas. He would then use his brush, fingers, or anything else at hand to spread the paint with swirling strokes.**

Vincent van Gogh. *Hospital at Saint-Remy.* 1889. The Armand Hammer Collection, Los Angeles, California.

▲ Figure 15–3   How many different objects draw attention to the figure on the left? How does the use of color help communicate the difference between the background and the main subject?

Paul Gauguin. *Ancestors of Tehamana*. 1893. Oil on canvas. 76.3 x 54.3 cm (30 x 21″). Art Institute of Chicago, Chicago, Illinois. Gift of Mr. and Mrs. Charles Deering McCormick.

Cézanne's main interest, however, was not showing the mountain as it really looked. It was to demonstrate how color patches could be turned in different directions to create a solid form. Notice how the artist uses the same color patches to form buildings, trees, and other objects. All are combined to create a richly colored pattern of geometric forms.

Content

The most famous of the Post-Impressionists was Vincent van Gogh (**goh**). Van Gogh's goal was not, like the Impressionists', to reproduce what the eye saw. It was to capture his own deepest feelings about a subject. He expresses these feelings with twisted lines and forms, intense colors, and rich textures.

Near the end of his short life, van Gogh suffered from mental illness. Hoping for a cure, he entered a private hospital. It was there that van Gogh painted the work in Figure 15–2 on page **227**. Take a moment to examine this picture. The artist treats the viewer to his private view of the world of the hospital. We see yellow walls and several small figures. But the twisting trees against a blue sky are the true focus of the painting. Through them, the artist communicates his mental agony and his sensitivity to the forces of nature. What principle of art is used to organize the curving lines of the trees?

Composition and Content

Paul Gauguin (goh-**ganh**) also used color and shapes in new and exciting ways. He also created art works that could be enjoyed for their decorative appearance.

The painting in Figure 15–3 shows a scene in the South Seas, where Gauguin spent part of his life. The artist has portrayed his wife against a decorated background. The painting has two parts, a portrait and a scene from the past. The composition hints at the relationship between past and present. Notice how the fan points to the small figure painted on the wall. Like most of Gauguin's other works, this one is filled with meaningful colors. **Arbitrary (ahr**-buh-trehr-ee)

colors are *colors chosen to communicate different feelings*. **Optical colors**, on the other hand, are *colors viewers actually see*. What feelings do you associate with each of the different colors in Gauguin's painting?

CHECK YOUR UNDERSTANDING

1. Define *Post-Impressionism*. Name two leading Post-Impressionists.
2. What were three different solutions Post-Impressionists found to the problems of Impressionism?
3. What was Cézanne's goal? What was van Gogh's goal?
4. What is arbitrary color? Which two Post-Impressionists used arbitrary color in their works?
5. What is optical color?

Painting in the Style of Post-Impressionists

The painting in Figure 15–4 shows yet another Post-Impressionist solution to the problems posed by Impressionism. The work is by an artist named Georges Seurat (**zhorzh** suh-**rah**). Like Cézanne, Seurat felt the Impressionists' attempt to show the blurring effect of sunlight on forms was misguided. Seurat's solution was to use *a technique in which small, carefully placed dots of color are used to create forms.* This technique, called **Pointillism** (**poynt**-uh-liz-uhm), reached its height in Seurat's painting of a sunny summer day in a park. When seen from close up, the picture looks like a grouping of tiny dots. When the viewer stands back, however, the picture totally changes. The dots seem to blend together to create new colors and clear shapes.

WHAT YOU WILL LEARN

You will create a painting in the style of Seurat or one of the other Post-Impressionists. Use color, line, shape, or texture in the manner of the artist you choose. (See Figure 15–5).

WHAT YOU WILL NEED

- Pencil
- Sheet of white paper, 9 x 12 inches (23 x 30 cm)
- Tempera paint, several brushes, and mixing tray

SAFETY TIP

When an assignment calls for paints, use watercolors, liquid tempera, or school acrylics.

▶ **Figure 15–4** This large painting is the artist's best known work. Thousands of colored dots are arranged with great precision to create the simple forms you see. Why do you suppose the artist made the work as large as he did? What kind of mood does it communicate to you?

Georges Seurat. *Sunday Afternoon on the Island of La Grande Jatte.* 1884–86. Oil on canvas. 207.6 x 308 cm (81½ x 121¼"). Art Institute of Chicago, Chicago, Illinois. Helen Birch Bartlett Memorial Collection.

WHAT YOU WILL DO

1. Look once again at the paintings in Figures 15–2, 15–3, and 15–4. With classmates, discuss the main features of each artist's style.
2. Look through the pages of a magazine or newspaper. Look for a black-and-white illustration that has an interesting design or communicates a mood.
3. Using pencil, lightly redo the illustration on the sheet of white paper. Make your drawing large enough to fill the whole sheet. Keep the shapes in your drawing simple. Do not include details.
4. Finish and paint your work using one of the following styles: (a) With a fine-tipped brush, cover your drawing with closely spaced tiny dots of paint. Use colors opposite each other on the color wheel to create new hues and intensities. In this way, your work will resemble the Pointillist style of Seurat. (b) With a medium brush, apply paint in a swirling motion, creating twisted lines and shapes. Use bright, arbitrary colors to express a certain mood or feeling. In this way, your work will look like that of van Gogh. (c) Paint your drawing as a pattern of flat, colorful shapes. Paint dark outlines around these shapes. This will give your painting the same decorative look as Gauguin's.
5. When the paint is dry, display your work alongside those of classmates. See whether you can identify the Post-Impressionist style in the works of your fellow students.

EXAMINING YOUR WORK

- **Describe**   Hold your painting next to the illustration on which it is based. Tell whether you can identify the objects in the illustration.
- **Analyze**   Explain how you used color, line, shape, and texture. Tell which Post-Impressionist artist you used as a guide in using these elements. Point to places in your work where your use of elements was similar to that of your chosen artist.
- **Interpret**   State what mood or feeling, if any, you were attempting to express. Note whether others are able to pinpoint this mood or feeling.
- **Judge**   Compare your work with that of the artist who served as your guide. Tell whether your painting is similar in style to that work. Show in what ways, if any, your work is different.

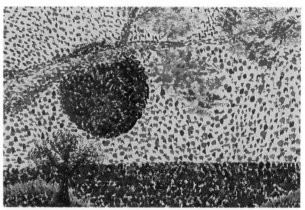

▲ Figure 15–5   Student work. Post-Impressionist painting.

OTHER STUDIO IDEAS

- Make another painting in the Post-Impressionist style, this time in the style of Cézanne. Base your painting on a familiar scene in your community or town. Use two hues of paint. Make sure to turn your color patches in different directions.

- ●● Complete a painting in which you combine Seurat's Pointillism style with van Gogh's concern for expressing emotions and feelings. When you are finished, tell whether you think the Pointillism style is an effective one to use when you are trying to express emotions. Explain why or why not.

American Painting in the Late 1800s

The 1800s was a period of great change and growth in the United States. The country grew in size as pioneers and the railroad pushed westward. It grew in wealth as trade and industry boomed. By the end of the century, America had taken its place as a world power. It had also emerged as a force to be reckoned with in the world of art.

In this lesson you will read about the artists who helped put America on the map.

AMERICAN REALIST ART

During the 1800s many American artists journeyed to the art centers of Europe to study. Some were greatly influenced by the art styles they encountered. Others were mainly unaffected by European art movements. They came home to develop styles that were unmistakably American. One of these was an artist named Thomas Eakins (**ay**-kuhnz).

▲ Figure 15–6   Everything in this picture is made to look real. The artist even included himself in the picture. He is the person in the center holding the oars.

Thomas Eakins. *Max Schmitt in a Single Scull (The Champion Single Sculls).* 1871. Oil on canvas. 81.9 x 117.5 cm (32¼ x 46¼"). The Metropolitan Museum of Art, New York, New York. Alfred N. Punnett Endowment Fund and George D. Pratt Gift.

▲ **Figure 15–7** Paintings like this capture the look and mood of the sea. With a little imagination, you can hear the roaring surf crashing against a rocky shore.

Winslow Homer. *Northeaster.* 1895. Oil on canvas. 87.4 x 127.6 cm (34⅜ x 50¼"). The Metropolitan Museum of Art, New York, New York. Gift of George A. Hearn.

Eakins, who painted only what he saw, is held to be one of America's first Realists. Realism was a movement that had its start in France in the mid-1800s. **Realism** is *a style of art in which everyday scenes and events are painted as they actually look.* Eakins, for example, stubbornly refused to show his subjects in a flattering light. As a result, he was scorned throughout his lifetime. His painting of a man in a racing boat in Figure 15–6 reveals Eakins's devotion to realism. The picture tells no story; it holds no suspense. What it does is offer a carefully studied and designed record of a simple scene that the artist witnessed. Note the care the artist took in painting even the reflections in the water.

Another artist who, like Eakins, painted exactly what he saw, was Winslow Homer.

Unlike Eakins, Homer painted pictures that often told stories, usually of people in the midst of some outdoor activity, such as hunting, fishing, or sailing.

Late in the 1880s Homer set up a studio on a rocky stretch of the Maine coast. There he painted scenes of the sea. At first his pictures were of action-filled struggles between nature and seafaring people. As time went on, the people in his works shrank in importance. His paintings began to focus instead on the power of the sea in its many moods. The work pictured in Figure 15–7 is from this later period. How would you describe the mood of the sea in this painting? What elements and principles of art help communicate this mood?

◀ Figure 15–8   Light is important in the artist's paintings. He often showed the source of light in the form of the sun or, as here, the moon.

Albert Pinkham Ryder. *Moonlight Marine (Toilers of the Sea)*. c. 1885. Oil on wood panel. 28.9 x 30.5 cm (11⅜ x 12″). The Metropolitan Museum of Art, New York, New York.

▶ Figure 15–9   Notice the looseness of the brush strokes. Does this take away from the impression of detail?

Mary Cassatt. *Sewing Woman*. c. 1880–1882. Oil on canvas. 92 x 63 cm (36 x 25″). Musee d' Orsay, Paris.

Portraying Realism

Two other artists who affected the development of American art in the 1800s were a colorful figure by the name of Albert Pinkham Ryder and Mary Cassatt.

A loner who paid little attention to the work of others, Ryder painted dreamlike images, often borrowed from literature. His style made use of large areas of color and thick layers of paint. The painting by him in Figure 15–8 shows the simple silhouette of a ship beneath a ghostly moon. The vessel seems to glide silently across the water, carrying its crew into a night filled with mystery and wonder.

Mary Cassatt, an American who studied at the Pennsylvania Academy of Fine Arts, went on to Paris for further training. There she met Degas and was influenced by his Impressionist paintings. She often chose women and children as her subjects, using the Impressionist play of light to enhance the gentle mood she created. Her work in Figure 15–9 shows why she is considered to be one of America's finest women painters.

STUDIO EXPERIENCE

One element that helps viewers sense the mood of the work in Figure 15–8 is texture. Look again at the painting. Notice how the sky and sea both appear alive, although in different ways.

Working lightly in pencil, sketch a nighttime landscape. Include trees, a lake, and the moon. Make your drawing large enough to fill a large sheet of paper. Switching to crayon, trace over all the pencil lines, pressing hard. Place a sheet of burlap beneath your paper. Using the side of an unwrapped crayon, rub over the sky in your drawing. Replace the burlap with bits of dried grass and leaves. Rub the crayon over the lake in your work. Examine the results. Use other materials with rough surfaces as a base for rubbing the remaining forms in your work. (For further information on rubbings, see Technique Tip **25**, *Handbook* page **286**.)

✔CHECK YOUR UNDERSTANDING

1. What is Realism?
2. Why were the works of Thomas Eakins shunned during his lifetime?
3. What were favorite subjects of Winslow Homer?
4. Name four artists who affected the development of American art in the 1800s.
5. What kinds of works did Albert Pinkham Ryder create? Where did he get the ideas for his works?

LESSON 4

Making an Expressive Watercolor Painting

Henry Tanner was a former student of Thomas Eakins and one of America's most talented black artists. Because his paintings did not sell in America, Tanner decided to move to Europe. Settling in Paris, he painted scenes from the Bible, which were well received. After one of his paintings was accepted in the Paris Salon, a highly respected French artist insisted that it be hung in a place of honor.

Although better known for his religious pictures, some of Tanner's best works were portraits and outdoor scenes. One of his scenes can be viewed in Figure 15–10. Notice the low-intensity hues, contrasting light and dark values, and fuzzy shapes in this painting. What kind of mood does Tanner create with these hues, values, and shapes?

WHAT YOU WILL LEARN

You will use watercolor paint to create your own expressive scene. Your scene will exhibit the same low-intensity hues, contrasting dark and light values, and fuzzy shapes found in Tanner's painting. Your painting will also express the same quiet stillness. (See Figure 15–11.)

▶ **Figure 15–10** The artist's interest in art was born when, as a child, he watched an artist at work in a park.

Henry O. Tanner. *The Seine*. 1902. Canvas. 23 x 32.9 cm (9 x 13"). National Gallery of Art, Washington, D.C. Gift of the Avalon Foundation.

WHAT YOU WILL NEED

- Container of water
- Sheet of white paper, 9 x 12 inches (23 x 30 cm)
- Watercolor paint and several brushes
- Tempera paint in different hues
- Pen and India ink

WHAT YOU WILL DO

1. With water, completely wet the sheet of white paper.
2. Load a medium-pointed brush with a light color paint, and apply this carefully to the damp paper. The area painted might represent a lake or river. Add other areas of light colors to suggest sky and clouds.
3. Use the same technique to add dark shapes to your paper. These could suggest the shoreline, distant rooftops, boats, a bridge, or other objects. Do not worry about details. Concern yourself with creating areas of color with different dark values.
4. While your picture is drying, study it carefully. Use your imagination to identify the general outlines of the different objects.
5. When your painting is dry, use a pen and India ink to outline the objects. Add details.
6. Use white paint to create highlights and additional details.

- **Describe** Identify the different objects in your scene. Name the hues you used.
- **Analyze** Point out the low-intensity hues, contrasting light and dark values, and fuzzy shapes.
- **Interpret** Explain how your work expresses a quiet, still mood.
- **Judge** Compare your work with that of Tanner. Tell how your picture is similar in content and composition. Point out the differences.

▲ **Figure 15–11 Student work. Expressive watercolor painting.**

OTHER STUDIO IDEAS

- Make another watercolor painting of the same outdoor scene. This time use high-intensity hues instead of low-intensity ones. Compare this second painting with the first. How does the use of high-intensity hues change the mood of the picture?

- ●● With colored chalk, create a picture of a different outdoor scene. Add a sense of space to your picture by using low-intensity hues to color background objects and high-intensity hues to color foreground objects.

CHAPTER 15 REVIEW

BUILDING VOCABULARY

Number a sheet of paper from 1 to 5. After each number, write the term from the box that best matches each description below.

arbitrary colors	Post-
optical colors	Impressionism
Pointillism	Realism

1. An art movement that appeared after the Impressionists.
2. Colors viewers actually see.
3. Colors chosen to communicate different feelings.
4. A technique in which small, carefully placed dots of color are used to create forms.
5. A style of art in which everyday scenes and events are painted as they actually look.

REVIEWING ART FACTS

Number a sheet of paper from 6 to 15. Answer each question in a complete sentence.

6. Name two problems and solutions some artists of the later 1800s found in the Impressionist style.
7. Which Post-Impressionist artist was a former Impressionist?
8. Which artist besides Cézanne was interested in making the forms in his paintings clearer and more solid-looking?
9. Which Post-Impressionist besides Gauguin used arbitrary colors in his works?
10. What painter filled his works with tiny dots of color? Why did he do this?
11. What was there about his works that made Eakins unpopular during his lifetime?
12. How did Homer's paintings change from his early to his later years in Maine?
13. Which two American artists of the late 1800s often painted pictures of the sea?
14. Name the artists who affected the development of American art in the 1800s.
15. Describe Ryder's painting techniques.

THINKING ABOUT ART

On a sheet of paper, answer each question in a sentence or two.

1. **Analyze.** Paul Cézanne claimed that all forms in nature are based on three forms: the sphere, the cone, and the cylinder. Examine his painting in Figure 15–1. Tell how his work supports this idea.
2. **Extend.** Like Claude Monet, Cézanne painted the same subject again and again. Explain his reasons for doing so.
3. **Compare and contrast.** Acting as a critic, interpret the works by Albert Pinkham Ryder (Figure 15–8) and Thomas Eakins (Figure 15–6). Tell how the two interpretations differ. Tell how they are alike.

MAKING ART CONNECTIONS

1. **Language Arts.** You are at a museum standing before the painting by Georges Seurat shown in Figure 15–4. As you are looking at the canvas, you overhear a viewer say, "Why, this painting is nothing but dots! Anyone can paint dots." What information could you give that would help the viewer better appreciate the work? What advice might you give?
2. **History.** Imagine you lived in America during the 1800s. Using history and literature books for reference, write a short report on what life would have been like for a teen growing up in this time. List some of the historical and social events that would shape your life.

LOOKING AT THE DETAILS

The detail shown below is from Edgar De-gas' *Dancers Practicing at the Bar.* Study the detail and answer the following questions using complete sentences.

1. What similarities to the Impressionist style do you see in this work? What differences do you see?
2. Where is the emphasis in this detail? Look at the entire work on page **224**. Has the emphasis changed? Explain your answer.

3. Look at the entire work on page **224**. Do you think Degas emphasized composition, content, or both? Explain your answer.
4. Both van Gogh and Degas are considered Post-Impressionist painters. Compare this work with Figure 15–2 on page **227**. What do the two works have in common? How are they different?

Edgar Degas. *Dancers Practicing at the Bar.* Date Unknown. Oil colors, mixed with turpentine, on canvas. (Detail.) 75.6 x 81.3 cm (29¾ x 32"). Metropolitan Museum of Art, New York, New York. H. O. Havemeyer Collection.

▲ Wassily Kandinsky's work was characterized by a sense of color and pattern. He experimented freely with established methods until he developed a new and exciting style to express feeling in his works.

Wassily Kandinsky. *Painting Number 200*. 1914. Oil on canvas. 162.5 x 80 cm (64 x 31½"). Museum of Modern Art, New York, New York. Mrs. Simon Guggenheim Fund.

CHAPTER 16

Art of the Early Twentieth Century

Art has the power to delight. Art has the power to teach. Art also has the power, as history has shown time and again, to shock. No style throughout art's long history shocked viewers more than the one highlighted in the painting at the left. This style, which developed early in the twentieth century, came about purely by accident. Do you know the name of this style? Can you identify its main features? In the pages that follow you will learn the answers to these and other questions.

OBJECTIVES

After completing this chapter, you will be able to:
- Identify the major art movements of the early twentieth century.
- Name the leaders of those movements.
- Describe art trends in the United States and Mexico in the early twentieth century.
- Use the elements and principles of art in the style of the Cubists.
- Create an art work showing rhythm and movement.

WORDS YOU WILL LEARN

Ashcan School
Cubism
The Eight
Expressionism

Fauvism
muralist
non-objective art
Regionalism

ARTISTS YOU WILL MEET

George Bellows
Georges Braque
John Steuart Curry
Wassily Kandinsky
Ernst Ludwig
   Kirchner

Käthe Kollwitz
Jacques Lipchitz
Henri Matisse
Diego Rivera
John Sloan
Alfred Stieglitz

Art of the Early Twentieth Century in Europe

Every age, it has been said, learns from and builds on the one before it. The truth of these words is clear from developments in art in the early 1900s. Several new styles came along, each borrowing in a different way from Post-Impressionism. These styles, which stunned the art world, continue to affect art through the present day. In this lesson you will learn about the pioneers behind these innovative ways of making art.

FAUVISM

In 1905 a showing by a group of French artists started the art community buzzing. The most striking feature of the works in the show was their raw, sizzling colors. No effort had been made to paint realistic pictures. The artists' goal was to express their feelings through sharply contrasting colors and heavy outlines. One angry critic wrote that the paintings looked as though they had

▶ **Figure 16–1** Describe the lines in this painting. How have the elements been used to give the work a sense of oneness?

Henri Matisse. *The Red Studio*. Issy-les-Moulineaux. 1911. Oil on canvas. 181 x 219.1 cm (71¼ x 86¼"). Museum of Modern Art, New York, New York. Mrs. Simon Guggenheim Fund.

been done by *fauves* (**fohvs**). This term, which is French for "wild beasts," gave the movement its name: Fauvism (**fohv**-iz-uhm). **Fauvism** is *an art movement in which artists used wild, intense color combinations in their paintings.*

The leader of the Fauves was a law student who chose to become an artist. His name was Henri Matisse (ahnh-**ree** mah-**tees**). For his paintings, Matisse chose colors that communicated a joyous or happy mood. He then combined them, as in the picture in Figure 16–1, to create rich, decorative patterns. To understand the importance of color in Matisse's works, try to imagine Figure 16–1 in black and white. In what way would the painting be different? How would its mood change?

EXPRESSIONISM

Matisse and the Fauves wanted to show feelings in their art. In Germany the same goal was shared by another group of artists, who developed a movement known as Expressionism (ek-**spresh**-uh-niz-uhm). Artists using **Expressionism** worked in *a style that emphasized the expression of innermost feelings.* They ignored the contemporary rules of art. They had the strength to experiment with, to exaggerate, and in other ways to change, the proportions of figures and objects.

Painting

An early leader of the Expressionist movement was an artist named Ernst Ludwig Kirchner (**ehrnst lood**-vig **keerk**-nuhr). Figure 16–2 shows Kirchner's inner view of a street scene. Note his use of brilliant, clashing colors and sharp, twisted shapes. The people in Kirchner's world are crammed together in a small space. Yet they manage not to notice one another. How might you sum up the artist's feelings toward these people and their world?

▲ **Figure 16–2** The artist has used twisted shapes to express his emotions. An earlier artist you read about did the same thing. Do you recall that artist's name?

Ernst Ludwig Kirchner. *Street, Berlin.* 1913. Oil on canvas. 120.6 x 91.1 cm (47½ x 35⅞"). Museum of Modern Art, New York, New York.

Printmaking

The power of Expressionism can also be seen in the prints and drawings of Käthe Kollwitz (**kay**-tuh **kohl**-wits). At a time when most artists were exploring color, Kollwitz created works mainly in black and white. Many, like the print in Figure 16–3, focus on the ills of working-class life. Can you identify the emotions on the faces of these people?

CUBISM

Paul Cézanne, you will remember, was interested in showing objects as solid-looking forms. A guiding idea behind Cubism was Cézanne's notion that all forms in nature are made up of three shapes. Those three are the sphere, cone, and cylinder. This idea led to the development of **Cubism**, *a style in which objects are shown from several different angles at once.*

▲ **Figure 16–3** This was from a series of prints showing an angry German peasant revolt in the 1500s. What might the artist's choice of subject tell us about events in her own time?

Käthe Kollwitz. *The Prisoners.* 1908. Etchings. Library of Congress, Washington, D.C.

Painting

The founder of Cubism was an artist you have met before in this book. Even if you had not met him here, his name is one you would instantly recognize. It is Pablo Picasso.

Picasso's early Cubist paintings were different arrangements of bits and pieces of his subject viewed from different angles. The subjects of these works are at times difficult to pick out. Later he began using brighter colors and larger shapes in his works. He also added texture and pattern, often by gluing found objects to his paintings. The picture in Figure 3–7 on page **42** is one of Picasso's later Cubist works. Are you able to identify the objects in this picture?

Sculpture

The Cubist style also found its way into sculpture of the early twentieth century. Jacques Lipchitz (**zhahk lip**-shuts), a Lithuanian-born sculptor who studied in Paris, used Cubism in his bronze castings. One of these works is pictured in Figure 16–4. Notice how the many fragments of a figure add up to a carefully designed three-dimensional whole. How has the artist used texture to give the work a sense of harmony?

▲ **Figure 16–4** What has the artist done to create different light and dark values? Can you point to places where a variety of lines and forms is used?

Jacques Lipchitz. *Bather*. 1923–25. Bronze. 198.5 x 79.1 x 70.5 cm (78⅛ x 31⅛ x 27¾"). Dallas Museum of Art, Dallas, Texas. Gift of Mr. & Mrs. Algur H. Meadows and the Meadows Foundation, Inc.

NON-OBJECTIVE ART

One evening in 1910 after painting outdoors all day, a weary artist returned to his studio. There he was greeted by a surprise that changed the course of art history. Perched on his easel was a painting unlike anything he had ever seen. Its brightly colored shapes and lines seemed to glow and shimmer in the dim light. Rushing to the canvas, the artist had his second surprise of the night. The work was his own; he had carelessly placed it upside down on the easel! The artist's name was Wassily Kandinsky (**vahs**-uh-lee kuhn-**din**-skee). His discovery led to the birth of a new style called **non-objective art**. These are *works in which no objects or subjects can be readily identified.*

In the experiments that followed, Kandinsky found he could express feelings using only colors, shapes, and lines. These elements could be arranged, just as the notes of a song are, to create a mood. Look at the painting that opens this chapter on page **240**. Imagine the colors, shapes, and lines to be musical notes. What kind of tune do these elements seem to play? Do they play a loud and brassy melody, or a soft and mellow one?

✔ CHECK YOUR UNDERSTANDING

1. What is Fauvism? Who was the leader of the Fauves?
2. What is Expressionism? In what way did the Expressionists ignore the rules of art?
3. To what movement did the artist Käthe Kollwitz belong? What media did she favor?
4. Define *Cubism*. Name the Post-Impressionist artist whose ideas influenced the Cubist movement.
5. Tell in what area of art Jacques Lipchitz worked. By what art movement was he influenced?
6. Tell how non-objective art got its start. Name the originator of the movement.

Making a Cubist Chalk Drawing

A co-founder of the Cubist movement was an artist named Georges Braque (**zhorzh brahk**). A favorite form of expression for Braque was the still life. Instead of fruits or flowers, he usually chose household objects as subjects. Figure 16–5 shows one of his still lifes. Notice how the table, other objects, and background are combined to make a flat, decorative design. All parts of the work are equally interesting to look at. The different colors, shapes, lines, and textures are organized into an interesting whole.

In this lesson you will use the elements and principles of art in the same way.

WHAT YOU WILL LEARN

You will create a still life with chalk in the later style of the Cubists. You will repeat colors, shapes, lines, and textures to make a flat, decorative pattern. Your pattern will fill the paper. A warm or cool color scheme will be used to add harmony and express a mood. (See Figure 16–6.)

WHAT YOU WILL NEED

- Pencil and sheets of sketch paper
- Sheet of white paper, 18 x 24 inches (46 x 60 cm)
- Colored chalk and spray fixative
- Sheets of facial tissue

▶ **Figure 16–5** How many different objects can you identify? What other objects could be used to make an interesting still life? Describe the different textures. How has the artist added unity to this design?

Georges Braque. *Still Life: Le Jour.* 1929. Canvas. 150 x 146.7 cm (45¼ x 57¾"). National Gallery of Art, Washington, D.C. Chester Dale Collection.

WHAT YOU WILL DO

1. Bring to class an object with an interesting shape. Some possibilities are an old violin or guitar, an oddly shaped bottle, or a house plant. Working with three other students, arrange the objects on a tabletop. Each student should have a clear view of the objects.

2. Make several rough pencil sketches for a still life. You may exaggerate or in other ways change shapes and lines for added interest. Shapes should be shown as simple, flat planes. Repeat the lines of the objects in the background areas.

3. Working lightly in chalk, transfer your best sketch to the sheet of white paper. Fill the whole sheet with your design.

4. Choose four or five sticks of chalk to create either a warm or cool color scheme. As you choose, keep in mind the mood you want your work to communicate.

5. Color your still life. Color some shapes by blending two or more hues with facial tissue. Repeat colors throughout the picture to add harmony. Make some shapes stand out clearly by adding heavy contour lines. Use the chalk to create different textures in some shapes.

6. Spray your still life with fixative. Compare it with the one in Figure 16–5 and those by other students.

EXAMINING YOUR WORK

- **Describe** Point to and name the different objects in your picture. Explain how and why you changed the shapes and lines of those objects.
- **Analyze** Point out places where you have repeated colors, shapes, and lines. Explain how these elements have been used to create a flat, decorative pattern. Tell whether your design fills the whole sheet of paper.
- **Interpret** Tell how the warm or cool color scheme adds a mood to your work. Identify this mood.
- **Judge** Tell whether you feel your work succeeds. Explain your answer.

▲ **Figure 16–6 Student work. Cubist chalk drawing.**

OTHER STUDIO IDEAS

- Make another still life, this time using a different color scheme. Some possibilities are split complementary or analogous colors. (See the color wheel on page **2**.)

- ● Make another still life, this time using India ink thinned with water. Using a pen, create different shades of gray. Leave some shapes white for contrast. Use different parts of the pen point to add texture and contour lines.

Art of the Early Twentieth Century in America

In the early twentieth century the pace of life quickened in the United States. The airplane, assembly line, and telephone were all part of a new fascination with speed. A search for new formulas in American art mirrored the restlessness of the age. In this lesson you will learn about the most important of the new art movements. You will also learn about developments in the art of Mexico.

THE ASHCAN SCHOOL

As the 1800s gave way to the 1900s, the important names in American art remained unchanged. Homer, Eakins, and Ryder continued on as the unchallenged leaders. In New York a group of lesser-known painters felt a change was overdue. Since there were eight members in all, they called themselves, simply, **The Eight**. This was a *group of artists who created art work that reflected the spirit of the times in which they lived, the early 1900s.*

The members of The Eight were all one-time newspaper cartoonists or magazine illustrators. These experiences influenced their choice of subjects for their paintings. Their works drew on images from everyday life in the big city. These pictures of crowded city streets, dark alleys, and gray slums were recorded in a no-nonsense, realistic style. When The Eight held their first public showing in 1908, viewers politely examined their works. Then they laughed. A more fitting name for these chroniclers of working-class American life, some decided, was the **Ashcan School**. This became *the popular name given to the group of artists who made realistic paintings of working-class America.*

Painting

One of the most talented members of the Ashcan School was John Sloan. His pictures capture the color, movement, and humor of big-city life. Look at the painting by Sloan in Figure 16–7. The hairdresser in the picture goes about her business with hardly a care. Below, meanwhile, passersby stop and stare as if witnessing an important event. Locate the girls at the bottom of the picture. One, you will notice, seems to be talking excitedly. What do you suppose she is saying?

▲ Figure 16–7 What has the artist done to emphasize the figures in the second-story window? How has movement been introduced?

John Sloan. *Hairdresser's Window.* 1907. Oil on canvas. 81 x 66 cm (31⅞ x 26"). Wadsworth Atheneum, Hartford, Connecticut. Ella Gallup Sumner and Mary Catlin Sumner Collection.

An artist who was closely tied to the Ashcan School, though not one of The Eight, was George Bellows. His painting in Figure 16–8 is of one of his favorite subjects, a prizefight. The work shows two boxers clashing furiously at center ring while onlookers cheer them on. Study the faces of the crowd. The quick, slashing brush strokes with which they are captured match the action in the ring.

Photography

The Ashcan painters were not alone in using city scenes as subjects for art. The same look and feel was achieved in the works of artist Alfred Stieglitz (**steeg**-luhts). Stieglitz played an important part in the early development of photography as a new art form. Examine his photograph in Figure 16–9. What details in the work reveal it to be of a bitterly cold winter day? What mood does the picture communicate?

REGIONALISM

After World War I a different brand of realistic art enjoyed brief popularity in the United States. Several artists used a style that became known as **Regionalism** (**reej**-uhn-uhl-iz-uhm) to record *local scenes and events from the artist's own region, or area, of the country.*

An example of the Regionalist style may be found in Figure 16–10. The artist of the work, John Steuart Curry (**stoo**-urt **ker**-ee), was a native of Kansas. In this painting he shows a preacher about to baptize, or spiritually cleanse, a young girl. The setting is a Kansas farm. Relatives and friends have gathered to witness this ritual of passage. They all look at the preacher and girl, automatically directing the viewer's eyes there. The legs of a windmill point to the scene as well as to the glowing clouds in the sky.

ART IN MEXICO

The early twentieth century was a time of unrest and revolution in Mexico. Hardworking peasants, treated like slaves by rich landlords, struggled to free themselves. Several artists witnessed the struggle. They used their art to lend their support to the people. One who did so was Mexico's foremost muralist (**myoor**-uh-luhst). A **muralist** is *an artist who paints large art works directly onto walls or ceilings.* His name was Diego Rivera (dee-**ay**-goh rih-**vehr**-uh). In the mural in Figure 16–11, the artist tells of the only true escape for the poor: death. Several soldiers of the common people kneel around one of their own who has fallen in battle. In the distance flames rise from the landlord's house; the peasant's death has already been avenged.

CHECK YOUR UNDERSTANDING

1. Who were The Eight? What were their backgrounds as artists? What kinds of paintings did they create?
2. When did The Eight stage their first showing? How did the public react? What nickname were The Eight given?
3. What art form was the specialty of Alfred Stieglitz?
4. What style of art became popular after World War I? Name an artist who created works in this style.
5. What is a muralist? Who was Mexico's foremost muralist?
6. What theme appears in the work of Diego Rivera?

STUDIO EXPERIENCE

Look again at Figure 16–11. The work, you will notice, is both abstract and expressive.

Choose one of the following words: *war*, *hunger*, *anger*. Look through magazines, tearing out pages showing objects that capture the idea of this word. Using pencil and tracing paper, carefully transfer the images you have found to a sheet of paper. Overlap the drawings to create an abstract effect. Use India ink to create contrasts of light and dark shapes. Display your work. Ask classmates to guess which word you used as the theme of your work.

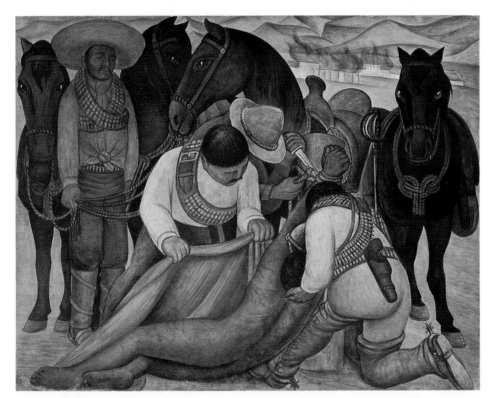

◀ **Figure 16–11** Describe the way in which these soldiers care for the dead. What feelings do you think this painting stirred up in Mexican viewers of the artist's day?

Diego Rivera. *Liberation of the Peon*. 1931. Fresco on plaster. 187.9 x 241.3 cm (74 x 95"). Philadelphia Museum of Art, Philadelphia, Pennsylvania. Gift of Mr. & Mrs. Herbert Cameron Morris.

Making a Print of a Figure in Action

Figure 16–12 shows another action scene by George Bellows. This is one of six paintings the artist made on the subject of prizefights. He also made many prints and countless drawings. Here, as elsewhere, he uses slashing diagonal lines to show movement. In this lesson you will do the same.

WHAT YOU WILL LEARN

You will overlap a series of prints showing a figure in action. You will use diagonal lines to complete the figure. These lines will add to a feeling of rhythm or movement. (See Figure 16–13.)

WHAT YOU WILL NEED

- Pencil and sheets of sketch paper
- Ballpoint pen and paper towels
- Styrofoam meat tray
- Brayer
- Water-based printing ink and shallow tray
- Scissors
- Sheet of drawing paper, 10 x 12 inches (25 x 30 cm)

▶ **Figure 16–12** **What has been done to emphasize the two figures? What kinds of lines have been used?**

George Wesley Bellows. *Stag at Sharkey's*. 1909. Oil on canvas. 93 x 122.5 cm (36¼ x 48¼"). The Cleveland Museum of Art, Cleveland, Ohio. Hinman B. Hurlbut Collection.

WHAT YOU WILL DO

1. Take turns with your classmates in acting as models. Each model will strike an action pose, such as running, reaching, or pushing.
2. Make a series of gesture drawings of students in different poses. Quickly drawn diagonal lines will help you catch a sense of action. Avoid details. Focus on showing movement. (For more on gesture drawing, see Technique Tip **1**, *Handbook* page **277**.)
3. Select your best drawing. Place it on top of the styrofoam meat tray and transfer the figure to the tray by tracing over it firmly with a ballpoint pen. Cut your figure out of the tray with scissors. This is to be your printing plate.
4. Squeeze a small amount of water-based printing ink into the tray. Roll the brayer back and forth through the ink until the whole brayer is covered with ink.
5. Put the figure on a paper towel. Roll the brayer over the figure. Pick up the figure by the edges and place it ink-side down on your sheet of drawing paper. Press the back of the figure firmly all over to transfer ink.
6. Ink the plate again and make another print. This time overlap images on your paper until you are satisfied with your design. Arrange your images in a horizontal or vertical line to add a feeling of rhythm.
7. Title your work, sign it, and place it on display.

- **Describe** Identify the figure in your print. Point out different features of the figure.
- **Analyze** Explain how the diagonal lines in your print carry a sense of rhythm.
- **Interpret** Find out whether viewers can identify the action in your print. Reveal the action you were trying to show.
- **Judge** Tell whether you feel your work succeeds. Tell what you would do to improve your work on a second effort.

▲ **Figure 16–13 Student work. Figure in action.**

OTHER STUDIO IDEAS

- Print your image again, this time using complementary colors of paper and ink. Compare the result with your first print. Tell which gives more of a sense of movement.
- •• Have a model act out a series of poses showing one non-stop act. One possibility would be walking, stopping, and bending to pick up something. Make a printing plate for each pose. Print your images horizontally on a long sheet of paper. Make sure the different images overlap.

BUILDING VOCABULARY

Number a sheet of paper from 1 to 8. After each number, write the term from the box that best matches each description below.

Ashcan School	Fauvism
Cubism	muralist
The Eight	non-objective art
Expressionism	Regionalism

1. An art movement in which artists used wild, intense color combinations in their paintings.
2. A style that emphasized the expression of innermost feelings.
3. A style in which objects are shown from several different angles at once.
4. A style in which no objects or subjects can be readily identified.
5. A group of New York artists who created art work that reflected the spirit of the times in which they lived, the early 1900s.
6. The popular name given to the group of artists who made realistic paintings of working-class America.
7. A style that records local scenes and events from an artist's own region, or area, of the country.
8. An artist who paints large art works directly onto walls or ceilings.

REVIEWING ART FACTS

Number a sheet of paper from 9 to 14. Answer each question in a complete sentence.

9. What feature did Expressionism and Fauvism have in common?
10. Identify the artist whose idea led to the forming of the Cubist movement.
11. What artist is credited with developing the non-objective style?
12. In what way were the photographs of Alfred Stieglitz linked to the work of the Ashcan painters?
13. When did the Regionalist movement begin? Name a member of the movement.
14. Which artist that you read about in this chapter was a muralist?

THINKING ABOUT ART

On a sheet of paper, answer each question in a sentence or two.

1. **Extend.** Imagine that Käthe Kollwitz had chosen to do her print *The Prisoners* (Figure 16–3) in color. Do you think such a decision would have added to the power of the work? Explain your answer.
2. **Interpret.** Cubists, it has been noted, relied mostly on their minds to think their way through a painting. Think of a verb you might use in place of *think* to make this statement fit the work of the German Expressionists.
3. **Analyze.** The work by John Steuart Curry (Figure 16–10) offers an excellent example of an artist's use of emphasis. Find another work in this chapter that uses emphasis. Explain what the artist of that work does to lead the viewer's eye to the most important feature.

MAKING ART CONNECTIONS

1. **Language Arts.** Divide a sheet of paper into three columns. Label one column *Subject*, one *Composition*, and one *Content*. Then, going through the art works in this chapter one by one, decide in which column or columns each artist's name belongs. Compare your completed list with those of other students in your class.
2. **Language Arts.** What might you say to someone who claimed photography is not art? Would you agree or disagree? How might you use the work by Alfred Stieglitz (Figure 16–9) to support your argument?

LOOKING AT THE DETAILS

The detail shown below is from Wassily Kandinsky's *Painting Number 200*. Study the detail and answer the following questions using complete sentences.

1. What do you notice in this work that suggests that a drawing medium has been used. Explain your answer.
2. Which aesthetic view would you use in judging this work? Give reasons to support your answer.

3. Look at the entire work on page **240**. The viewer's eye tends to follow this image from the center of the canvas to the lower left, then upward through the middle. Which elements of art help to define this path?
4. Which principles of art unify this work?

Wassily Kandinsky. *Painting Number 200*. 1914. Oil on canvas. (Detail.) 162.5 x 80 cm (64 x 31½"). Museum of Modern Art, New York, New York. Mrs. Simon Guggenheim Fund.

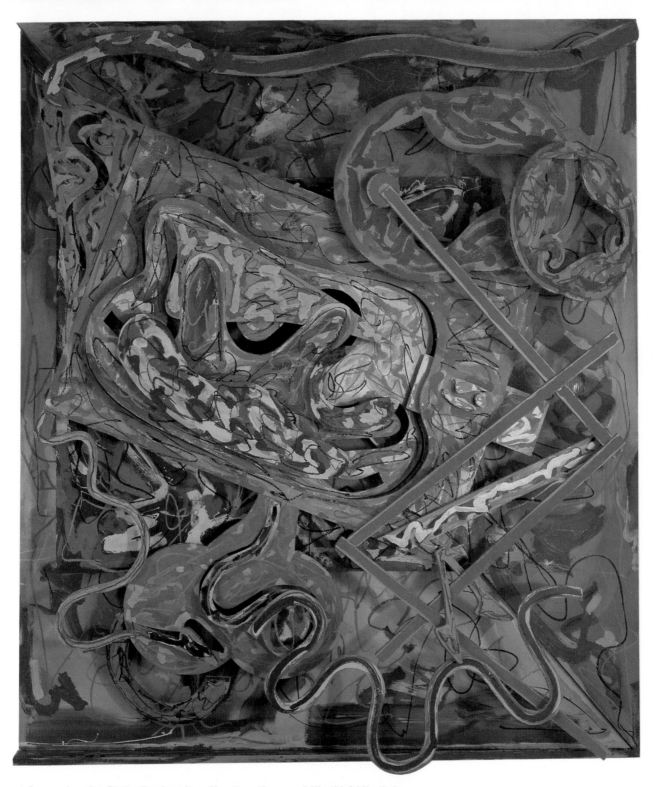

▲ **Can you imagine Giotto, Rembrandt, or Monet creating a work like this? Like their paintings, this one was made using media, techniques, and ideas of its time.**

Frank Stella. *Shards III*. 1983. Mixed media on aluminum. 346.7 x 304.2 x 62.2 cm (136½ x 119¾ x 24½"). Leo Castelli Gallery, New York, New York.

CHAPTER 17

Art of Today

The story of art is a story of change. With each passing age, the search for untried forms of expression is renewed. A style that shocks viewers of one generation becomes part of the mainstream in the next.

At no time in history has the search for new directions been more visible than now. The last 40 years have seen more changes in art styles and techniques than all the thousand years before. One recent style appears in the work at the left. How does this style differ from those developed earlier? In this chapter you will learn how this and other recent styles originated.

OBJECTIVES

After completing this chapter, you will be able to:

- Identify major art movements of the last 50 years.
- Identify the characteristics and leaders of those art movements.
- Create a painting in the Surrealist style.
- Create a work using contemporary styles and techniques.

WORDS YOU WILL LEARN

Abstract Expressionism	multi-media art
Dada	New Realism
Hard-Edge painting	Op Art
kinetic art	social protest painting
mobile	Surrealism

ARTISTS YOU WILL MEET

Alexander Calder	Marino Marini
Giorgio de Chirico	Joan Miró
Gene Davis	Henry Moore
Arshile Gorky	Louise Nevelson
Duane Hanson	Nam June Paik
Barbara Hepworth	Judy Pfaff
Ellsworth Kelly	Sandy Skoglund
Paul Klee	Frank Stella
Jacob Lawrence	Andrew Wyeth
René Magritte	

European Art Today

The Impressionists went outdoors to find ideas. The Expressionists looked to their own hearts. The second decade of the twentieth century found artists exploring still another source for art ideas. That was the inner workings of the mind.

FANTASY ART

Imagine yourself a visitor at a showing of new art. Suddenly your eye falls upon a work that is at once familiar and shocking. It is familiar because it is a photograph of the *Mona Lisa*. It is shocking because someone has drawn a mustache on Leonardo da Vinci's world-famous portrait.

It was this very experience that outraged members of Europe's art community in 1916. The artist behind the work was a one-time Cubist named Marcel Duchamp (mar-**sel** doo-**shahnh**). The movement he belonged to, **Dada** (**dahd**-ah) was *founded on the belief that Western culture had lost its meaning*. For Dadaists (**dahd**-uah-ists), the beauty of art was in the *mind*, not the eye, of the beholder. Art, in other words, did not have to be beautiful or express important ideas. Usually the point was driven home, as in Duchamp's photograph, by poking fun at art of the past.

SURREALISM

Although Dada lasted only six years, it paved the way for other art explorations of the mind. The most important of these was **Surrealism** (suh-**ree**-uh-liz-uhm). This movement *probed the unconscious world of dreams* for ideas, and was touched off by the works of a Greek-born Italian artist named Giorgio de Chirico (**jor**-joh duh **kir**-ih-koh). Like the artists who followed him, de Chirico created mysterious, nightmarish landscapes

▲ **Figure 17–1   What gives this picture its dreamlike appearance? What kinds of feelings does it arouse in you?**

Giorgio de Chirico. *The Nostalgia of the Infinite*. 1911. Oil on canvas. 135.2 x 64.8 cm (53¼ x 25½"). The Museum of Modern Art, New York, New York.

where time had no meaning. One of these is shown in Figure 17–1. Notice the two small figures seen as silhouettes at the center of the work. Their importance seems to shrink before the huge tower looming behind them. In the stillness a sudden breeze begins whipping at some flags atop the tower. Who are these people? What is the meaning of the tower and the flags? Like a dream, the painting raises many unanswerable questions. Attempts to answer these questions only adds to the feeling that the viewers are experiencing a nightmare from which they cannot awaken.

By the end of the 1920s the Surrealist movement had spread to many countries. One artist who seemed comfortable with the movement was the Spanish painter Joan Miró (**zhoo**-ahn mee-**roh**). Miró created fantasy worlds that were free not only of rhyme and reason but also of realism. In the work in Figure 17–2 he brings the viewer face-to-face with a scene depicting strange, imaginary creatures. See how the subjects whirl and twist in a playful ballet.

◀ **Figure 17–2   Why do you suppose the artist called this painting "Dutch Interior"? Are there any shapes that look like animals or musical instruments?**

Joan Miró. *Dutch Interior.* 1928. Guggenheim Collection. Venice.

Fantasy and humor are key ingredients also in the art of Swiss-born Paul Klee (**klay**). Though not a Surrealist, Klee based his work on images glimpsed through his mind's eye. Most, like his picture of a tightrope walker (Figure 17–3), are like simple, childlike creations. Notice how the walker makes his way boldly across a wire supported by a flimsy network of thin lines. These lines look as though they will collapse at any second. What statement might the artist be making about people who foolishly enter situations without weighing the consequences?

SCULPTURE

Over the last 40 years sculptors have also explored new areas of self-expression. Some have continued to create recognizable images. Others have taken the path toward non-objective art.

The works of Marino Marini (muh-**reen**-oh muh-**reen**-ee), an Italian sculptor, draw on a single haunting image. That image — peasants fleeing their villages on horseback during bombing raids — was one the artist witnessed during World War II. Sculptures like the one in Figure 17–4 are attempts to capture the suffering of civilians during wartime.

▲ **Figure 17–3   What has the artist done to add a sense of harmony? Can you point to places where variety is used? What property of this work is most important — its realism, its design, or its meaning?**

Paul Klee. *Tightrope Walker.* 1923. Color lithograph. 43.1 x 26.7 cm (17 x 10½"). McNay Art Museum, San Antonio, Texas.

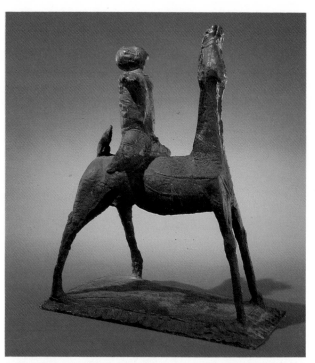

▲ **Figure 17–4   What kinds of real and imaginary lines help add a feeling of tension? What makes this work successful or unsuccessful?**

Marino Marini. *Horse and Rider.* 1951. Bronze. 55.7 x 31.1 x 43.5 cm (21⅞ x 12¼ x 17⅛"). Hirshhorn Museum and Sculpture Garden, Smithsonian Institution, Washington, D.C. Gift of the Lily Harmon Foundation.

An artist best known for her non-objective creations was English sculptor Barbara Hepworth. A trademark of her work is the use of holes. As in the work in Figure 17–5, these create centers of interest within gently curving forms.

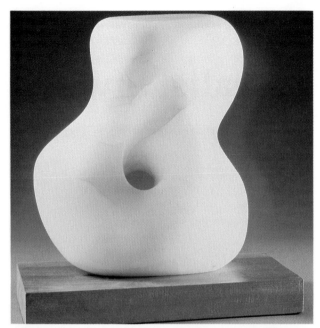

▲ Figure 17–5   Notice the smooth texture of the alabaster. Would you be tempted to run your hands over the surface of the work?

Barbara Hepworth. *Merryn*. 1962. Alabaster. 33 x 29 x 20 cm (13 x 11½ x 8″). National Museum of Women in the Arts. Washington, D.C., Gift of Wallace and Wilhelmina Holladay.

▲ Figure 17–6   Notice how the sculptor gave the family members a feeling of unity. How did he provide variety?

Henry Moore. *Family Group*. 1948–49. Cast 1950. Bronze. 150.5 x 118.1, base 114.3 x 75.9 cm (59¼ x 46½, base 45 x 29⅞″). Museum of Modern Art, New York, New York. A Conger Goodyear Fund.

Another sculptor, Henry Moore, created both non-objective works and works that were sometimes nearer to realism. The close relationship of family members is expressed in Figure 17–6. Moore stylized the figures and yet clearly defined them as mother, father, and child. The figures of the parents are linked by the child, the touching knees, and the husband's hand on his wife's shoulder, providing a unified whole.

✔ CHECK YOUR UNDERSTANDING

1. What did the Dadaists believe? How did they usually give expression to this belief?
2. What is Surrealism? What artist's works initiated the movement? Name another Surrealist.
3. For what kinds of works is Paul Klee best known?
4. What image turns up again and again in the works of Marino Marini?
5. What is the trademark of sculptor Barbara Hepworth?

Painting in the Surrealist Style

Another artist who painted in the Surrealist style was Belgian painter René Magritte (ren-**ay** muh-**greet**). Magritte was a painter of riddles. In his pictures, familiar objects turn up together in unusual relationships or strange settings. Look at the work in Figure 17–7. At first glance this appears to be little more than a realistic painting of an ordinary looking room with a fireplace suggesting stillness and peace. The clock on the mantle notes the slow, regular passing of time. But bursting out of the wall is a steaming locomotive! This is an image of speed, energy and noise that disturbs the peacefulness of the room. What does it mean? Perhaps the only purpose here is to create surprise. We are shocked to see ordinary objects put together in ways that make no sense at all.

WHAT YOU WILL LEARN

You will draw and paint a work in the Surrealist style. You will combine familiar objects in strange, surprising ways. Objects will be painted realistically with a variety of hues, values, and intensities. (See Figure 17–8.)

WHAT YOU WILL NEED

- Pencil and sheets of sketch paper
- Sheet of white drawing paper, 10 x 12 inches (25 x 30 cm)
- Tempera paint
- Assorted brushes
- Mixing tray

▲ Figure 17–7   How does Magritte's dream world differ from de Chirico's (see Figure 17–1)? Does the realistic painting style add to or take away from the idea the work communicates?

René Magritte. *Time Transfixed*. 1938. Oil on canvas. 147 x 98.7 cm (58 x 39″). The Art Institute of Chicago, Chicago, Illinois. Joseph Winterbotham Collection.

WHAT YOU WILL DO

1. Pick a common object to be featured in your picture. Using your imagination, sketch this object in a setting that makes little or no sense. You might, for instance, feature a thumbtack as tall as a house. You might choose to draw a bed on which eggs are frying. Make your image as offbeat and surprising as you can.

2. Carefully transfer your best sketch to the sheet of drawing paper. Make your finished drawing as realistic as possible. Using tempera, paint your work. Add details. Mix and blend hues, values, and intensities of color to make your objects lifelike.

4. Give your work a title unrelated to the objects in it. Write this title on the back of the picture.

5. Exchange paintings with a classmate. Write a brief explanation of the painting you receive. Your explanation, like the painting itself, can be offbeat.

6. Display your work along with its explanation. Compare it with those done by other students. Which were most surprising? What qualities in them caused you to react this way?

EXAMINING YOUR WORK

- **Describe**   Identify the objects in your picture. Explain what steps you took to make these objects appear lifelike.
- **Analyze**   Point to the variety of hues, values, and intensities in your work. Identify any other elements and principles you used to make objects more real-looking.
- **Interpret**   Explain what steps you took to surprise and shock viewers.
- **Judge**   Tell whether you feel your work succeeds. State what aesthetic view you feel would be best for judging your work.

▲ **Figure 17–8   Student work. Surrealist painting.**

OTHER STUDIO IDEAS

- Think about two animals that look nothing alike. On a sheet of paper, list the features of each. Make a drawing of an imaginary animal that has features from both lists. Color your animal with watercolors. Add a background scene. Title your work.

●● Walk around your school grounds searching for an object that people might normally overlook. Two possibilities are a door to a storage closet and a flag pole. Design a picture in which this object is the center of attention. Do not change the appearance of the object. Instead, use your imagination to place it in a new and unusual setting.

American Art Today

In the late 1800s the United States was recognized as a global power. It began slowly but surely to emerge as a world leader in art. By 1950 the change was complete. New York replaced Paris as the center of painting and sculpture.

Art since that time has been rocked by one new style after another. Countless new materials and techniques have been tried as artists attempt to solve an age-old problem. That problem is how best to speak to viewers through the language of art. In this lesson you will look at some solutions.

ABSTRACT EXPRESSIONISM

The first new form of expression was a bold style that was influenced by several past styles. Its name is **Abstract Expressionism**. In this art style, *paint was dribbled, spilled, or splashed onto huge canvases to express painting as an action*. Abstract Expressionist artists rejected the use of subject matter in their work. They dripped, spilled, and splashed rich colors on canvas to create their paintings. The *act* of painting was so tied to their work that the Abstract Expressionists became labeled "action painters."

One of the first members of the Abstract Expressionist movement was an Armenian-born artist named Arshile Gorky (**ar**-shuhl **gor**-kee). Gorky's early works show strong traces of Surrealism. By the mid-1940s, however, he was showing real objects as doodle-like lines and shapes in his paintings. Figure 17–9 shows a painting completed a year before his death. To appreciate such works demands that viewers open themselves to the artist's one-of-a-kind blending of colors, shapes, and lines.

▲ Figure 17–9   Does a viewer need to see things in a painting to enjoy it? Can a painting be enjoyed for the beauty of the visual elements?

Arshile Gorky. *Golden Brown Painting*. 1947. Oil on canvas. 110.8 x 141.3 cm (43⅝ x 55⅝"). Washington University Gallery of Art, St. Louis, Missouri.

▲ Figure 17–10   What is the positive shape in this work? What is the negative shape?

Ellsworth Kelly. *Red/White*. 1964. Oil on canvas. 95.3 x 91.4 cm (37½ x 36"). Courtesy Blum Helman Gallery, New York, New York.

Equally dazzling in their use of color are the paintings of Helen Frankenthaler (**frank-uhn-tahl-uhr**), another Abstract Expressionist. Frankenthaler's action paintings often begin on the floor of her studio. Standing above a blank canvas, the artist pours on layer after layer of thinned color. With each new addition, the work grows. Study the painting by Frankenthaler in Figure 2–5 on page **20**. Like most works by the artist, edges of shapes are sometimes sharp, sometimes blurred. Find the flamelike shape at the center. Notice how it appears to be spreading outward to other parts of the canvas.

OTHER DIRECTIONS IN PAINTING

It was not long after Abstract Expressionism appeared on the scene that other artists began challenging it. The style, they argued, was too personal—too much in the mind of the artist. Among the solutions that arose were:

- **Hard-Edge painting**. This was *a style that emphasized clear, crisp-edged shapes*. The work shown in Figure 17–10 is by Hard-Edge painter Ellsworth Kelly. Notice how the square shape of the canvas shows off the simple positive and negative shapes. What would you see first if the colors were reversed?
- **Social protest painting**. Emerging in the 1930s, this was *an art style that attacked the ills of big-city life*. It remained alive through the 1960s in the works of Jacob Lawrence, a black artist. Study the painting by Lawrence in Figure 17–11. Like the artist's other works, this one tells a story. What words would you use to describe the story?
- **New Realism**. Not all artists of the past few decades have been content to use non-objective styles. Some formed a movement called **New Realism**, *an art movement that rediscovered the importance of realistic detail*. Figure 17–12 shows a work by Andrew Wyeth, who has been a realist throughout his long career. The painting, you will notice, offers more than just a photographic record of its subject. It gives a glimpse of the kind of person the man is. Notice that he is turned away from the viewer. In this way he cannot see the pity in our eyes. Alone in his empty room he stubbornly guards the possessions left to him—his pride and dignity.

◀ **Figure 17–11** This is an example of social protest painting. What symbols did the artist use to convey his ideas?

Jacob Lawrence. *Toussaint L'Overture Series*. 1938. Tempera on paper. 46.4 x 61.6 cm (18¼ x 24¼"). Fisk University.

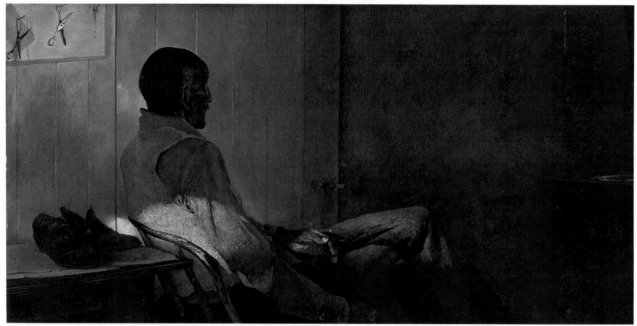

▲ Figure 17–12   Notice how the man in the picture is turned away from the viewer. What reason might the artist have had for positioning him this way?

Andrew Wyeth. *That Gentleman*. 1960. Tempera on panel. 59.7 x 45.1 cm (23½ x 17¾"). Dallas Museum of Art, Dallas, Texas.

SCULPTURE

Painters have not been alone in the search for new methods of self-expression. Sculptors, too, have experimented with new styles. One of them, Alexander Calder, was able to number among his contributions the invention of a new term. That term, **mobile** (**moh**-beel), was used to describe a *sculpture made of carefully balanced shapes hung on wires*. Most of Calder's mobiles, like the one in Figure 17–13, are non-objective. Imagine this moving sculpture as it might appear as you stand near it. Try to picture the ever-changing patterns created by the bobbing and twisting of the shapes. What images do you think might come to mind?

A different approach to non-objective sculpture is found in the three-dimensional collages of Louise Nevelson (**nev**-uhl-suhn). Her works, one of which appears in Figure 17–14, were assembled from found objects and wood scraps. Viewers often experience these sculptures as at once familiar and foreign. The wood scraps in Figure 17–14 are easily identified. They are combined in such a way, however, that they create something

entirely new and different. Are they gates or doors? If so, what kind of fascinating world lies beyond?

Just as some painters of recent times have made realism their goal, so have some sculptors. One is artist Duane Hanson. Hanson's sculptures are so lifelike they are often mistaken for real people. Imagine yourself

▲ Figure 17–13   What shape is emphasized in this mobile? How is this emphasis achieved? Is pattern an important principle? How is pattern shown?

Alexander Calder. *Zarabanda* (Un Disco Blanco). 1955. Painted sheet metal, metal rods and wire. 106.6 x 166.1 cm (42 x 65⅜"). Hirshhorn Museum and Sculpture Garden, Smithsonian Institution, Washington, D.C. Gift of Joseph H. Hirshhorn.

▲ Figure 17–14 What would happen if this sculpture were painted in several different colors? Would it be as successful? Why or why not?

Louise Nevelson. *Mrs. N's Palace*. 1971. Painted wood, mirror. 355.6 x 607 x 457.2 cm (140 x 239 x 180″). The Metropolitan Museum of Art, New York, New York. Gift of the artist.

▲ Figure 17–15 The people in this work are types you might pass on the street or at a shopping mall. Why do you think the artist has chosen to freeze these types in time? What are we able to learn about them? What can we learn about ourselves?

Duane Hanson. *Tourists*. 1970. Polyester and fiberglass. Lifesize. OK Harris Works of Art, New York, New York.

standing before Hanson's sculpture of tourists in Figure 17–15. Typical of his work, these people are average-looking and wear everyday clothing. What reaction do you suppose the artist wants viewers to have? What message about life in present-day America might he be sending?

✔CHECK YOUR UNDERSTANDING

1. What is Abstract Expressionism? Name two members of the movement.
2. Besides Abstract Expressionism, name three directions painting has taken in the last 40 years. Define each school.
3. What term did Alexander Calder invent? Describe the kinds of sculptures he created.
4. Which of the artists you learned about in this lesson created three-dimensional collages?

Making a Hard-Edge Op Art Work

The painting in Figure 17–16, by artist Gene Davis, is typical of another movement of the second half of the twentieth century. The movement's name is **Op Art**. Artists working in this style *made use of precise lines and shapes to create optical illusion*. Stare at Davis' painting for a moment. Notice how the vertical lines in the picture appear to vibrate with color.

Compare this work with the Hard-Edge painting on page **264**. Imagine the artists of the two had decided to combine their styles in a single painting. What would it look like?

WHAT YOU WILL LEARN

Using India ink, you will create a pattern of black and white values. You will create this design over another made up of simple positive and negative shapes. The finished work—a blend of Op Art and Hard-Edge styles—will give a feeling of dizzying movement. (See Figure 17–17.)

WHAT YOU WILL NEED

- Pencil, sheets of sketch paper, and ruler
- Piece of illustration board, 12 x 12 inches (30 x 30 cm)
- India ink
- Pen holder and assorted points, or nibs

▶ **Figure 17–16** How does the artist add variety to this composition? Where are the most intense colors found? When you stare at it, does this picture seem to vibrate?

Gene Davis. *Cool Buzz Saw.* 1964. Acrylic on canvas. 189.9 x 291.1 cm (113¾ x 115"). San Francisco Museum of Modern Art, San Francisco, California. Gift of the Women's Board.

WHAT YOU WILL DO

1. Look once again at the Hard-Edge painting by Kelly on page **264**. Draw several pencil sketches of a single Hard-Edge shape. The negative and positive shapes on your paper should be equally interesting.
2. Pick your best sketch. Using pencil and ruler, draw it on the piece of illustration board.
3. Study the Op Art painting by Gene Davis in Figure 17–16. Again working with ruler and pencil, cover the illustration board with closely spaced vertical lines. The spaces between the lines need not be exact. No two lines, however, should be more than a half inch apart.
4. With a pen and India ink, fill in the shape at the top left corner of your design. Be careful to stay within the lines. Working downward, leave the next shape white. Ink in every other shape until you reach the bottom of the illustration board. Repeat the process for the next vertical strip, this time leaving the topmost shape white. Continue in this fashion until all the strips have been completed.
5. Display your work alongside those of classmates. Which have the most interesting Hard-Edge designs? Which give the same kind of vibrating effect found in Figure 17–16?

EXAMINING YOUR WORK

- **Describe**   Point out the positive and negative shapes in your work.
- **Analyze**   Explain how the pattern of dark and light values causes the picture to seem to vibrate.
- **Interpret**   Tell whether your work gives a dizzying feeling.
- **Judge**   Tell whether you feel your work succeeds. State which aesthetic view you would use in explaining your judgment.

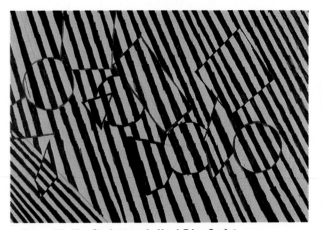

▲ **Figure 17–17**   **Student work. Hard-Edge Op Art.**

OTHER STUDIO IDEAS

- Do a second version of the work, this time using two complementary colors of tempera paint. Use horizontal lines in place of vertical ones if you like.

- ●● Create a simple landscape or still life. Use India ink or tempera and the Op Art technique detailed in the lesson.

Art of the Next Frontier

Artists have never been content to stay in one place for long. They are a restless breed, forever moving on, thirsting after new challenges. As we move swiftly toward the year 2000, questions arise: What challenges will open themselves to the artists of tomorrow? What will art be like in the twenty-first century?

Answering these questions would take a crystal ball. Still, possible glimpses of the art of tomorrow are afforded by innovative developments in the art of today. In this lesson you will look at some of these developments.

ART AND TECHNOLOGY

If there is one word most closely identified with art of today, it is *technology*. Technology is the use of science to make life better. Art of the past few years has drawn on such technological advances as the computer and laser. It has also redefined the boundaries between one branch of art and the next.

Staged Photography

In the late 1800s the new art of photography changed the way painters looked at their subjects. In more recent times another new art—filmmaking—has had the same effect on photographers. Some have begun staging pictures in much the way movie directors set up a scene.

Figure 17–18 shows a staged photograph by artist Sandy Skoglund (**skoh**-gluhnd). For this work the artist sculpted each of the goldfish individually from clay. She also painted the room and directed the location of the two people. What twentieth-century style of painting does this work call to mind? What message might the photographer be sending to viewers?

▲ **Figure 17–18** How would you describe the artist's use of color? Would this work have a different appearance if it had been shot in black and white?

Sandy Skoglund. *Revenge of the Goldfish.* 1981. Staged Photograph. Lorence Monk Gallery. New York, New York.

Multi-Media Art

The ancient Hindus, you may recall, believed temples to be as much sculpture as architecture. This idea has been carried forward in recent years by artists of multi-media works. **Multi-media art** is *a work that makes use of tools and techniques from two or more areas of art.*

A careful merging of architecture and sculpture is found in the expressions of sculptor Judy Pfaff (**faf**). Study the multi-media work by her in Figure 17–19. Parts of the work are the floor of the room, walls, and ceiling themselves. The viewer is able to move not only around this sculpture but also *within* it.

Kinetic Art

Examine the "sculpture" in Figure 17–20 by Nam June Paik. This work loosely belongs to a movement begun in the 1960s called **kinetic** (kuh-**net**-ik) **art**. This is *a style in which parts of works are set into motion.* The motion can be triggered by a form of energy or by

▲ **Figure 17–19** In what ways has the artist created a "real" landscape? What other branches of art besides sculpture and architecture are brought into play in this multi-media work?

Judy Pfaff. *Kabuki (Formula Atlantic)*. 1981. Mixed media. Hirshhorn Museum and Sculpture Garden, Smithsonian Institution, Washington, D.C.

the viewer moving past the work. Some art gives the impression of movement without actually moving. The work in Figure 17–20 is made up in part of 300 television screens. The viewer experiences a number of different images and sounds all at the same time. What do you imagine this experience would be like? What statement might the artist be making about the age of television?

STUDIO EXPERIENCE

Art, it has been said, mirrors the time in which it is created. This holds especially true for the branch of art called architecture.

Brainstorm with classmates about what dwellings of the future will be like. Let your imagination guide you. On a sheet of paper, make a pencil drawing of your dream dwelling of the future. Allow in your design for solutions to such growing problems as pollution and thinning of the ozone layer. Share your finished work with classmates. Which design is the most interesting? Why?

✔ CHECK YOUR UNDERSTANDING

1. What is technology? What part has technology played in art of the present?
2. What is a staged photograph?
3. Define *multi-media art*.
4. To what two art movements does the painting in Figure 17–16 belong?

▲ **Figure 17–20** A computer is used to "flip" and enlarge images on the different screens in this work. How many different images can you count?

Nam June Paik. *Fin de Siècle II*. 1989. Video installation: Approximately 300 television sets. Originally shown at the Whitney Museum of American Art, New York, New York.

BUILDING VOCABULARY

Number a sheet of paper from 1 to 10. After each number, write the term from the box that best matches each description below.

Abstract Expressionism	multi-media art
Dada	New Realism
Hard-Edge painting	Op Art
kinetic art	social protest painting
mobile	Surrealism

1. An art movement founded on the belief that Western culture had lost its meaning.
2. An art movement that probed the unconscious world of dreams.
3. An art style in which paint was dribbled, spilled, or splashed onto huge canvases to express painting as an action.
4. An art style that emphasized clear, crisp-edged shapes.
5. An art style that attacked the ills of big-city life.
6. An art movement that rediscovered the importance of realistic detail.
7. A sculpture made of carefully balanced shapes hung on wires.
8. An art style that made use of precise lines and shapes to create optical illusion.
9. A work that makes use of tools and techniques from two or more areas of art.
10. An art style in which parts of works are set into motion by a form of energy.

REVIEWING ART FACTS

Number a sheet of paper from 11 to 18. Answer each question in a complete sentence.

11. Name an artist of the Dada movement.
12. Describe the works of Paul Klee.
13. What sculptor did works of Italian peasants fleeing a bombing raid?
14. For which type of sculpture was Barbara Hepworth best known?
15. In what art movement was Arshile Gorky a pioneer?
16. What sculptor you learned about created three-dimensional collages?
17. Name an artist who works in the area of staged photography.
18. For what kinds of works is Judy Pfaff known?

THINKING ABOUT ART

On a sheet of paper, answer each question in a sentence or two.

1. **Analyze**. React to the opinion that art must be serious to be good. Find works from the chapter that support your position.
2. **Compare and contrast**. Compare the works in Figure 17–2 and Figure 17–13. Aside from the fact one is a painting and the other a sculpture, how do they differ? What do they have in common? Would you use the same aesthetic view in judging the two? Explain.

MAKING ART CONNECTIONS

1. **Language Arts**. Choose one of the non-objective works you learned about in this chapter. Make a list of points about this work you would bring up in a debate with someone who claimed a two-year-old could create the same "art."
2. **History**. In this chapter you learned of some art movements that appeared in the late twentieth century. The following are several others: Pop Art, Earth Art, and Concept Art. Using an encyclopedia or other library resource, find out the names of artists who worked in the movement, and identify their goals. Report your findings to the class.

LOOKING AT THE DETAILS

The detail shown below is from Frank Stella's *Shards III*. Study the detail and answer the following questions using complete sentences.

1. How would you know that this was a multi-media work if a credit line was not available?

2. Identify the two art media that Stella used to create this work.
3. How has the artist created depth?
4. Look at the entire work on page **256**. What shape has been used to unify the art work?

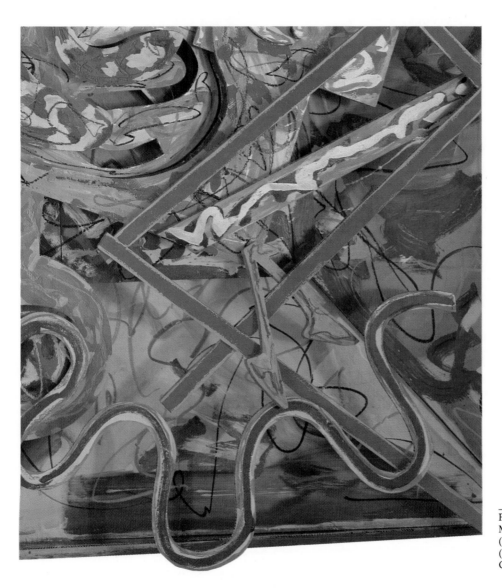

Frank Stella. *Shards III*. 1983. Mixed media on aluminum. (Detail.) 346.7 x 304.2 x 62.2 cm (136½ x 119¾ x 24½"). Leo Castelli Gallery, New York, New York.

▲ Working on group murals is an excellent way to practice artistic skills, gain recognition, and at the same time, have fun.

HANDBOOK CONTENTS

PART 1: Technique Tips

Drawing Tips

1. Making Gesture Drawings   277
2. Making Contour Drawings   277
3. Drawing with Oil Pastels   277
4. Drawing Thin Lines with a Brush   277
5. Making a Grid for Enlarging   277
6. Using Shading Techniques   278
7. Using Sighting Techniques   278
8. Using a Viewing Frame   279
9. Using a Ruler   279

Painting Tips

10. Cleaning a Paint Brush   279
11. Making Natural Earth Pigments   280
12. Mixing Paint to Change
    the Value of Color   280
13. Working with Poster Paints   281
    (School Tempera)
14. Working with Watercolors   281

Printmaking Tip

15. Making a Stamp Printing   281

Sculpting Tips

16. Working with Clay   281
17. Joining Clay   281
18. Making a Clay Mold
    for a Plaster Relief   282
19. Mixing Plaster   282
20. Working with Paper Mâché   283
21. Making a Paper Sculpture   284

Other Tips

22. Measuring Rectangles   284
23. Making a Mat   285
24. Mounting a Two-Dimensional Work   286
25. Making Rubbings   286
26. Scoring Paper   286
27. Making a Tissue Paper Collage   287
28. Working with Glue   287

PART 2: Artist Profiles

Paul Cézanne   289
Giotto (di Bondone)   289
Francisco Goya   290
Lucy Lewis   290
Judith Leyster   291
Michelangelo (Buonarroti)   291
Joan Miró   292
Claude Monet   292
Berthe Morisot   293
Louise Nevelson   293
Albert Pinkham Ryder   294
Diego Rivera   294
Alfred Stieglitz   295
Henry O. Tanner   295

PART 3: Career Spotlights

Art Director	297
Art Teacher	297
Computer Graphics Specialist	298
Editorial Cartoonist	298
Exhibit and Display Designer	299
Graphic Designer	299
Industrial Designer	300
Interior Designer	300
Magazine Designer	301
Medical Illustrator	301
Museum Curator	302
Photojournalist	302
Special Effects Designer	303
Urban Planner	303

PART 4: Additional Studios

Lesson 1 Computer-Type Drawing	304
• Examining Your Work	305
Lesson 2 Coil Pot	306
• Examining Your Work	307
Lesson 3 Photo Essay	308
• Examining Your Work	309
Lesson 4 False Face Mask	310
• Examining Your Work	311
Lesson 5 Space Colony	312
• Examining Your Work	313

1. Making Gesture Drawings

Gesture drawing is a way of showing movement in a sketch. Gesture drawings have no outlines or details. You are not expected to draw the figure. Instead, you are expected to draw the movement, or what the figure is doing. Follow these guidelines:

- Use the side of the drawing tool. Do not hold the medium as you would if you were writing.
- Find the lines of movement that show the direction in which the figure is bending. Draw the main line showing this movement.
- Use quickly drawn lines to build up the shape of the person.

2. Making Contour Drawings

Contour drawing is a way of capturing the feel of a subject. When doing a contour drawing, remember the following pointers:

- If you accidentally pick up your pen or pencil, don't stop working. Place your pen or pencil back where you stopped. Begin again from that point.
- If you have trouble keeping your eyes off the paper, ask a friend to hold a piece of paper between your eyes and your drawing paper. Another trick is to place your drawing paper inside a large paper bag as you work.
- Tape your paper to the table so it will not slide around. With a finger of your free hand, trace the outline of the object. Record the movement with your drawing hand.

- Contour lines show ridges and wrinkles in addition to outlines. Adding these lines gives roundness to the object.

3. Drawing with Oil Pastels

Oil pastels are sticks of pigment held together with an oily binder. The colors are brighter than wax crayon colors. If you press heavily you will make a brilliant-colored line. If you press lightly you will create a fuzzy line. You can fill in shapes with the brilliant colors. You can blend a variety of color combinations. For example, you can fill a shape with a soft layer of a hue and then color over the hue with a heavy layer of white to create a unique tint of that hue.

If you use oil pastels on colored paper, you can put a layer of white under the layer of hue to block the color of the paper.

4. Drawing Thin Lines with a Brush

Drawing thin lines with a brush can be learned with a little practice. Just follow these steps:

1. Dip your brush in the ink or paint. Wipe the brush slowly against the side, twirling it between your fingers until the bristles form a point.
2. Hold the brush at the beginning of the metal band near the tip. Hold the brush straight up and down.
3. Imagine that the brush is a pencil with a very sharp point. Pretend that pressing too hard will break the point. Now touch the paper lightly with the tip of the brush and draw a line. The line should be quite thin.

To make a thinner line still, lift up on the brush as you draw. After a while, you will be able to make lines in a variety of thicknesses.

5. Making a Grid for Enlarging

Sometimes the need arises to make a bigger version of a small drawing. An example is when you create a mural based on a small sketch. Follow these steps:

1. Using a ruler, draw evenly spaced lines across and up and down your original drawing (Figure T–1). Count

▲ **Figure T–1**

the number of squares you made from side to side. Count the number of squares running up and down.

2. Measure the width of the surface to which the drawing is to be transferred. Divide that figure by the number of side-to-side squares. The resulting number will be the horizontal measure of each square. You may work in inches or centimeters. Using a ruler or yardstick, mark off the squares. Draw in light rules.

3. Measure the height of the surface to which the drawing is to be transferred. Divide that figure by the number of up-and-down squares. The resulting number will be the vertical measure of each square. Mark off the squares. Draw in pencil lines.

4. Starting at the upper left, number each square on the original drawing. Give the same number to each square on the large grid. Working a square at a time, transfer your image. (See Figure T–2.)

6. Using Shading Techniques

When using shading techniques, keep in mind the following:

• Lines or dots placed close together create dark values.

• Lines or dots placed far apart, on the other hand, create light values. To show a change from light to dark, start with lines or dots far apart and little by little bring them close together.

• Use care also to follow the shape of the object when adding lines. Straight lines are used to shade an object with a flat surface. Rounded lines are used to shade an object with a curved surface.

7. Using Sighting Techniques

Sighting is a technique that will help you draw objects in proportion.

1. Face the object you plan to draw. Hold a pencil straight up and down at arm's length. Your thumb should rest against the side of the pencil and be even with the tip.

2. Close one eye. With your other eye, focus on the object.

3. Slide your thumb down the pencil until the exposed part of the pencil matches the object's height. (See Figure T–3.)

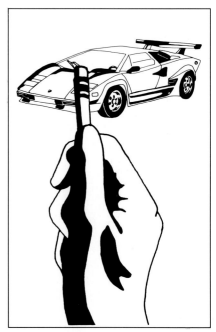

▲ **Figure T–3**

4. Now, without moving your thumb or bending your arm, turn the pencil sideways.

5. Focus on the width of the object. If the height is greater, figure out how many "widths" will fit in one "height." If the width is greater, figure out how many "heights" will fit in one "width."

▲ **Figure T–2**

8. Using a Viewing Frame

Much in the way a camera is used to focus on one area of a scene, you can better zero in on an object you plan to draw by using a viewing frame (Figure T–4). To make a viewing frame do the following:

1. Cut a rectangular hole in a piece of paper about 2 inches (3 to 5 cm) in from the paper's edges.
2. Hold the paper at arm's length and look through the hole at your subject. Imagine that the hole represents your drawing paper.
3. Decide how much of the subject you want to have in your drawing.
4. By moving the frame up, down, sideways, nearer, or farther, you can change the focus of your drawing.

9. Using a Ruler

There are times when you need to draw a crisp, straight line. By using the following techniques, you will be able to do so.

1. Hold the ruler with one hand and the pencil with the other.
2. Place the ruler where you wish to draw a straight line.
3. Hold the ruler with your thumb and first two fingers. Be careful that your fingers do not stick out beyond the edge of the ruler.
4. Press heavily on the ruler so it will not slide while you're drawing.
5. Hold the pencil lightly against the ruler.
6. Pull the pencil quickly and lightly along the edge of the ruler. The object is to keep the ruler from moving while the pencil moves along its edge.

▲ Figure T–4

PAINTING TIPS

10. Cleaning a Paint Brush

Cleaning a paint brush properly helps it last a long time. *Always*:

1. Rinse the thick paint out of the brush under running water. Do not use hot water.
2. Gently paint the brush over a cake of mild soap, or dip it in a mild liquid detergent (Figure T–5).

▲ Figure T–5

3. Gently scrub the brush against the palm of your hand to work the soap into the brush. This removes paint you may not have realized was still in the brush.

4. Rinse the brush under running water while you continue to scrub your palm against it (Figure T–6).

▲ Figure T–6

5. Repeat steps 2, 3, and 4 as needed.

When it is thoroughly rinsed and excess water has been squeezed from the brush, shape your brush into a point with your fingers (Figure T–7). Place the brush in a container with the bristles up so that it will keep its shape as it dries.

▲ Figure T–7

11. Making Natural Earth Pigments

Anywhere there is dirt, clay, or sand, there is natural pigment. To create your own pigments, gather as many different kinds of earth colors as you can. Grind these as finely as possible. (If you can, borrow a mortar and pestle.) (See Figure T–8.) Do not worry if the pigment is slightly gritty.

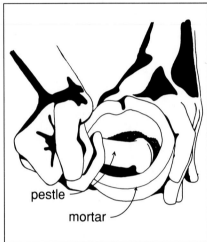

pestle

mortar

▲ Figure T–8

To make the binder, mix equal parts of white glue and water. Place a few spoonfuls of your powdered pigment into a small jar. Add a little of the binder. Experiment with different amounts of each.

When you work with natural pigments, remember always to wash the brushes before the paint in them has a chance to dry. The glue from the binder can ruin a brush. As you work, stir the paint every now and then. This will keep the grains of pigment from settling to the bottom of the jar.

Make a fresh batch each time you paint.

12. Mixing Paint to Change the Value of Color

You can better control the colors in your work when you mix your own paint. In mixing paints, treat opaque paints (for example, tempera) differently from transparent paints (for example, watercolors).

• *For light values of opaque paints.* Mix only a small amount of the hue to white. The color can always be made stronger by adding more of the hue.

• *For dark values of opaque paints.* Add a small amount of black to the hue. Never add the hue to black.

• *For light values of transparent paints.* Thin a shaded area with water (Figure T–9). This allows more of the white of the paper to show through.

• *For dark values of transparent paints.* Carefully add a small amount of black to the hue.

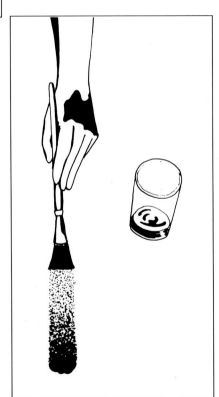

▲ Figure T–9

13. Working with Poster Paints (School Tempera)

When using poster paints (school tempera) remember the following:

- Poster paints run when wet. To keep this from happening, make sure one shape is dry before painting a wet color next to it.

14. Working with Watercolors

- If you apply wet paint to damp paper, you create lines and shapes with soft edges.
- If you apply wet paint to dry paper, you create lines and shapes with sharp, clear edges.
- If you dip a dry brush into damp paint and then brush across dry paper, you achieve a fuzzy effect.
- School watercolors come in semi-moist cakes. Before you use them, place a drop of water on each cake to let the paint soften. Watercolor paints are transparent. You can see the white paper through the paint. If you want a light value of a hue, dilute the paint with a large amount of water. If you want a bright hue, you must dissolve more pigment by swirling your brush around in the cake of paint until you have dissolved a great deal of paint. The paint you apply to the paper can be as bright as the paint in the cake.

PRINTMAKING TIP

15. Making a Stamp Printing

A stamp print is an easy way to make repetitive designs. The following are a few suggestions for making a stamp and printing with it. You may develop some other ideas after reading these hints. Remember, printing reverses your design, so if you use letters, be certain to cut or carve them backwards.

- Cut a simple design into the flat surface of an eraser with a knife that has a fine, precision blade.
- Cut a potato, carrot, or turnip in half. Use a paring knife to carve a design into the flat surface of the vegetable.
- Glue yarn to a bottle cap or a jar lid.
- Glue found objects to a piece of corrugated cardboard. Make a design with paper-clips, washers, nuts, leaves, feathers, or anything else you can find. Whatever object you use should have a fairly flat surface. Make a handle for the block with masking tape.
- Cut shapes out of a piece of inner tube material. Glue the shapes to a piece of heavy cardboard.

There are several ways to apply ink or paint to a stamp:

- Roll water-based printing ink on the stamp with a soft brayer.
- Roll water-based printing ink on a plate and press the stamp into the ink.
- Apply tempera paint or school acrylic to the stamp with a bristle brush.

SCULPTING TIPS

16. Working with Clay

To make your work with clay go smoothly, always do the following:

1. Dip one or two fingers in water.
2. Spread the moisture from your fingers over your palms.

Never dip your hands in water. Too much moisture turns clay into mud.

17. Joining Clay

If you are creating a piece of sculpture that requires joining pieces, do the following:

1. Gather the materials you will need. These include clay, slip, (a creamy mixture of clay and water), a paint brush, a scoring tool, (perhaps a kitchen fork) and clay tools.
2. Rough up or scratch the two surfaces to be joined (Figure T–10).

▲ Figure T–10

3. Apply slip to one of the two surfaces using a paint brush or your fingers (Figure T–11).

▲ **Figure T–11**

4. Gently press the two surfaces together so the slip oozes out of the joining seam (Figure T–12).

▲ **Figure T–12**

5. Using clay tools and/or your fingers, smooth away the slip that has oozed out of the seam (Figure T–13). You may wish to smooth out the seam as well, or you may wish to leave it for decorative purposes.

▲ **Figure T–13**

18. Making a Clay Mold for a Plaster Relief

One of the easiest ways to make a plaster relief is with a clay mold. When making a clay mold, remember the following:

• Plaster poured into the mold will come out with the opposite image. Design details cut into the mold will appear raised on the relief. Details built up within the mold will appear indented in the relief.

• Do not make impressions in your mold that have *undercuts* (Figure T–14). Undercuts trap plaster, which will break off when the relief is removed. When cutting impressions, keep the deepest parts the narrowest.

• In carving a raised area in the mold, take care not to create a reverse undercut (Figure T–15).

If you want to change the mold simply smooth the area with your fingers.

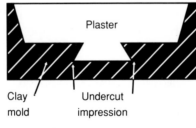

▲ **Figure T–14**

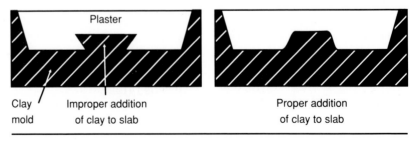

▲ **Figure T–15**

19. Mixing Plaster

Mixing plaster requires some technique and a certain amount of caution. It can also be a very simple matter when you are prepared. Always do the following:

• Use caution when working with dry plaster. Wear a dust mask or work in a well-ventilated room.

• Cover your work space to keep the dust from spreading.

• Always use a plastic bowl and a stick for mixing. Never use silverware you will later eat from.

• Always use plaster that is fine, like sifted flour. Plaster should never be grainy when dry.

• Always add the water to the bowl first. Sift in the plaster. Stir slowly.

• Never pour unused plaster down a drain. Allow it to dry in the bowl. To remove the dried plaster, twist the bowl. Crack the loose plaster into a lined trash can.

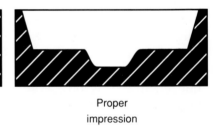

20. Working with Papier-Mâché

Papier-mâché (**pay**-puhr muh-**shay**) is a French term meaning "chewed paper." It is also the name of several sculpting methods using newspaper and liquid paste. These methods can be used to model tiny pieces of jewelry. They can also be used to create life-size creatures.

In creating papier-mâché sculptures, the paper-and-paste mixture is molded over a support. You will learn more about supports shortly. The molded newspaper dries to a hard finish. The following are three methods for working with papier-mâché:

- **Pulp Method**. Shred newspaper, paper towels, or tissue paper into tiny pieces. (Do not use glossy magazine paper; it will not soften.) Soak your paper in water overnight. Press the paper in a kitchen strainer to remove as much moisture as possible. Mix the mashed paper with commercially prepared papier-mâché paste or white glue. The mixture should have the consistency of soft clay. Add a few drops of oil of cloves to keep the mixture from spoiling. A spoonful of linseed oil makes the mixture smoother. (If needed, the mixture can be stored at this point in a plastic bag in the refrigerator.) Use the mixture to model small shapes. When your creations dry, they can be sanded. You will also be able to drill holes in them.
- **Strip Method**. Tear newspaper into strips. Either dip the strips in papier-mâché paste or rub paste on them. Apply the strips to your support (Figure T–16). If you do not want the strips to stick to your

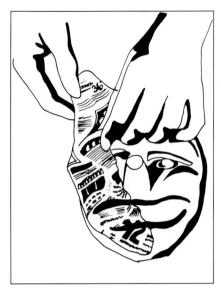

▲ Figure T–16

support, first cover it with plastic wrap. Use wide strips for large shapes. Use thin strips for smaller shapes. If you plan to remove your finished creation from the support, apply five or six layers. (Change directions with each layer so you can keep track of the number.) Otherwise, two or three layers should be enough. After applying the strips to your support, rub your fingers over the surface.

As a last layer, use torn paper towels. The brown paper towels that are found in schools produce an uncomplicated surface on which to paint. Make sure no rough edges are sticking up. Store any unused paste mixture in the refrigerator to keep it from spoiling.

- **Draping Method**. Spread papier-mâché paste on newspaper. Lay a second sheet on top of the first. Smooth the layers. Add another layer of paste and another sheet of paper. Repeat until you have four or five layers of paper. Use this method for making drapery on a figure. (See Figure T–17.) If you allow the lay-

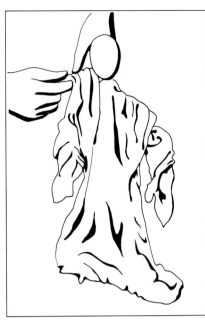

▲ Figure T–17

ers to dry for a day or two, they will become leathery. They can then be cut and molded as you like. Newspaper strips dipped in paste can be used to seal cracks.

Like papier-mâché, supports for papier-mâché creations can be made in several different ways. Dry newspaper may be wadded up and wrapped with string or tape (Figure T–18). Wire coat hangers may be padded with rags. For large figures, a wooden frame covered with chicken wire makes a good support.

▲ Figure T–18

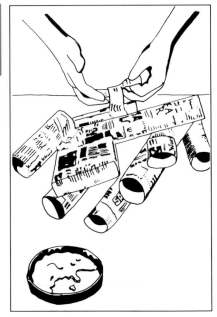

▲ **Figure T–19**

To create a base for your papier-mâché creations, tape together arrangements of found materials. Some materials you might combine are boxes, tubes, and bowls. (See Figure T–19.) Clay can also be modeled as a base. If clay is used, be sure there are no undercuts that would keep the papier-mâché from lifting off easily when dry. (For an explanation of undercuts, see Technique Tip **18**, *Handbook* page **276**.)

Always allow time for your papier-mâché creations to dry. The material needs extra drying time when thick layers are used or when the weather is damp. An electric fan blowing air on the material can shorten the drying time.

21. Making a Paper Sculpture

Another name for paper sculpture is origami. The process originated in Japan and means "folding paper." Paper sculpture begins with a flat piece of paper. The paper is then curved or bent to produce more than a flat

surface. Here are some ways to experiment with paper.

- **Scoring.** Place a square sheet of heavy construction paper, 12 x 12 inch (30 x 30 cm), on a flat surface. Position the ruler on the paper so that it is close to the center and parallel to the sides. Holding the ruler in place, run the point of a knife or a pair of scissors along one of the ruler's edges. Press down firmly but take care not to cut through the paper. Gently crease the paper along the line you made. Hold your paper with the crease facing upward.
- **Pleating.** Take a piece of paper and fold it one inch from the edge. Then fold the paper in the other direction. Continue folding back and forth.
- **Curling.** Hold one end of a long strip of paper with the thumb and forefinger of one hand. At a point right below where you are holding the strip, grip it lightly between the side of a pencil and the thumb of your other hand. In a quick motion, run the pencil along the strip. This will cause the strip to curl back on itself. Don't apply too much pressure, or the strip will tear. (See Figure T–20.)

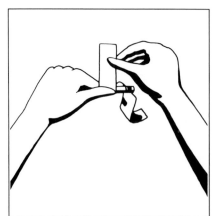

▲ **Figure T–20**

22. Measuring Rectangles

Do you find it hard to create perfectly formed rectangles? Here is a way of getting the job done:

1. Make a light pencil dot near the long edge of a sheet of paper. With a ruler, measure the exact distance between the dot and the edge. Make three more dots the same distance in from the edge. (See Figure T–21.)

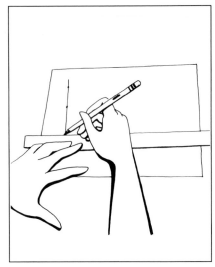

▲ **Figure T–21**

2. Line a ruler up along the dots. Make a light pencil line running the length of the paper.
3. Turn the paper so that a short side is facing you. Make four pencil dots equally distant from the short edge. Connect these with a light pencil rule. Stop when you reach the first line you drew. (See Figure T–22.)
4. Do the same for the remaining two sides. Erase any lines that may extend beyond the box you have made.
5. Trace over the lines with your ruler and pencil.

The box you have created will be a perfectly formed rectangle.

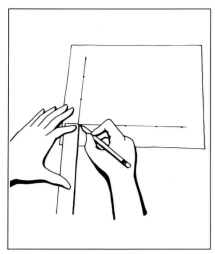

▲ Figure T–22

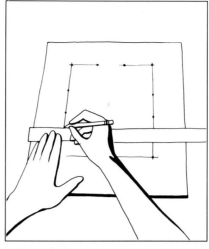

▲ Figure T–23

23. Making a Mat

You can add appeal to an art work by making a mat, using the following steps.

1. Gather the materials you will need. These include a metal rule, a pencil, mat board, cardboard backing, a sheet of heavy cardboard to protect your work surface, a mat knife with a sharp blade, and wide masking tape.

2. Wash your hands. Mat board should be kept very clean.

3. Measure the height and width of the work to be matted. Decide how large a border you want for your work. (A border of approximately 2½ inches on three sides with 3 inches on the bottom is aesthetically pleasing.) Your work will be behind the window you will cut.

4. Plan for the opening, or window, to be ¼ inch smaller on all sides than the size of your work. For example, if your work measures 9 by 12 inches, the mat window should measure 8½ inches (9 inches minus ¼ inch times two) by 11½ inches (12 inches minus ¼ inch times two). Using your metal rule and pencil, lightly draw your window rectangle on the back of the board 2½ inches from the top and left edge of the mat. (See Figure T–23.) Add a 2½ inch border to the right of the window and a 3 inch border to the bottom, lightly drawing cutting guidelines.

Note: If you are working with metric measurements, the window should overlap your work by 0.5 cm (centimeters) on all sides. Therefore, if your work measures 24 by 30 cm, the mat window measures 23 cm (24 − [2 x 0.5]) by 29 cm (30 − [2 x 0.5]).

▲ Figure T–24

5. Place the sheet of heavy, protective cardboard on your work surface. Place the mat board, pencil marks up, over the cardboard. Holding the metal rule firmly in place, score the first line with your knife. Always place the metal rule so that your blade is away from the frame. (See Figure T–24.) In case you make an error you will cut into the window hole or the extra mat that is not used for the frame. Do not try to cut through the board with one stroke. By the third or fourth stroke, you should be able to cut through the board easily.

6. Working in the same fashion, score and cut through the board along all the window lines. Be careful not to go beyond the lines. Remove the window.

7. Cut a cardboard backing for your art work that is slightly smaller than the overall size of your mat. Using a piece of broad masking tape, hinge the back of the mat to the backing. (See Figure T–25.)

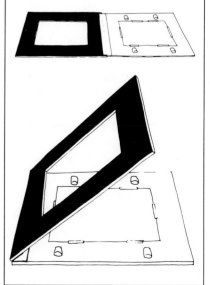

▲ Figure T–25

Position your art work between the backing and the mat and attach it with tape. Anchor the frame to the cardboard with a few pieces of rolled tape.

24. Mounting a Two-Dimensional Work

Mounting pictures that you make gives them a professional look. To mount a work, do the following:

1. Gather the materials you will need. These include a yardstick, a pencil, poster board, a sheet of heavy cardboard, a knife with a very sharp blade, a sheet of newspaper, and rubber cement.
2. Measure the height and width of the work to be mounted. Decide how large a border you want around the work. Plan your mount size using the work's measurements. To end up with a 3-inch (8 cm) border, for example, make your mount 6 inches (15 cm) wider and higher than your work. Record the measurements for your mount.
3. Using your yardstick and pencil, lightly draw your mount rectangle on the back of the poster board. Measure from the edges of the poster board. If you have a large paper cutter available, you may use it to cut your mount.
4. Place the sheet of heavy cardboard on your work surface. Place the poster board, pencil marks up, over the cardboard. Holding the yardstick firmly in place along one line, score the line with your knife. Do not try to cut through the board with one stroke. By the third try, you should be able to cut through the board.

▲ Figure T–26

5. Place the art work on the mount. Using the yardstick, center the work. Mark each corner with a dot. (See Figure T–26.)
6. Place the art work, face down, on a sheet of newspaper. Coat the back of the work with rubber cement. (*Safety Note:* Always use rubber cement in a room with plenty of ventilation.) *If your mount is to be permanent, skip to Step 8.*
7. Line up the corners of your work with the dots on the mounting board. Smooth the work into place. *Skip to Step 9.*
8. After coating the back of your art work, coat the poster board with rubber cement. Be careful not to add cement to the border area. Have a partner hold your art work in the air by the two top corners. Once the two glued surfaces meet, you will not be able to change the position of the work. Grasp the lower two corners. Carefully lower the work to the mounting board. Line up the two corners with the bottom dots. Little by little, lower the work into place (Figure T–27). Press it smooth.

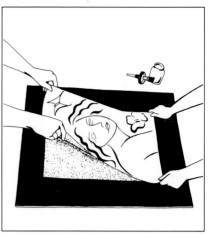

▲ Figure T–27

9. To remove any excess cement, create a small ball of nearly dry rubber cement. Use the ball of rubber cement to pick up excess cement.

25. Making Rubbings

Rubbings make interesting textures and designs. They may also be used with other media to create mixed-media art. To make a rubbing, place a sheet of thin paper on top of the surface to be rubbed. Hold the paper in place with one hand. With the other hand, rub the paper with the flat side of an unwrapped crayon. Always rub away from the hand holding the paper. Never rub back and forth, since this may cause the paper to slip.

26. Scoring Paper

The secret to creating neat, sharp folds in cardboard or paper is a technique called scoring. Here is how it is done:

1. Line up a ruler along the line you want to fold.
2. Lightly run a sharp knife or scissors along the fold line. Press down firmly enough to leave a light crease. Take care not to cut all the way through the paper (Figure T–28).

▲ **Figure T–28**

3. Gently crease the paper along the line you made. To score curved lines, use the same technique. Make sure your curves are wide enough to ensure a clean fold. Too tight a curve will cause the paper to wrinkle (Figure T–29).

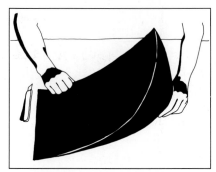

▲ **Figure T–29**

27. Making a Tissue Paper Collage

For your first experience with tissue, make a free design with the tissue colors. Start with the lightest colors of tissue first and save the darkest for last. It is difficult to change the color of dark tissue by overlapping it with other colors. If one area becomes too dark, you might cut out a piece of white paper, glue it over the dark area carefully, and apply new colors over the white area.

1. Apply a coat of adhesive to the area where you wish to place the tissue.
2. Place the tissue down carefully over the wet area (Figure T–30). Don't let your fingers get wet.
3. Then add another coat of adhesive over the tissue. If your brush picks up any color from the wet tissue, rinse your brush in water and let it dry before using it again.
4. Experiment by overlapping colors. Allow the tissue to wrinkle to create textures as you apply it. Be sure that all the loose edges of tissue are glued down.

28. Working with Glue

When applying glue, always start at the center of the surface you are coating and work outward.

• When gluing papers together don't use a lot of glue, just a dot will do. Use dots in the corners and along the edges. Press the two surfaces together. Keep dots at least ½ inch (1.3 cm) in from the edge of your paper.
• Handle a glued surface carefully with only your fingertips. Make sure your hands are clean before pressing the glued surface into place.
• *Note:* The glue should be as thin as possible. Thick or beaded glue will create ridges on your work.

▲ **Figure T–30**

▲ Artists, down through the ages, have helped us visualize what we learn about history. Art historians are responsible for much of what we know about the artists who have lived in the past.

Paul Cézanne

1839–1906
French Painter

The Card Player
page 19

Mont Sainte-Victoire
page 226

In 1839 the art of photography was born in France. Another French birth the same year — that of Paul Cézanne — would lead to equally important developments in the future of pictures.

Cézanne was born in the town of Aix (**ex**) in southern France. At the age of 22 he journeyed to Paris to study with the Romantics. He soon learned of other styles of painting that held even greater appeal for him.

By the end of the 1870s Cézanne began experimenting with an art style all his own. He returned to the south of France to perfect it. His goal, as he described it, was "to make of Impressionism something solid and permanent, like the art of the museums."

A loner, Cézanne struck the people of his little town as a strange figure. Who, they wondered, was this man who spent his days alone in the fields, making paintings no one bought? It was while out in the fields one rainy day during his sixty-seventh year that Cézanne developed a bad cough. A few days later he died of pneumonia.

Cézanne's one-of-a-kind use of color patches to create solid forms is showcased in *Mont Sainte-Victoire* (page **226**). This is one of over 60 views of a favorite subject the artist painted.

The widespread availability in the early 1300s of a product called paper ushered in a new era in writing. A new era in painting came about during this same period. The person responsible for this second development was a gifted Italian artist named Giotto di Bondone (**jah**-toh dee-bahn-**dohn**-ee).

Giotto's lifelong calling as an artist was clear from the time he was 10. The son of a shepherd, he liked to pass the time drawing on flat stones in the fields. According to a popular story, one day a famous artist named Cimabue (chee-muh-**boo**-ay) came across young Giotto at work. Amazed at the boy's skill, Cimabue took him into his studio. Soon Giotto's skill as a painter was recognized throughout Italy.

In the early 1300s Giotto was asked to paint a series of frescoes on the walls of a church in Padua, Italy. One of these, *The Flight into Egypt*, is shown on page **154**. Like other religious paintings of the day, Giotto's works focused on familiar stories from the Bible. Unlike anything ever done before, however, Giotto's paintings were peopled with flesh-and-blood figures. These figures moved about in what appeared to be real space. They also exhibited feelings and emotions with their facial expressions and gestures. Painting had taken a giant step forward.

So great was Giotto's contribution that when he died, a statue was created in his honor. On its base were the words "I am Giotto, that is all. The name alone is a victory poem."

Giotto (di Bondone)

c. 1266–1337
Italian Painter

The Flight into Egypt
page 154

Francisco Goya
1746–1828
Spanish Painter

*Cornered (From the Disasters
of War)*
   page 187

The early 1800s found the world on the move. The invention of the steamboat was followed quickly by the building of the first railroad. The art world, too, was on the move — into a realm of self-expression where it has stayed to this day. The artist most identified with this move is a free spirit named Francisco Goya (fran-**sis**-koh **goy**-uh).

Goya lived in Saragossa (sar-uh-**goh**-suh), Spain. As a young man he traveled to Italy. He was not impressed by the Renaissance masterpieces and returned home. There he went to work as a portrait painter. His works flattered the members of the Spanish ruling class, who were his subjects. In 1786 he was named personal painter to King Charles IV.

An illness six years later left the artist deaf. Far from plunging him into despair, his handicap seemed to fuel his imagination. When war broke out in 1808, the artist created a series of prints unlike anything done before. Goya's view of war has no heroes or acts of glory. Like *Cornered* (page **187**), the prints in this series speak, rather, of senseless waste and brutality.

As Goya grew older, his view of the world grew grimmer still. His later works drew more and more on his own inner dreams and visions.

By the mid-1890s the United States had entered the age of communication. The newly invented telephone and wireless telegraph made it possible for people to communicate with one another over great distances. Not all people benefited from these inventions, however. To Native Americans tucked away in the New Mexico wilderness, time had stood still. It was in that quiet place at this not-so-quiet time that an artist named Lucy Lewis was born.

Lucy Lewis was raised in a pueblo in the town of Acoma (uh-**coh**-muh). She learned early of the importance of pottery to her people. As a child, Lewis watched her aunt make wide-bellied pots called *ollas* (**oy**-uhs). She was taught where to dig for the best clay and how to mix the clay with water. As she grew, she began to experiment with different natural pigments. The pots she designed and crafted were unusually lightweight and handsome.

In time, people in the pueblo became aware that Lucy Lewis had a special gift. They encouraged her to enter craft fairs and shows. She followed their advice — and came away with many awards.

Today Lewis still lives in the Acoma area with her family. There she and her daughters teach others the fine craft of pottery.

Lucy Lewis
1897–
Native American Craftsperson

Polychrome Pots
   page 201

Judith Leyster

1609–1660
Dutch Painter

Self-Portrait
page 181

The late 1800s were a time of great discovery. In Germany a scientist named Roentgen (**rent**-guhn) discovered X-rays. In France a husband and wife named Curie (**kyu**-ree) discovered the element radium. Another discovery in France at the time had important consequences for the art world. It was the discovery of a signature on a painting long thought to be by the great Dutch artist Franz Hals. The surprising signature read "Judith Leyster" (**ly**-stuhr), not Franz Hals.

This "mystery" artist had been born some 250 years earlier in the Dutch city of Haarlem (**har**-luhm). At a time when women seeking art careers were often helped by artist fathers, Leyster—a brewer's daughter—had to rely on talent alone. Another difference between her and other female painters was her choice of subject matter. Instead of delicate still lifes, Leyster did robust genre paintings and portraits. One of these, her now-famous *Self-Portrait*, appears on page **181**. By 17 she had gained a reputation as an artist of great promise.

Leyster learned—and learned well—from other major painters of her day. Most notable among these are Hals, for his brush technique, and Caravaggio (see page **179**), for his use of light. Still, her works have a look that on careful inspection is unmistakably hers. Her portraits, especially, seem to invite the viewer in as if subject and viewer were close friends.

The voyages in the late 1400s of Christopher Columbus and Vasco da Gama broadened the world's horizons. So did the birth during that period of possibly the greatest artist the world has ever known. His name was Michelangelo Buonarroti (my-kuh-**lan**-juh-loh bwohn-uh-**rah**-tee).

Michelangelo was born in Florence to a poor family. At the age of six he was sent to live with the family of a stonecutter. There he came to love the feel of a sculptor's chisel and hammer in his hands. Art had found its way into his life.

Over the next 10 years Michelangelo's genius was given shape and direction through study with Florence's foremost artists. By the time he was 24, he had completed his first masterpiece, the *Pietà* (page **165**).

Despite his great talents, Michelangelo was hampered by some very human shortcomings. One was a hot temper, which made him hard to work with. Another was a need to see every project he took on in larger-than-life terms. Because of this second weakness, many of his works were never finished. One that was completed—and one of his most famous achievements—was his magnificent painting of the ceiling of the Sistine Chapel in Rome. The heroic job took four years to complete. During that time Michelangelo worked flat on his back on a platform he had built 68 feet (20 m) above the chapel floor!

Michelangelo (Buonarroti)

1475–1564
Italian Sculptor, Painter

Pietà
page 165

Joan Miró
1893–1983
Spanish Painter

Femme
page 27

Dutch Interior
page 259

The year was 1925. The world had scarcely recovered from "the war to end all wars" when it was shaken again. This time the explosion took place within the art world of Paris. It was caused by paintings like *Dutch Interior* (page **259**), created by a shy little Spanish artist named Joan Miró (zhoo-**ahn** meer-**roh**).

Miró was born in a town outside of Barcelona (bahr-suh-**loh**-nuh), Spain. As an art student, he was made to draw objects by "feeling" them rather than looking at them. For someone more fascinated by the world within than the one outside, the exercise was perfect training.

In 1919 Miró traveled to Paris, the capital of the art world. There he fell upon hard times. He was forced to get by on one meal a week. In between he ate dried figs to keep up his strength. It may have been the visions brought about by hunger that led to his first important Surrealist pictures.

After his first showing, Miró was hailed as a major new talent. He went to live on the island of Majorca (muh-**yor**-kuh), off the coast of Spain. There he painted in a room so small he had trouble moving around in it.

Later in his long career Miró broadened his interests to include sculpture. He also created huge weavings that, like *Femme* (page **27**), mirror the colorful designs of his paintings.

After the Brooklyn Bridge opened in the late 1800s, bridge building would never be the same. After a showing of paintings in Paris during this same period, art would never be the same. The showing was by a group of artists who had been turned down by the Salon. Their style, which became known as Impressionism, took its name from a work by one of the group's founders. His name was Claude Monet (**klohd** moh-**nay**).

Monet was born in Paris in 1840. His father, a grocer, moved the family to the port city of Le Havre (luh **hahv**-ruh) soon after his son's birth. Even as a child, Monet saw something magical in sunlight's effects on water. He studied with a noted landscape artist, who taught him the basics of Realist painting.

It was while a student that Monet met two other young artists, Auguste Renoir (oh-**guste** ren-**wahr**) and Alfred Sisley. The three soon became friends. They also began experimenting together, making paintings outdoors in natural sunlight. At first their works were laughed at by critics. Today the works of these three artists are among the most admired in the history of art.

It was during a stay in England that Monet painted *Waterloo Bridge, London* (page **220**). Like his other mature works, this work contains no solid lines or forms. Rather, these elements are hinted at through dabs and dots of color.

Claude Monet
1840–1926
French Painter

Banks of the Seine, Vetheuil
page 216

Waterloo Bridge, London
page 220

Berthe Morisot

1841–1895
French Painter

---

*The Artist's Sister at a
Window*
   page 218

The last decade of the 1800s was a time of change. In 1896 Thomas Edison burst on the scene with the invention of the motion picture. A year earlier the art world mourned the passing of a maker of pictures of a different sort. Her name was Berthe Morisot (**behrt** maw-ree-**zoh**).

Berthe Morisot was born into an art family. Her parents were art lovers and Jean-Honoré Fragonard (**zhahnh** oh-nor-**ay** frah-goh-**nahrh**), an important painter of the 1700s, may have been her great-grandfather. From the time she was a young girl, she knew she would become a painter. At 15 she met and became good friends with Edouard Manet (ay-doo-**ahrh** mah-**nay**), a leading artist of the day. Several years later she married Manet's brother.

Like Manet, Morisot focused on indoor scenes and portraits. Her portrait titled *The Artist's Sister at a Window* (page **218**) is one of her best-known works.

Although other artists praised her work, during her lifetime Morisot was ignored by critics. Many did so merely because she was a woman. It was not until her death that her work began receiving the respect it had always deserved.

In 1905 Albert Einstein published his theory of relativity. In so doing, he challenged age-old beliefs about the meaning of time and space. In that same year a young girl moved with her family from Russia to America. She would grow up to create art that would challenge age-old beliefs about the meaning of sculpture. Her name was Louise Nevelson (**nev**-uhl-suhn).

As a child in Maine, Nevelson spent long hours playing in her father's lumberyard. She loved to carve and build using the scraps of wood she found.

At the age of 20 Louise married and two years later gave birth to a child. In time, she came to resent the responsibilities of marriage and motherhood that took time away from her art. In 1931 she left her son with her parents and headed to Europe to study art.

Nevelson's first showing came in 1941. The reviews, which were favorable, spurred her on. In the decades that followed, she began more and more to experiment with "found" media. It was not uncommon to find her studio littered with wood scraps very much like the ones she had played with in her father's lumberyard. Most of Nevelson's works from the 1960s on are, like *Mrs. N's Palace* (page **267**), three-dimensional collages. Most invite viewers to use their imaginations as well as their eyes.

Louise Nevelson

1900–1988
American Sculptor

Mrs. N's Palace
   page 267

Albert Pinkham Ryder

1847–1917
American Painter

Moonlight Marine (Toilers of the Sea)
    page **234**

The first two decades of the twentieth century were a politically stormy time. The winds of revolution swept through Russia and China. In 1914 the world went to war. To take their minds off gloomy events of the day, some people turned inward. One who did—and came back to the world with a rare gift of art—was Albert Pinkham Ryder.

Ryder was born in New Bedford, Massachusetts. When he was a young man, his family moved to New York City. There an older brother helped pay his way through art school. Showing little interest in the works of other artists, Ryder forged his own one-of-a-kind style. Among the features of his style were paint layers so thick that his pictures sometimes looked three-dimensional.

Always given to strange personal habits, Ryder developed still odder ways during his middle years. He gave up his Greenwich Village apartment and moved into a run-down rooming house. Burdened by poor eyesight, he spent his days indoors, his nights roaming the streets alone. After 1900 he became a hermit altogether.

It may have been during his silent night walks that Ryder dreamed up ideas for his pictures. Most, like *Moonlight Marine* (page **234**), are glimpses of a dream world, which capture the viewer's imagination.

In 1921 a bitterly fought revolution in Mexico ended. Honest, hard-working people, long treated as slaves by rich landlords, were free at last. In that same year a talented Mexican artist returned from abroad. He began the first of many larger-than-life chronicles of the struggle for freedom. His name was Diego Rivera (dee-**ay**-goh rih-**vehr**-uh).

Rivera was born in the city of Guanajuato (gwahn-uh-**waht**-oh). As a young man, he journeyed to Paris, where he met Picasso and Matisse. While in Europe he also studied the art of the great Italian fresco painters. The size of the frescoes—some covered entire walls—appealed to him. Such an art form, he felt, would be a fitting tribute to those who had fought so bravely in the Mexican Revolution. It would also be a reminder to Mexico's rich of the power of the people.

Murals like *The Liberation of the Peon* (page **251**) reveal Rivera's skill as a storyteller. They also reveal the influences of both Giotto and Rivera's pre-Columbian ancestors.

After making a name for himself, Rivera was asked to paint murals in the United States. He created works that, like those in Mexico, were filled with people and action. These illustrated the American fascination with speed and the machine. Unfortunately, many of these magnificant murals were destroyed.

Diego Rivera

1886–1957
Mexican Painter

The Liberation of the Peon
    page **251**

Alfred Stieglitz

1864–1946
American Photographer

The Terminal
page 249

Around 1900 the United States opened its doors to Americans-to-be from all nations. To young Abstract painters hoping to enter the art world of the day, the door was firmly shut. Abstract painting was misunderstood and unappreciated by the public and most art critics. One free thinker who provided an outlet for these brave new talents was himself an artist. He was photographer Alfred Stieglitz (**steeg-luhts**).

Stieglitz was born in Hoboken, New Jersey. His interest in photography began when he was young. Early in his career he began seeing photography's potential as an art medium. He spent long hours — sometimes in swirling snow — waiting for just the right shot.

In 1902 he formed Photo-Secession, an organization devoted to the art of photography. Three years later he opened a gallery at 291 Fifth Avenue in New York City. Known as 291, the gallery became a haven for struggling young artists from all areas of art. One artist whose work was displayed at 291 was a native of Wisconsin named Georgia O'Keeffe. Stieglitz and O'Keeffe developed a friendship that grew over time. Despite an age difference of 23 years, the two were married in 1924.

Stieglitz spent his life championing the world of other photographers. Still, his own photographs are among the most sensitive ever taken. Through instant human studies, like *The Terminal* (page **249**), he carried photography to new heights.

In 1875 Congress passed an act giving African Americans the right to serve on juries. Eight years later the Supreme Court declared the act unconstitutional. It was not long after that decision that artist Henry Tanner made a decision of his own. Tanner, an African American artist having little success selling paintings in America, decided to set sail for Europe.

Tanner had been born 32 years earlier in Philadelphia, Pennsylvania. His father was a minister, who later became a bishop. Tanner's interest in art began when he was only 12. Walking through a park with his father, he saw a landscape painter at work. Tanner watched in fascination. As his fascination grew, so did his desire to become a painter.

Tanner entered the Pennsylvania Academy of Fine Arts, where his teacher was Thomas Eakins. Eakins advised his student to turn from landscapes to genre scenes — which Tanner did. But Tanner found there was little market for paintings of any kind by an African American. Wanting, in any case, to focus on Biblical subjects, he headed for Paris. Within five years one of his Biblical pictures was hanging in a place of honor at the Paris Salon.

While Tanner painted mostly religious works, he still found time now and then to exhibit his skills at painting landscapes. *The Seine* (page **236**) is one of these works.

Henry O. Tanner

1859–1937
American Painter

The Seine
page 236

▲ There are many career opportunities in art and art-related fields.

Art Director

You may know that movies are the work of hundreds of people. You may also know there is one person in charge of all others, called the director. But did you know that advertisements, books, and magazines also have directors?

Art directors are experienced artists whose job is to lead or supervise other artists. Like film directors, art directors are responsible for seeing that all other jobs in a project are done.

Art directors are hired by advertising agencies, book publishers, and television or radio stations. The specific tasks of the job may differ slightly from place to place. In general, the art director hires and oversees the work of illustrators, photographers, and graphic designers. Together, the art director and the people who report to him or her are called a team. The art director has the responsibility for signing off, or approving, all work done by team members.

Art Teacher

Many people with an interest in art and a desire to share their knowledge become art teachers.

A career in art teaching requires a college education. Part of that education is devoted to methods of teaching. Part is devoted to developing a broad background in the history of art and the use of art materials and techniques.

Good art teachers open their students to a wide variety of art experiences. They give students the chance to create their own art and to react to the art of others. They also make sure their students learn about such important areas as aesthetics, art criticism, and art history.

While most art teachers work in schools, some find employment opportunities in other areas. Some art teachers work in museums or hospitals. Some teachers work in retirement centers. Still others work in nursery schools and day-care centers.

Computer Graphics Specialist

What do computers have to do with art? To the person known as a computer graphics specialist, the answer is "everything!"

Computer graphics specialists are skilled professionals who use state-of-the-art electronic equipment to create designs. The work they do has brought the world of commercial art into the space age. A career in this field combines a strong background in design with a knowledge of computers.

The computer graphics specialist works with tools such as electric light pens on electronic tablets. With these tools, any image may be drawn and colored in. Such computer drawings may be stored permanently in the computer's memory. They can then be called up and reworked by the designer as needed.

Some computer graphics specialists work with systems that allow them to see their finished work in different sizes and colors. Computer-made designs can also be sent along telephone lines around the world.

Editorial Cartoonist

Newspaper editorials are written accounts that invite readers to form an opinion about important news topics. Editorial cartoons do the same work in pictures.

Editorial cartoonists, the people who create such pictures, work for newspapers and magazines. Their creations usually appear as single drawings without titles or captions. Sometimes editorial cartoons go hand-in-hand with the main editorial, which is printed nearby. At other times they comment on other issues figuring in current events.

Many editorial cartoonists use a style of art called *caricature* (**kar**-ih-kuh-chur). This is the exaggerating of facial features or expressions to poke fun at well-known figures. Some editorial cartoonists use symbols to communicate their meanings. A bear, for instance, is often used by editorial cartoonists to symbolize the Soviet Union.

Exhibit and Display Designer

The next time you pass a display of clothing or other goods in a department store, look carefully. Somewhere within that display will be a hidden message: artist at work.

Exhibit and display designers work in a number of retail and non-profit settings. Some of these settings are trade shows, department stores, showrooms, art galleries, and museums. Such designers plan presentations of collections, exhibits, and traveling shows of all kinds. They are responsible for such matters as deciding what items should be grouped together. They also take into account how displays should be arranged and lighted.

The display designer is an important part of the sales team. Displays attract customers. They can affect a customer's decision to buy. The way the display designer does his or her job can make all the difference between whether or not a sale is made.

Graphic Designer

There are artists all around us. They are there behind every billboard, street sign, and soup can label. These artists are called graphic designers. They use pictures and words to inform or decorate.

Graphic designers work in a great many areas. Each area has its own special tasks and title. Technical illustrator is one of these titles. Sign maker is another.

The field of graphic design has its roots in the 1500s. It was in that century that the printing press was invented. People were needed to arrange words and pictures on the printed page. To this day that task, known as layout, is a job of graphic designers. Graphic designers also pick type faces, or styles of lettering, for printed material. They must also decide how drawings or photographs will be used as illustrations.

Industrial Designer

What do toys, vacuum cleaners, and cars have in common? All are designed to work easily and have a pleasing look. These and countless other items you see and use each day are the work of industrial designers.

Industrial designers work for makers of products. These artists work closely with engineers who develop the products. Sometimes industrial designers are asked to work on things as simple as tamper-proof caps for medicines. At other times they are asked to work on projects as complicated as space vehicles. Before they begin work, industrial designers need to know how the product is to be used.

Because different brands of the same product are sold, industrial design sometimes crosses over into advertising. The appearance of a design becomes especially important in the case of very competitive products such as cars and entertainment systems, for example.

Interior Designer

Architects give us attractive, functional spaces in which to live, work, and play. Interior designers fill those spaces with attractive and useful furnishings and accessories.

The job of the interior designer is to plan the interior space. This includes choosing furniture, fabrics, floor coverings, lighting fixtures, and decorations. To do this job well, the designer must take into account the wants and needs of the users of the space. In planning a home, for example, the interior designer will learn as much as possible about the lifestyle of the family that lives there.

Interior designers help their clients envision their ideas through the use of floor plans, elevations, and sketches. Once a client has agreed to a plan, the designer makes arrangements for buying materials. He or she also oversees the work for builders, carpenters, painters, and other craftspeople.

Magazine Designer

Magazine designers are graphic designers who work for publications called *periodicals*. These are booklets or pamphlets that come out on a regular basis in issues.

There are two parts to a magazine design — the fixed design and the variable design. The fixed design includes the features of the magazine that seldom change. These include the different type faces and decorative elements such as page borders. The magazine designer works mostly on the variable design. This includes making sure all the pages in an issue are a standard length. Another part of variable design is figuring out where illustrations should go and how large they should be.

At times a magazine designer is called upon to create special features for a periodical. These are used to highlight a theme running throughout the issue.

Medical Illustrator

Among Leonardo da Vinci's many achievements were his drawings of *anatomy* or human body parts. Ever since his time there has been a call for medical illustrators.

Medical illustrators work for medical schools, teaching hospitals, and publishers of medical journals and textbooks. All have a basic knowledge of medicine and an ability to work with many different art media. Among these are transparencies (trans-**pare**-uhn-sees), or illustrations that are placed on overhead projectors.

The work of medical illustrators falls into two main areas. One is the drawing of diagrams showing various details, such as the heart and limbs. The second is doing step-by-step illustrations of surgical and other medical procedures.

At times medical illustrators are called upon to work with such medical equipment as X-ray machines, microscopes, and scanners.

Museum Curator

Like universities and libraries, museums have the job of preserving and passing on culture. The person in charge of seeing that the museum does its job is called the museum curator (**kyoor**-ayt-uhr).

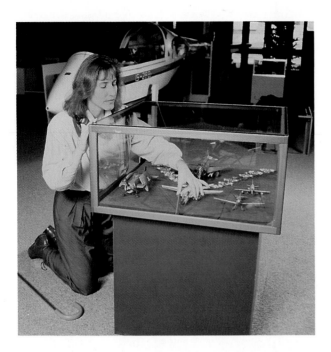

Curators are part custodian, part scholar, and part historian. The tasks of the curator are many. They include securing, caring for, displaying, and studying works of art. The curator makes sure works are arranged so they teach, inform, and delight.

As holders of advanced college degrees, curators carry on research in their own areas of interest. They report their findings in books, lectures, and journals.

Photojournalist

Photography, as you have learned, was unheard of until the mid-1800s. No sooner had photography emerged on the scene, however, than the field of photojournalism was born. Photojournalism is the taking of pictures for newspapers and magazines.

One of the earliest photojournalists was a photographer named Mathew Brady. Brady lived in America during the Civil War. His early black-and-white snapshots offer dramatic glimpses of life on and off the battlefield.

Since Brady's time the field of photojournalism has grown and with it, the responsibilities of the photographer. Photojournalists are expected to seek out and record newsworthy scenes. They must also be able to take action pictures quickly and process them with equal speed.

Some photojournalists in recent decades have chosen specialties for themselves. Two of these areas are politics and sports.

Special Effects Designer

Are you the sort of person whose imagination works overtime? Then maybe the field of special effects design is for you.

Unlike people in other art careers, special effects designers may not attend special schools. The field is very new. The people who have created film and television magic to date have come up through the ranks. They may have started by building sets for plays or designing film backgrounds.

Special effects artists are one part painter, one part sculptor, and one part engineer. They have the ability to imagine, and then create, fantasy scenes or creatures. They are masters of make-believe.

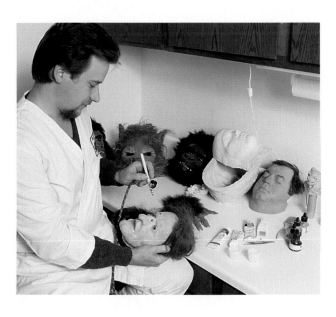

There is no limit to the tools used by special effects designers. Depending on the needs of a project, they might use papier-mâché, plaster, plastic molds, or paint. Makeup, trick photography, and computers are just a few of the other media they use.

Urban Planner

Have you ever wondered how big cities come to look the way they do? The two-word answer to this question is urban (or city) planners.

City planners are people whose job is to supervise the care and improvement of a city. Every large American city has a planner.

A main task of city planners is to enforce zoning laws. These are laws controlling what part of a city may be used for what purposes. Thanks to city planners, garbage dumps are not located in residential communities.

A second task of the city planner is to look after the growth and development of the urban areas. The planner works with the mayor and other city officials to create parks, harbors, and shopping malls.

City planners are trained as architects. Their knowledge of design helps them to plan a pleasing cityscape.

Computer-Type Drawing

Look back at the painting in Figure 15–4 on page **230**. The work illustrates the Pointillist technique of Georges Seurat. When you look at this work, your eye connects the dots to make forms and colors. Taking an approach similar to Seurat's, computer artists in recent years have started creating pictures like the one shown in Figure S–1. The tiny squares of color, called pixels (**piks**-els), work exactly as the dots do in a Seurat painting. When seen from a distance they blend together into a recognizable three-dimensional image.

WHAT YOU WILL LEARN

You will plan and create a computer-type drawing emphasizing a single three-dimensional form. You will use colored pencils and graph paper to create pixels of color. Warm and cool colors will be combined to suggest a three-dimensional form. (See Figure S–2.)

WHAT YOU WILL NEED

- Pencil, eraser, and colored pencils
- Sheet of graph paper, 9 x 12 inches (23 x 30 cm)

▶ **Figure S–1** How does the use of warm and cool hues help to show form in this computer-generated work?

WHAT YOU WILL DO

1. Pick colors for your work ranging from very warm to very cool. Choose an equal number of each type, no fewer than eight.
2. Working lightly in pencil, draw the outline of a large, interesting shape on the graph paper. The shape may be either organic or geometric but should fill most of the page. Use the eraser to make adjustments. When you are pleased with the shape you have created, trace over it in a very cool hue.
3. Find the square that is roughly in the center of your shape. Color in this first square using the warmest, brightest hue. This could be a bright orange or yellow. Using the same hue, fill in the squares directly above, below, and to either side.
4. Continue to work outward from the center square. As you do, switch little by little to warm hues that are less bright. When you reach roughly the halfway point between the center and outermost squares, begin to use bright cool colors. The squares closest to the outline of the shape should be filled with color.
5. When you have finished, display your work along with those of your classmates. Stand back and look at the different drawings. Which of the shapes look most three-dimensional?

EXAMINING YOUR WORK

- **Describe** Name the colors used. Identify those that are warm colors and those that are cool colors. Explain how the warm and cool colors have been used to suggest a three-dimensional form.
- **Analyze** Explain how step-by-step changes in color are used to change a shape into a form. Tell how this form is emphasized in the drawing.
- **Interpret** State what image, if any, your shape calls to mind. Create a title for your work.
- **Judge** Tell whether you have succeeded in suggesting a three-dimensional form. If you have not, tell what you could do to improve your work.

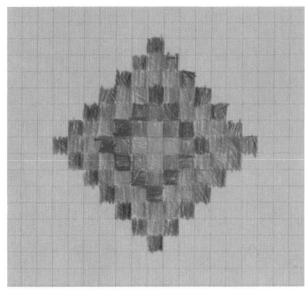

▲ Figure S–2 Student work. Computer-type drawing.

OTHER STUDIO IDEAS

- Repeat the assignment, this time using only lead pencil. Leave the squares closest to the center white. Press harder and harder as you move outward. The boxes at the outer edge should be as black as you can make them. Notice how gradual changes in value can also be used to suggest a three-dimensional form.

- ●● Repeat the assignment, this time using tempera paint in place of the colored pencils. Add a background of sky and clouds to your shape, painting freely. Identify what style of art the finished work most resembles.

LESSON 2

Coil Pot

Look at the object in Figure S–3. This is an example of an early Native American coil clay pot. Scientific dating of artifacts like this helps experts estimate the earliest time ancient people may have arrived on this continent. Works like this also provide a window on the way of life of those people.

WHAT YOU WILL LEARN

You will create a clay pot in the style of prehistoric Native Americans. You will give the work a sense of rhythm by increasing and then decreasing the size of coils. Your finished pot should be both useful and decorative.

WHAT YOU WILL NEED

- 2 pounds of clay, and slip
- Canvas-covered clay board
- Large plastic bag and bowl of water
- Scrap piece of heavy cardboard

WHAT YOU WILL DO

1. Review Technique Tip **16**, *Handbook* page **281**. It will give you some general background information on working with clay.
2. Gently throw your clay against the clay board. Doing this will remove any air pockets that might cause your work to explode when fired.

▶ **Figure S–3   What do you suppose were some of the functional uses of a pot like this in the Pueblo culture?**

Pueblo. Ceramic Jar. Prehistoric. White slip with black painted decoration. 10.8 x 15.8 cm (4¼ x 6¼"). Indian Arts Research Center, Santa Fe, New Mexico.

3. Pinch off a lump of clay about the size of a lemon. With the heel of your hand, flatten the lump into a circle about ½ inch (13 mm) thick. Set it aside. (See Figure S–4.)

4. Pinch off a second smaller lump, and roll it into a rope. The rope should be about ½ inch (13 mm) thick and 12 inches (30 cm) long. Form the rope into a ring, joining the two ends with slip. Seal the ring to the circle you made. This is to be the base of your pot.

5. Create four more ropes. All should be the same thickness as the first rope. Each, however, should be slightly longer than the one before it. Form the shortest rope into a ring, as you did earlier. Using slip, attach it to your base. Form the next longest rope into a ring. Attach it to the outer edges of the last coil. Continue to work in this fashion until your work is five coils high.

6. Roll out five more ropes, this time making each slightly shorter than the one before it. Form the longest into a ring. Attach it to the inner edges of the last coil on your pot. Continue working in this manner until you have used all your ropes. (*Hint:* If it takes longer than one class period to finish your pot, store it in the plastic bag. This will keep it moist until you are ready to work with it again.)

7. Allow your pot to dry to the greenware stage. Use the scrap of cardboard as a scraper to smooth out any bumps. Fire the pot in a kiln. Display your finished pot alongside those of classmates. Which pots succeed in showing a sense of rhythm?

EXAMINING YOUR WORK

- **Describe**   Tell whether all the coils in your pot have the same thickness. Describe the form of your pot. Explain what you did to obtain this form.
- **Analyze**   Tell which principles were used to organize the elements in your work. State whether your pot has a sense of rhythm. Explain how this sense of rhythm is realized.
- **Interpret**   Point out in what ways your pot is similar to a prehistoric Native American coil pot.
- **Judge**   Tell whether you have succeeded in creating a work that is both useful and decorative. Tell what changes you would make if you were going to redo your pot.

▲ Figure S–4   Student work in progress.

OTHER STUDIO IDEAS

- Make a second pot similar to the first one. This time, use your fingernails or a pencil point to dent each coil every inch (3 cm) or so. This will add an interesting texture. Compare your pot with the coiled pot in Figure 13–2 on page **194**.

- ●● Make a second pot similar to the first one. This time, use your cardboard scraper to smooth out the coils. Using a sharp clay tool, carve a geometric design in the surface of your pot. This design should be made so that it fits comfortably within the shape of your pot.

ADDITIONAL STUDIOS

Photo Essay

Dorothea Lange (dahr-uh-**thee**-uh **lang**) was a portrait photographer of the 1920s and 1930s who grew tired of making "pretty" pictures. Looking for a more meaningful outlet for her talents, she turned to photo essays. These are collections of photographs that together make a statement about the human condition. The photo essay in Figure S–5 is one from an essay Lange shot during the Great Depression of the 1930s. This was a time when many people were out of work. Hunger and homelessness were widespread. Study the photograph. In it, Lange offers more than just a portrait of a starving mother and her children. She captures the hopelessness and despair of a bleak time.

▶ **Figure S–5 Can you identify any of the elements of art that work to capture feeling or mood in this photograph?**

Dorothea Lange. *Migrant Mother.* Nipomo, California. 1936. Library of Congress, Washington, D.C.

WHAT YOU WILL LEARN

You will create a photo essay dealing with a theme that focuses on some aspect of the human condition today. You will contrast color and value to emphasize a center of interest in your photos. You will share your work with your class as part of a sound-sight presentation.

WHAT YOU WILL NEED

- Instant camera and color slide film
- Slide projector and screen
- Tape recorder or phonograph

WHAT YOU WILL DO

1. Pick a theme for your photo essay. The theme should deal with some aspect of the human condition today. Some possibilities are pollution, problems of the aging, overcrowding, or Americans' fascination with speed.
2. Carefully read the directions for using your camera and film. Think about the angle from which you will shoot your subjects. Decide whether shooting your subjects from above or below eye level might add to your statement. Decide whether close-ups or long shots will best serve your needs.
3. Explore your neighborhood or town looking for subjects for photos that fit your theme. Be creative in your search for ideas. An elderly person seated alone on a park bench might be used to support the theme of loneliness. A person looking impatiently at his or her watch might be used to illustrate the American "rat race."

EXAMINING YOUR WORK

- **Describe** Identify the theme you chose. Tell why you chose it. Explain how you decided what pictures to shoot to illustrate this theme.
- **Analyze** Tell whether your pictures were in focus. Tell from what angles you shot your pictures. Explain how your decisions affected your work. Point out the center of interest in your photos. Tell how you used color and value to emphasize this center of interest.
- **Interpret** State the theme of your essay. Tell whether viewers understood your theme. Give your photo essay a title.
- **Judge** Tell whether you were satisfied with your presentation. Explain what, if anything, you would do to improve it on a second try.

4. Photograph your subjects. Be sure to hold the camera still while shooting. When possible, rest the camera on a ledge or other stationary object. Consider contrasts of color and value to make your subject the center of interest.
5. Have your slides developed. While they are being developed, locate musical recordings that go along with your theme.
6. Present your work to the class. Do your classmates understand the theme? Do they get your message?

OTHER STUDIO IDEAS

- Repeat the activity, this time using photos clipped from magazines. Mount the photos on a sheet of poster board. Plan your arrangement so that it effectively expresses your theme. Include the title of your essay in your design.

- • Repeat the activity, this time using color or black-and-white print film. Mount the developed prints on a sheet of poster board. Plan your arrangement to express the theme. Include the title of your essay in your design.

ADDITIONAL STUDIOS

False Face Mask

Among the finest examples of early Native American art are the false face masks created by the Iroquois (**ir**-uh-kwoy). Carved from living trees, these masks were thought to be alive with spiritual powers. So completely did the Iroquois believe in the life force of these masks that they fed them!

Study the mask in Figure S–6. In what ways is this object similar to the African face mask in Figure 9–8 (page **136**)? In what ways are the two different?

WHAT YOU WILL LEARN

You will make a false face mask using papier-mâché or strips of cloth or gauze dipped in plaster. Your mask will stand for a particular guardian spirit and show that spirit's character. You will paint your mask using either an analogous or a complementary color scheme. You will use feathers, straw, or shredded paper for hair to add texture to your mask and increase its visual interest. (See Figure S–7.)

WHAT YOU WILL NEED

- Sketchbook and pencil
- Lifesize model of a human skull or Styrofoam wig support
- Plastic wrap, mixing bowl, and water
- Commercially prepared papier-mâché paste
- Strips of newspaper
- *Optional:* Plaster, strips of cloth or gauze instead of papier-mâché
- Sandpaper, scissors, and white glue
- Acrylic paint and several brushes
- Feathers, straw, or shredded paper
- String or ribbon

▶ **Figure S–6   Can you tell what the decoration on this mask is made from?**

Iroquoian. *Husk Face Mask.* National Museum of American History, Smithsonian Institution, Washington, D.C.

WHAT YOU WILL DO

1. Decide what guardian spirit your mask will stand for. Some possibilities are the spirit of good luck and the spirit of fair weather. Once you have chosen a spirit, make pencil sketches of how you believe your spirit should look. Your sketches should also show the character of the spirit — friendly, fierce, or frightening. Choose your best sketch.

2. Cover the skull model with plastic wrap. In the mixing bowl, combine commercially prepared papier-mâché paste and water. Soak strips of newspaper in the mixture, and apply these to the model's face. (For more on the use of papier-mâché, see Technique Tip **20**, *Handbook* page **283**.)

3. When the mask is thick enough to hold its shape, set it on a support to dry.

4. Remove the dried mask from the support. Use sandpaper to rid the mask of any rough spots. With the point of the scissors, carefully make eye and breathing holes. Cut a pinhole at eye level close to the edge on either side.

5. Using two or more hues of acrylic, paint your mask. Refer back to your pencil sketch. Use either an analogous or a complementary color scheme.

6. When the paint has dried, add hair in the form of feathers, straw, or shredded paper. Try to create a variety of textures. Attach the hair with white glue. Lace a piece of string or ribbon through the pinholes at the side. (Leave enough slack in the string so that the mask may be worn.)

7. Display your mask. Can classmates guess the guardian spirit living in your mask?

OTHER STUDIO IDEAS

• Using white glue, add feathers, beads, and other items to your mask in a decorative pattern. Use acrylic or tempera to paint shapes and lines that add to this decorative pattern. Tell whether this adds to or takes away from the mask's appeal.

EXAMINING YOUR WORK

• **Describe**   Identify the guardian spirit your mask stands for. Point out and describe the different textures you used. Tell what colors you used to paint your mask.

• **Analyze**   Explain what kind of color scheme you used. Show where texture variety adds visual interest to your mask.

• **Interpret**   Explain how your choice of color scheme helped identify the character of the guardian spirit it represents. Create a legend to go with your mask.

• **Judge**   Tell whether your work succeeds. Explain your answer.

▲ Figure S–7   Student work. False face mask.

•• Create another mask in which you use a color scheme that emphasizes the gentle or fierce character of the spirit. Colors and color combinations should be as expressive as possible. Determine if viewers can identify the character of your spirit.

Space Colony

The technological advances of each age give artists new subject ideas. In the 1800s artists could, if they chose, base a work on the locomotive. In the early twentieth century the car became an option as the basis for a painting or drawing. More recently artists have found still other frontiers to explore. One such frontier is illustrated in the painting in Figure S–8. What do you suppose an artist of today might find as a next subject?

WHAT YOU WILL LEARN

You will design a space colony that will provide housing on another planet for humans of the future. The colony should be both practical and pleasant to live in. The forms of buildings and other structures should vary in size and shape. They should also harmonize with the natural forms of the planet. You will use shading techniques to give your forms depth.

WHAT YOU WILL NEED

- Pencil and sketch paper
- Sheet of black construction paper, 12 x 18 inches (30 x 46 cm)
- Oil pastels

▲ Figure S–8   This art work appears at a national science museum. What kind of statement does this make about the role of art in our modern culture?

Robert McCall. *Space Station #1.* Poster created for the MGM film "2001: A Space Odyssey." National Air and Space Museum, Washington, D.C.

WHAT YOU WILL DO

1. Make pencil sketches of rock formations and other natural land features you might find on a strange, newly discovered planet. Be as imaginative as you can. Choose your best sketch. Make a second set of sketches that show the main features of your colony. Include buildings of different types and sizes. The building forms should appear to grow out of the landscape on the planet and should not look like buildings on our own planet Earth. Again, choose your most imaginative sketch.

2. Turn the sheet of construction paper so it is lengthwise. Using a white oil pastel crayon, fill in the lower third of the sheet. This is to serve as a foundation for other colors in your work. Fill the upper two-thirds of the sheet with white dots. These are to appear as stars in a night sky. You might wish to show far-off moons and other planets as well. (For more on the use of oil pastels, see Technique Tip **3**, *Handbook* page **277**.

3. Switching to a black crayon, lightly transfer features from the two sketches you chose. Blend the two into a harmonious whole by making the buildings appear to grow out of the landscape. Fill in the building forms with hues of pastel that add to the overall harmony. Use different shading techniques to give your forms depth. (For information on shading techniques, see Technique Tip **6**, *Handbook* page **278**.)

EXAMINING YOUR WORK

- **Describe** Describe the land features of the new planet. Describe the forms of the buildings and other structures in your colony. Tell what colors you used for your colony.
- **Analyze** Identify the variety of building forms in your drawing. Tell whether the natural forms of the planet harmonize with the humanmade forms of your colony. Point to the shading techniques you used to give depth to the forms in your picture.
- **Interpret** Identify the different purposes for which the buildings in your colony might be built. Tell whether the space colony would be a practical and comfortable place to live.
- **Judge** Tell whether your work succeeds. Explain your answer.

4. Display your works beside those of classmates. Decide which show the most imagination. Which seem most believable?

OTHER STUDIO IDEAS

- Make a map of the area in which your space colony is located. Create a color-coded legend for your map showing height of objects. Create a scale of miles (kilometers).

- ● Create a three-dimensional relief of your space colony. Create buildings and other structures out of heavy-duty cardboard. Paint the relief using the same colors you did in your oil pastel version.

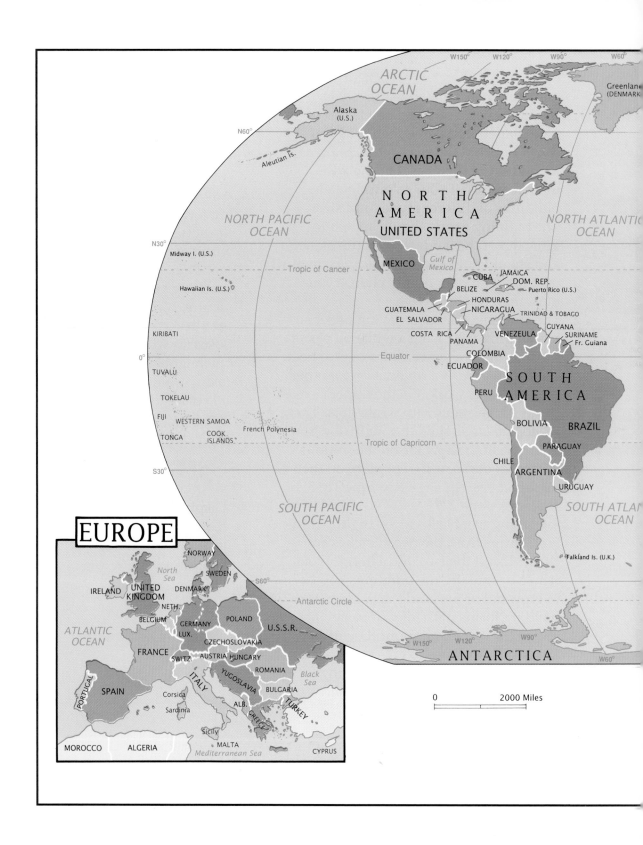

ARCTIC OCEAN

Greenland (DENMARK)

Alaska (U.S.)

Aleutian Is.

N60°

CANADA

NORTH PACIFIC OCEAN

N O R T H
A M E R I C A

UNITED STATES

NORTH ATLANTIC OCEAN

N30°

Midway I. (U.S.)

MEXICO

Gulf of Mexico

Tropic of Cancer

CUBA

JAMAICA
DOM. REP.
Puerto Rico (U.S.)

BELIZE

HONDURAS

Hawaiian Is. (U.S.)

GUATEMALA
EL SALVADOR

NICARAGUA

TRINIDAD & TOBAGO

KIRIBATI

COSTA RICA

PANAMA

VENEZEULA

GUYANA
SURINAME
Fr. Guiana

COLOMBIA

0°

ECUADOR

Equator

TUVALU

S O U T H
A M E R I C A

TOKELAU

PERU

FIJI

WESTERN SAMOA

French Polynesia

BOLIVIA

BRAZIL

TONGA

COOK ISLANDS

Tropic of Capricorn

PARAGUAY

CHILE

S30°

ARGENTINA

URUGUAY

SOUTH PACIFIC OCEAN

SOUTH ATLAN OCEAN

Falkland Is. (U.K.)

S60°

Antarctic Circle

W150°

W120°

W90°

W60°

ANTARCTICA

0   2000 Miles

EUROPE

NORWAY

North Sea

SWEDEN

IRELAND

UNITED KINGDOM

DENMARK

NETH.

BELGIUM

GERMANY
LUX.

POLAND

U.S.S.R.

ATLANTIC OCEAN

FRANCE

SWITZ.

CZECHOSLOVAKIA

AUSTRIA HUNGARY

ROMANIA

Black Sea

PORTUGAL

SPAIN

Corsica

ITALY

YUGOSLAVIA

BULGARIA

Sardinia

ALB.

GREECE

TURKEY

Sicily

MOROCCO

ALGERIA

MALTA

Mediterranean Sea

CYPRUS

THE CONTEMPORARY WORLD

Aubin, Barbara, American, 1928- , collage
I Dreamed I Saw a Pink Flamingo in the Salle de Bain, 22, *Fig.* 2-7

Bellows, George Wesley, American, 1882-1925, painter, printmaker
Both Members of This Club, 249, *Fig.* 16-8
Stag at Sharkey's, 252, *Fig.* 16-12

Bishop, Isabel, American, 1902- , painter
Men and Girls Walking, 21, *Fig.* 2-6

Bonheur, Rosa, French, 1822-99, painter
Plowing in the Niverne, xivT

Borromini, Francesco, Italian, 1599-1667, architect, sculptor
San Carlo alle Quattro Fontane, 178, *Fig.* 12-1

Braque, Georges, French, 1882-1963, painter
Still Life: Le Jour, 246, *Fig.* 16-5

Brooks, James, American, 1906-, painter
Rasalus, 34, *Fig.* 3-1

Calder, Alexander, American, 1898-1976, sculptor
Zarabanda (Un Disco Blanco), 266, *Fig.* 17-13

Cannon, T. C., Native American, 1946-78, painter
Turn of the Century Dandy, 202, *Fig.* 13-15

Caravaggio, Michelangelo Merisi da, Italian, c. 1573-1610, painter
The Deposition, 179, *Fig.* 12-2

Cassatt, Mary, American, 1845-1926, painter
Sewing Woman, 234, *Fig.* 15-9
Sleepy Baby, 18, *Fig.* 2-1

Cézanne, Paul, French, 1839-1906, painter
The Card Player, 19, *Fig.* 2-2
The Card Players, 19, *Fig.* 2-3
Mont Sainte-Victoire, 226, *Fig.* 15-1

Chagall, Marc, Russian, 1887-1985, painter
Green Violinist, 4, *Fig.* 1-3

Chao Meng-fu, Chinese, early 14th century, scroll painter
Twin Pines, Level Distance, 70, *Fig.* 5-3

Chardin, Jean-Baptiste Siméon, French, 1699-1779, painter
The Kitchen Maid, 186, *Fig.* 12-12

Curry, John Steuart, American, 1897-1946, painter
Baptism in Kansas, 250, *Fig.* 16-10

Dallas, Tony, Native American, contemporary, craftsperson
Koshare Clown, xiiiT, 200, *Fig.* 13-11

David, Jacques Louis, French, 1748-1825, painter
The Death of Socrates, 214, *Fig.* 14-4
The Oath of the Horatii, 210, *Fig.* 14-1

Davis, Gene, American, contemporary, painter
Cool Buzz Saw, 268, *Fig.* 17-16

da Vinci, Leonardo, Italian, 1452-1519, painter, sculptor
Ginevra de 'Benci, 164, *Fig.* 11-4
Studies of Male Shoulder, 166, *Fig.* 11-8

de Chirico, Giorgio, Italian, 1888-1978, painter
The Nostalgia of the Infinite, 258, *Fig.* 17-1

Degas, Edgar, French, 1834-1917, painter
Dancers Practicing at the Bar, 224, 239, *Chapter 15 Opener, Chapter 15 Review Detail*

Delacroix, Eugène, French, 1798-1863, painter
Arabs Skirmishing in the Mountains, 212, *Fig.* 14-2

del Castagno, Andrea, Italian, c. 1421-57, painter
Portrait of a Man, 160, 175, *Chapter 11 Opener, Chapter 11 Review Detail*

Demuth, Charles, American, 1883-1935, painter
I Saw the Figure 5 in Gold, 12, *Fig.* 1-10

Derain, André, French, 1880-1954, painter
The River Seine at Carrieres-sur-Seine, viiB

Eakins, Thomas, American, 1844-1916, painter
Max Schmitt in a Single Scull (The Champion Single Sculls), 232, *Fig.* 15-6

Eberle, Abastenia St. Leger, American, 1878-1942, sculptor
The Windy Doorstep, 25, *Fig.* 2-10

Escher, M. C., Dutch, 1898-1972, printmaker
Drawing Hands, 16, 31, *Chapter 2 Opener, Chapter 2 Review Detail*

Frankenthaler, Helen, American, 1928-, painter
Interior Landscape, 20, *Fig.* 2-5

Gaudi, Antonio, Spanish, 1852-1926, architect
Church of the Sacred Family, 26, *Fig.* 2-11

Gauguin, Paul, French, 1848-1903, painter
Ancestors of Tehamana, 228, *Fig.* 15-3

Gentileschi, Artemisia, Italian, c. 1593-c. 1652/3, painter
Judith and Maidservant with the Head of Holofernes, 176, 191, *Chapter 12 Opener, Chapter 12 Review Detail*

Giotto (di Bondone), Italian, c. 1266-1337, painter
The Flight into Egypt, 154, *Fig.* 10-14

Glackens, William, American, 1870-1938, painter
Family Group, xivB

Gorky, Arshile, Armenian, 1905-48, painter
Golden Brown Painting, 264, *Fig.* 17-9

Goya, Francisco, Spanish, 1746-1828, painter
Cornered (From the Disasters of War), 187, *Fig.* 12-13

Hanson, Duane, American, 1925- , sculptor
Tourists, 267, *Fig.* 17-15

Hardouin-Mansart, Jules, French, 1646-1708, architect
Palace at Versailles, 185, *Fig.* 12-9

Harnett, William Michael, American (b. County Cork, Ireland), 1848-92, painter
Munich Still Life, 3, *Fig.* 1-2

Hartigan, Grace, American, 1922- , painter
The Faraway Places, 6, *Fig.* 1-4

Hepworth, Barbara, English, 1903-75, sculptor
Merryn, 261, *Fig.* 17-5

Hokusai, Katsushika, Japanese, 1760-1849,
   printmaker
   View of Mt. Fuji from Seven-Ri Beach, ixT
Homer, Winslow, American, 1836-1910, painter
   Northeaster, 233, *Fig. 15-7*
Hopper, Edward, American, 1882-1967, painter
   Early Sunday Morning, 38, *Fig. 3-4*
   Room in New York, 40, *Fig. 3-6*
Houser, Allan, Native American, contemporary,
   sculptor
   Sacred Rain Arrow, 192, 207, *Chapter 13 Opener,
   Chapter 13 Review Detail*
Howe, Oscar, Native American, 1915-, painter
   Victory Dance, 203, *Fig. 13-16*
Hoxie, Vinnie Ream, American, 1847-1914, sculptor
   Abraham Lincoln, 24, *Fig. 2-8*
Kandinsky, Wassily, Russian, 1866-1944, painter
   Painting Number, 200, 240, 255, *Chapter 16 Opener,
   Chapter 16 Review Detail*
Kelly, Ellsworth, American, contemporary, painter
   Red/White, 264, *Fig. 17-10*
Kenojuak, Native American, 1927-, printmaker
   Owls, Ravens and Dogs, 204, *Fig. 13-18*
Kirchner, Ernst Ludwig, German, 1880-1938, painter
   Street, Berlin, 243, *Fig. 16-2*
Kiyotada, Torii, Japanese, printmaker
   An Actor of the Ichikawa Clan. 75, *Fig. 5-10*
Klee, Paul, Swiss, 1879-1940, painter
   Tightrope Walker, 260, *Fig. 17-3*
Kollwitz, Käthe, German, 1867-1945, painter,
   printmaker
   The Prisoners, 244, *Fig. 16-3*
Lange, Dorothea, American, 1895-1965, photo-journalist
   Migrant Mother, 308, *Fig. S-5*
Lawrence, Jacob, American, 1917- , painter
   Toussaint L'Overture Series, xvT, 265, *Fig. 17-11*
Le Vau, Louis, French, 1612-70, architect
   Palace at Versailles, 185, *Fig. 12-9*
Lewis, Lucy, Native American, 1897- , craftsperson
   Polychrome Pots, 201, *Fig. 13-12*
Leyster, Judith, Dutch, 1609-60, painter
   Self-Portrait, xiiB, 181, *Fig. 12-5*
Lindner, Richard, American, contemporary, painter
   Rock-Rock, viiT, 8, *Fig. 1-7*
Lipchitz, Jacques, French, 1891-1973, sculptor
   Bather, 245, *Fig. 16-4*
Magritte, René, Belgian, 1898-1967, painter
   Time Transfixed, 262, *Fig. 17-7*
Marini, Marino, Italian, 1901-80, sculptor
   Horse and Rider, 260, *Fig. 17-4*
Marin, John, American, 1870-1953, painter
   Sunset, Casco Bay, 20, *Fig. 2-4*
Masaccio, Italian, 1401-28, painter
   The Holy Trinity, 163, *Fig. 11-2*
Matisse, Henri, French, 1869-1954, painter
   The Red Studio, 242, *Fig. 16-1*

Michelangelo (Buonarroti), Italian, 1475-1564,
   sculptor, painter
   Pietà, 165, *Figs. 11-6, 11-7*
Miró, Joan, Spanish, 1893-1983, painter
   Dutch Interior, 259, *Fig. 17-2*
   Woman, 27, *Fig. 2-13*
Monet, Claude, French, 1840-1926, painter
   Banks of the Seine, Vetheuil, 216, *Fig. 14-5*
   Waterloo Bridge, London, 220, *Fig. 14-10*
Moore, Henry, English, 1898-1986, sculptor
   Family Group, 261, *Fig. 17-6*
Morisot, Berthe, French, 1841-95, painter
   In the Dining Room, xiiiB
   The Artist's Sister at a Window, 218, *Fig. 14-7*
Münter, Gabriele, German, 1877-1962, painter
   Staffelsee in Autumn, xviii, 15, *Chapter 1 Opener,
   Chapter 1 Review Detail*
Musawwir, 'Abd Allah, Islamic, 16th century,
   painter
   The Meeting of the Theologians, 124, *Fig. 8-15*
Myron, Greek, c. 480-440 B.C., sculptor
   The Discus Thrower, xT, 100, *Fig. 7-3*
Nadu, Tamil
   Shiva, King of the Dancers, 118, *Fig. 8-6*
Naminga, Dan, Native American, contemporary,
   painter
   Hopi Dwelling, 203, *Fig. 13-17*
Natzler, Gertrud, potter
   Pilgrim Bottle, 27, *Fig. 2-12*
Natzler, Otto, potter
   Pilgrim Bottle, 27, *Fig. 2-12*
Nevelson, Louise, American, 1900-88, sculptor
   Mrs. N's Palace, 267, *Fig. 17-14*
Paik, Nam June, Korean, 1932-, contemporary, kinetic
   artist
   Fin de Siècle II, 271, *Fig. 17-20*
Pfaff, Judy, English, 1946-, contemporary, multi-
   media artist
   Kabuki (Formula Atlantic), 271, *Fig. 17-19*
Phidias, Greek, c. 490-430 B.C., sculptor
   Horsemen Riding at a Gallop (Parthenon), 25, *Fig. 2-9*
Picasso, Pablo, Spanish, 1881-1973, painter, sculptor
   First Steps, 42, *Fig. 3-7*
Raphael, Italian, 1483-1520, painter
   Madonna and Child Enthroned with Saints, 164, *Fig. 11-5*
   The Small Cowper Madonna, xiiT
Rembrandt van Rijn, Dutch, 1606-69, painter
   Portrait of a Lady with an Ostrich-Feather Fan, 182,
   Fig. 12-6
Renoir, Auguste, French, 1841-1919, painter
   Madame Henriot, 217, *Fig. 14-6*
   Oarsmen at Chatou, 208, 223, *Chapter 14 Opener,
   Chapter 14 Review Detail*
   Young Spanish Woman with a Guitar, 9, *Fig. 1-8*
Resnick, Milton, American, 1917-, painter
   Genie, viiiT

Rivera, Diego, Mexican, 1886-1957, painter
Liberation of the Peon, 251, *Fig.* 16-11
Rodin, Auguste, French, 1840-1917, sculptor
Claude Lorrain, 219, *Fig.* 14-8
Rouault, Georges, French, 1871-1958, painter
Christ Mocked by Soldiers, 32, 45, *Chapter 3 Opener,*
Chapter 3 Review Detail
Rubens, Peter Paul, Flemish, 1577-1640, painter
The Assumption of the Virgin, 180, *Fig.* 12-4
Ryder, Albert Pinkham, American, 1847-1917, painter
Moonlight Marine (Toilers of the Sea), 234, *Fig.* 15-8
Seurat, Georges, French, 1859-91, painter
Sunday Afternoon on the Island of La Grande Jatte, 230,
Fig. 15-4
Skoglund, Sandy, American, contemporary,
photographer
Revenge of the Goldfish, 270, *Fig.* 17-18
Sloan, John, American, 1871-1951, painter
Hairdresser's Window, 248, *Fig.* 16-7
Steen, Jan, Dutch, c. 1626-79, painter
Eve of St. Nicholas, 35, *Fig.* 3-2
The Drawing Lesson, xvB
Stella, Frank, American, 1936- , painter, sculptor
Shards III, 256, 273, *Chapter 17 Opener, Chapter 17*
Review Detail
Stieglitz, Alfred, American, 1864-1946, photographer
The Terminal, 249, *Fig.* 16-9
Tafoya, Margaret, Native American, 1904-, potter
Jar, 201, *Fig.* 13-13

Tanner, Henry O., American, 1859-1937, painter
The Seine, 236, *Fig.* 15-10
Turner, Joseph M. W., English, 1775-1851, painter
The Grand Canal, Venice, 213, *Fig.* 14-3
Unknown, Native American, painter
Exploits of a Sioux Leader, 197, *Fig.* 13-7
van der Weyden, Rogier, Flemish, c. 1399-1464,
painter
Descent from the Cross, 170, *Fig.* 11-12
van Eyck, Jan, Flemish, before 1395-1441, painter
The Annunciation, 169, *Fig.* 11-11
Giovanni Arnolfini and His Bride, 172, *Fig.* 11-14
van Gogh, Vincent, Dutch, 1853-90, painter
Hospital at Saint-Remy, 227, *Fig.* 15-2
The Starry Night, 10, *Fig.* 1-9
van Ness, Beatrice Whitney, American, 1888-1981,
painter
Summer Sunlight, 36, *Fig.* 3-3
Velázques, Diego, Spanish, 1599-1660, painter
The Needlewoman, 179, *Fig.* 12-3
Vigée-Lebrun, Marie-Louise-Élisabeth, French, 1755-
1842, painter
Portrait of a Lady, 186, *Fig.* 12-11
Watteau, Antoine, French, 1684-1721, painter
Embarkation from Cythera, 188, *Fig.* 12-14
The Vista, 185, *Fig.* 12-10
Wyeth, Andrew, American, 1917- , painter
That Gentleman, 266, *Fig.* 17-12

Glossary

Abstract Expressionism An art style in which paint was dribbled, spilled, or splashed onto huge canvases to express a feeling. (Ch. 17-3)

Abstract work A work in which the artist uses a recognizable subject but portrays it in an unrealistic manner. (Ch. 9-1)

Adobe (uh-**doh**-bee) Sun-dried clay. (Ch. 6-3)

Aesthetic view (ess-**thet**-ik) An idea, or school of thought, on what is important in a work of art. (Ch. 3-1)

Amphora (**am**-fuh-ruh) A twin-handled vase. (Ch. 7-1)

Aqueduct (**ak**-wuh-duhkt) A network of channels meant to carry water to a town or city. (Ch. 7-3)

Arabesques (ar-uh-**besks**) Swirling geometric patterns of plant life used as decoration. (Ch. 8-3)

Arbitrary colors (**Ahr**-buh-trehr-ee) Colors chosen to communicate different feelings. (Ch. 15-1)

Architecture The planning and creating of buildings. (Ch. 2-3)

Art criticism Studying, understanding, and judging works of art. (Ch. 3-1)

Art history The study of art from past to present. (Ch. 3-3)

Artifacts Simple handmade tools or objects. (Ch. 6-1)

Art movement A trend formed when a group of artists band together to create works of a single style. (Ch. 14-3)

Ashcan School The popular name given to the group of artists who made realistic paintings of working-class America. (Ch. 16-3)

Balance A principle of art concerned with arranging the elements so that no one part of a work overpowers, or seems heavier than, any other part. (Ch. 1-3)

Baroque (buh-**rohk**) An art style emphasizing movement, contrast, and variety. (Ch. 12-1)

Batik (buh-**teek**) A method of designing on fabric using wax and dyes. (Ch. 8-2)

Binder A liquid that holds together the grains of pigment in paint. (Ch. 2-1)

Buttress A brace or support placed on the outside of a building. (Ch. 10-3)

Calligraphy (kuh-**ligg**-ruh-fee) A method of beautiful handwriting sometimes using a brush. (Ch. 8-3)

Castles Fortlike dwellings with high walls and towers. (Ch. 10-1)

Cathedral A large, complex church created as a seat of office for a bishop. (Ch. 10-3)

Coiled pot A pot formed by coiling long ropes of clay in a spiral. (Ch. 13-1)

Collage (kuh-**lahzh**) An art work made up of bits and pieces of two-dimensional materials pasted to a surface. (Ch. 8-4)

Color An element of art that refers to what the eyes see when light is reflected off an object. (Ch. 1-1)

Composition The way the art principles are used to organize the art elements of color, line, shape, form, space, and texture. (Ch. 3-1)

Concrete A finely ground mixture of small stones and powdered minerals used in building. (Ch. 7-3)

Content The idea, feeling, mood, or message expressed by an art work. (Ch. 3-1)

Contour drawing (**kahn**-toor) Drawing an object as though your drawing tool is touching the edges of the form. (Ch. 11-2)

Cradle board A harness worn on the shoulders and used to carry a small child. (Ch. 13-1)

Crafts The different areas of applied art in which craftspeople work. (Ch. 2-3)

Cubism An art style in which objects are shown from several different angles at once. (Ch. 10-1)

Culture The ideas, beliefs, and living customs of a people. (Ch. 4-1)

Dada (**dahd**-ah) An art movement founded on the belief that Western culture had lost its meaning. (Ch. 17-1)

Edition A series of identical prints made from a single plate. (Ch. 2-1)

Effigy (**eff**-uh-jee) An image that stands for ideas or beliefs. (Ch. 6-1)

The Eight A group of New York artists who created art work that reflected the spirit of the times in which they lived, the early 1900s. (Ch. 16-3)

Emphasis A principle of art concerned with making an element or object in a work stand out. (Ch. 1-3)

Etching An intaglio print made by scratching an image onto a specially treated copper plate. (Ch. 12-3)

Expressionism (ek-**spresh**-uh-niz-uhm) A style that emphasized the expression of innermost feelings. (Ch. 16-1)

Facade (fuh-**sahd**) The outside front of a building. (Ch. 12-1)

Face mask A mask worn to hide the identity of the wearer. (Ch. 9-3)

Fauvism (**fohv**-iz-uhm) An art movement in which artists use wild, intense color combinations in their paintings. (Ch. 16-1)

Form An element of art that refers to an object with three dimensions. (Ch. 1-1)

Freestanding sculpture Sculpture surrounded on all sides by space. (Ch. 2-3)

Fresco (**fres**-koh) A painting created when pigment is applied to a section of wall spread with fresh plaster. (Ch. 10-3)

Frieze (**freez**) A decorative band running across the upper part of a wall. (Ch. 7-1)

Funerary urns (**fyoo**-nuh-rehr-ee)   Decorative vases or vessels found at burial sites. (Ch. 6-2)

Gargoyle   A projecting ornament on a building carved in the shape of a fantastic animal or grotesque creature. (Ch. 10-4)

Genre pieces (**zhahn**-ruh)   Art works that focus on a subject or scene from everyday life. (Ch. 6-1)

Glaze   Glass-like finish on pottery. (Ch. 5-1)

Hard-Edge painting   An art style that emphasized clear, crisp-edged shapes. (Ch. 17-3)

Harmony   A principle of art concerned with blending elements to create a more calm, restful appearance. (Ch. 1-3)

Headpieces   Masks carved of wood and worn on the head like a cap. (Ch. 9-3)

Hieroglyphic (hy-ruh-**glif**-ik)   An early form of picture writing. (Ch. 4-3)

Illuminations   Hand-painted book illustrations. (Ch. 10-1)

Impressionism   An art style that attempted to capture the rapidly changing effects of light on objects. (Ch. 14-2)

Intaglio (in-**tal**-yoh)   A printmaking method in which the image to be printed is cut or scratched into a surface. (Ch. 9-2)

Kachina doll   A hand-carved statuette used to teach children about Pueblo rituals. (Ch. 13-1)

Kinetic art (kuh-**net**-ik)   An art style in which parts of works are set into motion by a form of energy. (Ch. 17-5)

Landscape   A drawing or painting focusing on mountains, trees, or other natural scenery. (Ch. 14-1)

Line   An element of art that refers to the path of a moving point through space. (Ch. 1-1)

Linear perspective (puhr-**spek**-tiv)   The use of slanted lines to make objects appear to extend back into space. (Ch. 11-1)

Loom   A frame holding a set of crisscrossing threads. (Ch. 13-2)

Madonna   A work showing the Virgin Mary with the Christ Child. (Ch. 11-1)

Media   The plural of *medium*. (Ch. 2-1)

Medium of art   A material used to create a work of art. (Ch. 2-1)

Megaliths   Large stone monuments, such as Stonehenge in England. (Ch. 4-1)

Mihrab (**meer**-ahb)   A highly decorated nook found in a mosque. (Ch. 8-3)

Minaret (min-uh-**ret**)   A slender tower from which Muslims are called to prayer. (Ch. 8-3)

Mixed media   The use of more than one medium in a work of art. (Ch. 3-1)

Mobile (**moh**-beel)   A sculpture made of carefully balanced shapes hung on wires. (Ch. 17-3)

Monolith (**mahn**-uh-lith)   A structure created from a single stone slab. (Ch. 6-3)

Mosque   A Muslim house of worship. (Ch. 8-3)

Motif (moh-**teef**)   Part of a design that is repeated over and over in a pattern or visual rhythm. (Ch. 6-2)

Movement   A principle of art used to create the look and feeling of action and to guide a viewer's eye throughout the work. (Ch. 1-3)

Multi-media art   A work that makes use of tools and techniques from two or more areas of art. (Ch. 17-5)

Muralist   An artist who paints large art works directly onto walls or ceilings. (Ch. 16-3)

Neoclassic (nee-oh-**klas**-ik)   An art style that borrowed from the early classical period of ancient Greece and Rome. (Ch. 14-1)

New Realism   An art movement that rediscovered the importance of realistic detail. (Ch. 17-3)

Non-objective   Having no recognizable subject matter. (Ch. 2-1)

Non-objective art (nahn-uhb-**jek**-tiv)   Art works in which no objects or subjects can be readily identified. (Ch. 1-2), (Ch. 16-1)

Oil paint   A mixture of pigment, linseed oil, and turpentine. (Ch. 11-3)

Op art   An art style that made use of precise lines and shapes to create optical illusion. (Ch. 17-4)

Optical colors   Colors viewers actually see. (Ch. 15-1)

Pagoda (puh-**gohd**-uh)   A tower several stories high with roofs curving slightly upward at the edges. (Ch. 5-3)

Papier-mâché (pap-yah-muh-**shay**)   A sculpting technique using newspaper and liquid paste. (Ch. 9-4)

Perceive   Look deeply at a subject. (Ch. 5-1)

Perceiving   Looking at and thinking deeply about what you see.

Petroglyphs (**peh**-truh-glifs)   Rock carvings and paintings. (Ch. 13-1)

Pietà (pee-ay-**tah**)   A work showing Mary mourning over the body of Christ. (Ch. 11-1)

Pigment   A finely ground powder that gives every paint its colors. (Ch. 2-1)

Pointed arch   A curved arrangement of stones reaching up to a central point. (Ch. 10-3)

Pointillism (**poynt**-uh-liz-uhm)   A technique in which small, carefully placed dots of color are used to create forms. (Ch. 15-2)

Polychrome (**pahl**-ee-krohm)   Having many colors. (Ch. 13-3)

Porcelain (**pore**-suh-luhn)   A fine-grained, high-quality form of pottery. (Ch. 5-1)

Portrait   A painting of a person. (Ch. 12-1)

Post and lintel system (**lint**-uhl)   An approach to building in which a crossbeam is placed above two uprights. (Ch. 4-3)

Post-Impressionism   An art movement that appeared after the Impressionists. (Ch. 15-1)

Printing plate   A surface onto or into which the image is placed. (Ch. 2-1)

Printmaking   A technique in which an inked image from a prepared surface is transferred onto another surface. (Ch. 2-1)

Proportion   A principle of art concerned with the relationship of one part to another and to the whole. (Ch. 1-3)

Pueblos   Stacked, many-family dwellings made of adobe. (Ch. 13-1)

Realism   A style of art in which everyday scenes and events are painted as they actually look. (Ch. 15-3)

Regionalism (**reej**-uhn-uhl-iz-uhm)   An art style that records local scenes and events from an artist's own region, or area, of the country. (Ch. 16-3)

Relief sculpture   Sculpture partly enclosed by space. (Ch. 2-3)

Renaissance (ren-uh-**sahns**)   A period of great awakening. (Ch. 11-1)

Rhythm   A principle of art concerned with repeating an element to make a work seem active or to suggest vibration. (Ch. 1-3)

Rococo (ruh-**koh**-koh)   An art style stressing free, graceful movement; a playful use of line; and bright colors. (Ch. 12-3)

Romanticism (roh-**mant**-uh-siz-uhm)   A style of art that found its subjects in the world of the dramatic and exotic. (Ch. 14-1)

Round arch   A curved arrangement of stones over an open space. (Ch. 7-3)

Salon (suh-**lahn**)   An annual exhibition of art. (Ch. 14-3)

Sand painting   The pouring of different colors of powdered rock on a flat section of earth to create an image or design. (Ch. 13-3)

Screen   A partition used as a wall to divide a room. (Ch. 5-3)

Scroll   A long roll of illustrated parchment or silk. (Ch. 5-1)

Shape   An element of art that refers to an area clearly set off by one or more of the other elements of art. (Ch. 1-1)

Shoulder masks   Large, carved masks made to rest on the shoulders of the wearer. (Ch. 9-3)

Social protest painting   An art style that attacked the ills of big-city life. (Ch. 17-3)

Solvent   A material used to thin a paint's binder. (Ch. 2-1)

Space   An element of art that refers to the distance between, around, above, below, and within things. (Ch. 1-1)

Stained glass   Colored glass pieces held in place with lead strips. (Ch. 10-3)

Stele (**stee**-lee)   A carved upright stone slab used as a monument. (Ch. 4-3)

Stupas (**stoop**-uhs)   Beehive-shaped domed places of worship. (Ch. 8-1)

Style   An artist's personal way of using the elements and principles of art and expressing feelings and ideas in art. (Ch. 3-3)

Stylized   Simplified or exaggerated to fit the rules of a specific type of design. (Ch. 6-3)

Subject   The image viewers can easily identify in an art work. (Ch. 3-1)

Surrealism (suh-**ree**-uh-liz-uhm)   An art movement that probed the unconscious world of dreams. (Ch. 17-1)

Symbolism   The use of an image to stand for a quality or an idea. (Ch. 11-3)

Tempera (**tem**-puh-ruh)   A painting medium in which pigment mixed with egg yolk and water is applied with tiny brush strokes. (Ch. 10-1)

Tepee (**tee**-pee)   A portable house. (Ch. 13-1)

Texture   An element of art that refers to the way a thing feels, or looks as though it might feel, if touched. (Ch. 1-1)

Totem pole   An upright log carving picturing stories of different families or clans. (Ch. 13-1)

Triumphal arch (try-**uhm**-fuhl)   A monument built to celebrate great army victories. (Ch. 7-3)

Ukiyo-e (oo-**kee**-yoh-ay)   An art style meaning "pictures of the floating world." (Ch. 5-3)

Unity   The arrangement of elements and principles with media to create a feeling of completeness or wholeness. (Ch. 1-3)

Urban planning   Arranging the construction and services of a city to best meet its people's needs. (Ch. 4-4)

Variety   A principle of art concerned with combining one or more elements to create interest by adding slight changes. (Ch. 1-3)

Warp   Threads running vertically and attached to the loom's frame. (Ch. 13-2)

Weaving   A craft in which fiber strands are interlocked to make cloth or objects. (Ch. 13-1)

Weft   Threads passed horizontally over and under the warp. (Ch. 13-2)

Woodblock printing   Making prints by carving images in blocks of wood. (Ch. 5-3)

Yamato-e (yah-**mah**-toh-ay)   An art style meaning "pictures in the Japanese manner." (Ch. 5-3)

Ziggurat (**zig**-uh-raht)   A stepped mountain made of brick-covered earth. (Ch. 4-4)

Index

A

Abraham Lincoln, 24, *Fig.* 2-8
Abstract Expressionism, 20, 264-265,
  Figs. 2-5, 17-9
Abstract works, 130, *Fig.* 9-2
  defined, 130
  sculpture, 261, *Fig.* 17-6
Acropolis, 98, 99, *Fig.* 7-2
Acrylic, 20, *Fig.* 2-5
Action painters, 264
  See also Abstract Expressionism
Actor of the Ichikawa Clan, An, 74, 75, *Fig.*
  5-10
Adobe, defined, 89
Aesthetic views
  composition view, 37
  content view, 37
  defined, 37
  subject view, 37
African art, 128-143
  abstract works, 130, 134
  figure sculptures, 134, *Fig.* 9-6
    carved wood, 130-131, *Figs.* 9-2. 9-3
    cast bronze, 132-133, *Figs.* 9-4, 9-5
  map of Africa, 130, *Fig.* 9-1
  masks
    face mask, 136, *Fig.* 9-8
    headpieces, 128-129, 136-137, 143,
      *Chapter 9 Opener, Chapter 9 Review
      Detail,* Fig. 9-9
    shoulder (helmet) masks, 138-139,
      140, Figs. 9-10, 9-12
  studio lessons
    abstract self-portrait, 134-135
    mood mask relief, 140-141
Agra, Taj Mahal, 122, 123, *Fig.* 8-12
American art, 232-237, 248-253
  Abstract Expressionism, 20, 264-265,
    Figs. 2-5, 17-9
  Ashcan school, 248-249, 252, *Figs.* 16-7,
    16-8, 16-9, 16-12
  Hard-Edge painting, 264, 265, 268-269,
    Fig. 17-10
  New Realism, 265-266, *Fig.* 17-12
  Op art, 268-269, *Fig.* 17-16
  Realism, 232-237, *Figs.* 15-6, 15-7, 15-8,
    15-9, 15-10
  Regionalism, 250, *Fig.* 16-10
  sculpture today, 266-267, *Figs.* 17-13,
    17-14, 17-15
  Social protest painting, 265, *Fig.* 17-11
  studio lessons
    expressive watercolor, 236-237
    Hard-Edge Op art, 268-269
    print of figure in action, 252-253
Amphora
  ancient Greek, 100-101, 102, *Fig.* 7-4,
    7-5, 7-7
  defined, 100
Analogous color scheme, 3
Analyzing (art criticism), 36
Analyzing (art history), 41
Ancestors of Tehamana, 228, 229, *Fig.* 15-3
Ancient Chinese art, 54, 58-59
  ancient Chinese culture, 58
  crafts, 58, 59, *Fig.* 4-14

map of ancient China, 58, *Fig.* 4-13
  sculpture, 58
Ancient Egyptian art, 54-57
  architecture, 54-55, *Figs.* 4-10, 4-11
    post and lintel system, 54, 55, *Fig.* 4-11
    pyramids, 54, 55, *Fig.* 4-10
  map of ancient Egypt, 54, *Fig.* 4-9
  painting, 56, 57, 62, *Figs.* 4-12, 4-18
    coffin painting, 56, 57, *Fig.* 4-12
    hieroglyphics, 57
    wall painting, 62, *Fig.* 4-18
  sculpture, 46, 57, 65, *Chapter 4 Opener,
    Chapter 4 Review Detail*
  stele, 46, 47, 65, *Chapter 4 Opener,
    Chapter 4 Review Detail*
  studio lesson, 62-63
Ancient Greek art, 96-103
  architecture, 98, 99, 7-2
  beginning of Greek culture, 98
  crafts, 100-101, *Figs.* 7-4, 7-5, 7-6
  influence on Roman art, 104
  map of Aegean civilization, 98, *Fig.* 7-1
  painting, 99-101, *Figs.* 7-4, 7-5
  sculpture, 25, 99, 100, *Figs.* 2-9, 7-3
  studio lesson, 102-103
Ancient Indian art, 54, 59-60
  ancient Indian culture, 59
  architecture, 60
  map of ancient India, 58, Fig. 4-13
  relief sculpture, 59, *Fig.* 4-15
Ancient Roman art, 104-109
  ancient Roman culture, 104
  architecture, 104-106, *Figs.* 7-10, 7-11,
    7-12, 7-13
  Greek influence on, 104
  map of ancient Rome, 104, *Fig.* 7-9
  sculpture, 106-107, *Figs.* 7-14, 7-15
  studio lesson, 108-109
Andean art, 88-91
  Chavín, 88-89 *Fig.* 6-11
  Incan, 90-91, *Figs.* 6-16, 6-17
  map of Andes Mountains region, 88,
    Fig. 6-10
  Mochica art, 89, *Figs.* 6-12, 6-13
  Tihuanaco art, 90, *Figs.* 6-14, 6-15
Andrea del Castagno, 160-161, 175
  Portrait of a Man, 160-161, 175, *Chapter
    11 Opener, Chapter 11 Review Detail*
Anersall-Romanesque Church, 147,
  Figs. 10-3, 10-4
Annunciation, The, 168-169, *Fig.* 11-11
Antelope headpieces, 136-137, *Fig.* 9-9
AP (Approved Product) paint label, 13
Applied art, 26
  See also Crafts
Approved Product (AP) paint label, 13
Aqueduct, 106, *Fig.* 7-12
Arabesques, 120-121, *Fig.* 8-9
Arabs Skirmishing in the Mountains, 211,
  212, *Fig.* 14-2
Arbitrary colors, defined, 229
Arches
  pointed, 152, 153, *Fig.* 10-11
  round, 104
  triumphal, 106, 107, 108-109, *Figs.* 7-13,
    7-16

Architecture, 26
  ancient Egyptian, 54-55, *Figs.* 4-10,
    4-11
  ancient Greek, 98, 99, *Fig.* 7-2
  ancient Indian, 60
  ancient Roman, 104-106, *Figs.* 7-10,
    7-11, 7-12, 7-13
  Baroque style, 178
  defined, 26
  design features
    buttresses, 152
    facades, 178
    flying buttresses, 152, 153
    gargoyles, 156
    pointed arches, 152, 153
    post and lintel system, 51, 54, 98
    round arches, 104
    windows, 147, 152
  Gothic, 150, 152-153, *Figs.* 10-8, 10-10,
    10-11, 10-12
  Indian, 114-115
    ancient, 60
  Japanese, 72, 73, *Figs.* 5-6, 5-7
  materials
    adobe, 89
    concrete, 104
  Native American
    Plains Indian, 196
    Pueblo, 195, 196, *Fig.* 13-4
  New Stone Age (Neolithic), 50-51,
    Fig. 4-5
  Palace at Versailles, 184, 185, *Fig.* 12-9
  Pre-Columbian
    Incan, 91, *Fig.* 6-16
    Mayan, 84, *Figs.* 6-4, 6-5
    Tiahuanaco, 90, *Fig.* 6-14
  purposes of, 26
  Romanesque, 146-147, *Figs.* 10-1, 10-2,
    10-3, 10-4
  studio lessons
    gargoyles, 156-157
    Romanesque castle relief, 150-151
    triumphal arch, 108-109
  types of structures
    aqueducts, 106, *Fig.* 7-12
    business, 26
    castles, 146, 150, *Figs.* 10-1, 10-7, 10-8
    megaliths, 50, 51, *Fig.* 4-5
    monoliths, 90, *Fig.* 6-14
    pagodas, 72, 73, *Fig.* 5-7
    prayer, 26, *Fig.* 2-11
    pueblos, 195, 196, *Fig.* 13-4
    stupas, 114, *Fig.* 8-1
    tepees, 196
    triumphal arches, 106, *Fig.* 7-13
    walled cities, 147, *Fig.* 10-2
  urban planning, 60
    studio lesson, 312-313
Arch of Constantine, 106, *Fig.* 7-13
  relief sculpture, 106, 107, *Fig.* 7-15
Arch of Septimus, 108, *Fig.* 7-16
Art connections
  history, 158, 222, 238, 272
  language arts, 14, 44, 78, 94, 110, 126,
    158, 174, 238, 254, 272

mathematics, 64
music, 190
science, 14, 30, 142, 206
social studies, 30, 44, 64, 78, 94, 110,
126, 142, 174, 190, 206, 222
Art criticism, 34-37
aesthetic views and, 37
Art director, 297
Art historian, 41
Art history, 40-43
See also specific periods of art history
Artifacts
defined, 82
Olmec, 82
Artist profiles
Cézanne, Paul, 289
Giotto (di Bondone), 289
Goya, Francisco, 290
Lewis, Lucy, 290
Leyster, Judith, 291
Michelangelo (Buonarroti), 291
Miró, Joan, 292
Monet, Claude, 292
Morisot, Berthe, 293
Nevelson, Louise, 293
Rivera, Diego, 294
Ryder, Albert Pinkham, 294
Stieglitz, Alfred, 295
Tanner, Henry O., 295
Artist's Sister at a Window, The, 218, 293,
Fig. 14-7
Art movements
Abstract Expressionism, 20, 264-265
Ashcan school, 248-249, 252
Cubism, 42, 134, 243-245
Dada, 258
defined, 216
Expressionism, 243, 244
Fauvism, 242-243
Hard-Edge, 265, 268-269
Impressionism, 217-221
Kinetic art, 270-271
Neoclassicism, 210-211, 214
New Realism, 265-266
Op art, 268-269
Post-Impressionism, 226-231
Realism, 232-235
Romanticism, 211-213
social protest painting, 265
Surrealism, 258-259
See also specific movements and periods
Art teacher, 297
Ashcan school, 248-249, 252
Assembling, 25, 28, *Fig.* 2-14
Assumption of the Virgin, The, 180-181,
Fig. 12-4
Asymmetrical (informal) balance, 9,
Fig. 1-8
Athena, 98
Athens, Acropolis, 98, 99, *Fig.* 7-2
Aubin, Barbara, 22, 23
*I Dreamed I Saw a Pink Flamingo in the
Salle de Bain*, 22, 23, *Fig.* 2-7
Avila Cathedral, 152, 153, *Fig.* 10-11
Aztec art, 85
Aztec culture, 85
calendar stone, 85, *Fig.* 6-7
sculpture, 85, *Figs.* 6-6, 6-7

B
Babylon, tower of, 60
Bach, Johann Sebastian, 190
Balance, 9
formal (symmetrical), 8, 9, *Fig.* 1-7
informal (asymmetrical), 9, *Fig.* 1-8
radial, 9, 10, *Fig.* 1-9
triangular or pyramid plan, 165, *Fig.*
11-7
Bambara headpieces, 136-137, *Fig.* 9-9
Banks of the Seine, Vetheuil, 216, 217, *Fig.*
14-5
Baptism in Kansas, 250, *Fig.* 16-10
Baroque style
architecture, 178
defined, 178
in Italy, 176-177, 178-179, 191, *Chapter
12 Opener, Chapter 12 Review Detail,
Figs.* 12-1, 12-2
in Northern Europe, 180-181, 182, *Figs.*
12-4, 12-5, 12-6
painting, 178-181
in Spain, 179, *Fig.* 12-3
Bather, 244, 245, *Fig.* 16-4
Batik, 118-119
Bear tooth necklace, 49, *Fig.* 4-3
Bellows, George Wesley, 249, 252
Both Members of This Club, 249,
Fig. 16-8
Stag at Sharkey's, 252, *Fig.* 16-12
Bible
illuminations, 149, *Fig.* 10-6
in sculpture, 148, *Fig.* 10-5
in stained glass, 154, *Fig.* 10-13
Bighorn sheep petroglyph, 195, *Fig.* 13-3
Binder
defined, 19
for oil paint, 19
for watercolor, 20
Bishop, Isabel, 21
Men and Girls Walking, 21, *Fig.* 2-6
Bison
cave painting (Lascaux), 48-49, *Fig.* 4-1
sculpture (Le Tuc d'Audoubert Cave),
49, *Fig.* 4-2
Bonheur, Rosa
Plowing in the Niverne, xivT
Borromini, Francesco, 178
San Carlo alle Quattro Fontane, 178,
Fig. 12-1
Both Members of This Club, 249, *Fig.* 16-8
Brady, Mathew, 301
Braque, Georges, 246
Still Life: Le Jour, 246, *Fig.* 16-5
Brooks, James, 34, 37
Rasalus, 34, 37, *Fig.* 3-1
Brunelleschi, Filippo, 162
Brush
cleaning, 279-280
drawing thin lines with, 277
Buddha, 72
bronze Buddha of Todai-Ji, 73, *Fig.* 5-8
Gautama Buddha in Contemplation, 116,
117, *Fig.* 8-4
Buddhism, 68, 72, 114,
Buttresses, flying, 152, 153, *Fig.* 10-12

C
Calder, Alexander, 266
Zarabanda (Un Disco Blanco), 266, *Fig.*
17-13
Calendar stone (Aztec), 85, *Fig.* 6-7
Calligraphy, 120-121, *Fig.* 8-9
Cannon, T. C., 202
Turn of the Century Dandy, 202,
Fig. 13-15
Caravaggio, Michelangelo Merisi da,
178-179, 291
The Deposition, 178-179, *Fig.* 12-2
Carcasonne, walled city of, 147, *Fig.* 10-2
Card Player, The, 18, 19, *Fig.* 2-2
Card Players, The, 18, 19, *Fig.* 2-3
Careers, 297-302
art director, 297
art teacher, 297
computer graphics specialist, 298
editorial cartoonist, 298
exhibit and display designer, 299
graphic designer, 299
industrial designer, 300
interior designer, 300
magazine designer, 301
medical illustrator, 301
museum curator, 302
photojournalist, 302
special effects designer, 303
urban planner, 303
Caricature, defined, 298
Cartoonist, editorial, 298
Carving, 24, *Fig.* 2-8
African wood figures, 130-131,
Figs. 9-2, 9-3
Cassatt, Mary, 18
Sewing Woman, 234, *Fig.* 15-9
Sleepy Baby, 18, *Fig.* 2-1
Castagno, Andrea del. *See* Andrea del
Castagno
Casting, 25, *Fig.* 2-10
African bronze figures, 132-133,
Figs. 9-4, 9-5
Castles
defined, 146
La Calahorra Castle, 146, *Fig.* 10-1
Penafiel, 150, *Fig.* 10-7
Rio Esla, 150, *Fig.* 10-8
Cathedral of Leon, 144-145, 159, *Chapter
10 Opener, Chapter 10 Review Detail*
stained glass from, 154, *Fig.* 10-13
Cathedrals
defined, 152
flying buttresses and, 152, 153,
Fig. 10-12
gargoyles on, 156, *Fig.* 10-16
Gothic, 144-145, 152-153, 159, *Chapter
10 Opener, Chapter 10 Review Detail,
Figs.* 10-10, 10-11, 10-12
pointed arches and, 152, 153, *Fig.* 10-11
Cave art
bison painting (Lascaux), 48-49, *Fig.* 4-1
bison sculpture (Le Tuc d'Audoubert
Cave), 49, *Fig.* 4-2
horse painting (Lascaux), 52, *Fig.* 4-7
Ceramics, 27
Jomon culture, 72
See also Pottery

Certified Product (CP) paint label, 13
Cézanne, Paul, 18, 19, 226, 227, 229, 289
　artist profile, 289
　The Card Player, 18, 19, *Fig.* 2-2
　The Card Players, 18, 19, *Fig.* 2-3
　Cubism and, 243
　Mont Sainte-Victoire, 226, 227, 229,
　　289, *Fig.* 15-1
Chagall, Marc, 4, 5
　Green Violinist, 4, 5, *Fig.* 1-3
Chalk
　safety tip for, 247
　studio lesson, 246-247
Chao Meng-fu, 70
　Twin Pines, Level Distance, 70, *Fig.* 5-3
Chardin, Jean-Baptiste Siméon, 186, 187
　The Kitchen Maid, 186, 187, *Fig.* 12-12
Chavín art, 88-89
　Chavín culture, 88
　Chavín de Húantar, 88
　crafts, 88-89, *Fig.* 6-11
Chinese art
　ancient, 54, 58-59
　crafts, 69, *Fig.* 5-2
　influence on Japanese art, 72
　landscape painting, 66, 68, 79,
　　*Chapter 5 Opener, Chapter 5
　　Review Detail*
　modern Chinese culture, 68-69
　scroll painting, 68, 70, *Fig.* 5-3
　sculpture, 68, 69, *Fig.* 5-1
　See also Ancient Chinese art
Chinese horse (Lascaux cave painting),
　52, *Fig.* 4-7
Christ Mocked by Soldiers, 32, 33,
　*Chapter 3 Opener, Chapter 3 Review
　Detail*
Churches. *See* Structures for prayer
Church of the Sacred Family, 26, *Fig.* 2-11
Claude Lorrain, 218, 219, *Fig.* 14-8
Clay, *See also* Ceramics; Pottery
Coffin painting (ancient Egyptian), 56,
　57, *Fig.* 4-12
Coiled pots, 194, 306, *Figs.* 13-2, S-3, S-4
　defined, 194
　Pueblo, 194, *Fig.* 13-2
　studio lesson, 306-307
Colima, 82
Collage, 124, 251, 287
Color, 2-3
　arbitrary, 229
　defined, 2
　hue, 2
　intensity, 3
　optical, 229
　polychrome, 200
　proportion in, 11
　schemes, 3
　value, 2
　　technique tips, 280
Color schemes, 3
　analogous, 3
　cool, 3
　monochromatic, 3
　warm, 3
Color wheel, 2, 3, *Fig.* 1-1
Composition
　aesthetic view based on, 37

defined, 36
Post-Impressionism and, 226-229,
　Figs. 15-1, 15-3
Computer graphics specialist, 298
Concrete
　defined, 104
　Roman architecture and, 104, 105,
　　Figs. 7-10, 7-11
Constantine, Arch of, 106, 107,
　Figs. 7-13, 7-15
Content
　aesthetic view based on, 37
　defined, 36
　Post-Impressionism and, 227-229,
　　Figs. 15-2, 15-3
Contour drawing, technique tips, 277
Cool Buzz Saw, 268, *Fig.* 17-16
Cool color scheme, 3
Cordoba
　Great Mosque of Abd ar-Rahman,
　　121, 122, *Figs.* 8-10, 8-11
　mosques in, 120
Cornered (From the Disasters of War), 187,
　290, *Fig.* 12-13
Counter-Reformation, 178
CP (Certified Product) paint label, 13
Cradle board, 196, *Fig.* 13-6
Crafts, 26-27
　ancient Chinese, 58, 59, *Fig.* 4-14
　ancient Greek, 100-101, *Figs.* 7-4,
　　7-5, 7-6
　Chinese, 69, *Fig.* 5-2
　defined, 26
　glassblowing, 27
　Gothic, 154, *Figs.* 10-13
　Islamic, 123, *Fig.* 8-13
　media of, 27
　Native American, 194, 196, 200-201,
　　Figs. 13-2, 13-6, 13-11, 13-12, 13-13
　New Stone Age (Neolithic), 50, *Fig.* 4-4
　Old Stone Age (paleolithic), 49,
　　Fig. 4-3
　pottery, 27, *Fig.* 2-12
　Pre-Columbian
　　Chavín, 88-89, *Fig.* 6-11
　　Incan, 91, *Fig.* 6-17
　　Mochica, 89, *Figs.* 6-12, 6-13
　　Tiahuanaco, 90, *Fig.* 6-15
　rugs, Persian or knotted-pile, 123,
　　Fig. 8-13
　stained glass, 154, *Fig.* 10-13
　weaving, 27, *Fig.* 2-13
　See also specific crafts
Criticism. *See* Art criticism
Cubism, 42, 243-245
　African sculpture and, 134
　art history and, 42
　Cézanne and, 243
　defined, 143
　painting, 42, 244, *Fig.* 3-7
　sculpture, 134, 244, 245, *Fig.* 16-4
Cultures
　African, 130-133, 136-139
　ancient Chinese, 58
　ancient Egyptian, 54-57
　ancient Greek, 98-100
　ancient Indian, 59
　ancient Roman, 104-106

defined, 48
Indian
　ancient, 59
　modern, 114
Islamic, 120-121
Japanese, 72-75
Mesopotamian, 60-61
modern Chinese, 68-69
Native American
　Northwest Coast Indian, 195, 196
　Plains Indian, 195-196, 197
　Pueblo, 194-195, 196
　Woodlands Indian, 196-197
New Stone Age (Neolithic), 50-51
Old Stone Age (Paleolithic), 48-49
pre-Columbian
　Aztec, 85
　Chavín, 88
　Incan, 90-91
　Mayan, 83-84
　Moche, 89
　Olmec, 82
　Tiahuanaco, 90
　West Mexican, 82-83
*See also specific cultures and periods of
　art history*
Cuneiform writing, 61
Curator, 302
Curry, John Steuart, 250
　Baptism in Kansas, 250, *Fig.* 16-10
Cutting tools, safety tip for, 109

D
Dada movement, defined, 258
Dallas, Tony, 200
　Koshare Clown, xiiiT, 200, *Fig.* 13-11
Dance Headdress, 128-129, 143, *Chapter 9
　Opener, Chapter 9 Review Detail*
Dancers Practicing at the Bar, 224-225,
　239, *Chapter 15 Opener, Chapter 15
　Review Detail*
Dark Ages. *See* Middle Ages
David, Jacques Louis, 210, 211, 214
　The Death of Socrates, 214, *Fig.* 14-4
　The Oath of the Horatii, 210, 211,
　　Fig. 14-1
da Vinci, Leonardo. *See* Leonardo da
　Vinci
Davis, Gene, 268
　Cool Buzz Saw, 268, *Fig.* 17-16
Death of Socrates, The, 214, *Fig.* 14-4
de Chirico, Giorgio, 258-259
　The Nostalgia of the Infinite, 258-259,
　　Fig. 17-1
Degas, Edgar, 224-225, 239
　Dancers Practicing at the Bar, 224-225,
　　239, *Chapter 15 Opener, Chapter 15
　　Review Detail*
Delacroix, Eugéne, 211, 212
　Arabs Skirmishing in the Mountains,
　　211, 212, *Fig.* 14-2
Demuth, Charles, 12
　I Saw the Figure 5 in Gold, 12, *Fig.* 1-10
Deposition, The, 178-179, *Fig.* 12-2
Derain, André
　The River Seine at Carrieres-sur-Seine,
　　viiB

Descent from the Cross, 170, *Fig*. 11-12
Describing (art criticism), 35
  details, 35
  elements, 35
  medium, 35
  object, 35
  process, 35
  size, 35
  subject, 35
Describing (art history), 41
Designer (careers)
  exhibit and display designer, 299
  graphic designer, 299
  industrial designer, 300
  interior designer, 300
  magazine designer, 301
  special effects designer, 303
Discus Thrower, The, xT, 99, 100, *Fig*. 7-3
Dogs, West Mexican effigies, 82-83,
  Fig. 6-3
Drawing, 18, 19, *Figs*. 2-1, 2-2
  contour drawing, 277
  gesture drawing, 277
  media of, 18
  purposes of, 18
  studio experience, 171
  studio lessons
    computer-type drawing, 304-305
    Cubist chalk drawing, 246-247
    expressive hands, 182-183
    still life, 166-167
  technique tips, 277-279
    contour drawings, 277
    enlarging using a grid, 277-278
    gesture drawings, 277
    oil pastels, 277
    ruler, using, 279
    shading, 278
    sighting, 278
    thin lines with a brush, 277
    viewing frame, using, 279
Drawing Hands, 16, 31, *Chapter 2 Opener*,
  Chapter 2 Review Detail
Drawing Lesson, The, xvB
Duchamp, Marcel, 258
Dutch Interior, 259, 292, *Fig*. 17-2
Dynasties, Chinese, 58, 68, 69, 70

E
Eakins, Thomas, 232-233
  influence on Tanner, 236, 295
  Max Schmitt in a Single Scull
    (The Champion Single Sculls),
    232-233, *Fig*. 15-6
Early Sunday Morning, 38, 39, 40, 41,
  Fig. 3-4
Earth pigments, 52-53, 280
Eastern art. *See* Ancient Chinese art;
    Ancient Indian art; Chinese art;
    Indian art; Japanese art
Eberle, Abastenia St. Leger, 25
  The Windy Doorstep, 25, *Fig*. 2-10
Effigies
  defined, 83
  West Mexican dog effigies, 82-83,
    Fig. 6-3
Egyptian art. *See* Ancient Egyptian art

Elements of art, 2-7
  color, 2-3
  describing, 35
  form, 5
  line, 4-5
  shape, 5
  space, 5
  texture, 5
  See also specific elements
Embarkation from Cythera, 188, *Fig*. 12-14
Emphasis, 11
English art
  Romanticism, 211, 213, *Fig*. 14-3
  See also specific art movements
Enlarging drawings using a grid,
  277-278
Environmental design, studio lesson,
  28-29
Equestrian figure, 131, *Fig*. 9-3
Escher, M. C., 16, 31
  Drawing Hands, 16, 31, *Chapter
    2 Opener, Chapter 2 Review Detail*
Eskimo art. *See* Inuit art
Etching, 187, *Fig*. 12-13
  See also Intaglio
Evening in Spring Hills, 66, 68, 79,
  *Chapter 5 Opener, Chapter 5 Review
    Detail*
Eve of St. Nicholas, 35, 36, 37, *Fig*. 3-2
Exploits of a Sioux Leader, 197, *Fig*. 13-7
Expressionism, 243, 244
  defined, 243
  painting, 243, *Fig*. 16-2
  printmaking, 243, 244, *Fig*. 16-3
Eyck, Jan van. *See* van Eyck, Jan

F
Facades, 178, *Fig*. 12-1
Face masks
  African, 136, *Fig*. 9-8
  defined, 136
  Iroquois, 197, 310, *Fig*. S-7
False face masks, 197, 310, *Fig*. S-7
Family Group (Glackens), xivB
Family Group (Moore), 261, *Fig*. 17-6
Fan, Chinese, 66, 68, 79, *Chapter 5
    Opener, Chapter 5 Review Detail*
Fantasy art, 258-260
  Dada, 258
  Surrealism, 258-259
Faraway Places, The, 6, *Fig*. 1-4
Far Eastern art. *See* Ancient Chinese art;
    Chinese art; Japanese art
Fauvism, 242-243, *Fig*. 16-1
Fin de Siècle II, 270-271, *Fig*. 17-20
Firespitter headpiece, 140, *Fig*. 9-12
First Steps, 42, 43, *Fig*. 3-7
Flight into Egypt, The, 154, 289, *Fig*. 10-14
Floating world, pictures of, 74, 75, *Fig*.
  5-10
Flying buttresses, 152, 153, *Fig*. 10-12
Form, 5
Formal (symmetrical) balance, 8, 9, *Fig*.
  1-7
Four Ladies of the Court Playing Polo, 68,
  69, *Fig*. 5-1

Fragonard, Jean-Honoré, 293
Frankenthaler, Helen, 20, 265
  Interior Landscape, 20, 265, *Fig*. 2-5
Freestanding sculpture, 24, *Fig*. 2-8
French art
  map of France, 184, *Fig*. 12-8
  Palace at Versailles, 184, 185, *Fig*. 12-9
  Rococo style, 184-185, 188, *Figs*. 12-10,
    12-11, 12-13, 12-14
  Romanticism, 211, 212, *Fig*. 14-2
  See also specific art movements
Fresco
  defined, 155
  Gothic, 155, *Fig*. 10-14
Friezes, 25, 99, *Fig*. 2-9
  defined, 99
Funerary Feast Stele of Nefertiabet, 46, 57,
  65, *Chapter 4 Opener, Chapter 4 Review
    Detail*
Funerary urns
  defined, 86
  Mexican (Zapotec), 80, 86, 95, *Chapter
    6 Opener, Chapter 6 Review Detail*

G
Gargoyles
  defined, 156
  Gothic, 156, *Fig*. 10-16
Gate of Sun Creator-God (Tiahuanaco),
  90, *Fig*. 6-14
Gaudi, Antonio, 26
  Church of the Sacred Family, 25, *Fig*. 2-11
Gauguin, Paul, 228, 229
  Ancestors of Tehamana, 228, 229,
    Fig. 15-3
Gautama Buddha in Contemplation, 116,
  117, *Fig*. 8-4
Genie, viiiT
Genre piece, defined, 83
Gentileschi, Artemisia, 176-177, 179, 191
  *Judith and Maidservant with the Head of
    Holofernes*, 176-177, 179, 191,
    *Chapter 12 Opener, Chapter 12
    Review Detail*
Gesture drawing, technique tips, 277
Ginevra de 'Benci, 164, *Fig*. 11-4
Giotto (di Bondone), 154, 289
  artist profile, 289
  The Flight into Egypt, 154, 289,
    Fig. 10-14
Giovanni Arnolfini and His Bride, 172,
  Fig. 11-14
Glackens, William
  Family Group, xivB
Glassblowing, 27
Glaze, 69, *Fig*. 5-2
Glue, technique tips, 287
Gogh, Vincent van. *See* van Gogh,
    Vincent
Golden Brown Painting, 264, *Fig*. 17-9
Gorky, Arshile, 264
  Golden Brown Painting, 264, *Fig*. 17-9
Gothic period, 146, 152-157
  architecture, 152-153, *Figs*. 10-8, 10-10,
    10-11, 10-12, 10-16
  crafts, 154, *Figs*. 10-13
  painting, 154, 155, *Fig*. 10-14

Goya, Francisco, 187, 290
  artist profile, 290
  Cornered (From the Disasters of War),
    187, 290, *Fig. 12-13*
  Grand Canal, Venice, The, 211, 213,
    Fig. 14-3
Great Mosque of Abd ar-Rahman, 121,
  122, *Figs. 8-10, 8-11*
Great Stupa at Sanchi, 114, *Fig. 8-1*
Greek art. *See* Ancient Greek art
Green Violinist, 4, 5, *Fig. 1-3*

H

Hairdresser's Window, 248, *Fig. 16-7*
Hals, Franz, Leyster painting attributed
  to, 291
Hanson, Duane, 266-267
  Tourists, 266-267, *Fig. 17-15*
Harappa, 59, 60
Hard-Edge painting, 264, 265, 268-269,
  Fig. 17-10
Hardouin-Mansart, Jules, 184, 185
  Palace at Versailles, 184, 185, *Fig. 12-9*
Harmony, 10
Harnett, William Michael, 2, 3, 5
  Munich Still Life, 2, 3, 5, *Fig. 1-2*
Hartigan, Grace, 6
  The Faraway Places, 6, *Fig. 1-4*
Head, Olmec, 82, 83, *Fig. 6-2*
Headdresses. *See* Headpieces
Head of a Prophet, 154, *Fig. 10-13*
Headpieces
  African, 128-129, 136-137, 143,
    *Chapter 9 Opener, Chapter 9 Review
    Detail, Fig. 9-9*
  defined, 136
Health Label (HL) paint label, 13
Helmet masks. *See* Shoulder masks
Hepworth, Barbara, 260, 261
  Merryn, 260, 261, *Fig. 17-5*
Hieroglyphics, 57
Hinduism, 114
History connections, 158, 222, 238, 272
History of art. *See* Art history
HL (Health Label) paint label, 13
Hokusai, Katsushika
  View of Mt. Fuji from Seven-Ri Beach,
    ixT
Holy Trinity, The, 162, *Fig. 11-2*
Homer, Winslow, 233
  Northeaster, 233, *Fig. 15-7*
Hopi Dwelling, 203, *Fig. 13-17*
Hopper, Edward, 38, 39, 40, 41
  Early Sunday Morning, 38, 39, 40, 41,
    Fig. 3-4
  Room in New York, 40, 41, *Fig. 3-6*
Horse and Rider, 260, *Fig. 17-4*
Horsemen Riding at a Gallop (Parthenon),
  24, 25, 99, *Fig. 2-9*
Horses
  cave painting (Lascaux), 52, *Fig. 4-7*
  sculpture
    African equestrian figure, 131,
      Fig. 9-3
    ancient Japanese, 76, *Fig. 5-12*
    Mounted King and Attendants,
      132, *Fig. 9-4*

Horyu-Ji, Nara Horyu-Ji Temple
  Pagoda, 72, 73, *Fig. 5-7*
Hospital at Saint-Remy, 227, 229, *Fig. 15-2*
Houser, Allan, 192-193, 202, 207
  Sacred Rain Arrow, 192-193, 207,
    *Chapter 13 Opener, Chapter 13
    Review Detail*
Howe, Oscar, 203
  Victory Dance, 203, *Fig. 13-16*
Hoxie, Vinnie Ream, 24
  Abraham Lincoln, 24, *Fig. 2-8*

I

*I Dreamed I Saw a Pink Flamingo in the
  Salle de Bain*, 22, 23, *Fig. 2-7*
Illuminations
  defined, 149
  Romanesque, 149, *Fig. 10-6*
Impression: Sunrise, 217
Impressionism, 217-221
  defined, 217
  painting
    Monet, 216, 217, 292, *Fig. 14-5*
    Morisot, 218, 293, *Fig. 14-7*
    Renoir, 208-209, 217, 223, *Chapter 14
      Opener, Chapter 14 Review
      Detail, Fig. 14-6*
  sculpture, 218, 219, *Fig. 14-8*
Incan art, 90-91
  architecture, 91, *Fig. 6-16*
  crafts, 91, *Fig. 6-17*
  Incan culture, 90-91
  Machu Picchu, 91, *Fig. 6-16*
Indian art
  ancient, 54, 59-60
  architecture, 60, 114-115
  map of India
    ancient, 58, *Fig. 4-13*
    modern, 115, *Fig. 8-2*
  modern, 114-119
  religions and, 114
  sculpture, 118, *Fig. 8-6*
    ancient, 59, *Fig. 4-15*
    modern, 116-117, 118, *Figs. 8-4, 8-5, 8-6*
  studio lesson, 118-119
  See also Ancient Indian art
Indian (Native American) art. *See*
  Native American art;
  Pre-Columbian art
Informal (asymmetrical) balance, 9,
  Fig. 1-8
Intaglio, 21, *Fig. 2-6*
  See also Etching
Intensity of hue, 3
Interior Landscape, 20, 265, *Fig. 2-5*
Interpreting (art criticism), 36-37
Interpreting (art history), 41
In the Dining Room, xiiiB
Inuit art, 204, *Fig. 13-18*
Iroquois art, 196-197
  false face masks, 197, 310, *Fig. S-7*
  studio lesson, 310-311
I Saw the Figure 5 in Gold, 12, *Fig. 1-10*
Islam, 120-121
Islamic art, 120-125
  architecture, mosques, 120-122,
    Figs. 8-10, 8-11, 8-12

calligraphy, 120, 121, *Fig. 8-9*
  crafts, 123, *Fig. 8-13*
  Islam and, 120-121
  map of Arabian peninsula, 120,
    Fig. 8-8
  painting
    calligraphy, 120, 121, *Fig. 8-9*
    miniatures, 112-113, 124, 127,
      *Chapter 8 Opener, Chapter 8 Review
      Detail, Fig. 8-15*
  studio lesson, 124-125
Italian art
  Baroque style, 176-177, 178-179, 191,
    *Chapter 12 Opener, Chapter 12
    Review Detail, Figs. 12-1, 12-2*
  Renaissance period, 162-167
    map of Renaissance Italy, 162,
      Fig. 11-1
  See also specific art movements

J

Jaguar pitcher (Chavín), 88-89, *Fig. 6-11*
Jaguar Temple (Mayan), 84, *Fig. 6-4*
Japanese art, 72-77
  architecture, 72, 73, *Figs. 5-6, 5-7*
  Japanese culture, 72
  Jomon culture, 72
  map of Japan, 72, *Fig. 5-5*
  painting, 74, *Fig. 5-9*
  printmaking, 74, 75, *Fig. 5-10*
  sculpture, 73, 76, *Fig. 5-8, Fig. 5-12*
  Ukiyo-e style, 74, 75, *Fig. 5-10*
  Yamato-e style, 74, *Fig. 5-9*
Jar, with removable head, 86, *Fig. 6-8*
Jar (Tafoya), 201, *Fig. 13-13*
Jewelry
  Mochica turquoise earring, 89,
    Fig. 6-12
  Old Stone Age (Paleolithic), 49,
    Fig. 4-3
Jomon culture, 72
Judging (art criticism), 37
Judging (art history), 41
*Judith and Maidservant with the Head of
  Holofernes*,
  176-177, 179, 191, *Chapter 12 Opener,
    Chapter 12 Review Detail*

K

Kabuki (Formula Atlantic), 270, 271, *Fig.
  17-19*
Kachina dolls
  defined, 200
  traditional Native American, 200, *Fig.
    13-11*
Kandinsky, Wassily, 240-241, 245, 255
  Painting Number, 200, 240-241, 255,
    *Chapter 16 Opener, Chapter 16
    Review Detail*
Kelly, Ellsworth, 265, 268
  Red/White, 264, 265, 268, *Fig. 17-10*
Kenojuak, 204
  Owls, Ravens and Dogs, 204, *Fig. 13-18*
Kinetic art, 270-271, *Fig. 17-20*
Kirchner, Ernst Ludwig, 243
  Street, Berlin, 243, *Fig. 16-2*

Kitchen Maid, The, 186, 187, *Fig.* 12-12
Kiyotada, Torii, 74, 75
  An Actor of the Ichikawa Clan, 74, 75, *Fig.* 5-10
Klee, Paul, 260
  Tightrope Walker, 260, *Fig.* 17-3
Knotted-pile rugs, 123, *Fig.* 8-13
Kollwitz, Käthe, 243, 244
  The Prisoners, 243, 244, *Fig.* 16-3
Korean art, influence on Japanese art, 72
Koshare Clown, xiiiT, 200, *Fig.* 13-11

L

La Calahorra Castle, 146, *Fig.* 10-1
Lake Titicaca, 90
Landscape painting
  Chinese, 66, 68, 79, *Chapter 5 Opener, Chapter 5 Review Detail*
  defined, 211
  Romantic, 211, 213, *Fig.* 14-3
Lange, Dorothea, 308
  Migrant Mother, 308, *Fig.* S-5
Language arts connections, 14, 44, 78, 94, 110, 126, 158, 174, 238, 254, 272
Lascaux cave paintings
  bison, 48-49, *Fig.* 4-1
  horse, 52, *Fig.* 4-7
Lawrence, Jacob, 265
  Toussaint L'Overture Series, xvT, 265, *Fig.* 17-11
Leonardo da Vinci, 162-164, 166
  Ginevra de 'Benci, 164, *Fig.* 11-4
  medical illustrations of, 300
  Mona Lisa, 164, 258
  Studies of Male Shoulder, 166, *Fig.* 11-8
Leon, Cathedral of, 144-145, 159, *Chapter 10 Opener, Chapter 10 Review Detail*
  stained glass from, 154, *Fig.* 10-13
Le Tuc d'Audoubert Cave, clay bison from, 49, *Fig.* 4-2
Le Vau, Louis, 184, 185
  Palace at Versailles, 184, 185, *Fig.* 12-9
Lewis, Lucy, 200, 201, 290
  artist profile, 290
  Polychrome Pots, 200, 201, *Fig.* 13-12
Leyster, Judith, 181, 291
  artist profile, 291
  Self-Portrait, xiiB, 181, 291, *Fig.* 12-5
Liberation of the Peon, 250, 251, 294, *Fig.* 16-11
Lindner, Richard, 8, 9
  Rock-Rock, viiT, 8, 9, *Fig.* 1-7
Line, 4-5
Linear perspective, defined, 162
Lion tooth necklace, 49, *Fig.* 4-3
Lipchitz, Jacques, 244, 245
  Bather, 244, 245, *Fig.* 16-4
Lithography, 21
Loom, 27
  defined, 198
  See also Weaving
Louis XIV, king, 184
Luxor, temple of, 54, 55, *Fig.* 4-11

M

Machu Picchu, 91, *Fig.* 6-16
Madame Henriot, 217, *Fig.* 14-6

Madonna and Child Enthroned with Saints, 164, *Fig.* 11-5
Madonnas
  defined, 164
  Renaissance, 164, *Fig.* 11-5
Magazine designer, 301
Magritte, René, 262
  Time Transfixed, 262, *Fig.* 17-7
Maps
  Aegean civilization, 98, *Fig.* 7-1
  Africa, 130, *Fig.* 9-1
  ancient China, 58, *Fig.* 4-13
  ancient Egypt, 54, *Fig.* 4-9
  ancient India, 58, *Fig.* 4-13
  ancient Rome, 104, *Fig.* 7-9
  Arabian peninsula, 120, *Fig.* 8-8
  France, 184, *Fig.* 12-8
  India
    ancient, 58, *Fig.* 4-13
    modern, 115, *Fig.* 8-2
  Japan, 72, *Fig.* 5-5
  Lands of Islam, 88, *Fig.* 6-10
  Mesopotamia, 58, *Fig.* 4-13
  Native American cultures, 194, *Fig.* 13-1
  Pre-Columbian Mesoamerica, 82, *Fig.* 6-1
  Renaissance Europe, 168, *Fig.* 11-10
  Renaissance Italy, 162, *Fig.* 11-1
  World Map, 314-315
Marini, Marino, 260
  Horse and Rider, 260, *Fig.* 17-4
Marin, John, 20
  Sunset, Casco Bay, 20, *Fig.* 2-4
Markers, safety tip for, 71
Masks
  African
    face masks, 136, *Fig.* 9-8
    headpieces, 128-129, 136-137, 143, *Chapter 9 Opener, Chapter 9 Review Detail, Fig.* 9-9
    shoulder (helmet) masks, 138-139, 140, *Figs.* 9-10, 9-12
  Iroquois, 197, 310, *Fig.* S-7
  studio lessons
    false face mask, 310-311
    mood mask relief, 140-141
Masaccio, 162
  The Holy Trinity, 162, *Fig.* 11-2
Mathematics connections, 64
Matisse, Henri, 242, 243
  The Red Studio, 242, 243, Fig. 16-1
Max Schmitt in a Single Scull (The Campion Single Sculls), 232-233, *Fig.* 15-6
Mayan art, 83-84
  architecture, 84, *Figs.* 6-4, 6-5
  Mayan culture, 83
  sculpture, 84, *Fig.* 6-5
Mecca, 120, 121
Media, 16-31
  of architecture, 26
  of crafts, 26-27
  defined, 18
  describing, 35
  of drawing, 18
  mixed, 18
  multi-media art, 270, 271, *Fig.* 17-19

  of painting, 18-20
  of printmaking, 21
  of sculpture, 24-25
  of special effects, 302
  technology and art, 270-271
Medieval period. *See* Middle Ages
Medium of art, 18
Meeting of the Theologians, The, 124, *Fig.* 8-15
Megaliths
  defined, 51
  Stonehenge, 50, 51, *Fig.* 4-5
Men and Girls Walking, 21, *Fig.* 2-6
Merryn, 260, 261, *Fig.* 17-5
Mesoamerican art
  Aztec, 85, *Figs.* 6-6 6-7
  Mayan, 83-84, *Figs.* 6-4, 6-5
  Olmec, 82, 83, *Fig.* 6-2
  West Mexican, 82-83, *Fig.* 6-3
Mesopotamian art, 54, 60-61
  architecture, 61
  map of Mesopotamia, 58, *Fig.* 4-13
  Mesopotamian culture, 60-61
  sculpture, 61, *Fig.* 4-17
Mexican art
  murals, 250, 251, *Fig.* 16-11
  See also Mesoamerican art
Michelangelo (Buonarroti), 164-165, 291
  artist profile, 291
  Pietà, 164-165, *Figs.* 11-6, 11-7
Middle Ages, 144-159
  Gothic period, 146, 152-157
    studio lesson, 156-157
  Romanesque period, 146-151
    studio lesson, 150-151
  See also Gothic period; Romanesque period
Mihrab, 121, 122, *Fig.* 8-10
Milan Cathedral, 152, *Fig.* 10-10
Minarets, 121, 122, *Fig.* 8-12
Ming dynasty, 69, *Fig.* 5-2
Miniatures, Islamic, 112-113, 124, 127, *Chapter 8 Opener, Chapter 8 Review Detail, Fig.* 8-15
Minister Kibi's Trip to China, 74, *Fig.* 5-9
Miró, Joan, 27, 259, 292
  artist profile, 292
  Dutch Interior, 259, 292, *Fig.* 17-2
  Woman, 27, 292, *Fig.* 2-13
Mixed media, 18
Mixing paint for value, 280
Mobiles, 266, *Fig.* 17-13
Moche art, 89
  crafts, 89, *Figs.* 6-12, 6-13
  Moche culture, 89
Modeling, 25, 27, *Fig.* 2-12
  studio lesson, 76-77
Mohenjo-Daro, 60
Mold for plaster relief, making from clay, 282
Mona Lisa, 164, 258
Monet, Claude, 216, 217, 220, 292
  artist profile, 292
  Banks of the Seine, Vetheuil, 216, 217, *Fig.* 14-5
  Impression: Sunrise, 217
  Waterloo Bridge, London, 220, 292, *Fig.* 14-10

Monochromatic color scheme, 3
Monolith
  defined, 90
  Tiahuanaco, 90, *Fig. 6-14*
Mont Sainte-Victoire, 226, 227, 229, 289,
  Fig. 15-1
Moonlight Marine (Toilers of the Sea), 234,
  235, 294, *Fig. 15-8*
Moore, Henry, 261
  Family Group, 261, *Fig. 17-6*
Morisot, Berthe, 218, 293
  artist profile, 293
  The Artist's Sister at a Window, 218,
    293, *Fig. 14-7*
  In the Dining Room, xiiiB
Mosques, 120-122, *Figs. 8-10, 8-11, 8-12*
  defined, 120
Motif
  defined, 86
  studio lessons
    clay urn, 86-87
    stylized motif, 92-93
Mounted King and Attendants, xiT, 132,
  Fig. 9-4
Mounting two-dimensional works, 286
Movement, 11
Mrs. N's Palace, 266, 267, 293, *Fig. 17-14*
Muhammad, 120-121
Multi-media art, 270, 271, *Fig. 17-19*
Munich Still Life, 2, 3, 5, *Fig. 1-2*
Münter, Gabriele, xviii, 15
  Staffelsee in Autumn, xviii, 15, *Chapter 1
    Opener, Chapter 1 Review Detail*
Muralist, defined, 250
Murals, Mexican, 250, 251, *Fig. 16-11*
Musawwir, 'Abd Allah, 124
  The Meeting of the Theologians, 124,
    Fig. 8-15
Museum curator, 302
Music connections, 190
Muslims, 120-121
Myron, 99, 100
  The Discus Thrower, xT, 99, 100, *Fig. 7-3*

N
Nadu, Tamil, 118
  Shiva, King of the Dancers, 118, *Fig. 8-6*
Nakht and his Wife, 62, *Fig. 4-18*
Naminga, Dan, 203
  Hopi Dwelling, 203, *Fig. 13-17*
Napoléon Bonaparte, 210
Nara Horyu-Ji Temple Pagoda, 72, 73,
  Fig. 5-7
Nara Todai-Ji Temple, 72, 73, *Fig. 5-6*
Narbonne, gargoyle at, 156, *Fig. 10-16*
Native American art, 192-207
  architecture
    Plains Indian, 196
    Pueblo, 195, 196, *Fig. 13-4*
  crafts
    Plains Indian, 196, 197, *Fig. 13-6*
    Pueblo, 194, *Fig. 13-2*
    traditional, 200-201, *Figs. 13-11,
      13-12, 13-13*
    Inuit, 204-205
    Kachina dolls, 200, *Fig. 13-11*

map of Native American cultures, 194,
  Fig. 13-1
modern, 202-203
Northwest Coast Indian, 195, 196
painting
  modern, 202-203, *Figs. 13-15, 13-16,
    13-17*
  Plains Indian, 197, *Fig. 13-7*
  Pueblo, 195, *Fig. 13-3*
  traditional sand painting, 201,
    Fig. 13-14
petroglyphs, 195, *Fig. 13-3*
Plains Indian, 195-196, 197
Pueblo, 194-195, 196
sculpture
  modern, 192-193, 202, 207, *Chapter 13
    Opener, Chapter 13 Review Detail*
  Northwest Coast Indian, 195, 196,
    Fig. 13-5
studio lessons
  false face mask, 310-311
  Inuit-style print, 204-205
  round weaving, 198-199
  Woodlands culture, 196-197
Natural earth pigments
  making, 280
  studio lesson, 52-53
Natzler, Gertrud and Otto, 25, 27
  Pilgrim Bottle, 25, 27, *Fig. 2-12*
Necklace of bear and lion teeth, 49,
  Fig. 4-3
Needlewoman, The, 179, *Fig. 12-3*
Nefertiabet, funerary feast stele of, 46,
  57, 65, *Chapter 4 Opener, Chapter 4
  Review Detail*
Neoclassic style, 210-211, 214, *Figs. 14-1,
  14-4*
  defined, 211
  studio lesson, 214-215
Neolithic art. *See* New Stone Age
  (Neolithic) art
Ness, Beatrice Whitney van. *See* van
  Ness, Beatrice Whitney
Nevelson, Louise, 266, 267, 293
  artist profile, 293
  Mrs. N's Palace, 266, 267, 293, *Fig. 17-14*
New Realism, 265-266, *Fig. 17-12*
  defined, 265
New Stone Age (Neolithic) art, 50-51
  architecture, 50-51, *Fig. 4-5*
  crafts, 50, *Fig. 4-4*
Nightmare, studio experience, 261
Nō drama, 75
  headband, 75, *Fig. 5-11*
Non-objective art, 6, 240-241, 245, 255,
  *Chapter 16 Opener, Chapter 16 Review
  Detail, Fig. 1-4*
  defined, 6, 245
  sculpture, 260, 261, 266, 267, *Figs. 17-5,
    17-13, 17-14*
Northeaster, 233, *Fig. 15-7*
Northern European art
  Baroque style, 180-181, 182, *Figs. 12-4,
    12-5, 12-6*
  map of Renaissance Europe, 168,
    Fig. 11-10
  Renaissance period, 168-173

Northwest Coast Indian art, 195, 196
  sculpture, 195, 196, *Fig. 13-5*
  totem pole, 195, 196, *Fig. 13-5*
Nostalgia of the Infinite, The, 258-259,
  Fig. 17-1
Notre Dame Cathedral, 152, 153, *Fig. 10-12*

O
Oarsmen at Chatou, 208-209, 223, *Chapter
  14 Opener, Chapter 14 Review Detail*
Oath of the Horatii, The, 210, 211, *Fig. 14-1*
Oil paint, 19, *Fig. 2-3*
  binder for, 19
  defined, 168
  discovery of, 168
  solvent for, 19
  technique tips
    cleaning a brush, 279-280
    mixing paint to change value of
      color, 280
Oil pastels, technique tips, 277
O'Keeffe, Georgia, marriage to Stieglitz,
  295
Old Stone Age (Paleolithic) art, 48-49
  crafts, 49, *Fig. 4-3*
  painting, 48-49, *Fig. 4-1*
  sculpture, 49, *Fig. 4-2*
Olmec art, 82
  Olmec culture, 82
  sculpture, 82, 83, *Fig. 6-2*
Op art, 268-269, *Fig. 17-16*
Optical colors, defined, 229
Organic shapes, 5
Oriental art. *See* Ancient Chinese art;
  Chinese art; Japanese art
Owls, Ravens and Dogs, 204, *Fig. 13-18*

P
Pagodas, 72, 73, *Fig. 5-7*
Paik, Nam June, 270-271
  Fin de Siècle II, 270-271, *Fig. 17-20*
Paint
  acrylic, 20, *Fig. 2-5*
  binder, 19
  tempera, 20,
  fresco, 155, *Fig. 10-14*
  oil paint, 19, 168, *Fig. 2-3*
    technique tips, 279-280
  pigment, 19
    earth pigments, 52-53, 280
  poster paint (school tempera), 20
    safety tip for, 102
    technique tips, 281
  safety tips for, 13, 102, 230
  sand painting, 201
  solvent, 19
  technique tips
    applying paint to a stamp, 281
    cleaning a brush, 279-280
    making natural earth pigments, 280
    mixing paint to change value of
      color, 280
    poster paints (school tempera), 281
    watercolors, 281
  watercolor, 20, 281, *Fig. 2-4*
  See also specific paints

Painting
  Abstract Expressionism, 20, 264-265,
    Figs. 2-5, 17-9
  American Realism, 232-237, *Figs.* 15-6,
    15-7, 15-8, 15-9, 15-10
  ancient Greek, 99-101, *Figs.* 7-4, 7-5
  Ashcan school, 248-249, *Figs.* 16-7, 16-8
  Baroque
    in Italy, 176-177, 178-179, 191,
      *Chapter 12 Opener, Chapter 12
      Review Detail, Fig.* 12-2
    in Northern Europe, 180-181, 182,
      Figs. 12-4, 12-5, 12-6
    in Spain, 179, *Fig.* 12-3
    studio lesson, 182-183
  Chinese
    landscape painting, 66, 68, 79,
      *Chapter 5 Opener, Chapter 5 Review
      Detail*
    scroll painting, 68, 70, *Fig.* 5-3
  Cubist, 42, 244, *Fig.* 3-7
  European today, 258-260, *Figs.* 17-1,
    17-2, 17-3
  Expressionist, 243, *Fig.* 16-2
  Fauvist, 242-243, *Fig.* 16-1
  fresco, 155, *Fig.* 10-14
  Gothic, 154, 155, *Fig.* 10-14
  Hard-Edge, 264, 265, 268-269,
    Fig. 17-10
  illuminations, 149, *Fig.* 10-6
  Impressionist, 208-209, 216-218, 223,
    *Chapter 14 Opener, Chapter 14
    Review Detail, Figs.* 14-5, 14-6, 14-7
  Islamic
    calligraphy, 120, 121, *Fig.* 8-9
    miniatures, 112-113, 124, 127, *Chapter
      8 Opener, Chapter 8 Review Detail,
      Fig.* 8-15
  Japanese, 74, *Fig.* 5-9
  landscape painting
    Chinese, 66, 68, 79, *Chapter 5 Opener,
      Chapter 5 Review Detail*
    Romantic, 211, 213, *Fig.* 14-3
  Madonnas, 164
  media of, 19-20
  murals, 250, 251, *Fig.* 16-11
  Native American, 197, 201, 202-203
  Neoclassic, 210-211, 214,
    Figs. 14-1, 14-4
  New Realism, 265-266, *Fig.* 17-12
  non-objective, 240-241, 245, 255,
    *Chapter 16 Opener, Chapter 16
    Review Detail*
  Old Stone Age (paleolithic), 48-49,
    Fig. 4-1
  Op art, 268-269, *Fig.* 17-16
  petroglyphs, 195, *Fig.* 13-3
  portraits, 181
  Post-Impressionist, 224-225, 226-231,
    *Chapter 15 Opener, Chapter 15
    Review Detail, Figs.* 15-1, 15-2, 15-3,
    15-4
  Regionalist, 250, *Fig.* 16-10
  Renaissance
    in Italy, 160-161, 162-167, 175,
      *Chapter 11 Opener, Chapter 11
      Review Detail, Figs.* 11-2, 11-4,
      11-5, 11-6, 11-7, 11-8

    in Northern Europe, 168-173,
      Figs. 11-11, 11-12, 11-14
  Rococo
    in France, 184-186, 188, *Figs.* 12-10,
      12-11, 12-12, 12-13 12-14
    in Spain, 187
  Romanesque, 149, *Fig.* 10-6
  Romanticism
    in England, 211, 213, *Fig.* 14-3
    in France, 211, 212, *Fig.* 14-2
  studio lessons
    Cubist style, 42-43
    earth pigments, 52-53
    expressive scene, 38-39
    expressive watercolor, 236-237
    Greek vase, 102-103
    Hard-Edge Op art, 268-269
    Impressionist landscape, 220-221
    picture story, 62-63
    scroll, 70-71
    still life, 166-167
    Surrealism, 262-263
    tempera batik, 118-119
    visual symbols, 172-173
  surface materials for, 18
  Surrealist, 258-259, 262-263,
    Figs. 17-1, 17-2, 17-7
  technique tips, 279-281
    cleaning a brush, 279-280
    making natural earth pigments, 280
    mixing paint to change value of
      color, 280
    poster paints (school tempera), 281
    watercolors, 281
Painting Number 200, 240-241, 255,
  *Chapter 16 Opener, Chapter 16 Review
  Detail*
Palace at Versailles, 184, 185, *Fig.* 12-9
Paleolithic art. *See* Old Stone Age
  (Paleolithic) art
Pantheon, 104, 105, *Figs.* 7-10, 7-11
Paper
  curling, 284
  pleating, 284
  scoring, 284, 286
  technique tips
    papier-mâché, 283-284
    scoring, 284, 286
    sculpture, 284
    tissue paper collage, 287
  tissue paper collage, 287
Papier-mâché, 283-284
  defined, 140
  studio lessons
    false face mask, 310-311
    mood mask relief, 140-141
  technique tips
    draping method, 283
    pulp method, 283
    strip method, 283
    supports for creations, 283-284
Parthenon, 96-97, 98, 111, *Chapter 7
  Opener, Chapter 7 Review Detail*
  frieze, 25, 99, *Fig.* 2-9
  Horsemen Riding at a Gallop (relief
    sculpture), 24, 25, *Fig.* 2-9
Pavilions, 68
Penafiel, castle at, 150, *Fig.* 10-7

Perception
  "perceive" defined, 69
  studio experience, 69
Persian knot, 123, *Fig.* 8-14
Persian rugs, 123, *Fig.* 8-13
Perspective, linear, 162
Peruvian art. *See* Andean art
Petroglyphs
  defined, 195
  Pueblo, 195, *Fig.* 13-3
Pfaff, Judy, 270, 271
  Kabuki (Formula Atlantic), 270, 271,
    Fig. 17-19
Pharoahs, 54
Phidias, 24, 25, 99
  Horsemen Riding at a Gallop
    (Parthenon), 24, 25, 99, *Fig.* 2-9
Phillip the Arab, 106, 107, *Fig.* 7-14
Photo essay, studio lesson, 308-309
Photography
  Ashcan school, 249, *Fig.* 16-9
  staged, 270, *Fig.* 17-18
  studio lesson, 308-309
Photojournalist, 302
  studio lesson, 308-309
Picasso, Pablo, 42, 43, 244
  First Steps, 42, 43, *Fig.* 3-7
Pietà (Michelangelo), 164-165, *Figs.* 11-6,
  11-7
Pietàs
  defined, 164
  Renaissance, 164-165, *Figs.* 11-6, 11-7
Pigment
  defined, 19
  earth pigments, 52-53, 280
Pilgrim Bottle, 27, *Fig.* 2-12
Pitchers
  bronze (ancient Chinese), 58, 59,
    Fig. 4-14
  stirrup-spout deer (Mochica), 89,
    Fig. 6-12
  stirrup-spout jaguar (Chavín), 88,
    Fig. 6-11
Pixels, defined, 304
Place, art history interpretation and, 41
Plains Indian art, 195-196, 197
  architecture, 196
  cradle board, 196, 197, *Fig.* 13-6
  crafts, 196, 197, *Fig.* 13-6
  painting, 197, *Fig.* 13-7
  studio experience, 197
  tepees, 196
Plaster
  mixing, 282
  relief, technique tips, 282
Plowing in the Niverne, xivT
Pointed arches, 152, 153, *Fig.* 10-11
  defined, 152
Pointillism, 230, *Fig.* 15-4
  defined, 230
Polychrome, defined, 200
Polychrome Pots, 200, 201, *Fig.* 13-12
Pont du Gard, 106, *Fig.* 7-12
Porcelain
  defined, 69
  Ming dynasty vases, 69, *Fig.* 5-2
Portrait, defined, 181
Portrait of a Lady, 186, *Fig.* 12-11

Portrait of a Lady with an Ostrich Feather Fan, 182, *Fig.* 12-6
Portrait of a Man, 160-161, 175, *Chapter 11 Opener, Chapter 11 Review Detail*
Post and lintel system
  defined, 51
  Parthenon, 96-97, 98, 111, *Chapter 7 Opener, Chapter 7 Review Detail*
  Stonehenge, 50, 51, *Fig.* 4-5
  Temple of Luxor, 54, 55, *Fig.* 4-11
Poster paint (school tempera)
  applying to a stamp, 281
  safety tip for, 102
  technique tips, 281
Post-Impressionism, 226-231
  composition and, 226, 227, 229, *Fig.* 15-1
  composition and content and, 228, 229, *Fig.* 15-3
  content and, 227, 229, *Fig.* 15-2
  defined, 226
  Pointillism, 230, *Fig.* 15-4
Pottery, 27, *Fig.* 2-12
  amphora, 100-101, *Figs.* 7-4, 7-5
  ancient Chinese, 69, *Fig.* 5-2
  ancient Greek, 99-101, *Figs.* 7-4, 7-5, 7-6
  coiled pot, 194, 306, *Figs.* 13-2, S-3, S-4
    studio lesson, 306-307
  glaze, 69
  Native American
    Pueblo, 194, *Fig.* 13-2
    traditional, 200-201, *Figs.* 13-12, 13-13
  New Stone Age (Neolithic), 50, *Fig.* 4-4
  porcelain, 69, *Fig.* 5-2
  Pre-Columbian
    Chavín, 88, *Fig.* 6-11
    Mochica, 89, *Fig.* 6-13
  studio lessons
    clay urn, 86-87
    coiled pot, 306-307
    painting for Greek vase, 102-103
    time capsule, 76-77
  technique tips, 281-282
    clay mold for plaster relief, 282
    joining clay, 281-282
    working with clay, 281
  See also Ceramics
Powdered tempera
  safety tip for, 102
  See also Poster paint (school tempera)
Pre-Columbian art, 80-95
  Andean, 88-91
  Aztec, 85, *Figs.* 6-6, 6-7
  Mayan, 83-84, *Figs.* 6-4, 6-5
  Mesoamerican, 82-85
  Olmec, 82, 83, *Fig.* 6-2
  studio lessons
    clay urn, 86-87
    stylized motif, 92-93
  West Mexican, 82-83, *Fig.* 6-3
  See also Native American art
Prehistoric art, 48-53
  Chinese, 54, 58-59
  Egyptian, 54-57
    studio lesson, 62-63

Indian, 54, 59
Mesopotamian, 54, 60-61
New Stone Age (Neolithic period), 50-51
Old Stone Age (Paleolithic period), 48-49
studio lessons
  earth pigments (cave painting), 52-53
  picture story (Egyptian art), 62-63
Principles of art, 8-13
  balance, 8, 9, 10, *Figs.* 1-7, 1-8, 1-9
  emphasis, 11
  harmony, 10
  movement, 11
  proportion, 11
  rhythm, 11
  unity, 11
  variety, 10
Printmaking
  defined, 21
  Expressionist, 243, 244, *Fig.* 16-3
  intaglio, 21, *Fig.* 2-6
  Inuit, 204, *Fig.* 13-18
  Japanese, 74, 75, *Fig.* 5-10
  lithography, 21
  methods of, 21
  relief printing, 21
  Rococo, 187, *Fig.* 12-13
  screen printing, 21
  stamp printing techniques, 281
  studio lessons
    figure in action, 252-253
    Inuit-style print, 204-205
  technique tips, 281
  woodblock printing, 74, 75, *Fig.* 5-10
Prisoners, The, 243, 244, *Fig.* 16-3
Process, describing, 35
Profiles. *See* Artist profiles
Proportion, 11
  defined, 11
  studio lesson, 12-13
Protestant Reformation, 178
Pueblo art, 194-195, 196, *Fig.* 13-2, 13-3, 13-4
Pueblos, 195, 196, *Fig.* 13-4
  defined, 195
Pyramid plan (balance), 165, *Fig.* 11-7
Pyramids
  adobe (Mochica), 89
  Egyptian, 54, 55, *Fig.* 4-10
  Mayan, 84, *Fig.* 6-4

R ═══════════════

Radial balance, 9, 10, *Fig.* 1-9
Raphael, 164
  Madonna and Child Enthroned, 164, *Fig.* 11-5
  The Small Cowper Madonna, xiiT
Rasalus, 34, 37, *Fig.* 3-1
Realism
  American, 232-237, *Figs.* 15-6, 15-7, 15-8, 15-9, 15-10
  Ashcan school, 248-249
  defined, 233
  New Realism, 265-266, *Fig.* 17-12
  sculpture, 266-267, *Fig.* 17-15
The Red Studio, 242, 243, *Fig.* 16-1

Red/White, 264, 265, 268, *Fig.* 17-10
Reformation, Protestant, 178
Regionalism, 250, *Fig.* 16-10
  defined, 250
Relief printing, 21
Relief sculpture, 24, 25, *Fig.* 2-9
  African, 132-133, *Fig.* 9-4
  ancient Indian, 59, *Fig.* 4-15
  ancient Roman, 106, 107, *Fig.* 7-15
  defined, 24
  frieze, 25, 99, *Fig.* 2-9
  Mayan, 84, *Fig.* 6-5
  plaster relief, 282
  studio lesson, 150-151
  technique tips
    clay mold for plaster relief, 282
    mixing plaster, 282
Rembrandt van Rijn, 182
  Portrait of a Lady with an Ostrich Feather Fan, 182, *Fig.* 12-6
Renaissance period, 160-175
  defined, 162
  in Italy, 162-167
  in Northern Europe, 168-173
  painting
    in Italy, 162-164, *Figs.* 11-2, 11-4, 11-5
    in Northern Europe, 168-173, *Figs.* 11-11, 11-12, 11-14
  sculpture, in Italy, 164-165, *Figs.* 11-6, 11-7
  studio lessons
    still life, 166-167
    visual symbols, 172-173
Renoir, Auguste, 9, 208-209, 217, 223, 292
  Madame Henriot, 217, *Fig.* 14-6
  Oarsmen at Chatou, 208-209, 223, *Chapter 14 Opener, Chapter 14 Review Detail*
  Young Spanish Woman with a Guitar, 9, *Fig.* 1-8
Resnick, Milton
  Genie, viiiT
Revenge of the Goldfish, 270, *Fig.* 17-18
Rhythm, 11
Rio Esla, castle on, 150, *Fig.* 10-8
Rivera, Diego, 250, 251, 294
  artist profile, 294
  Liberation of the Peon, 250, 251, 294, *Fig.* 16-11
River Seine at Carrieres-sur-Seine, The, viiB
Rock carvings and paintings. *See* Cave art; Petroglyphs
Rock-Rock, viiT, 8, 9, *Fig.* 1-7
Rococo style, 184-189
  architecture, 184, 185, *Fig.* 12-9
  defined, 184
  painting
    in France, 184-186, 188, *Figs.* 12-10, 12-11, 12-13, 12-14
    in Spain, 187
  studio experience, 187
  studio lesson, 188-189
Rodin, Auguste, 218, 219
  Claude Lorrain, 218, 219, *Fig.* 14-8
Roentgen, Wilhelm Conrad, 291
Roman art. *See* Ancient Roman art

Romanesque period, 146-151
  architecture, 146-147, *Figs.* 10-1, 10-2, 10-3, 10-4
    castles, 146-147, *Fig.* 10-1
    churches, 147, *Figs.* 10-3, 10-4
    studio lesson, 150-151
    walled cities, 147, *Fig.* 10-2
  illuminations, 149, *Fig.* 10-6
  painting, 149, *Fig.* 10-6
  sculpture, 148, *Fig.* 10-5
Romanticism, 211-213
Room in New York, 40, 41, *Fig.* 3-6
Rouault, Georges, 32, 33
  Christ Mocked by Soldiers, 32, 33, 45, *Chapter 3 Opener, Chapter 3 Review Detail*
Round arches
  ancient Roman, 104
  defined, 104
Rubbing, technique tips, 286
Rubens, Peter Paul, 180-181
  The Assumption of the Virgin, 180-181, *Fig.* 12-4
Rugs
  Persian or knotted-pile, 123, *Fig.* 8-13
  studio experience, 123
Runners in a Race, 100, 101, *Fig.* 7-5
Ryder, Albert Pinkham, 234, 235, 294
  artist profile, 294
  Moonlight Marine (Toilers of the Sea), 234, 235, 294, *Fig.* 15-8

S

Sacred Rain Arrow, 192-193, 207, *Chapter 13 Opener, Chapter 13 Review Detail*
Safety tips
  chalk, 247
  cutting tools, 109
  markers, 71
  paints, 13, 102, 230
  waterproof ink, 119
Salon
  defined, 216
  Impressionism and, 216-217
San Carlo alle Quattro Fontane, 178, *Fig.* 12-1
Sanchi, Great Stupa at, 114, *Fig.* 8-1
Santa Maria la Real Church, 148, *Fig.* 10-5
School tempera. *See* Poster paint
Science connections, 14, 30, 142, 206
Scissors, safety tip for, 109
Scoring paper, 284, 286
Screen printing, 21
Scroll
  Chinese scroll painting, 68, 70, *Fig.* 5-3
  defined, 68
  Japanese scroll painting, 74, *Fig.* 5-9
Sculpture, 24-25
  abstract, 261, *Fig.* 17-6
  African
    figure sculptures, 130-135, *Figs.* 9-2, 9-3, 9-4, 9-5, 9-6
    masks, 128-129, 136-141, 143, *Chapter 9 Opener, Chapter 9 Review Detail, Figs.* 9-8, 9-9, 9-10, 9-12

studio lessons, 134-135, 140-141
American today, 266-267, *Figs.* 17-13, 17-14, 17-15
ancient Chinese, 58
ancient Egyptian, 46, 57, 65, *Chapter 4 Opener, Chapter 4 Review Detail*
ancient Greek, 25, 99, 100, *Figs.* 2-9, 7-3
ancient Roman, 106-107, *Figs.* 7-14, 7-15
Chinese, 68, 69, *Fig.* 5-1
Cubist, 134, 244, 245, *Fig.* 16-4
European today, 260-261, *Figs.* 17-4, 17-5, 17-6
freestanding, 24, *Fig.* 2-8
frieze, 25, 99, *Fig.* 2-9
Impressionist, 218, 219, *Fig.* 14-8
Indian
  ancient, 59, *Fig.* 4-15
  modern, 116-117, 118, *Figs.* 8-4, 8-5, 8-6
Japanese, 73, 76, *Fig.* 5-8, *Fig.* 5-12
media of, 24-25
Mesopotamian, 61, *Fig.* 4-17
methods, 24-25
  assembling, 25, 28, *Fig.* 2-14
  carving, 24, *Fig.* 2-8
  casting, 25, *Fig.* 2-10
  modeling, 25, 27, *Fig.* 2-12
  studio lesson, 28-29
mobiles, 266
Native American
  modern, 192-193, 202, 207, *Chapter 13 Opener, Chapter 13 Review Detail*
  Northwest Coast Indian, 195, 196, *Fig.* 13-5
non-objective, 260, 261, 266, 267, *Figs.* 17-5, *Figs.* 17-13, 17-13, 17-14
Old Stone Age (paleolithic), 49, *Fig.* 4-2
Pietàs, 164
Pre-Columbian
  Aztec, 85, *Figs.* 6-6, 6-7
  Mayan, 84, *Fig.* 6-5
  Olmec, 82, 83, *Fig.* 6-2
  West Mexican, 82-83, *Fig.* 6-3
relief, 24, 25, *Fig.* 2-9
  African, 132-133, *Fig.* 9-4
  ancient Indian, 59, *Fig.* 4-15
  ancient Roman, 106, 107, *Fig.* 7-15
  Mayan, 84, *Fig.* 6-5
  technique tips, 282
Renaissance, in Italy, 164-165, *Figs.* 11-6, 11-7
Romanesque, 148, *Fig.* 10-5
studio lessons
  abstract self-portrait cutout, 134-135
  environmental design, 28-29
  mood mask relief, 140-141
technique tips, 281-284
  clay, joining, 281-282
  clay mold for plaster relief, 282
  clay, working with, 281
  paper sculpture, 284
  papier-mâché, 283-284
  plaster, clay mold for plaster relief, 282
  plaster, mixing, 282
Seals, ancient Indian, 59, *Fig.* 4-15

Seine, The, 236, 295, *Fig.* 15-10
Self-portrait
  studio experience, 133
  studio lesson, 134-135
Self-Portrait (Leyster), xiiB, 181, 291, *Fig.* 12-5
Septimus, Arch of, 108, *Fig.* 7-16
Serigraphs
  defined, 21
  See also Screen printing
Seurat, Georges, 230, 304
  Pointillism of, 230
  Sunday Afternoon on the Island of La Grande Jatte, 230, 304, *Fig.* 15-4
Shading, techniques, 278
Shang dynasty, 58
Shape, 5
  defined, 5
  geometric, 5
  organic, 5
Shards III, 256-257, 273, *Chapter 17 Opener, Chapter 17 Review Detail*
Shiva, King of the Dancers, xB, 118, *Fig.* 8-6
Shoulder masks
  African, 138-139, 140, *Figs.* 9-10, 9-12
  defined, 138
Sighting techniques, 278
Silk screen printing. *See* Screen printing
Sipan, 89
Sisley, Alfred, 292
Skoglund, Sandy, 270
  Revenge of the Goldfish, 270, *Fig.* 17-18
Sleepy Baby, 18, *Fig.* 2-1
Sloan, John, 248
  Hairdresser's Window, 248, *Fig.* 16-7
Small Cowper Madonna, The, xiiT
Social protest painting, 265, *Fig.* 17-11
  defined, 265
Social studies connections, 30, 44, 64, 78, 94, 110, 126, 142, 174, 190, 206, 222
Solvents
  for acrylic, 20
  defined, 19
  for oil paint, 19
  for watercolor, 19, 20
Space, 5
Space colony, studio lesson, 312-313
Spanish art
  Baroque style, 179, *Fig.* 12-3
  Rococo style, 187, *Fig.* 12-13
  See also specific art movements
Special effects designer, 303
Staffelsee in Autumn, xviii, 15, *Chapter 1 Opener, Chapter 1 Review Detail*
Stag at Sharkey's, 252, *Fig.* 16-12
Staged photography, 270, *Fig.* 17-18
Stained glass
  Gothic, 154, *Figs.* 10-13
  studio experience, 155
Stairway, Mayan, 84, *Fig.* 6-5
Stamp printing techniques, 281
Starry Night, The, 9, 10, *Fig.* 1-9
Statua di Donna, 61, *Fig.* 4-17
Steen, Jan, 35, 36, 37
  Eve of St. Nicholas, 35, 36, 37, *Fig.* 3-2
  The Drawing Lesson, xvB

Stele
  defined, 57
  Funerary Feast Stele of Nefertiabet, 46,
    57, 65, *Chapter 4 Opener, Chapter 4
    Review Detail*
Stella, Frank, 256-257, 273
  Shards III, 256-257, 273, *Chapter 17
    Opener, Chapter 17 Review Detail*
Stieglitz, Alfred, 249, 295
  artist profile, 295
  The Terminal, 249, 295, *Fig.* 16-9
Still Life: Le Jour, 246, *Fig.* 16-5
Stirrup-spout pitchers
  Chavín, 88, *Fig.* 6-11
  Mochica, 89, *Fig.* 6-12
Stonehenge, 50, 51, *Fig.* 4-5
Street, Berlin, 243, *Fig.* 16-2
Structures for prayer, 26
  ancient Egyptian, *Temple of Luxor*, 54,
    55, *Fig.* 4-11
  Baroque, San Carlo alle Quattro
    Fontane, 178, *Fig.* 12-1
  Church of the Sacred Family, 26, *Fig.* 2-11
  Gothic
    Avila Cathedral, 152, 153, *Fig.* 10-11
    Cathedral of Leon, 144-145, 159,
      *Chapter 10 Opener, Chapter 10 Review
      Detail*
    Milan Cathedral, 152, *Fig.* 10-10
    Notre Dame Cathedral, 152, 153,
      Fig. 10-12
  Indian
    Great Stupa at Sanchi, 114, *Fig.* 8-1
    rock cut temple, 115, *Fig.* 8-3
    Taj Mahal, 122, 123, *Fig.* 8-12
  Islamic
    Great Mosque of Abd ar-Rahman,
      121, 122, *Figs.* 8-10, 8-11
    Taj Mahal, 122, 123, *Fig.* 8-12
  Japanese Buddhist
    Nara Horyu-Ji Temple Pagoda, 72,
      73, *Fig.* 5-7
    Nara Todai-Ji Temple, 72, 73, *Fig.* 5-6
  Mayan, *Jaguar Temple*, 84, *Fig.* 6-4
  Romanesque
    Anersall-Romanesque Church, 147,
      Figs. 10-3, 10-4
    Santa Maria la Real Church, 148,
      Fig. 10-5
Studies of Male Shoulder, 166, *Fig.* 11-8
studio experiences
  Abstract Expressionism, 267
  abstract expressiveness, 251
  action painting, 267
  architecture of the future, 271
  detailed drawing, 171
  Expressionist collage, 245
  hieroglyphics, 57
  illuminations, 149
  images from sound, 213
  images in natural forms, 51
  Impressionism, 219
  Japanese headband, 75
  masks, 139
  meditation, 69
  nightmare scene, 261
  the ordinary as extraordinary, 187
  perception, 69

Persian knot, 123
Plains Indian story painting, 197
Post-Impressionism, 229
rose window design, 155
self-portrait as ancestor, 133
texture, 235
tree of life, 117
triangular balance, 165
triumphal arch, 107
vase shapes, 101
Studio lessons
  African art
    abstract self-portrait, 134-135
    mood mask relief, 140-141
  ancient Egyptian art, 62-63
  ancient Greek art, 102-103
  ancient Roman art, 108-109
  architecture
    gargoyles, 156-157
    Romanesque castle relief, 150-151
    triumphal arch, 108-109
  Ashcan school, 252-253
  Baroque style, 182-183
  Chinese art, 70-71
  collage, 124-125
  Cubism
    chalk drawing, 246-247
    painting in Cubist style, 42-43
  drawing
    computer-type drawing, 304-305
    Cubist chalk drawing, 246-247
    expressive hands, 182-183
    still life, 166-167
  elements of art, 6-7
  Gothic period, 156-157
  Hard-Edge Op art, 268-269
  Impressionist landscape, 220-221
  Indian art, 118-119
  Islamic art, 124-125
  media
    environmental design, 28-29
    mixed media, 22-23
  motif
    clay urn, 86-87
    stylized, 92-93
  Native American art
    false face mask, 310-311
    Inuit-style print, 204-205
    round weaving, 198-199
  Neoclassic stage set, 214-215
  non-objective art, 6-7
  painting
    Cubist style, 42-43
    earth pigments, 52-53
    expressive scene, 38-39
    expressive watercolor, 236-237
    for Greek vase, 102-103
    Hard-Edge Op art, 268-269
    Impressionist landscape, 220-221
    picture story, 62-63
    scroll, 70-71
    still life, 166-167
    Surrealism, 262-263
    tempera batik, 118-119
    visual symbols, 172-173
  photo essay, 308-309
  Post-Impressionism, 230
  pottery

clay urn, 86-87
coiled pot, 306-307
painting for Greek vase, 102-103
time capsule, 76-77
  Pre-Columbian art
    clay urn, 86-87
    stylized motif, 92-93
  principles of art, 12-13
  printmaking
    figure in action, 252-253
    Inuit-style print, 204-205
  Renaissance
    still life, 166-167
    visual symbols, 172-173
  Rococo style, 188-189
  Romanesque castle relief, 150-151
  sculpture
    abstract self-portrait cutout, 134-135
    environmental design, 28-29
    mood mask relief, 140-141
  space colony, 312-313
  Surrealism, 262-263
  symbolism, 172-173
  time capsule, 76-77
  weaving, 198-199
Stupas, 114, *Figs.* 8-1
  defined, 114
Style, defined, 41
Stylized, defined, 89
Stylized motif, studio lesson, 92-93
Subject
  aesthetic view based on, 37
  defined, 35
  describing, 35
Sumerians, 61
Summer Sunlight, 35, 36, 37, *Fig.* 3-3
*Sunday Afternoon on the Island of La
  Grande Jatte*, 230, 304, *Fig.* 15-4
Sun King (Louis XIV), 184
Sunset, Casco Bay, 20, *Fig.* 2-4
Surrealism, 258-259, 262-263, *Figs.* 17-1,
  17-2, 17-7
  defined, 258
  studio lesson, 262-263
Symbolism
  defined, 168
  in editorial cartoons, 298
Symmetrical (formal) balance, 8, 9,
  Fig. 1-7

T

Tafoya, Margaret, 201
  Jar, 201, *Fig.* 13-13
Taj Mahal, 122, 123, *Fig.* 8-12
Tanner, Henry O., 236, 295
  artist profile, 295
  The Seine, 236, 295, *Fig.* 15-10
Teacher, art, 297
Technique tips, 277-287
  drawing, 277-279
    contour drawings, 277
    enlarging using a grid, 277-278
    gesture drawings, 277
    oil pastels, 277
    ruler, using, 279
    shading, 278
    sighting, 278

thin lines with a brush, 277
viewing frame, using, 279
miscellaneous, 284-287
glue, working with, 287
making a mat, 285
measuring rectangles, 284
mounting two-dimensional
works, 286
rubbings, 286
tissue paper collage, 287
painting, 279-281
cleaning a brush, 279-280
making natural earth pigments, 280
mixing paint to change value of
color, 280
poster paints (school tempera), 281
watercolors, 281
printmaking, 281
sculpting, 281-284
clay, joining, 281-282
clay mold for plaster relief, 282
clay, working with, 281
paper sculpture, 284, 286
papier-mâché, 283-284
plaster, clay mold for plaster
relief, 282
plaster, mixing, 282
Technology
art and, 270-271
space colony studio lesson, 312-313
Tempera, 20, *See* Poster paint (school
tempera)
Temple of Luxor (ancient Egyptian), 54,
55, *Fig.* 4-11
Temples. *See* Structures for prayer
Tenochtitlán, 85
Terminal, The, 249, 295, *Fig.* 16-9
Texture, 5
That Gentleman, 265-266, *Fig.* 17-12
Three-dimensional art, 24
form, 5
space, 5
Tiahuanaco art, 90
architecture, 90, *Fig.* 6-14
crafts, 90, *Fig.* 6-15
monolith, 90, *Fig.* 6-14
Tiahuanaco culture, 90
Tightrope Walker, 260, *Fig.* 17-3
Tikal, 84, *Fig.* 6-4
Time Transfixed, 262, *Fig.* 17-7
Tissue paper collage, 287
Todai-Ji
bronze Buddha of, 73, *Fig.* 5-8
Nara Todai-Ji Temple, 72, 73, *Fig.* 5-6
Tomb of Nakht, wall painting from, 62,
Fig. 4-18
Totem poles
defined, 195
Northwest Coast Indian, 195, 196,
Fig. 13-5
Tourists, 266-267, *Fig.* 17-15
Toussaint L'Overture Series, xvT, 265,
Fig. 17-11
Tower of Babylon, 60
Transparencies, defined, 300
Tree of Life and Knowledge, 117, *Fig.* 8-5

Triangular balance, 165, *Fig.* 11-7
studio experience, 165
Triumphal arches
ancient Roman, 106, 107, 108,
Figs. 7-13, 7-15, 7-16
defined, 106
Turner, Joseph M. W., 211, 213
The Grand Canal, Venice, 211, 213,
Fig. 14-3
Turn of the Century Dandy, 202, *Fig.* 13-15
Turpentine, 19
Twin Pines, Level Distance, 70, *Fig.* 5-3
Two-dimensional art
form, 7
matting, 285
mounting, 286
shape, 5
space, 5
Tyi Wara, 136

U
Ukiyo-e style
defined, 74
woodcut, 74, 75, *Fig.* 5-10
United States art. *See* American art
Unity, 11
defined, 11
Urban planning
ancient Indian, 60
defined, 60
Urn, funerary. *See* Funerary urns

V
Value, 2
mixing paint for, 280
studio lesson, 6-7
van der Weyden, Rogier, 170, 171
Descent from the Cross, 170, *Fig.* 11-12
van Eyck, Jan, 168-169, 171, 172
The Annunciation, 168-169, *Fig.* 11-11
Giovanni Arnolfini and His Bride, 172,
Fig. 11-14
van Gogh, Vincent, 9, 10, 227, 229
Hospital at Saint-Remy, 227, 229,
Fig. 15-2
The Starry Night, 9, 10, *Fig.* 1-9
van Ness, Beatrice Whitney, 35, 36, 37
Summer Sunlight, 35, 36, 37, *Fig.* 3-3
van Rijn, Rembrandt. *See* Rembrandt
van Rijn
Variety, 10
Vasco da Gama, 291
Vases
ancient Greek, shapes, 101, *Fig.* 7-6
See also Amphora
Vau, Louis Le. *See* Le Vau, Louis
Velázques, Diego, 179
The Needlewoman, 179, *Fig.* 12-3
Versailles, Palace at, 184, 185, *Fig.* 12-9
Victory Dance, 203, *Fig.* 13-16
View of Mt. Fuji from Seven-Ri Beach, ixT
Viewing frame techniques, 279
Vigée-Lebrun, Élisabeth, 186
Portrait of a Lady, 186, *Fig.* 12-11
Vista, The, 184-186, *Fig.* 12-10

W
Walled city of Carcassone, 147, *Fig.* 10-2
Wall painting from the tomb of Nakht,
62, *Fig.* 4-18
Warm color scheme, 3
Warp, defined, 198
Watercolor, 20, *Fig.* 2-4
technique tips, 281
Waterloo Bridge, London, 220, 292,
Fig. 14-10
Watteau, Antoine, 184-186, 188
Embarkation from Cythera, 188,
Fig. 12-14
The Vista, 184-186, *Fig.* 12-10
Weaving, 27, *Fig.* 2-13
loom, 198
Native American, Plains Indian,
196, 197, *Fig.* 13-6
Persian rugs, 123, *Figs.* 8-13, 8-14
Pre-Columbian
Incan, 91, *Fig.* 6-17
Tiahuanaco, 90, *Fig.* 6-15
Weft, defined, 198
West Mexican art, 82-83
dog effigies, 82-83, *Fig.* 6-3
sculpture, 82-83, *Fig.* 6-3
West Mexican culture, 82
Zapotec funerary urn, 80, 86, 95,
*Chapter 6 Opener, Chapter 6 Review
Detail*
Weyden, Rogier van der. *See* van der
Weyden, Rogier
Windy Doorstep, The, 25, *Fig.* 2-10
Woman, 27, 292, *Fig.* 2-13
Woodblock printing
defined, 74
Japanese Ukiyo-e style, 74, 75,
Fig. 5-10
Woodcut, Ukiyo-e style, 74, 75, *Fig.* 5-10
Woodlands Indian art, 196-197
Wyeth, Andrew, 265-266
That Gentleman, 265-266, *Fig.* 17-12

X
Xochipilli, Lord of the Flowers, 85, *Fig.* 6-6

Y
Yamato-e style
defined, 74
scroll, 74, *Fig.* 5-9
Young Spanish Woman with a Guitar, 9,
Fig. 1-8

Z
Zapotec funerary urn, 80, 86, 95, *Chapter
6 Opener, Chapter 6 Review Detail*
Zarabanda (Un Disco Blanco), 266, *Fig.*
17-13
Ziggurat, 60, 61, *Fig.* 4-16
defined, 61

Acknowledgements: The art work executed and submitted by the following students was exemplary. Because of book design constraints, all of the student work could not be included. The authors feel, however, that each student who contributed should be recognized.

Jennifer Alexander, Taylor Road Middle School; Dina Anderson, Colonial Junior High; Amy Antonini, Taylor Road Middle School; Andrea Armstrong, Highlands Junior High School; Chris Bayliss, Standon College Preparatory School; Jennifer Beaver, Taylor Road Middle School; Daniel Bense, Taylor Road Middle School; Angelia Black, Taylor Road Middle School; Ryan Bray, Marvin Pittman Laboratory School; Erin Brock, Stanton College Preparatory School; Natalie Brown, North Augusta High School; Bertina Brunson, North Augusta High School; Shawn Burke, Telfare County High School; Christine Camplone, Taylor Road Middle School; Robbee Coates, Taylor Road Middle School; Pat Cone, Marvin Pittman Laboratory School; Krisha Craven, Marvin Pittman Laboratory School; Dee Dee Crawford, Stanton College Preparatory; Kris DeMasse, Taylor Road Middle School; Elizabeth Dewey, Marvin Pittman Laboratory School; Chris Drago, Taylor Road Middle School; Maria Carolina Dugue, Savannah County Day School; Liza Dupont, North Augusta High School; Jason Easley, Taylor Road Middle School; Eric Elliot, Marvin Pittman Laboratory School; Shari Erwin, Taylor Road Middle School; Steve Eubanks, North Augusta High School; Rachel Ferrara, Savannah County Day School; Danny Fredt, Taylor Road Middle School; Robert Freemantle, Taylor Road Middle School; Heather Gatlin, Telfare County High School; Rachel Goossen, Taylor Road Middle School; Brandy Hartman, Hillside School; Sierra Hartman, Mountain View School; Jason Hebert, Tecumseh Middle School; Jennifer Herron, Stanton College Preparatory School; Wendy Hester, Telfare County High School; Matt Hickman, Marvin Pittman Laboratory School; Charlotte Hollingsworth, Fletcher Junior High School; Chris Holsapple, Fletcher Junior High School; Chad Hope, Taylor Road Middle School; Jennifer Howard, Taylor Road Middle School; Ashley Hoynowski, Taylor Road Middle School; Raymond Hubbard, Bradwell Institute High School; Kyle Ivey, Marvin Pittman Laboratory School; Kim Jones, Marvin Pittman Laboratory School; Rick Jones, Taylor Road Middle School; Ryan Kight, North Augusta High School; Cornelius Lewis, Marvin Pittman Laboratory School; Cindy Sang-Ching Li, Stanton College Preparatory School; Myron Linder, Marvin Pittman Laboratory School; Joshua A. Lipps, Ridgeway Junior/Senior High School; Alice Long, Tecumseh Middle School; Mahrien Louis, Colonial Junior High School; Todd Lowe, North Augusta High School; Tara Martin, Telfare County High School; Jimmy McCrory, Taylor Road Middle School; Mark McGlen, Taylor Road Middle School; Jenifer Meeks, Ridgeway Junior/Senior High School; Kelvin Mercer, Marvin Pittman Laboratory School; Mazi Merritt, Marvin Pittman Laboratory School; Kouthy Mom, Colonial Junior High; Brian Monaco, Taylor Road Middle School; Paola Morrongiello, Stanton College Preparatory School; Douglass Myers III, Stanton College Preparatory School; Artis Nails, Highlands Junior High School; Danielle Nelson, Highlands Junior High School; Jason Nelson, Fletcher Junior High School; Wichelle Norton, Marvin Pittman Laboratory School; Dana Odom, Marvin Pittman Laboratory School; Marina Patrick, Taylor Road Middle School; Melanie Pearson, Mabry Middle School; Shanti Persad, Savannah County Day School; Eloy Powell, North Augusta High School; David Reed, John Sevier Middle School; J. R. Rees, Tecumseh Middle School; Sindye Reich, Taylor Road Middle School; Sharon Reinertsen, Stanton College Preparatory School; Sharon Muse Renfrow, Savannah County Day School; Matthew Richmond, Douglas Anderson School of the Arts; Rebecca Ritter, Mabry Middle School; Loretta Rosenfeld, Taylor Road Middle School; Kristen Rudi, Taylor Road Middle School; Shani Russeau, Stanton College Preparatory; P. J. Samara, Taylor Road Middle School; Katie Schnellman, Savannah County Day School; Fred Shackelford, Ridgeway Junior/Senior High School; Garrett Shook, Stanton College Preparatory School; Jason Slider, Taylor Road Middle School; Alexia Strauch, North Augusta High School; Kelli Sumerau, North Augusta High School; Tiffany-Claire Teague, Mabry Middle School; Anna Thomas, Savannah County Day School; Marilyn Touchstone, Colonial Junior High; James Vaughan, Taylor Road Middle School; Amy Wallace, Marvin Pittman Laboratory School; Matthew Werner, Tecumseh Middle School; Deborah Wilcox, Telfare County High School; Latoya Wiley, Marvin Pittman Laboratory School; Andre Wilkey, Marvin Pittman Laboratory School; Matt Williams, Telfare County High School; Donna Wilson, Telfare County High School; Heather Wilson, North Augusta High School; Coretta Wintz, Bradwell Institute High School; Monica Woodruff, Taylor Road Middle School; Chad Yonell, North Augusta High School.